DESIGN FOR ASSISTED LIVING

DESIGN FOR ASSISTED LIVING

Guidelines for Housing the Physically and Mentally Frail

Victor Regnier, FAIA

JOHN WILEY & SONS, INC.

Copyright © 2002 by John Wiley & Sons, New York. All rights reserved.

Published simultaneously in Canada.

This publication is designed to provide accurate and authoritative information in regard to the subject matter covered. It is sold with the understanding that the publisher is not engaged in rendering professional services. If professional advice or other expert assistance is required, the services of a competent professional person should be sought.

Wiley also publishes its books in a variety of electronic formats. Some content that appears in print may not be available in electronic books. For more information about Wiley products, visit our web site at www.wiley.com.

Library of Congress Cataloging-in-Publication Data:
Regnier, Victor, 1947–
   Designing for assisted living : guidelines for housing the physically and mentally frail / Victor Regnier.
      p. cm.
   Includes index.
   ISBN 0-471-35182-2 (cloth : alk. paper)
    1. Aged—Housing.   2. Architecture and the physically handicapped.   3. Congregate housing. 4. Aged—Dwellings. 5. Aged—Care. I. Title.
   RA564.8 .R455 2002
   725'.5—dc21   2001046743

Printed in the United States of America.

10 9 8 7 6 5 4 3

To my father, Victor, and my mother, Helen, who have both taught me about long-term care from the inside out; my friend and colleague Powell Lawton, who provided me with the professional encouragement to take on this topic; my patient wife, Judy, and my wonderful children, Jennifer and Heather, who have tolerated my weird hours and my paripatetic schedule during the last decade.

CONTENTS

PREFACE

Looking Back from the Future

I suspect that in 2030, when we look back at the history of long-term care design during the last third of the twentieth century, we will be amazed at how society could have ever tolerated such an oppressive institutional system of care and support. I am sure we will be amazed at how long-term care was regulated and how little influence residents and their family members had on the system. We will have a hard time understanding why people with dementia were placed in hospital-like settings and why so little attention was paid to movement therapy, exercise, and physical therapy. We will wonder why residents had to live in semiprivate rooms and why so little attention was paid to fostering independence and autonomy. We will wonder why we stayed with a long-term care model that was so clearly based on a short-term hospital template. Today we look back at the 1960s and find it hard to believe that residents were regularly institutionalized because they were incontinent—a muscle control problem, not a health care problem.

In 2030 I will be 83, and if I am still alive, I suspect that many of my contemporaries and their families will be thinking very seriously about long-term care. The purpose of this book is to stimulate your thinking about what long-term care could be in the future. I hope that in 25 to 30 years, when we contemplate the housing choices available for persons who are growing older and frailer, we will be faced with not just one option but a variety of choices. These should be choices that pay homage to our past experience and are more consistent with our present desires.

A Short Exploratory History

In 1991, with support from the Retirement Research Foundation, I published a monograph that dealt with a new long-term care alternative that at the time was variously labeled *assisted care, catered living,* and *assisted living* (Regnier, 1991). Although alternatives to institutionalization had occurred before then, the late 1980s saw small groups of people throughout the country reinventing long-term care. Their solutions rejected the traditional notion of institutionalization in favor of a homelike setting with a management structure that put older persons and their families first and rules and regulations second. There was great enthusiasm for the possibilities that existed and a desire to create a new way to allow older frail people to age with dignity and independence.

After that initial work, with encouragement from colleagues and the convenient timing of a sabbatical leave, I planned a trip to study northern European housing alternatives for the frail. It was financed by a Fulbright research award and support from several other sources including the American Institute of Architects (AIA), the Swedish American Association, and the Retirement Research Foundation. This trip took me to 100 projects in five northern European countries. There I saw the promise of assisted living fully implemented in systems, procedures, and philosophies at a much larger scale and in a more ubiquitous fashion. What my North American colleagues were struggling to gain recognition for was already fully realized. Two books followed in 1994 and 1995 (Regnier, 1994; Regnier, Hamilton and Yatabe, 1995) that chronicled the work in Europe and examined the basic assumptions underlying the design, management, and financing of this early work. Since that time, a lot has happened. Assisted living has come into its own, experiencing the exhilarating highs of testing new concepts, as well as dealing with the challenges of a quick expansion that found too many projects built throughout the country in places where too few older frail people wanted to live.

The proprietary and nonprofit organizations involved in the development of assisted living facilities are currently taking a break to assess the future. Some are expanding into other countries, as well as pursuing sites in urban areas that were initially skipped because they were more difficult to develop. Others are catching up by training more personnel and working on increasing the occupancy of existing facilities.

In 1999 I earned another sabbatical leave and made a return visit to 95 new projects in the same five countries. The purpose of this trip was to discover new ideas, as well as chronicle the changes that had occurred during the 1990s. During that period, I made over 50 presentations at conferences on the design of housing for the frail and consulted on the design of over 100 new assisted living buildings throughout the United States. I also completed a one-day postoccupancy evaluation (POE) in each quarter to see how design ideas were being implemented in the field.

This book, for me, is like an evaluation. It is about taking stock of what we have learned and what needs to be explored further.

Personal and Profession Worlds Collide

Personally as well as professionally, the last ten years have been eventful. My father and mother both grew mentally and physically frail, and my search for what constituted the best environment took on personal dimensions. Along with my brother, Bob, and my sister, Cathy, we experienced as a family the problems of dealing with a rigid long-term care system. We learned how the *rules rule* with a nursing home that was more interested in achieving a perfect score on its state assessment than creating a perfect environment for residents and family members.

I met staff members who were truly dedicated, compassionate people whom I admired greatly and found others (usually at middle to upper level management) who had lost touch with the purpose of their work. I saw how the environment limited the program for activities and services and how a narrow vision of the program limited the potential use of the environment.

My appreciation for the little things that make life stimulating and interesting in these settings grew. The simple pleasures of connecting with children, plants, and pets that Bill Thomas (1996) has revealed in his Eden Alternative work became clearer. I started to spend more time thinking about the building from the inside out rather than from the outside in. For example, I argued more about the need for bigger windows with more continuous glass rather than the "punched openings" my architectural colleagues promoted. I thought about the pleasure that passive observation provided residents when they could overlook a playground or a ball field.

The experience of the place was not just about the environment but encompassed the activities of other residents, the staff, family, and friends. I conceptualized the place as a series of sequenced, linked, or overlapped behavioral settings that supported the program yet stimulated opportunities for improvisational use. I began to see the building as the backdrop and support mechanism for the day-to-day narrative of life. The space took on those transactional characteristics of place that imbue a setting with meaning and human connection.

How This Book Is Organized

Many ideas have influenced the way this book is organized. To start with, the book has over 200 photographs and drawings. In addition, the detailed heading structure captures the essence of the text so that it is easy to skim and read. Most of the captions are long and descriptive, pointing out what is worth paying attention to in the drawing or the photograph.

Part I begins by asking the simple question "What is assisted living?" Starting with a simple official definition, it explores the issue of what assisted living should be now and what it can be in the future. The work of environmental design researchers, as well as researchers who are chronicling the programs and environments of the newest collection of assisted living housing, is used to establish benchmarks. Qualities of the environment are established as criteria against which new programs and designs can be evaluated.

Part II identifies 100 issues, qualities, and characteristics of successful environments that make these settings stimulating and noteworthy. These issues relate to basic design and development decisions, which are the basis for creating the environment. Using a general-to-specific format, neighborhood and site considerations are identified, followed by more detailed building and program considerations. This part is divided into ten chapters that deal comprehensively with the social and physical context. These chapters focus on larger conceptual ideas rather than on the more practical and mundane. However, enough detail is sprinkled throughout the chapters to give them specificity and meaning for application.

Part III uses 15 case study buildings from northern Europe and the United States to demonstrate how issues discussed in Part II have been integrated into fully realized examples. Attributes of each building and their programs are identified in a narrative accompanied by illustrations of each building. Each case study demonstrates a unique assemblage of programmatic and physical concepts reconciled with the climate and geography of different places.

Part IV consists of a series of concluding thoughts. Lessons learned from these five countries in northern Europe are identified and related to U.S. practice.

Twenty concluding design and management directives summarize the major findings of the book into a list of critical topics. Future predictions and trends are identified from the general literature on assisted living and from European experiences. Finally, several overarching concluding thoughts serve as a bridge to future work.

What About Your "Perfect World" Vision?

In 2000, I was interviewed on Terry Gross's National Public Radio program "Fresh Air." Her style is to mix personal and professional commentary in a way that makes you feel as well as think about important topics of the day. She asked me if I had "seen, experienced, or imagined a place where I would want to grow old and frail." This is a difficult question because no one looks forward to coping with the problems of old age. Maintaining continuity appears to be the best response, which is why so many people want to stay at home as they become more impaired. I still think this is the best solution for most people until they reach a point where their needs require ongoing support and attention.

For me, the perfect environment embraces many of the concepts discussed in this book. First is the idea of an apartment for life (*Humanitas*, page 158). This has great appeal because it speaks to the desire for environmental continuity. Stay in your apartment and let the services you need change rather than changing the environment. This also allows you to control the separation between yourself and the staff, which in a conventional staff-dominated nursing home is often impossible.

Second is the Dutch concept of *op maat* (care fitted to your needs), which involves scheduling needed care around your preferences and desires rather than shaping your life to fit the schedule of the institution It is perhaps best demonstrated at *Wilhelmiina* (page 163) but also occurs in many other Dutch facilities including *Humanitas* (page 158). For example, does everyone really want or need to get up when the first shift arrives at 6 AM?

Third is the need to keep physically active and engaged in an exercise and physical therapy program linked to your own unique physiological needs—like the program in *Gyngemosegård* (page 174). Because we can't choose our parents, we are saddled with their gene pool. Keeping active is one of the most important things we can do to maintain ambulation and independence. Too many programs kill us with kindness by encouraging a passive lifestyle.

Fourth is the desire for healthy, good-tasting, and nutritious meals. Food is often one of the most important things residents receive. It not only sustains life but also brings immediate gratification. When you are old and frail, there are few pleasurable experiences that equal taking a meal for its overall impact on quality of life. Most of the projects claim to have excellent food service, but you know what they say about the "proof of the pudding."

Fifth is the ability to visit a range of interesting places outside of your unit. These should be places inside and outside where you can host friends and family members, like many of those available in the *Sunrise* at Richmond (page 196). Along with this should be a frequently scheduled transportation van that will take you to neighborhood destinations and for pleasure rides. In a perfect world, you would also have nearby stores and service places that are easy to walk to.

Sixth is continuity in care. Having the same caregiver, who knows your habits and pleasures, who cares about your comfort and can understand you as a person, is invaluable. Many of the case studies have designated caregiver programs that value and provide continuity in the caregiving staff.

My list would go on to include a pet, a place for plants, a version of the Danish vacation program, and a few other minor options—but enough about my ideal setting. What about your fantasy? How would you answer Terry Gross's question for yourself? I hope that you will find some of the answers in the following pages.

Victor Regnier FAIA
Los Angeles, California
email: regnier@usc.edu

ACKNOWLEDGMENTS

A book like this is mostly about experience and interaction. There are hundreds of people I came in contact with while preparing for and making my second study visit to assisted living facilities in the United States and Northern Europe in 1990. The ideas in this book came from site visits, interviews, consulting experiences, conference presentations, postoccupancy evaluations, classroom seminars, and discussions with colleagues and friends. All of them have played an important role in clarifying the ideas and beliefs presented here.

Informants, Hosts, and Publications

Several publications were useful in identifying the best facilities. The most useful sources included Fich, Mortensen, et al. (1995), Gotesborg Stad (1992), Gottschalk and Potter (1993), Houben and Mulder (1999), Jensen (1997), Kristiansen (1997), Lindstrom (1989, 1995), and Zahle (1998). However, by far the most useful informants were the northern Europeans who helped me make appointments and gave me advice about places to visit. These included:

▲ Jacque Smit and Roelie Post, of Breda, the Netherlands, who set up appointments in the Netherlands and hosted part of my stay there.

▲ Hans van Beek, of Pro Atelier, Architects, who accompanied me to several projects and hosted me for several days in the Netherlands.

▲ Heli Kotilanen, of the National Research and Development Center for Welfare and Health in Helsinki, Finland, who set up or verified the 20 site visits in Finland.

▲ Jorma Ohman of NVO architects, Helsinki, Finland, who accompanied me to several of his buildings in Finland (including Virranranta and Metsätähti).

▲ Hakan Josefsson, of White Arkitekter, Göteborg, Sweden, who suggested buildings and accompanied me to projects around Göteborg.

▲ Elenora Alaoui, of the Swedish Institute, Stockholm, Sweden.

▲ Ulla Broen, National Board of Social Welfare, Copenhagen, Denmark.

▲ Bente Lindstrom, Professor, School of Architecture, Åarhus, Denmark.

▲ Jan Paulsson, Chalmers Institute of Technology, Goteborg, Sweden.

▲ Lisbeth Kristiansen, Architect, Viby, Denmark.

▲ Margrethe Dobloug, Professor, Oslo School of Architecture, Oslo, Norway.

▲ Edvard Hiorthoy, of the Trondheim Division of Architectural Design, Trondheim, Norway.

▲ Karen Zahle, Professor, Royal Danish Academy of Fine Arts, Copenhagen, Denmark.

▲ Esa Laaksonen, editor of *Arkkitehti*, the Finnish architectural journal, Helsinki, Finland.

I interviewed several hundred people in facilities throughout these five countries. Most were extremely patient with me and very generous with their time. Their honest and frank responses to my questions made it possible for me to ascertain the most interesting characteristics of these projects. Although it is impossible for me to name them all, they contributed the most valuable insights to this work.

Professional Colleagues

Among the most interesting experiences I have had in the past decade has been the opportunity to work with Paul and Terry Klaassen of Sunrise Assisted Living. Paul and I have had many conversations about the power of the environment to change the lives of older frail people. His insight and perspective on assisted living in the United States, as well as his familiarity with European models, made him a great source and a wonderful colleague.

Working with the Sunrise organization brought me into contact with numerous individuals. Among the most influential have been Martha Child, President of Martha Child Interiors; Harley Cook, Executive Vice President of Development; and Billy Shields, Senior Vice President of Development. All three have been instrumental in helping me pursue my ideas about the nature of assisted living environments.

Many other Sunrise Assisted Living colleagues have contributed to substantive personal and professional conversations. These include Sean Ambrose, Maribeth Bersani, Nancy Card, Bill Carney, Elaine Chandler, Tim Cox, Marian De Meire, David Driscoll, Carol Edelstein, Eddie Edwards, David Faeder, Becky Fix, Dan Gorham, Caitlin Heagy, Tim Hedges, Laura Hester, Dana Keegan, Brenda Kuhn, Willie Long, Bob MacNamara, Elizabeth Masar-Woolhouse, Joe McElwee, Joe Miklich, Tom Newell, John Noone, Mark Owens, Jose de Pablo, Mike Parsells, Diane Perrymore, Jay Pope, Jim Schaffer, Gene Schoenfelder, Steve Shear, Chris Slavin, Brian Swinton, Chris Tatum, Susan Timoner, Tiffany Tomasso, Brian Williams, Jeff Wright, and Dan Zemanek.

In developing these ideas, I also worked closely with the following project architects at Berry Rio and Associates: Andy Coelho, Daba Dabic, Tim Danforth, Haydn Heman-Ackah, Parviz Izadjoo, Dora Kay, Teeja Manan, John Mills, Long Nguyen, Steve Ruiz, Elise Schoer, and John Walker.

Several colleagues at Senior Resource Group in San Diego, California, also deserve special recognition. They include Michael Grust, Bill Drake, and Martin Fenton.

The last seven years, I have had the pleasure of working closely with a number of architects on a range of projects. Our consultations have helped me clarify through application many of my own ideas. Their perspectives on projects here and abroad have challenged my thinking and sharpened my ideas. These architects include:

▲ Whit Wagner AIA, Eka Rehardjo, AIA, and Chuck Heath, AIA, of Berry Rio and Associates, Springfield, Virginia

▲ Jerry McDivett, AIA, and Don Doman, AIA, of Mithun Architects, Seattle, Washington

▲ Wolfgang Hack, AIA, Mark Hendrickson, AIA, and John Paris, AIA, of Hill Partnership, Newport Beach, California

Case Study Contributors

Several of the architects responsible for the case studies helped by sending drawings and photographs. A special thank-you to:

▲ Maury Childs, FAIA, CBT Architects, Boston, Massachusetts
▲ Frank Dimella, AIA, Dimella-Shafer Architects, Boston, Massachusetts
▲ Wolfgang Hack, AIA, Hill Partnership, Newport Beach, California
▲ Chuck Heath, AIA, Berry Rio and Associates, Springfield, Virginia
▲ Lars Hetland, Nielson and Rubow, Copenhagen, Denmark
▲ David Hoglund, FAIA, Perkins-Eastman Architects, Pittsburgh, Pennsylvania
▲ Don Jacobs, AIA, JBZ Architecture and Planning, Newport Beach, California
▲ Bjorn Karlsson, ANOVA Architects, Stockholm, Sweden
▲ Henrik Lading, Domus Architects, Lyngby, Denmark
▲ Karen Lindstrom, White Arkitekter, Malmö, Sweden
▲ Jerry McDivett, AIA, Mithun Architects, Seattle, Washington
▲ Kevin Mantz, AIA, KM Development, Milwaukee, Wisconsin
▲ Jorma Ohman, NVO Architects, Helsinki, Finland
▲ Freek Prins, EGM Architecten, Dordrecht, the Netherlands
▲ Tuomo Siitonen, Tuomo Siitonen Architects, Helsinki, Finland

Friends and Colleagues

My colleagues (and former colleagues) at USC were, as always, helpful and curious. Through numerous interactions, they helped me to think about this work. I thank Jon Pynoos, Phoebe Liebig, Bob Harris, Neal Cutler, Eileen Crimmens, John Mutlow, Julie Overton, Bob Timme, Chuck Lagreco, Bob Wiswell, Aaron Hagedorn, and especially Maria Henke, who reviewed an early draft of Chapter 2.

Jim Birren, a friend, mentor, and colleague from USC and UCLA, was generous with his ideas and his Roladex. He helped enrich my second visit by suggesting additional contacts.

My professional colleagues, John Zeisel, Ph.D., and

David Hoglund, FAIA, continued the dialog through discussions of their own work (both represented here) and during seminars at dozens of professional conferences and six consecutive summer courses at Harvard. We have learned how to share ideas and learn from one another in a most productive way.

I had the pleasure of enjoying the company of some special friends who flew over to join me in touring buildings. Tom Safran, a senior housing developer in Los Angeles, joined me in the Netherlands for several days to visit projects. Elise Nakhnikian, former editor of *Contemporary Long Term Care* magazine, joined me in Stockholm for two days of site visits. Finally, Len Fishman took time out of his busy schedule as CEO of the American Association of Housing and Services for the Aging to spend four days with me in Finland. All of them were wonderful traveling companions, and each of them helped me to see the pros and cons of projects from their own fresh perspectives.

The graphics for the case study chapter, when necessary, were placed on CAD by Asawari Marathe. Others who were instrumental in helping with CAD file coordination were Doug Noble, Karen Kensak, Shon Garzan and, John Walker

I can't end without thanking my family. My spouse, Judy Gonda, has been more than patient with my wanderlust. She kept everything running smoothly and was often mother and father to our two wonderful children, Jennifer and Heather. My brother, Bob, and my sister, Cathy, and I have learned a great deal from our parents and their struggle against brain cancer and dementia. I am especially indebted to my sister for an editing review of the final manuscript. Dealing with the emotional as well as the professional side of aging has helped me to better understand older people and their special relationship with family members.

Although I attribute many of the insights in this book to my long list of personal and professional informants, any shortcomings in this work can be directly attributed to my need to get at least six hours sleep per night. Thanks, everyone, for making this experience a great one. I hope that by sharing it with others, the next generation of housing arrangements will profit from our mistakes and benefit from our experiences.

Hofje van Staats in Haarlem, the Netherlands, dates from 1731.

PART I
ASSISTED LIVING DEFINED

It is often said that the value and meaning of a civilization can be determined from the record it leaves in the form of architecture and that the true measure of the compassion and civility of a society lies in how well it treats its frail older people.

—Regnier, 1994, p. vii

As we settle into the new millennium and think about the challenges that face our society in the next 50 years, it is hard to ignore the demographic imperative that has led to the aging of society. Today we view this trend from a much broader perspective because changes in longevity and public health have made it a worldwide issue.

As people age and experience a greater number of years filled with chronic health problems and disability, the question of how they are going to live out those remaining years in a dignified and positive way increases in perplexity. Although making home modifications and receiving home-delivered services can lengthen the time one can spend independently at home, if you live long enough and are frail enough, there is a certain inevitability associated with moving to a setting where services and monitoring can be provided on an ongoing basis. Although only 5 percent of the 65+ population live in nursing homes, about half of women and a third of men who turned 60 in 1990 are expected to enter a nursing home at least once in their lifetime (Treas, 1995).

The purpose of this book is to explore how to design a more satisfying physical environment and caregiving milieu for older, mentally and physically frail people—an environment that is more satisfying than the traditional nursing home. Moreover, this book seeks to analyze the attributes of building designs and service interventions that allow residents to live a more independent and satisfying life in a setting that supports their physical, emotional, and health care needs. Because the book gathers examples and practices from both the United States and northern European countries, the conclusions that are drawn are not just reflective of what we have come to expect in the United States.

Twenty years ago, there were few options for mentally or physically frail people other than placement in a nursing home. Today, the options abound. The rich experiences of the Scandinavians in exploring new ways of conceptualizing long-term care are exhilarating and eye-opening. In northern Europe, nursing homes, as we know them in the United States, were difficult to find ten years ago. Today they have all but disappeared from the long-term care landscape. New buildings designed for a frail population have dwelling units that are single occupied, and these buildings embrace the characteristics we associate with assisted living environments in this country. The ability of the Scandinavians to enhance home care delivery systems while creating community-based housing environments that support very old, frail people in highly residential environments is truly refreshing. As we approach the steady transition of "boomers" into older age cohorts, there has never been a better time to question current practice and think creatively about the options that could exist if we approached the problem in a bolder, more innovative way.

1

WHAT IS ASSISTED LIVING?

Answering this question in 1993 was easier than in 1989, when no one had a clear idea of just what *assisted living* meant. In 2001 we have a well-accepted definition, but exceptions to that definition continue to emerge. The definition of assisted living has clearly evolved over the last decade and has come to symbolize a setting that is resident-centered, family friendly, and residential in character. The definition of assisted living from the Assisted Living Federation of America (ALFA) is perhaps the most widely accepted:

> . . . [A] special combination of housing, supportive services, personalized assistance and healthcare designed to respond to the individual needs of those who require help with activities of daily living (ADL) and instrumental activities of daily living (IADL). Supportive services are available, 24 hours a day, to meet scheduled and unscheduled needs, in a way that promotes maximum dignity and independence for each resident and involves the resident's family, neighbors and friends. . . . (ALFA, 2000)

Like many widely accepted definitions, this one is broadly worded to fit as many situations as possible. However, identifying the qualities and characteristics that all projects should strive to include is perhaps a better way of focusing on the specific attributes of the environment and the caregiving philosophy that enhance the quality of life for the residents of these communities.

DEFINING FEATURES OF ASSISTED LIVING

Based on experiences from northern Europe and knowledge of the best settings in the United States, the following nine criteria provide a normative standard against which the physical and operational environment of assisted living housing can be measured. Although even excellent projects are not likely to include all nine of these features, they are nonetheless a useful checklist of items that can be used to rate the strengths and weaknesses of an environment.

▲ Appear residential in character

▲ Be perceived as small in size

▲ Provide residential privacy and completeness

▲ Recognize the uniqueness of each resident

▲ Foster independence, interdependence, and individuality

▲ Focus on health maintenance, physical movement, and mental stimulation

▲ Support family involvement

▲ Maintain connections with the surrounding community

▲ Serve the frail

The following expanded description of each feature provides a more detailed understanding of how these attributes can be used to create a more satisfying environment.

Traditional crafts are less common with today's elderly population: This intricate weaving is as interesting to watch as it is beautiful to behold.

Appear Residential in Character

The character, appearance, and imagery of assisted living buildings should be related to residential housing. These associations can be explored through the color, materiality, configuration, massing, detailing, and design of the building and its interior spaces. The building should employ residential elements such as sloped roofs, attached porches, and dormers for scale and association purposes. Residential materials, finishes, and treatments should be used to clad and enclose the building. The building should also fit into the surrounding neighborhood. Interior rooms should be consistent with residential proportions. Larger-scale spaces like the dining room should be broken up into smaller separate rooms. Residential materials should be specified for interior finishes and furnishings. Rooms should have variety in character and purpose, as in a typical house. Open stairs should connect floors, and units should be clustered into small groups to stimulate the development of friendships and helping behaviors. In other words, the building should be as much like a house and as little like a hospital as possible.

Be Perceived as Small in Size

The minimum number of units to achieve economies of scale will vary by region, state, and urban context. In a small town, one may be able to operate with as few as 25–30 units. Nevertheless, most settings will require 40–60 units to offer competitive rental rates and provide reliable 24-hour care. (However, the larger the building, the more likely its scale will overwhelm residents.) When residents know one another and the administrator knows each resident, a feeling of familiarity develops. This creates a second "family" for residents in addition to their own related family members. Creating a building that resembles a big house or courtyard villa can achieve compactness in plan and solidarity in community relationships. One of the major mistakes inexperienced providers make is loading a site with too many units. Except in unusual circumstances, where the cost of land and construction may require it, projects with more than 90–100 units are usually too many for a residential-scale assisted living building.

Provide Residential Privacy and Completeness

A small kitchenette and a full bathroom make the dwelling unit complete. Providing extra space for an overnight guest or family member can be achieved even in units as small as a studio alcove. Privacy should be achieved through a combination of efforts, including leasing policies that encourage single occupancy, design features such as locks on doors, and management practices that require staff to identify themselves before entering residents' dwellings. To personalize their units, residents should be able to bring in their own furniture as well as display photos, artwork, and special collectibles. Keep in mind that some residents enjoy the company of another person and feel more secure when they are sharing a unit. If this occurs, the room should be large enough or configured in a way that avoids a side-by-side bed placement.

Recognize the Uniqueness of Each Resident

Each older person who enters assisted living has lived a unique life. Each has a multiplicity of experiences, which have nurtured diverse interests, abilities, and values, through the acquisition of a highly personalized knowledge base. Gerontologists like James E. Birren argue that as we age, life's experiences and our own differentiated interests make us unique rather than uniform in our understanding and appreciation of daily life events. Capturing that diversity within a group living environment is important. Welch and her colleagues (1984) describe the various resident personality profiles in group housing, which vary from passive joiners to active leaders. These differences suggest resident roles that can make the programming and activity process a dynamic one. Encouraging small-group participation and nurturing individual interests can make a setting extraordinarily rich. It is almost always better to have a program that recognizes different interests through clubs and small-group participation than one that is highly dependent on large-group activities.

Foster Independence, Interdependence, and Individuality

Resident assessments should inventory the unique capabilities and competencies of each person and should lead to a program that treats each person as an individual with respect and dignity. Even for the most impaired residents, we must search for ways in which the community can provide help, as well as ways in which these persons can contribute to the community. When residents are treated as objects and are not expected to demonstrate any independent behaviors, they become victims of learned helplessness and eventually become more dependent. When assessments identify strengths and behaviors that can be the subject of therapy, then residents can preserve and build competencies. Helping one another is a wonderful practice that often develops naturally among residents who become friends. Peer support and encouragement is highly motivating and are almost always

Alcove used to personalize unit entry: A small corridor alcove next to a resident's entry door contains several items that refer to the artistic achievements of her granddaughter.

provided on the basis of affection. It should be treasured and encouraged.

Focus on Health Maintenance, Physical Movement, and Mental Stimulation

Avoiding institutionalization for as long as possible is a major motivation for most residents. Monitoring health through preventive checks, good nutritional habits, and careful attention to medications constructs a safety net of assurance. Physical challenges in the form of exercise therapy can build upper and lower body strength, increase aerobic capacity, and achieve muscle control over problems like incontinence. Spiduso and Gilliam-McRae (1991) underscore the impact sedentary behavior has on human frailty when medications and physical restraints are used in nursing homes. They describe in detail the effects of exercise on the four chronic diseases (cardiovascular disease, diabetes mellitus, chronic lung disease, and arthritis) that cause the greatest amount of disability in the elderly. Maria Fiatarone (1994) emphasizes exercise, weight training, and nutritional supplementation in strength-building regimens. Activities that stimulate the mind, like reading and discussion groups, also create opportunities for friendship formation, informal social exchange, and the sharing of personal feelings. Such activities counteract depression by replacing friendships that have been lost through attrition or relocation.

Support Family Involvement

Most institutions treat patients like a baton in a relay race. Family responsibility ends when the resident moves into an institution. The baton is handed off, and in most conventional nursing home facilities, there is usually no way to get it back. Maintaining strong connections with a family member is often difficult after institutionalization unless the family is involved in the caregiving process. A family-based assessment can develop a caregiving partnership that allows family members a more important role in making critical decisions and in providing direct care. The building should be designed with a range of different spaces where residents and family members can spend time together. Encouraging overnight stays outside the facility at the family's house or within a resident's unit can also add to family connectivity. When family members become participating partners in the life of a place, they add vitality and energy. Their social participation can also be a source of enjoyment for other residents.

Maintain Connections with the Surrounding Community

Encouraging residents to visit their old neighborhood to attend church or have their hair styled maintains connections with old friends and familiar places. Interaction with the old neighborhood allows residents to draw on a wider range of interactions rather than narrowing their choices. Housing projects that develop inventive ways to serve the surrounding community become less internally focused and better connected to the community. Institutions by their vary nature are divorced from the surrounding context. When a building connects to the community by, for example, creating a sidewalk linkage to an adjacent church, school, or library, it makes a gesture of

Double pocket doors link the living room and bedroom: In the *Zion* housing project in Trondheim, Norway, doors allow this wide portal to be opened or closed. When it is closed, bedroom privacy is maintained. When it is opened, the unit is perceived as being much larger.

friendship and connection. Intergenerational exchange programs with schools have been successful in forging relationships between older people and children. Foster grandparents receive affection, admiration, and increased self-esteem as a result of these programs.

Serve the Frail

The average resident of an assisted living facility is likely to be in the 82- to 87-year age range. Furthermore, facilities should conform to the 30/40/50 rule, which suggests that about 30 percent of the population are incontinent, 40 percent are wheelchair and/or walker dependent, and 50 percent have the beginning of memory loss. It is not at all uncommon for as many as 60 percent of residents to be in need of bathing assistance and 25 percent to be in need of toileting assistance. A population with this level of impairment is the appropriate target group for an assisted living building. Residents who have less serious impairments can best be better served in the community by home health care workers.

FACTORS AFFECTING THE GROWTH OF ASSISTED LIVING

A number of factors are responsible for the meteoric rise of assisted living as the current long-term care alternative of choice. Many of these are basic issues representing underlying concerns that have characterized nursing home environments for years. In the last 15 years, these forces, both individually and collectively, have forced a rethinking of what defines long-term care in America. The following ten factors appear to be among the most powerful influences affecting the growth of assisted living.

Growth in the Oldest-Old Population

The single most important factor affecting the demand for assisted living housing is the growth in the oldest segment of the U.S. population. The U.S. Bureau of the Census (middle series projection) anticipates nearly a doubling of the 85+ population between 1990 (3.1 million) and 2010 (5.8 million). This will be followed by a further doubling of this population in the next 30 years (2010 [5.8 million] to 2040 [14.3 million]). A 300 percent increase in 50 years is huge, but Guralnik, Yanagishita, and Schneider (1988) argue that pending biomedical breakthroughs and advances in disease prevention and therapy could maintain the 2 percent decline in mortality experienced by the United States in the last 20 years. If this is the case, the increase would be closer to 440 percent, rising from 4.3 million people over age 85 in 2000 to 23.3 million in 2040. The growth of the 85+ population will be especially great after 2030. As a result, nearly one-fourth of the elderly population is expected to be 85 years or over by the year 2050 (Wallman, 2000).

International Trends

The trend toward an older, frailer population is not just an American phenomenon. Japan is projected to experience a 274 percent increase in the 80+ population between 1990 and 2025 (U.S. Senate Special Committee on Aging, 1991). However, the major increase in the oldest-old population worldwide will occur in less developed countries, outpacing that of more developed countries in the next 35 years by a factor of 3 (Myers, 1990). Today's problems with the oldest old appear to exist in North America, Europe, and Japan. However,

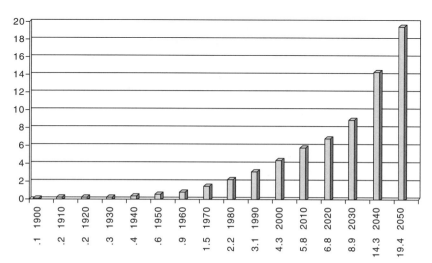

85+ Population: The actual and projected population increase of the United States from 1990 to 2050 (Wallman, 2000).

Alternative Projections of Life Expectancy for the Population aged 65+ and 85+, 1980, 1990, 2000, 2020, and 2040

	1980[1]	*1990*[2]	*Middle Series Mortality 2000*	*Middle Series Mortality 2020*[4]	*Middle Series Mortality 2040*[4]	*High Series Mortality 2040*[4]	*Assumption of 2% Annual Mortality 2040*[5]
Life Expectancy From birth (yrs)							
Male	70.0	72.1	72.7[3]	—	75.0	77.8	85.9
Female	77.4	79.0	80.3[3]	—	83.1	86.7	91.5
Population (thousands)							
Age 85+	2.2	3.3	4.3[4]	6.8	14.3	16.8	23.3
Age 65	25.5	31.6	34.8[4]	53.7	77.2	87.1	86.8
Percentage of 65+ population age 85 and over	8.7%	10.3%	12.4%	12.7%	18.5%	19.3%	26.9%

Sources:

[1] U.S. Bureau of the Census, tabulated from Decennial Census of the Population, 1983.

[2] U.S. Bureau of the Census, 1989.

[3] U.S. Bureau of the Census, 1984.

[4] Wallman, 2000.

[5] Guralnik, Yanagishita, et al. 1988.

by 2025, China (with 33.5 million people aged 80+) and India (15.9 million) will push the United States into third place (2025—14.3 million people aged 80+) (U.S. Bureau of the Census, 2001)

The Oldest Old and Service Needs

The older the population, the greater the likelihood that formal service intervention will be necessary to support personal independence. Rivlin and Weiner (1988) estimate that more than 60 percent of the current 85+ population is disabled compared to 18.4 percent of the younger old (65–84). Although informal care provision

World Population Projections for Ages 80+, 2000 and 2025

Country	2000	Rank	2025	Rank
China	11,514	1	33,590	1
USA	9,225	2	14,800	3
India	6,175	3	15,956	2
Japan	4,671	4	11,221	4
Russia	2,936	5	4,514	6
Germany	2,910	6	6,049	5

Source: U.S. Bureau of the Census. *World Population 2001*, accessed online at www.census.gov/ipc/www/idbsum.html on July 3, 2001.

accounts for the vast majority of help provided to the elderly, as the population ages the percentage that relies on formal support increases (Chappell, 1990). For example, while only 1.1 percent of the younger old (age 65–84) are in nursing homes, this percentage increases 20-fold for the 85+ age group. Of those over the age of 65 who are severely disabled, approximately 35 percent are in nursing homes. Thus, the probability that more intensive assistance from the formal support system will be needed grows dramatically with an increase in age and disability.

Although the number of people over the age of 85 grew in the 1990s by 37 percent (compared to the general population growth of 13 percent), fewer disabled people were housed in nursing homes than in 1994. The elderly today are in better physical shape than their predecessors, and more are choosing to stay in assisted living than in traditional nursing home environments (Wallman, 2000).

Approximately 6.9 million people over the age of 65 were in need of long-term care in 1990. By the year 2000, this number had increased 30 percent to 9 million. During the next 40 years, it will double to 18 million (U.S. Senate Special Committee on Aging, 1991). Current nursing home stock will care for only a fraction of this population. Home care and assisted living will be the answer for the vast majority of this continually growing segment of the older frail.

Cost Differences Between Assisted Living and Skilled Nursing Care

One of the major challenges to long-term care is making it more affordable. The continuing increase in long-term care costs has concerned both policy makers and consumers. Some believe that the increase in dementia residents in long-term care may even bankrupt the Medicaid system by 2010. Current nursing home care costs are estimated to rise from $18.2 billion in 2000 to $33.0 billion by 2010. Both policy makers and politicians see the cost of long-term care burgeoning out of control. Consumers are increasingly questioning the value of services provided by nursing homes, especially in light of other growing alternatives. Rivlin and Weiner (1988) estimate that long-term care costs will triple in the next decade and will likely continue to increase exponentially unless we discover new ways to care for an increasingly dependent older-old population. Assisted living has generally proven to be less expensive than conventional nursing home care.

In a comparative study carried out by Marion Merrill Dow and Healthcare Financial Management Association (ALFA, 2000) around 1996, the average cost of a private assisted living unit was $72 compared with $111 for a private pay/private bed in a skilled nursing environment—a 54 percent increase over assisted living. In the same report, subacute care averaged $250/day and acute hospital care, $821/day. Surprisingly, home health nursing visits averaged $83. Of course, the resident of an assisted living unit generally requires less care than someone in a skilled nursing facility. However, compared with the rapidly increasing cost of skilled care, assisted living costs for the most common unit (private, one bedroom) have increased by only 16 percent during the last four years (ALFA, 2000).

Changing Preferences of Consumers and Their Advocates

Older consumers, many of whom have themselves institutionalized a parent, are increasingly reluctant to accept a skilled nursing home placement for themselves. In fact, the total rate of nursing home placement on a per capita basis declined from 54 persons per 1000 (age 65+) in 1985 to 45 persons per 1000 (age 65+) in 1997. In the 85+ population, this represented a 13 percent decline (Wallman, 2000). Many older people have grown accustomed to the choice, control, autonomy, and privacy that living at home provides (AARP, 1996). The increased cost and the institutional lifestyle associated with a conventional nursing home facility are unappealing to the vast majority of older persons. Furthermore, middle-aged children who increasingly make decisions about placements are seeking value and responsiveness from providers. Many delay placement as long as possible and then search for an environment that is residential in character, as well as friendly and appealing to visit. Nursing homes so closely resemble hospitals that many older people and their families avoid this alternative at all costs.

Convenient bench near the elevator: This bench seating at the *De Overloop* in Almere, the Netherlands, is convenient for residents who are waiting for the elevator or for friends to join them. Some residents like to sit here and greet others.

Questioning of the Hospital-Based Care Model

The minimizing of hospital stays brought about by cost-saving controls on insurance reimbursement and the increasing reliance on outpatient care have altered the image of the hospital from its traditional role as an inpatient setting. This change has also called into question the appropriateness of the nursing home as a long-term care environment. Just as the minimum hospital stay was challenged by diagnosis related groups (DRGs), the need for nursing home care has been questioned for those who are not acutely ill but are nonetheless placed in an expensive health care environment. At the same time, nursing homes are experiencing an increase in the number of very frail older people. For example, between 1985 and 1997, the percentage of persons requiring assistance in eating jumped from 41 to 45 percent and the percentage of persons who needed help with mobility increased from 76 to 79 percent percent. When these very sick residents are combined with the financially indigent and with older people with dementia, the resulting mixture raises questions about the role of the nursing home in long-term care. Increasingly, nursing homes see themselves as subacute settings that are oriented toward medically indigent residents in need of rehabilitation services or heavy care. Regulations that recognize this increasing level of acuity have encouraged nursing homes to move in this direction. As the medical service needs of the older population increase, it makes less sense to use the nursing home for others who are in better physical condition.

Growth of New Technologies and Care Systems

The last 15 years have seen an explosion in electronic communication technology: cell phones, laptop computers, fax machines, remote sensing devices, noninvasive medical diagnostic equipment, and the Internet. These new technologies have also had profound impacts on medical care. Incontinence, which was once considered a rationale for institutionalization, has been redefined by incontinence products and self-managed incontinence programs. Electronic communication systems such as Lifeline, Wanderguard, and TeleAlarm are redefining the way older people are monitored and receive care in a range of housing environments. Portable medical devices are allowing more older people to die at home. Given the monitoring and sensing technologies available in buildings today, most of these structures are increasingly safe. In fact, the probability of dying in a fire within a sprinkled building is extremely low compared to the probability of a serious life-threatening car or airplane accident. Decentralized technologies have made it increasingly feasible to care safely for older, sicker people in noninstitutional environments.

Questioning of the Concept of Institutionalization

The movement toward decentralized home care over the last 15–20 years has allowed many older, frail people to live in the community safely and effectively. As a result of the success of movements like this one, older residents and their families are increasingly questioning whether it is necessary to enter a nursing home. The availability of community-based care and the increasing number of other options like assisted living have left many older people and their families wondering if nursing home placement is a concept of the past. Many older people see themselves "aging in place" until they can no longer care for themselves. At that point, an assisted living environment appears to be a better fit for their needs. A nursing home doesn't make sense unless the resident requires 24-hour medical care provision. This level of care is necessary for a relatively small number of aging individuals. In fact, a study of nursing home residents conducted in six states found that 39 percent of them received no care from a registered nurse during a 24-hour period. The remainder who did receive care used it for an average of only 7.9 minutes (Friedlob, 1993). Both nursing homes and assisted living are primarily involved in the delivery of personal care assistance.

Lack of Informal Family-Based Care Opportunities

Middle-aged women, who traditionally have been caregivers for their parents, are increasingly engaged in work outside of the home. In 1915, 20.5 percent of the labor force was made up of women; today it is more than 50 percent. As a result, women must juggle competing demands or decrease their paid employment to provide care (Stone, 2000). Adult children provide the majority of care to older people, followed by spouses. Currently, the number of persons over age 70 with activity limitations is 8.5 million. This will more than double to 21 million by the year 2030 (National Academy on an Aging Society, 2000). With the pressing demands of the workplace, informal caregivers are seeking housing alternatives that allow them to provide care on a more flexible basis. This has long been a pattern in northern European countries, which have some of the highest percentages of working women in the world. In northern Europe, the system of elder care is highly dependent on assisted living housing alternatives for the frail segment of this population.

Dutch doors open the room to the corridor: The half-doors used as unit entry doors at *Woodside Place* in Oakmont, Pennsylvania, are not used by residents or staff. Reports from Copper Ridge (page 201), where they were also employed, reflect the same pattern of use (Kershner, Roques, et al., 1999).

Changing Attitudes Regarding Regulation

The increasingly stringent nursing home regulations implemented over the last 20 years in response to abuses have failed to provide better, more attractive facilities. Consumers in search of cost-effective, humane, and attractive residential environments generally avoid highly regulated nursing homes. Policy makers questioning the effectiveness of nursing homes in producing attractive alternatives have encouraged states and service providers to seek other approaches. Oregon and Washington started what has since become a widespread movement by introducing a special licensing category for assisted living. According to Mollica (1995, 2000), nearly 60 percent of U.S. states are considering, developing, or implementing new regulations that apply to assisted living.

Another factor encouraging the development of new standards has been the growth in unlicensed facilities that are seeking to satisfy the demand for more flexible housing and service arrangements.

Awareness of Cross-Cultural Solutions

Today, countries located thousands of miles apart are connected through finance, political cooperation, and world trade. Greater familiarity with other cultures through world travel has also allowed us to appreciate and understand how other countries deal with similar problems. Most countries are struggling with the problem of a burgeoning older-old population. Sweden, with a 65+ population of 17.2 percent, has one of the highest percentages of elderly in the world (Wallman, 2000). As a result, in the last 25 years, it has devised systems that deal more humanely with the needs and preferences of older people for noninstitutional supportive housing. These buildings and service systems make a great deal of sense today as we seek to learn from one another through cross-cultural examinations. As the United States struggles to understand how best to deal with its aging population, so do other countries. Our ability to learn from one another increases the probability that new models will successfully adapt ideas from other countries.

Interest of Corporate America in Responding to Opportunities

Corporate America has responded aggressively to the creative opportunities developing as our society ages. Of particular interest is the mismatch between what consumers want and what is available to satisfy their demand. Assisted living is perceived as a far better choice for personal care than the traditional nursing home. In response to the perceived need for assisted living, public companies, hospitality organizations, and private nonprofit providers are creating assisted living buildings. Between 1997 and 2000, the American Seniors Housing Association (2000) estimated that 1321 assisted living properties were constructed throughout the United States. Assisted living construction accounted for more than two-thirds of the purpose-built senior housing created during this period.

TYPICAL PROFILES OF ASSISTED LIVING RESIDENTS

Assisted living is seen as a housing type for both the physically and mentally frail. Although these two groups have very different needs, the assisted living model of care serves both of them well. Mentally frail residents are al-

Flexible cabinet serves as a religious altar: In a multipurpose room, a simple piece of furniture, when properly designed, can transform the space from a secular to a sacred use.

most always cared for in a separate unit that is designed to accommodate their special needs. These units are either separated in a stand-alone building or are carved out of a larger building as a secured cluster of dwelling units and common spaces. Part III of this book contains several examples of buildings of this type. A typical assisted living building attracts individuals who are both mentally and physically impaired.

Because dementia is a progressive ailment that affects every resident in a slightly different way, there is tremendous variability in this population. Some residents can mask their mental frailty well after it develops, while others exhibit antisocial behaviors from the beginning. Assisted living buildings with a secured wing or floor for dementia make it possible to move initially to assisted living and then move again when the disease progresses to the point where special care and more security are required. Because memory loss is common among the oldest old (National Institute of Aging, 1999), every assisted living building has residents with some memory impairment.

Mentally Impaired Residents

The move to a separate secured dementia unit is normally triggered when residents become a hazard to themselves or begin to disturb others. Dementia units are normally

designed around a cluster of units and limited to 12–20 residents. Northern European models utilize much smaller clusters—6–10 residents. The profile of a mentally frail resident varies, but many experience disorientation, confusion, agitation, and frustration. As the disease progresses, restlessness, aimless wandering, occasional verbal outbursts, and behavioral aggressiveness may develop. However, many residents remain passive and pleasant until the end. As residents age, they may become both physically and mentally frail. In the United States, it is becoming increasingly common for residents to die in assisted living buildings rather than be moved to a nursing home. New regulations in Michigan and Texas are allowing families to stay in assisted living if the facility and the family are satisfied that their needs can be met in this setting. In northern Europe, residents rarely move from a dementia unit unless they become violent or require major medical interventions. In fact, in both cultures, there is little reason to move a resident to an institutional setting. Memory loss alone is not a good enough reason to institutionalize an older person in a health care setting.

Physically Impaired Residents

Assisted living residents with physical problems are the other type of resident. Typically, these residents move to assisted living in response to an acute or chronic medical problem. The aftermath of a broken hip or heart attack might trigger a move, but most likely it is the increasing chronic disability of mobility impairment, arthritis, or balance control that motivates a change in residence. Residents with physical impairments often have a difficult time walking. A few are in wheelchairs, but most are dependent on a walking stick, four-prong cane, or walker to get around. Many have limitations that are not apparent, such as hypertension, heart disease, diabetes, inconti-nence, hearing loss, or visual impairment. When these limitations are mild, they make preparing meals, driving a car, shopping for groceries, and managing medications difficult. When these conditions become more disabling, they make it difficult to take a shower, dress without assistance, go to the bathroom alone, and eat without as-sistance. These disabilities can be easily managed in assisted living unless they are so disabling that they require 24-hour supervised nursing care.

2

BENCHMARKING ASSISTED LIVING BUILDINGS AND RESIDENTS

During the last ten years, a number of efforts have been made to understand the nature of assisted living. Reviews of the empirical literature (Wylde and Zimmerman, 1999) have attempted to define the major issues, and guidebooks have suggested practical development and management approaches (Gordon, 1998; Harrigan, Raiser, et al., Raiser, 1998; Moore, 1996, 2000, 2001; Pearce, 1998; Porter, 1995). Environmental design researchers (Brumett, 1997; Golant, 2000; Moore, 1998) have written focused studies, and several new edited books regarding design and policy have appeared on the topic (Schwartz and Brent, 1999; Zimmerman, Sloane, et al., 2001). The experiences of other countries have been presented from a broader policy perspective (Pynoos and Liebig, 1995) and from a more practical design perspective (Centre for Accessible Environments, 1998; Hoglund, 1985; Salmon, 1993; Valins, 1988; Weal and Weal, 1988). Most of these works have been useful in understanding the role the environment plays in assisted living. However, they do not clarify the state of assisted living housing today.

To understand this more fully, we must turn to several national surveys that have pieced together an accurate picture of what constituted assisted living in the United States at the end of the 1990s. The study that most people rely on is *ALFA's Overview of the Assisted Living Industry* (ALFA, 2000). This is an annual self-report survey of ALFA membership that was first conducted in 1995 (ALFA, 1996). The most recent survey conducted in 1999 but published in 2000, is the fourth in this series of annual reports and contains comparisons from previous years. The survey has grown in size and complexity over the years. In 1996, it was a sample of 268 ALFA member buildings (14,927 units) focused solely on assisted living in 35 states. The 2000 study of 373 facilities (27,011 units) in 44 states was expanded to include independent living. The major limitation of the study is the fact that it reflects only ALFA members and that it relies on self-reported data from project administrators.

In 1998 ALFA, in conjunction with the National Investment Conference (NIC), published a survey of assisted living buildings from the 48 contiguous states. The report, entitled "National Survey of Assisted Living Residents: Who Is the Customer?", was an important publication because it employed a much more scientific sampling procedure. However, it was also oriented toward contemporary projects, limiting itself to buildings that had been constructed or substantially remodeled in the last 15 years. This research contained a survey of administrators that focused on characteristics of the setting and an interview that was completed by a random sample of residents or their caregivers. Altogether, 178 buildings were included in the sample profile. Each facility also yielded a random sample of five or six residents, for a total of 1023 resident respondents. To be included in the research, assisted living communities had to meet the following criteria:

▲ Contain eight or more units

▲ Have a freestanding or separately staffed assisted living services section

▲ Be built or substantially renovated after 1982

▲ Have a minimum service package of two meals per day and personal care assistance

▲ Be a setting where 70 percent of the residents are over 60 years of age

▲ Provide 24-hour protective oversight

Also included in the survey is a special subsample of "modern" assisted living buildings. These communities are analyzed as a separate subgroup. They include settings that meet the following additional criteria:

▲ Opened since 1990

▲ Freestanding buildings

▲ Purpose built as assisted living, and

▲ Developed by the for-profit sector

These projects are generally most representative of the assisted living facilities that are being developed for today's older population.

WHAT ARE THE CHARACTERISTICS OF THE RESIDENTS IN ASSISTED LIVING FACILITIES?

Age and Gender

Because women outlive men in this country by nearly seven years, it is no surprise that the majority of people in assisted living are female. Although the numbers have changed slightly in each of the four years the ALFA (2000) study has been conducted, the population is 75 to 78 percent female. Women are also more likely to end up in assisted living because many of them are widowed and no longer have a spouse to care for them. Because women often outlive their spouses, they are more likely to have been their caregiver. Three-quarters of men over age 70 are married and live with their spouses, but only a third of women aged 70+ have a spouse present. By age 90 as many as 40 percent of men are married, compared with only 5 percent of women (Schaefer, 2000).

In many cases, married women have gone to great lengths to take care of their spouse at home. However, when they are old and frail and need personal care assistance, few husbands are around to provide it. The av-

Exercise equipment placed in the atrium: Several easily accessible pieces of exercise equipment are located on the first floor of the three-story Saga garden atrium in Helsinki, Finland.

Assisted Living: Basic Demographic Profile

Resident Personal Statistics	ALFA[1] 2000	NIC[2] 1998
1. Female	75.3%	78.0%
2. Male	24.7%	22.0%
3. Average age	83.8 years	—
3. Average age (female)	84.3 years	84.5 years
4. Average age (male)	82.5 years	83.2 years
5. Average height (female)	—	5'2"
6. Average weight (female)	—	135.8#
7. Average height (male)	—	5'7 1/2"
8. Average weight (male)	—	162.3#
9. % w/annual income below $25,000	—	64.0%
10. % w/net worth of less than $100,000	—	63.0%
11. Couples (per building)	1.8	—
12. Average length of stay	24.5 months	30.8 months

[1] ALFA: ALFA statistics are from an annual national survey of assisted living providers who are ALFA members. The 1999 assisted living portion of the survey involved responses from 350 assisted living providers representing 18,019 units and 18,272 residents. Because the survey is limited to ALFA members, it does not necessarily represent the universe of assisted living environments available to older people. (ALFA, 2000)

[2] NIC: The NIC study is the result of a study of 178 assisted living communities located in the contiguous 48 states and of 1023 residents living in those communities. The survey instruments consisted of a facility survey completed by facility personnel and a resident survey with a resident assessment instrument completed by older residents with assistance from family members and staff. (NIC, 1998)

erage age of male residents in assisted care facilities, according to the ALFA (2000) study, is 82.5 years. The average age of female residents is 84.3 years. Interestingly, the average age of residents in nursing facilities is close to these numbers. However, residents of nursing homes are generally in much poorer health. The table above contains basic demographic information related to both the NIC and ALFA surveys.

Income and Net Worth

One surprising finding of the NIC study was that almost two-thirds of the resident population had an income of less than $25,000 per year. Yet the average daily fee of $67 amounted to $24,433 per year. Residents were spending down their net assets to stay in assisted living, and a surprising 16 percent of all residents were relying on financial help of at least $200 a month from family members (NIC, 1998). Net assets for two-thirds of the resident population were less than $100,000.

Married Couples

Couples are not very common in assisted living facilities. The ALFA survey found that, on the average, 1.8 mar-

ried couples are found at each assisted living facility (average size: 52.5 units). Often, married couples maintain their independence by possessing differential competencies. For example, one spouse might use a walker, while the other is partially sighted but ambulatory. Each one carries out tasks the other spouse cannot accomplish. Together they help one another to maintain independence.

Average Length of Stay

The average length of stay in assisted living is 24.5 months (ALFA, 2000), although it has trended downward from a 1996 high of 28.5 months. The NIC study showed a slightly longer 30.8-month average length of stay. In general, it is in the best interest of an assisted living facility, and often the desire of family members, to keep residents for as long as possible. This decision can sometimes be controversial if the facility is not equipped to deal with the increasing medical needs of the resident.

Five Levels of Service Need

More than half of the older people who seek the support of an assisted living environment do so for a health reason or because increasing mental and/or physical frailty makes it difficult for them to live alone (NIC, 1998). In fact, only 7 to 10 percent need no services to live independently. Examining the services that residents use is a good way to form a mental picture of the disabilities this group experiences every day. A quick perusal of the 18 different services or disabilities rank ordered in the following table reveals a number of interesting insights.

The 60 Percent Service Need Level

Nearly two-thirds of residents have such complex drug regimens that they need help with the organization and timing of medications. This is one reason why nursing personnel are considered to be important in many facilities. Drug interactions and side effects need to be iden-

tified, interpreted, and communicated to physicians and family members. Bathing assistance is another highly sought-after service. The potential for slipping or experiencing a balance control problem in the shower is feared by many older people. About half of the 61 percent of residents who needed help with bathing in the NIC study needed supervision assistance only. The remainder needed help transferring to and from the bathtub/shower or were totally dependent (NIC, 1998).

The 50 Percent Service Need Level

Cognitive impairment is also a prevalent condition. Research projections show that the incidence of this condition will triple over the next 50 years (Evans, 1990). Nationwide, between 35 and 37 percent of the 85+ pop-

Assisted Living: Percentage of Residents Needing/Receiving Assistance

	ALFA[1] 2000	NIC[2] 1998	NIC-Modern[3] 1998
1. Medication dispensing	66.5%	—	—
2. Bathing	65.5%	61.0%	62%
3. Dressing	47.8%	35.0%	39.6%
4. % cognitively impaired	45.0%	—	—
5. % hospitalized in last year	—	45.0%	—
6. Personal hygiene	43.9%	—	—
7. Wheelchair/walker users	41.0%	—	—
8. Toileting	28.9%	25.1%	30.7%
9. Daily incontinence	26.4%	—	—
10. Locomotion (mobility asst.)	24.4%	16.2%	20.2%
11. Eating	16.3%	6.2%	5.8%
12. Using home health services	—	11.3%	15.7%
13. Transferring assistance	—	11.9%	—
13. Diabetes	10.4%	—	—
14. Wheelchair users	—	11.7%	—
15. Who could live independently	—	10.9%	7.7%
16. Parkinson's disease	6.1%	—	—
17. Residents with automobiles	—	5.2%	4.7%
18. Nonambulatory/bedridden	.9%	—	—

[1] ALFA: ALFA statistics are from an annual national survey of assisted living providers who are ALFA members. The 1999 assisted living portion of the survey involved responses from 350 assisted living providers representing 18,019 units and 18,272 residents. Because the survey is limited to ALFA members, it does not necessarily represent the universe of assisted living environments available to older people. (ALFA, 2000)

[2] NIC: The NIC study is the result of a study of 178 assisted living communities located in the contiguous 48 states and of 1023 residents living in those communities. The survey instruments consisted of a facility survey completed by facility personnel and a resident survey with a resident assessment instrument completed by older residents with assistance from family members and staff. (NIC, 1998)

[3] NIC-Modern: The "modern subsample" of the NIC study consists of newer facilities that have opened since 1990. They were also screened to meet the following three criteria: (a) free-standing, (b) purpose-built, and (c) sponsored by for-profit sponsors. (NIC, 1998)

ulation have moderate to severe memory loss (Wallman, 2000). In assisted living buildings, the ALFA (2000) survey estimates that 45 percent of the resident population suffers from cognitive impairment. In nursing homes the number is slightly higher, with 54 percent having dementia (Krauss and Altman, 1998).

The 40 Percent Service Need Level

Dressing assistance is also a common personal care service because arthritis, a chronic condition that affects nearly 50 percent of the 65+ population (CDC, 1999), can become a disabling problem as one grows older and more infirm. The data show that 35 to 47 percent of the assisted living population need or receive this form of help. The combination of walkers and wheelchair users reaches approximately 41 percent of the assisted living population, according to the ALFA (2000) survey. Referring to an earlier statistic from the NIC (1998) survey, which shows 11.7 percent of the population use a wheelchair, we can assume that walkers and other walking aides are far more prevalent than wheelchairs.

The 30 Percent Service Need Level

Toileting assistance and the problem of incontinence affect 25–30 percent of the population (ALFA, 2000; NIC, 1998). An incontinence program can help residents manage this condition with greater dignity. Providing help with toileting is necessary when residents find it difficult to transfer on and off the commode or to self-manage their continence.

The 10 Percent Service Need Level

A number of special problems affect smaller segments of the older population. Difficulty with eating and chronic diseases like diabetes and Parkinson's disease, as well as wheelchair dependence, affect 6 to 15 percent of this population.

Relationships with Family and Friends

Family support is one of the most cherished forms of friendship and assistance. Regardless of the competence and friendliness of paid personnel, they can never replace the emotional bond and support of family members. Of course, not every resident has this support network. Some families are alienated as a result of conflicts over caring for their parents. In the NIC study (see the table below), 11.3 percent of residents openly expressed conflict or anger with family or friends. Additionally, 25 per-

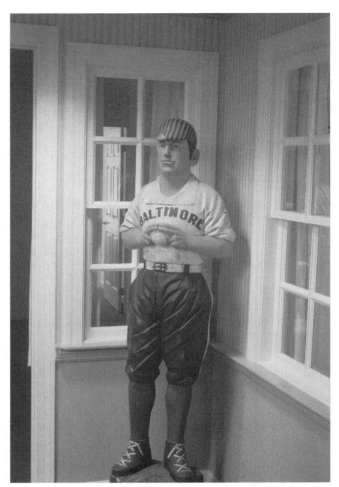

Large sculpture works well for orientation purposes: This full-sized statue, which is unusual in size and memorable in appearance, creates a landmark in a facility where symmetrical corridors have been confusing to some assisted living residents.

cent of residents did not have children to look after them. For many, the decision to move into assisted living involved family input. Daughters were the most influential in the decision-making process, followed by sons (NIC, 1998).

Although family members do a lot of the research in exploring assisted living alternatives, a surprising 47.8 percent of residents in the NIC (1998) study felt that the idea to make the move was mostly their own. As a result of the move, nearly 75 percent of residents live either closer to their family or at about the same distance (NIC, 1998). Additionally, the move often leads to a more positive family relationship. Although the majority of residents had the same family relation-

Assisted Living: Satisfaction with Family and Friends

	NIC[1] 1998
1. Average number of living children	1.79 children
2. % who said it was mostly their idea to move	47.8%
3. % with no children	25.0%
4. % who saw family more after move	27.0%
5. % who saw family about as often	47.1%
6. % with better family relationship	21.6%
7. % with the same family relationship	69.0%
8. % very satisfied with quality of life	49.6%
9. % satisfied with quality of life	39.4%
10. % very dissatisfied with quality of life	0.6%
11. % dissatisfied with quality of life	1.7%

[1] NIC: The NIC study is the result of a study of 178 assisted living communites located in the contiguous 48 states and of 1023 residents living in those communities. The survey instruments consisted of a facility survey completed by facility personnel and a resident survey with a resident assessment instrument completed by older residents with assistance from family members and staff.

ship (69.0 percent) after the move to assisted living, 21.6 percent reported a better relationship, while only 2.9 percent reported a worse relationship after the move.

Satisfaction with the Quality of Life

An improving family relationship is wonderful, but are residents any happier? The NIC study asked a very interesting summary question: "How satisfied are you with the quality of life in this residence?" The answers were equally revealing. Almost half (49.6 percent) of the respondents were very satisfied, and nearly 40 percent (39.4 percent) were satisfied. Less than 1 percent (.6 percent) were very dissatisfied, and less than 2 percent (1.7 percent) were dissatisfied. The remainder (8.7 percent) were neither more nor less satisfied. A cross-correlation analysis involving the relationship with family members was also revealing (NIC, 1998). Among the residents who experienced a better relationship with family members after moving (21.6 percent of the sample), 57.7 percent were very satisfied with the quality of their lives. This demonstrates again how important family connections are to a successful adjustment in a new assisted living environment.

WHAT TYPES OF SERVICES AND ACTIVITIES ARE AVAILABLE TO RESIDENTS?

Core Services Available to Residents

One way to conceptualize assisted living is to think of it as housing with a strategic collection of services. Thus, the availability of a range of services, more than anything else, defines the level of assistance available. The following table rank orders the percentage of buildings that provide different types of services. These services may or may not be included in the monthly fee. The percentages reflect the number of buildings that make these services available to residents. The first 14 are provided by more than 92 percent of the assisted living buildings in both surveys and represent the "core service package" associated with assisted living. This core list includes food, personal care assistance, help with medications, laundry, and transportation. These 14 core services include:

Three meals per day
Housekeeping service
Assistance with basic ADLs
Personal laundry
Snacks
Medication assistance
Escort service within the building
Wellness activities
Assistance with bathing
Beauty/barber shop services
Emergency call system
Linen service
Special diets
Transportation to shopping

Secondary Services Available to Residents

The next group on the list includes services that are provided by at least 80 percent of assisted living providers. Here we begin to see some of the differences reflected in the ALFA and NIC surveys. The availability of transportation service ranks in the 90s in the ALFA survey and in the mid-80s in the NIC survey. Some state regulations require that residents be given transportation to doctors' offices. Others are far less specific and assume that family members will arrange for transportation. Also included is incontinence management, which is provided by more ALFA than NIC survey respondents. Specialized services like respite care and home health services from external providers are included here as well.

Assisted Living: Services Available to Residents

	ALFA[1] 2000	NIC[2] 1998	NIC-Modern[3] 1998
1. Three meals/day	99.7%	—	—
2. Housekeeping	97.5%	99.4%	—
3. Assistance w/ADLs	96.3%	99.4%	—
4. Personal laundry	99.1%	98.2%	—
5. Snacks	98.1%	—	—
6. Medication assistance	96.0%	97.7%	—
7. Escort service within bldg.	—	97.7%	—
8. Wellness activities	97.2%	—	—
9. Assistance w/bathing	—	97.1%	—
10. Beauty/barber shop	—	97.0%	—
11. Emergency call system	96.3%	—	—
12. Linen service	—	94.2%	—
13. Special diets	92.7%	—	—
14. Transp. to shopping	95.6%	88.9%	—
15. Access to auto/van	—	84.2%	73.6%
16. Home health services	—	85%	93.9%
16. Toileting assistance	—	87.7%	—
15. Transp. to medical appts.	—	83.7%	—
17. Respite care	81.4%	—	—
18. Incontinence management	92.7%	80.6%	—
19. Nursing services	77.7%	—	—
20. Licensed to administer meds.	—	72.0%	77.6%
21. Weekly health checkup	69.8%	—	—
22. Physical therapy	48.2%	—	—

[1] ALFA: ALFA statistics are from an annual national survey of assisted living providers who are ALFA members. The 1999 survey involved responses from 350 assisted living providers representing 18,019 units and 18,272 residents. Because the survey is limited to ALFA members, it does not necessarily represent the universe of assisted living environments available to older people. (ALFA, 2000)

[2] NIC: The NIC study is the result of a study of 178 assisted living communities located in the contiguous 48 states and of 1023 residents living in those communities. The survey instruments consisted of a facility survey completed by facility personnel and a resident survey with a resident assessment instrument completed by older residents with assistance from family members and staff. (NIC, 1998)

[3] NIC-Modern: The "modern subsample" of the NIC study consists of newer facilities that have opened since 1990. They were also screened to meet the following three criteria: (a) free-standing, (b) purpose-built, and (c) sponsored by for-profit sponsors. (NIC, 1998)

Finally, the last four services are related to more intensive medical assistance and rehabilitation. Although most facilities provide assistance with medications, some are not licensed to administer medications. Usually this requires a more highly trained professional staff. Nursing services including weekly health assessments may or may not be required by state regulation. Finally, physical therapy is an expensive and complicated service if provided on site. When provided off site, it requires transportation to appointments. Although this is one of the most important services for assisted living facilities in the future to embrace, according to the ALFA survey it is now available in less than half of the facilities.

Core Activities Available to Residents

Knowing how older residents spend their time in an assisted living environment gives us a more enlightened view of how to design a building that supports activity patterns and residents' daily interests. The following table describes 14 different activities in which varying percentages of the resident population engage. The most common activities are somewhat passive and can be carried out in common areas of the building or within the resident's dwelling unit. The social activity of talking is the most popular, with nearly three-fourths of the population (73.9 percent) engaging in it. Social exchange

Garments near the door signal dementia residents to dress warmly: Outer garments located on these pegs next to a garden exit door encourage residents to put on warmer clothing if they want to walk outside during cold or inclement weather.

that can lead to friendships is an important contributor to well-being. Rowe and Kahn (1998) devote a chapter of their book to "relating to others" and conclude that "social support in its many forms . . . has direct positive effects on health." When a building design supports this goal, the building is more friendly and the quantity and quality of interaction are enhanced.

Watching TV, listening to music, reading, and writing are very popular passive activities. To enhance the enjoyment of these activities, acoustical environments should be designed to overcome the problem of hearing loss. Furthermore, audiovisual equipment that produces high-quality images and sound should be available. Dwelling units as well as common space should be designed to support these popular activities.

Activities Available to Many Residents

There are six middle-range activities that appeal to 33–46 percent of the resident population. These include more specialized group activities like card playing, crafts, and religious services. These activities also require more physical movement and include trips and shopping, walking and wheeling outdoors, and exercise sports. It is important to point out the focus on activities that take place outside the building. These activities underscore the need for an activity room, an indoor room for exercise, walking pathways that surround the site, and transportation to local shopping centers.

Least Common Activities Available to Residents

The last four activities are popular with smaller subsamples—10 to 31 percent of the population. Two of these represent the desire of many residents to engage in volunteer/helping activities in the community. David Wolfe (1990), in his book on marketing to older adults, refers to *The Altruistic Principle*. He contends that the older person often seeks activities that are less self-gratifying and more beneficial to others. In assisted living settings, helping others or carrying out tasks in the community also reinforces a sense of self-mastery that residents find appealing. The most competent individuals are those who have the energy and ability to help others; thus, there is status associated with this role.

The final two activities require considerable energy—dancing and gardening. They are both appealing to 10 percent of the population. Both require facility support, which can be managed in a modest or more elaborate fashion. Garden plots are easy to develop. When they are raised 16 to 24 inches off the ground, handicapped individuals, as well as those with chronic back pain, do not have to bend over. A resilient hard surface area for dancing is also of great benefit. With the range of wood and wood grain vinyl products available, a dance floor can be easily managed in a cost-effective, low-maintenance, attractive way. Finally, only 2.3 percent of residents reported no engagement in any activities. Clearly, most residents see a benefit to engaging in the life of the place.

Assisted Living: Activities Available for Residents

1999	ALFA[1] 2000	NIC[2] 1998	NIC-Modern[3] 1998
Activities			
1. Talking or conversing	—	73.9%	—
2. Watching TV	—	68.3%	—
3. Listening to music	—	60.8%	—
4. Reading and writing	—	57.8%	—
5. Spiritual/religious	—	46.1%	—
6. Card and other games	—	44.2%	—
7. Trips and shopping	—	42.6%	—
8. Walking and wheeling outdoors	—	42.2%	—
9. Crafts/art	—	35.4%	—
10. Exercise sports	—	33.6%	—
11. Helping others	—	31.0%	—
12. Doing chores around hse./comm.	—	18.5%	—
13. Dancing	—	11.0%	—
14. Gardening/plants	—	10.3%	—
15. None of the above	—	2.3%	—
Activities Allowed			
1. Visitors allowed anytime	—	90.6%	90.0%
2. Overnight guests	77.7%	—	—
3. Leave w/o obtaining permission	—	71.8%	65.0%
4. Community pets	69.9%	—	—
5. Resident owned pets	65.9%	—	—
6. Alcohol	65.2%	—	—
7. Smoking (in designated areas)	59.1%	—	—

[1] ALFA: ALFA statistics are from an annual national survey of assisted living providers who are ALFA members. The 1999 survey involved responses from 350 assisted living providers representing 18,019 units and 18,272 residents. Because the survey is limited to ALFA members, it does not necessarily represent the universe of assisted living environments available to older people. (ALFA, 2000)

[2] NIC: The NIC study is the result of a study of 178 assisted living communities located in the contiguous 48 states and of 1023 residents living in those communities. The survey instruments consisted of a facility survey completed by facility personnel and a resident survey with a resident assessment instrument completed by older residents with assistance from family members and staff. (NIC, 1998)

[3] NIC-Modern: The "modern subsample" of the NIC study consists of newer facilities that have opened since 1990. They were also screened to meet the following three criteria: (a) free-standing, (b) purpose-built, and (c) sponsored by for-profit sponsors. (NIC, 1998)

Activities Allowed in Assisted Living Buildings

The last seven features listed in the table represent freedoms and choices available to residents. The responses to the survey questions demonstrate the freedom and the constraints residents experience. A majority of buildings allowed all of these activities. Although most of these activities would be taken for granted in independent housing, many are not allowed in skilled nursing homes. For example, visitors were allowed anytime (90.6 percent), could bring an overnight guest (77.7 percent), and could leave without obtaining permission (71.8 percent) in the vast majority of settings. The privilege of owning or caring for a community pet was sanctioned in 69.9 percent of the buildings. In 65.9 percent of the buildings, residents were allowed to bring their own pets. Finally, drinking alcohol and smoking, both of which can compromise safety, were allowed by 65.2 percent (drinking) and 59.1 percent (smoking) of facilities. Smoking was almost always restricted to designated areas, and drinking was often limited if a resident had a previous history of alcohol abuse.

Enclosed balconies are popular in the cold climate of northern Europe: Some residents in the *Folkhälsen* service house apartments, in Helsinki, Finland, have enclosed their balconies with movable glass panels so that they can be used during three seasons.

Assisted Living: Staffing Patterns

	NIC[1] 1998	NIC-Modern[2] 1998
1. Average No. of FTE employees	25.4 employ.	27.3 employ.
2. Median FTE/resident ratio	.50	.55
3. % w/licensed nurse[3]	83.2%	86%
4. % w/resident assessment	93.0%	—

[1] NIC: The NIC study is the result of a study of 178 assisted living communities located in the contiguous 48 states and of 1023 residents living in those communities. The survey instruments consisted of a facility survey completed by facility personnel and a resident survey with a resident assessment instrument completed by older residents with assistance from family members and staff.

[2] NIC-Modern: The "modern subsample" of the NIC study consists of newer facilities that have opened since 1990. They were also screened to meet the following three criteria: (a) free-standing, (b) purpose-built, and (c) sponsored by for-profit sponsors.

[3] Includes registered nurse (RN), licensed practical nurse (LPN), or licensed vocational nurse (LVN).

Staffing Levels and Patterns

Very few staffing statistics are available through these two surveys. However, the NIC (1998) study has collected data regarding overall staff ratios displayed in the following table. The assisted living buildings studied have an average of 25.4 full-time equivalent (FTE) employees. The modern building, which has a slightly larger average size and a slightly more impaired population, has 27.3 FTE employees. This translates into a median FTE staff to resident ratio of 0.50 for the universal sample and 0.55 for the modern subsample. In comparison, most nursing homes have FTE ratios that are closer to 1.0. Health care considerations are important in assisted living environments. That is why 93.0 percent of the buildings go through a resident health assessment process and 83.2 percent have a licensed nurse on staff. Obviously, the more chronically impaired a resident is, the more sophisticated the nursing component must be.

WHAT ARE THE BUILDING'S CHARACTERISTICS AND AMENITIES?

Size of the Building

Data that describe the physical characteristics of assisted living buildings are among the most interesting and useful statistics for our purposes (see the following table). ALFA (2000) data-gathering periods have reflected some abrupt changes in these statistics during the last four years. For example, the average size of buildings has decreased from 59 units in 1996 to a low of 48.7 units in 1998 and then back to 52.5 units in 1999. Some of this variation is probably due to changes in ALFA membership, which in 1998 reflected a merger with the National Association of Residential Care Facilities. This organization had a membership that traditionally served smaller buildings with fewer residents.

The data from the NIC study, however, provide an interesting contrast. The NIC (1998) study shows that unit averages vary from 50.6 for all facilities to 51.2 for the modern facilities. The modern buildings are newer. The average age of the NIC Modern subsample is 3.3 years versus the 7.5 years that characterizes the total sample. The ALFA statistics also include recently developed buildings. Although not documented in the newest study, the ALFA (1999) study showed that nearly three-fourths of the sample (73.3 percent) represented building that were opened in the last four years.

A building of 40–60 units is ideal from a caregiving and management perspective. Larger buildings, although often less expensive to run, can be more difficult to maintain at full capacity. An average-sized building of 52.5

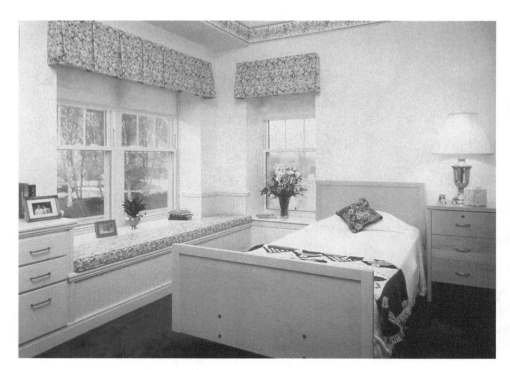

Low window seat links the bed with a view: This detail at *Copper Ridge* (page 201) has been popular for displaying items as well as for seating. The top is hinged for storage below. (Photo: Robert Ruschak)

units has a capacity of approximately 61.6 licensed beds, according to the ALFA (2000) survey. The difference between these two numbers accounts for double occupancies that can result from married couples, related siblings, and individuals who are sharing their unit with an unrelated individual.

Frequency of Double Occupancy

Neither study gives us an accurate picture of how many units were actually occupied by two people. The statistics gathered in the ALFA (2000) study show that 12 percent of the units were designed for double occupancy. The NIC (1998) study measured this in a slightly different way and found that 22 percent of the units were for semiprivate occupancy. Although licensed bed figures rarely reflect the actual occupancy, the difference between units and beds results in a multiplier of between 1.17 (ALFA) and 1.27 (NIC). In other words, approximately 17–25 percent of the units are capable of being double occupied. There has been a lot of controversy regarding double versus single occupancy. In 1998, a coalition of six housing and aging consumer organizations, called the Assisted Living Quality Coalition, agreed on a set of quality standards for assisted living. One of the issues they could not agree on was that of single- versus double-occupancy units. Some members of the coalition were concerned that allowing double occupancies would reduce the standard of privacy to a level similar to that of

skilled nursing facilities. The report noted that the overwhelming preference was for single private units. However, concerns about affordability and the benefits of companionship for some individuals led to the impasse.

Gross Building Statistics

In making assessments about the size of a building, one useful statistic is the number of gross square feet per dwelling unit. This is calculated by taking the total average gross square footage of the building and dividing it by the number of units. The ALFA (2000) survey showed that approximately 790 square feet (SF) per unit was available. The NIC study did not collect comparable data. This gross square footage number reflects the amount of space that is designated for common spaces, residential units, corridors, back-of-the-house areas, and wall construction. The percentage of gross square footage allocated to common areas or to residential space is another important figure that is often used to compare building philosophies. However, neither survey collected these data.

Based on an extrapolation of average residential unit sizes, the ALFA averages appear to allocate approximately 45 percent of the building's square footage to residential units and the remainder to all other spaces. In buildings with larger dwelling units, the ratios are normally reversed, with approximately 60 percent of the space dedicated to residential units and 40 percent to other

Assisted Living: General Building and Cost Statistics

	ALFA[1] 2000	*NIC[2]* 1998	*NIC-Modern[3]* 1998
Building Statistics			
1. Average size of project	52.5 units	50.6 units	51.2 units
2. Average capacity (licensed beds)	61.6 beds	64.2 beds	61.7 beds
3. Average number of residents	—	49.7 residents	42.6 residents
4. Average total building size	41,472 SF	—	—
5. Average square footage per unit	790 SF/unit	—	—
6. Average number of floors of building	—	1.8 floors	—
7. Occupancy rate (opened 18 mo.+)	—	91.4%	93.6%
8. Mean age of the facility	—	7.5 years	3.3 years
Location and Type Statistics			
1. % of projects in metropolitan area	57.5%	—	—
2. % of projects in nonmetropolitan area	42.5%	—	—
3. % of purpose-built buildings	—	70.0%	100.0%
4. % free-standing AL	63.6%	61.2%	100.0%
5. % part of a CCRC	13.2%	19.4%	—
6. % part of congregate community	12.1%	12.0%	—
7. % part of a nursing home	5.0%	7.0%	—
Construction Statistics			
1. Units per acre[4]	13 units/acre	—	—
2. Average square footage per unit[4]	769SF/Unit	—	—
3. Total development cost of project[4]	$8,370,488	—	—
4. Building construction cost per SF[4]	$93.82	—	—
5. Building construction cost per unit[4]	$72,144	—	—

[1] ALFA: ALFA statistics are from an annual national survey of assisted living providers who are ALFA members. The 1999 survey involved responses from 350 assisted living providers representing 18,019 units and 18,272 residents. Because the survey is limited to ALFA members, it does not necessarily represent the universe of assisted living environments available to older people. (ALFA, 2000)

[2] NIC: The NIC study is the result of a study of 178 assisted living communities located in the contiguous 48 states and of 1023 residents living in those communities. The survey instruments consisted of a facility survey completed by facility personnel and a resident survey with a resident assessment instrument completed by older residents with assistance from family members and staff. (NIC, 1998)

[3] NIC-Modern: The "modern subsample" of the NIC study consists of newer facilities that have opened since 1990. They were also screened to meet the following three criteria: (a) free-standing, (b) purpose-built, and (c) sponsored by for-profit sponsors. (NIC, 1998)

[4] These statistics are from another study by Herman/Turner Group LLC. This study encompassed 89 assisted living facilities. Forty contained fewer than 60 units, 28 contained 60 to 100 units and 21 contained more than 100 units. The building sizes were slightly larger. The buildings averaged 70 units in size and averaged 53,827 SF in size. This is 769 SF/unit, which is within 3% of the ALFA sample size of 790 SF/unit. (ALFA, 2000)

uses. Although little if any empirical data are available to contrast these two square footage allocation philosophies, they appear to lead to buildings that operate in fundamentally different ways. When units are smaller and common spaces are larger, a resident is likely to spend more of her time outside of her unit. When the unit is generous and the common spaces tight, the opposite pattern prevails. Another interesting statistic is the average

height in stories. According to the NIC (1998) survey, it appears to be 1.8 stories.

Construction Cost Statistics

Supplementary construction data in the ALFA (2000) survey were also gathered from other sources. A survey of 89 recently completed buildings by the Herman

Sculptural balcony design provides a sheltered area: This balcony design for the *Oulusalon* service house in Oulunsalo, Finland, is both beautiful and functional.

Assisted Living: Dwelling Unit Statistics

	ALFA[1] 2000	NIC[2] 1998	NIC-Modern[3] 1998
Dwelling Units by Type			
1. % semi-private rooms[4]	12.6%	22.0%	19.9%
Average square footage	315.5 SF	—	—
Average daily rate	$63.35	—	—
2. % of private (studio) units	61.0%	60.5%	60.3%
Average square footage	300.2 SF	317.8 SF	317.0 SF
Average daily rate	$73.97	$60.21	$60.58
Average occupancy	—	94.2%	85.5%
3. % of one-bedroom units	21.9%	31.3%	29.3%
Average square footage	515.2 SF	448.1 SF	448.2 SF
Average daily rate	$84.61	$71.33	$76.59
Average occupancy	—	93.8%	87.4%
4. % of two-bedroom units	2.5%	8.2%	10.4%
Average square footage	727.1 SF	597.1 SF	544.0 SF
Average daily rate	$101.55	$72.54	$77.80
Average occupancy	—	85.3%	86.3%
5. Average daily rate (all unit sizes)	—	$66.94	$70.78

[1] ALFA: ALFA statistics are from an annual national survey of assisted living providers who are ALFA members. The 1999 survey involved responses from 350 assisted living providers representing 18,019 units and 18,272 residents. Because the survey is limited to ALFA members, it does not necessarily represent the universe of assisted living environments available to older people. (ALFA, 2000)

[2] NIC: The NIC study is the result of a study of 178 assisted living communities located in the contiguous 48 states and of 1023 residents living in those communities. The survey instruments consisted of a facility survey completed by facility personnel and a resident survey with a resident assessment instrument completed by older residents with assistance from family members and staff. (NIC, 1998)

[3] NIC-Modern: The "modern subsample" of the NIC study consists of newer facilities that have opened since 1990. They were also screened to meet the following three criteria: (a) free-standing, (b) purpose-built, and (c) sponsored by for-profit sponsors. (NIC, 1998)

[4] The two surveys calculated units types differently. In the ALFA survey, semiprivate units were counted as a separate unit type. In the NIC study units were counted by three sizes. The number of units designed to be shared by another person were calculated separately.

Turner group provides additional data regarding price and size. In this supplemental survey, the average total building size was 70 units or 53,827 SF. The gross square footage per unit was 769 SF, which is slightly lower than the ALFA figure of 790 SF per unit. This difference might be accounted for by the larger unit count and presumably the more efficient building size in the Herman Turner sample. Total development costs in this sample were $8,370,488, or approximately $155 per SF. Construction costs for the building were $93.82, or $72,144 per dwelling unit. Total development costs per unit amount to $119,578.

Dwelling Unit Statistics

The ALFA and NIC studies gathered unit data in slightly different ways, making comparisons difficult. As shown in the following table, ALFA created five categories of units including special categories for double occupancy and "other." The NIC (1998) survey recognized only three unit categories: studios, one bedroom, and two bedrooms. One way to reconcile the two data sources is to add the double-occupancy units to the one-bedroom category and the other units to the two-bedroom category. When this is done, the data are much more comparable. They reveal a unit mixture that is about 60–65 percent studios, 30–35 percent one-bedroom units, and 7–10 percent two-bedroom units. Unit sizes between the two samples also vary. The studio units are closest together, averaging 300–317 SF. The one-bedroom units from the two samples vary by 15 percent from 448 to 515 SF. The 448 SF figure appears to be low given the difficulties of designing this size unit in a way that allows natural light to reach both the bedroom and the living room. A 500–550 SF size would fit a greater range of conditions. The 727 SF ALFA (2000) two-bedroom unit average also seems a little large, and the 597 SF NIC (1998) two-bedroom unit average seems a little small. An intermediate figure of 650 SF for an average-size two-bedroom unit would be more appropriate.

Assisted Living: Unit Amenities and Features

	ALFA[1] 2000	NIC[2] 1998	NIC-Modern[3] 1998
Unit Amenities and Features			
1. Grab bars in shower/tub	—	100.0%	—
2. Fire sprinkler system	—	87.2%	91.6%
3. Call buttons (bathrooms)	—	85.5%	77.7%
4. Private toilet	83.2%	—	—
5. Call buttons (bedrooms)	—	81.8%	75.1%
6. Private shower	74.8%	75.8%	60.1%
7. Higher elevated toilets	—	69.5%	66.7%
8. Refrigerator in room	58.7%	57.6%	60.8%
9. Commercial bather (access to)	—	53.9%	63.4%
10. Sink in room	55.7%	—	—
11. Toasters/toaster-ovens	—	43.0%	42.9%
12. Microwave oven in room	33.5%	30.5%	43.9%
13. Private bathtub in unit	18.4%	30.9%	8.8%
14. Roll-in showers	—	28.2%	39.0%
15. Stove in room	14.4%	18.8%	9.9%
16. Portable help buttons	—	—	10.6%

[1] ALFA: ALFA statistics are from an annual national survey of assisted living providers who are ALFA members. The 1999 survey involved responses from 350 assisted living providers representing 18,019 units and 18,272 residents. Because the survey is limited to ALFA members, it does not necessarily represent the universe of assisted living environments available to older people. (ALFA, 2000)

[2] NIC: The NIC study is the result of a study of 178 assisted living communities located in the contiguous 48 states and of 1023 residents living in those communities. The survey instruments consisted of a facility survey completed by facility personnel and a resident survey with a resident assessment instrument completed by older residents with assistance from family members and staff. (NIC, 1998)

[3] NIC-Modern: The "modern subsample" of the NIC study consists of newer facilities that have opened since 1990. They were also screened to meet the following three criteria: (a) free-standing, (b) purpose-built, and (c) sponsored by for-profit sponsors. (NIC, 1998)

Assisted Living: Buildings for People with Dementia

	ALFA[1] 2000
General Dementia Statistics	
1. % of properties w/dedicated alz. unit	23.6%
2. Designed specifically for alz. residents	8.5%
2. Average number of alz. units in DU	24.2 units
3. Average resident capacity in DU	27.0 people
4. Average occupancy of alz. DU	82.8%
Specific Dementia-Only Unit Statistics	
1. Average size of dementia-only bldg.	47 units
2. Average resident capacity	52 residents
3. Average occupancy rate	89.3%
4. Average age (males)	79.1 years
5. Average age (females)	81.6 years
6. Average length of stay	20.9 months
7. % semiprivate rooms	36.8%
8. % private studios	53.5%
9. % one-bedroom units	9.2%
10. Average cost—semiprivate unit	$94.23
11. Average cost—private unit	$106.69

[1] ALFA: ALFA statistics are from an annual national survey of assisted living providers who are ALFA members. The 1999 survey involved responses from 350 assisted living providers representing 18,019 units and 18,272 residents. Because the survey is limited to ALFA members, it does not necessarily represent the universe of assisted living environments available to older people. (ALFA, 2000)

Dwelling Units Costs and Occupancy

The average daily rate for a studio unit was recorded as $73.97 for the ALFA (2000) study and $60.21 for the NIC (1998) study. Costs varied from an average low of $60.21 for a one-bedroom unit (NIC, 1998) to a high of $101.54 for a two-bedroom unit (ALFA, 2000). In general, the ALFA pricing was 19–40 percent higher, depending on unit size. Unit costs can be expected to increase over time, and the NIC (1998) study is older than the ALFA (2000) study. Occupancy rates vary, depending on when they are measured. Because it takes a building 12–24 months to stabilize, most occupancy figures are gathered after 18 months of occupancy. According to the NIC study, studio and one-bedroom occupancies are the highest, with two-bedroom rates lagging approximately 8 percent behind.

Dwelling Unit Amenities and Features

The popularity of 16 unit features was recorded between the two studies, and these features are rank ordered in the table on page 27. All but one of these features can be categorized as either a bathroom feature, a kitchen feature, or a safety feature. Two of the features are both bathroom amenities and safety features. Safety features like grab bars in the shower, fire sprinklers, and call buttons were among the most popular unit amenities. Bathroom features like a private toilet, a private shower, and an elevated toilet seat were next in popularity. Only a few exotic bathroom features like a roll-in shower and a private bathtub were ranked in the lowest third of the list. Kitchen features were ranked in the middle to lowest third. Midrange items included a refrigerator, sink, toaster oven, or microwave in the room. These are all items that together form a simple tea kitchen. The inclusion of a stove in the room appeared in only 10–19 percent of the units. The only nonunit feature included in this table is access to a commercial bather. Between 53.9 percent and 63.4 percent of the units in the NIC universal and modern (1998) samples included this feature. Items like control of heat, ventilation, and air conditioning (HVAC), window size, medicine storage, handicapped access, lighting, ventilation, and adequacy of storage were unfortunately not included in this data set.

Buildings and Settings for People with Dementia

Two types of dementia units were reviewed by the ALFA (2000) study. The first type is assisted living buildings that include a dementia unit cluster. These clusters are typically located in a secured wing or floor of the building. The other type is a building that stands alone and has only dementia residents. Both types of units have pros and cons. According to the ALFA (2000) study (see the adjacent table), nearly a quarter (23.6 percent) of all assisted living buildings had a dedicated wing or floor for persons with cognitive impairment. However, only 8.5 percent (about one-third of the units) were built specifically for residents with dementia. These buildings are generally small. They have an average of 24.2 units with 27.0 people. The average occupancy of these units is 82.8 percent.

Buildings for People with Dementia

The ALFA (2000) study also gathered data on buildings that contained only residents with dementia. These buildings averaged 47 units, which is slightly smaller than the assisted living unit average. On average, residents with dementia were approximately two to three years younger than the assisted living population. Dementia facilities have a much higher percentage of residents in semipri-

Assisted Living: Reason Residence Was Selected

	NIC[1] 1998
1. Services offered	31.9%
2. Convenient to family and friends	21.7%
3. Appearance of residence	12.9%
4. Staff	6.6%
5. Only choice available	5.4%
6. Lower monthly fee	3.3%
7. Apartment selection	2.6%
8. Family member selected	2.5%
9. Convenient shopping/services	2.0%
10. Size of apartment	2.0%
11. Referral	1.3%
12. Other	7.8%

[1] NIC: The NIC study is the result of a study of 178 assisted living communities located in the contiguous 48 states and of 1023 residents living in those communities. The survey instruments consisted of a facility survey completed by facility personnel and a resident survey with a resident assessment instrument completed by older residents with assistance from family members and staff. (NIC, 1998)

vate rooms (36.8 percent), with 53.5 percent in private studios but only 9.2 percent in one-bedroom units. The average length of stay in a dementia-specific unit is 20.9 months compared to 24.5 months in assisted living. Finally, the costs are considerably higher, at $94.23 for a semiprivate unit and $106.69 for a private unit.

Reasons Residents Selected a Particular Residence

One of the most interesting responses was to the NIC (1998) question about why a particular residence was selected. The rank-ordered responses are presented in the adjacent table. The most important reason, given by 31.9 percent of the sample, was the "services offered." In other words, families and older residents were seeking the particular services provided by assisted living. The second reason, given by 21.7 percent of the sample, was location. They wanted the building to be convenient to family members and friends. The third reason had to do with the physical appearance of the residence— presumably both inside and outside. This accounted for 12.9 percent of the reasons. Eight more specific reasons were provided that accounted for 25.7 percent of the reasons why the residence was selected. Included in this list are two more physical design factors.

These include the apartment selection (2.6 percent) and size of the apartment (2.0 percent). Collectively, building appearance, apartment size, and apartment selection account for 17.5 percent of the total number of reasons. This is more than 2.5 times larger than the fourth reason, which is the quality of the staff (6.6 percent). Some claim that the decision to move is based on the attractiveness of the building, but the decision to stay is based on the quality of the staff. Clearly, one of the most surprising findings in this table is how little "lower monthly fee" contributed to the reason to move, at 3.3 percent. Money may be important, but the decision to move rarely appears to hinge on that consideration alone.

3

DEFINING CONCEPTUAL FRAMEWORKS FOR ASSISTED LIVING ENVIRONMENTS AND SERVICES

Every theorist concerned with environmental evaluation hopes to reduce the salient factors associated with a successful setting to a few well-chosen concepts. The eight frameworks shown in the following table are taken from the work of both researchers and practitioners. Each lists a series of salient goals, objectives, or concepts that underlie its conceptual grasp of assisted living or dementia environments for frail elderly residents. These are very powerful frameworks. Each of them could be used as a diagnostic consideration when evaluating a setting. Together they describe a hierarchy of considerations that define the essence of what well-designed assisted living environments are seeking to provide.

These frameworks are grouped by function. The first two, by Regnier and Pynoos (1992) and Weisman and Calkins (1999), are composite lists that come from the evaluation of the work of other researchers. The second two come from providers who are pioneers in the assisted living provider movement. It is fair to say that their facilities, which embodied these goals, established the conceptual lead for other assisted living sponsors and for

ALFA. The third group reflects the work of Cohen and Weisman (1991) and Zeisel (1999) in establishing specific goals for the design and management of facilities for people with dementia. The last two frameworks are specialized. The first comes from the assisted living research work of Brummett (1997), who seeks a connection between concepts of home and assisted living design. The second is from the work of Martha Tyson (1998) and is oriented toward landscape architecture. The 27 therapeutic goals articulated by her work are subdivided into goals for the environment, the staff, and the family.

FRAMEWORK COMMONALTIES AND OVERLAPS

Taking these frameworks together as a group (see the following table) allows us to see the commonalties and overlaps between them. The single most important goal appears to be *privacy*. Following this are two interrelated concepts: *independence and autonomy* and *choice and control*. Every study identified a cluster of concerns re-

Eight Conceptual Frameworks for Environmental Evaluation

Composite Frameworks

1. Regnier and Pynoos (1992)—Environment-behavior principles for housing the aged
2. Weisman and Calkins (1999)—Concepts from a comparative examination of the work of eight other environmental design researchers

Provider Frameworks

3. Wilson (1990)—Concept development and management principles used to develop the philosophy for the provider—Assisted Living Concepts
4. Klaassen—Concepts and operating principles established by the provider—Sunrise Assisted Living

Dementia Frameworks

5. Cohen and Weisman (1991)—Therapeutic goals for dementia housing
6. Zeisel (1999)—Criteria for the design and management criteria of dementia facilities

Specialized Frameworks

7. Brummett (1997)—Concepts of home
8. Tyson (1998)—Therapeutic design goals for landscape architecture

garding the basic issue of the freedoms residents could exercise. Next was the ability to *personalize the environment* and be *treated as a individual.* Following this, but still identified by the majority of frameworks, are the concern for *safety and security* and the desire for *social interaction.* Next is the *homelike appearance* of the building and its sense of *familiarity* to occupants. Finally, near the bottom of the list, is the ability of the environment to *stimulate the senses,* to *orient* residents, to *adapt to changing circumstances,* and to provide a *relationship to the family.*

COMPOSITE FRAMEWORKS

Regnier and Pynoos's Environment-Behavior Principles

This list of 12 principles was taken from a review article (Regnier and Pynoos, 1992) that focused on identifying a critical collection of attributes for housing design. This list is meant to be somewhat broad and could apply to assisted living for elderly residents, dementia facilities, nursing homes, or congregate housing. Some of the characteristics, like privacy and social interaction, are in

opposition to one another. All environments, however, should support a range of options for both social engagement and privacy. Another pair of opposed principles is safety/security and stimulation/challenge. In developing a balanced housing environment, we must recognize that each person has both a need for support and a need for challenge.

Other principles presented in this list are timeless qualities of stimulating architecture relevant to all populations. However, in many cases, the special needs of the elderly for more accommodating architecture further underscore their meaning and importance. Orientation and wayfinding is a good example. Many older people have difficulties in complex environments where few cues are available for navigation. However, older frail people with spatial memory impairments are more easily confused by a symmetrical plan and less able to differentiate similar residential floors from one another.

Another important factor is operational policies, which can reinforce or reduce the effectiveness of each principle. For example, a lock on the door does little to maintain privacy when staff members have passkeys and do not knock before entering. Operational policies and environmental design attributes must be considered as complementing and affecting one another.

1. Privacy

Provide Opportunities for a Place of Seclusion from Company or Observation Where One Can Be Free from Unauthorized Intrusion.   This is important because: it provides the older person with a sense of self and of separateness from others. Auditory and visual privacy are important components of physical separation. Privacy is more difficult to ensure in group living arrangements. Nursing home settings that rely on double-occupancy rooms severely limit privacy.

2. Social Interaction

Provide Opportunities for Social Interaction and Exchange.   This is important because one of the basic reasons for creating age-segregated group living arrangements is to stimulate informal social exchange, recreational activities, discussion groups, and friendship development. Social interaction counters depression by allowing older people to share problems, life experiences, and daily events.

3. Control, Choice/Autonomy

Provide Opportunities for Residents to Make Choices and to Control Events That Influence Outcomes.   This is important because older people are often more alienated, less satisfied, and more task dependent in settings

Conceptual Framework Commonalties and Overlaps

	Composite Frameworks		Provider Frameworks		Dementia Frameworks		Specialized Frameworks	
Regnier and Pynoos, 1992	Weisman and Calkins (1999)	Wilson (1990)	Klaassen	Cohen and Weisman, 1991	Zeisel (1999)	Brummett (1997)	Tyson (1998)
1. Privacy	Privacy	Privacy	Privacy	Privacy	Privacy	Privacy	Create privacy
2. Contl/chce/auto	Autonomy	Independence	Independence	Auton + control	Autonomy	Autonomy	Sense of freedom
3. Res. control	Choice/control	Choice	Choice	Auton + control	Contl/chce/auto	Personal ownership	
4. Personalization	Personalization	Individuality	Individuality Personal serv.		Individuality		
5. Safety	Safety			Safety	Safety	Safety	Sense of security
6. Social Interaction	Social inter.			+ social milieu	Social Inter.		Social opportunities
7. Aesthetics/appear		Homelike				Homelike environment	
8. Familiarity				Familiar	Homelike	Familiarity	Connect to the familiar
9.		Dignity	Dignity				
10. Sensory stim. Stimulation				Stim. + challng.	Sensory stim.		Compensate for losses
11.			Family		Family respons. Family		Family involvement
12. Adaptability				Adaptability			Maintain flexibility to adapt
13. Orientation				Orientation			

Entry allows for a connection between the corridor and the unit: At *De Overloop* in Almere, the Netherlands, this includes a Dutch door, a corner window by the kitchen, a transom window above the door, and a shelf for delivering items.

that are highly restricted and regimented. Having a sense of mastery and control has been found to have pronounced positive effects on life satisfaction. Independence is often defined by our ability to make choices, control events, and be autonomous.

4. Orientation/Wayfinding

Foster a Sense of Orientation Within the Environment That Reduces Confusion and Facilitates Wayfinding. This is important because feeling lost or being disoriented within a building is a frightening and disconcerting feeling that can lessen confidence and self-esteem. Older people who have experienced some memory loss are more easily disoriented within a featureless, symmetrical, complex environment. Signs can overcome some problems, but they never provide a person with the

confidence of knowing exactly where they are within the larger environment.

5. Safety/Security

Provide an Environment That Ensures That Each User Will Sustain No Harm, Injury, or Undue Risk. Older people may experience physiological and sensory problems such as visual impairments, balance control difficulties, loss of lower body strength, and arthritis, which make them more susceptible to falls and burns. Reductions in bone calcium levels with aging can also increase their susceptibility to broken bones and hips. The elderly experience a high rate of injury from home accidents.

6. Accessibility and Functioning

Consider Manipulation and Accessibility as Basic Requirements for Any Functional Environment. This is important because older people often experience difficulties manipulating the environment. Windows, doors, HVAC controls, and bathroom fixtures can be hard to twist turn, and lift. Furthermore, older people confined to a wheelchair or dependent on a walker must have environments that are adaptable enough to accommodate these devices. Reach capacity and strength limitations are therefore important considerations in the layout of bathrooms and kitchens and in the specification of finishes.

7. Stimulation/Challenge

Provide a Stimulating Environment That is Safe But Challenging. This is important because a stimulating environment keeps the older person alert and engaged. Stimulation can result from color, spatial variety, visual pattern, and contrast. Stimulation can also involve animating the setting with intergenerational activities, pet therapy, or a music program. Environments overly concerned with maintenance and cleanability are often uniform in color and pattern, noisy and disconcerting to the ear, and glaring and reflective in appearance. Each resident is different and should be allowed to experience an optimum level of complexity and challenge.

8. Sensory Aspects

Changes in Visual, Auditory, and Olfactory Senses Should Be Accounted for in the Environment. This is important because older people tend to suffer age-related sensory losses. Smell, touch, sight, hearing, and taste decrease in intensity as a person ages. Sensory stimulation can involve aromas from the kitchen or garden, colors and patterns from furnishings, laughter from conversations, and the texture of certain fabrics. A range of sensory inputs can be used to make a setting more stimulating and interesting.

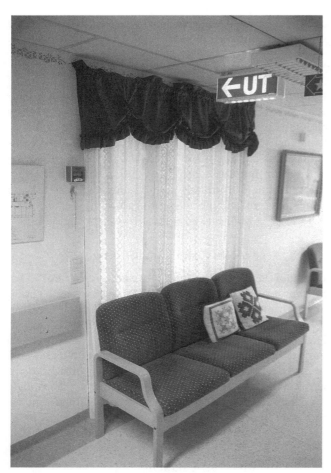

Corridor exit is camouflaged with a light curtain and a movable bench: Unlike the United States, where this strategy would be discouraged, the *Ensjøtunet* in Oslo, Norway, has looked for simple ways to keep residents from eloping from this dementia cluster.

9. Familiarity

Environments That Use Historical References and Solutions Influenced by Local Tradition Provide a Sense of the Familiar and Enhance Continuity. This is important because moving into a new housing environment is a very disorienting experience for some older people. Creating continuity and connection with the past is reassuring and facilitates the transition. Residents take cues from the environment. When it is designed to accommodate traditional events and fits into the regional housing vernacular, it appears more predictable and understandable. Institutional environments often use imagery that does not come from housing examples and therefore appears cold and alienating.

10. Aesthetics and Appearance

Design Environments That Appear Attractive, Provoking, and Noninstitutional. This is important because the overall appearance of the environment sends a strong symbolic message to visitors, friends, and relatives about the older person. Housing that appears institutional provides negative cues to others about the competence, well-being, and independence of residents. Staff and caregiving personnel are also highly affected by the appearance of the physical and policy environment. Personnel working in a building that resembles a nursing home will reduce cognitive dissonance and act in ways that are consistent with an institutional context.

11. Personalization

Provide Opportunities to Make the Environment Personal and to Mark It as the Property of a Unique Single Individual. This is important because it allows older residents to express self-identity and individuality. In nursing homes, individual expression is often very limited. Patients do not have much personal space in compact two-bed rooms furnished with hospital beds and over-the-bed trays. Personal items used for display and decoration are often very important and salient to the older person. Collectible items may trigger memories of travel to other countries or emotional bonds with family and friends. These items can animate a room by recalling past associations.

12. Adaptability

An Adaptable or Flexible Environment Can Be Made to Fit Changing Personal Characteristics. This is important because older people age differently. Some have mental impairments, while others suffer visual losses. Chronic arthritis keeps some persons from performing ADLs, while for others, arthritis is an occasional annoyance rather than a disabling disease. The environment has the capacity to compensate for many deficits and to adapt to changing resident needs. Bathrooms and kitchens are the major rooms where work activities take place and where safety is a major consideration. Environments should be designed to be adaptable to a range of users, including those who need wheelchairs and walkers.

Calkins and Weisman's Composite Therapeutic Goals

In a chapter devoted to conceptualizing models for environmental assessment, Calkins and Weisman (1999) assembled in a single table the therapeutic goals associated with eight environmental design researchers. They found

Dementia garden combines antique farm items with landscaping: The secured garden at *Sunrise of Severna Park,* Maryland, uses objects in combination with plant materials to add interest and variety.

a surprising amount of overlap from these separate studies (Calkins, 1988; Cohen and Weisman, 1991; Lawton, Fulcomer, et al., 1984; Regnier and Pynoos, 1992; Sloane, Weisman, et al., 1993; Zeisel, Hyde, et al., 1994). The table ranked ordered from highest to lowest the degree of similarity between these salient social and environmental attributes. Although the table arrayed 15 therapeutic goals, the 7 most popular characteristics were identified by at least five of the eight studies. These included the following:

▲ Orientation and wayfinding
▲ Opportunities for social interaction
▲ Increased autonomy and functioning
▲ Personalization and familiarity
▲ Privacy
▲ Safety and security
▲ Resident control/autonomy

PROVIDER FRAMEWORKS

Wilson's Assisted Living Concepts and Attributes

Keren Brown Wilson, a pioneer in the development of assisted living and former CEO of Assisted Living Concepts, began her exploration of assisted living in Oregon. She coauthored an important publication with Rosalie Kane (Kane and Wilson, 1993) that helped to document

the emerging nature of assisted living projects at the beginning of the 1990s. Wilson's approach to assisted living was greatly influenced by her belief that congregate housing, when combined with the right operational infrastructure, could keep older frail people out of nursing homes. Her model of assisted living (Wilson, 1990) recognizes six attributes of the physical and operational environment and identifies four concepts that underlie her management philosophy for housing the frail elderly. The attributes include:

▲ Privacy
▲ Dignity
▲ Choice
▲ Independence
▲ Individuality
▲ Homelike surroundings

The following four concepts are accompanied by suggestions about how to implement them through a consistent management philosophy.

Create a Place of One's Own

Assure privacy through a locked door, a private bathroom, and the ability to prepare one's own food.

Serve the Unique Individual

Each resident's needs and abilities are different. Recognizing these differences is the basis for an effective personal therapeutic strategy for each resident.

Share Responsibility Among Caretakers, Family Members, and Residents

Creating partnerships between formal providers and the family gives everyone, including the older person, the option of participating in care management.

Allow Resident Choice and Control

Simplifying choices can expand the number of decisions residents can make. The more residents can exercise choice, the more control they have over a given situation.

Klaassen's Sunrise Assisted Living Core Values

Paul and Terry Klaassen are early innovators in assisted living and the cocreators of Sunrise Assisted Living of McLean, Virginia. They got many of their initial ideas from the housing environments for the elderly that Paul visited as a child in the Netherlands. He visited his grandmother, who lived in a small-group setting with services that was inviting and *gezellig* (a Dutch term meaning warm, cozy, and friendly). These environments were in stark contrast to the United States nursing homes, where Paul and Terry often volunteered with a local singing group.

They started Sunrise Assisted Living in the mid-1980s in reaction to what they didn't find in many of the homes they visited in northern Virginia. As their corporation grew, it became necessary to formalize their approach to assisted living, and they did so by identifying eight principles of service that created the foundation for an operating model of caregiving. They consider it so important that employees take to heart the core values of the organization that they print the following eight principles and the pictograph illustrating their caregiving philosophy on the back of every employee's business card. The principles of service include:

▲ Encouraging *independence*
▲ Preserving *dignity*
▲ *Personalizing* services
▲ Enabling *freedom of choice*
▲ Fostering *individuality*
▲ Protecting *privacy*
▲ *Nurturing* the spirit
▲ Involving *family and friends*

These principles are seen in conjunction with other factors that operationalize them as part of a philosophy of care. The pictogram that Paul Klaassen uses to explain his approach is a classical building façade. His vision literally depicts a foundation, a base and four columns that support a pediment. His philosophy is based on *the belief in the sacred value of human life*. He borrows freely from his own moral and ethical values to establish this as the foundation for the corporate philosophy. Above this foundation they envision a base which includes the *eight principles of service*. Coupled with a verb, each of these descriptive principles is given a more active emphasis.

Above these two foundation elements are four columns. Each column represents a different attitude about the provision of service.

Respect for All—Column One

This emphasizes the need to be respectful to every member of the caregiving team. Providing personal care assistance is hard work, and its success depends on teamwork. Everyone has a role to play, and every role is significant in achieving overall success.

Sense of Mission—Column Two

Every employee must recognize that the work he or she is doing is important and vital to the happiness of every resident. Enthusiasm and a "serving heart" are important personal attributes that the best employees bring to their work.

Devoted Stewards—Column Three

Every resource used to bring life, activity, and independence to residents should be carefully expended. The financial resources of residents and families support the salaries of employees and the operating expense of each home. These resources should be employed wisely for maximum benefit.

Joy in Service—Column Four

For most residents, this will be their last home, and for many their days are numbered. Every day is precious and should be lived to the fullest. Employees must recognize the need to bring joy into the life of each resident.

These four attitudes (columns) support the fundamental outcome measure of a *high quality of life for all seniors*. This final statement is made in a way that includes a broader cross section of individuals. Klaassen is not just speaking to the obligation of caring for residents; he defines the mission as one that affects all older people. He strongly believes that the work of the company produces a standard of excellence that is "redefining how seniors age in this country."

DEMENTIA FRAMEWORKS

Cohen and Weisman's Therapeutic Goals for Dementia Facilities

In establishing a basis for operationalizing their model of design, management, and resident interaction, Cohen and Weisman (1991) have identified nine therapeutic goals that form the basis for operational policies, physical design solutions, and social interaction. These goals were originally established to apply to people with dementia, but they appear to apply equally well to those with physical impairments. They include the following:

▲ Ensure safety and security.

▲ Support functional ability through meaningful activity.

▲ Heighten awareness and orientation.

▲ Provide appropriate environmental stimulation and challenge.

▲ Develop a positive social milieu.

▲ Maximize autonomy and control.

▲ Adapt to changing needs.

▲ Establish links to the healthy and the familiar.

▲ Protect the need for privacy.

Zeisel's Criteria for Design and Management of Dementia Facilities

John Zeisel and his colleagues (Zeisel, 1999) have identified eight environment-behavior criteria for the design of settings for people with dementia. These criteria, identified through their extensive research activities with dementia residents (Zeisel, Hyde, et al., 1994), describe tangible ways to formulate a design that supports the patterns of behavior characteristic of dementia residents. In addition to these "environmental" criteria, Zeisel has identified eight management-type criteria. These he labels as *individual-organization operational criteria*. These criteria identify the conflicting and consensual forces between the needs of the individual dementia resident and the needs of the entity which takes responsibility for the care of all residents. Taken together, they address the worlds of design and management. Of particular importance is Zeisel's direct operational experience through Hearthstone Alzheimer's Care. This experience adds to the usefulness of this construct and also adds additional richness to the interpretation of person-environment-organization relationships.

Eight Environment-Behavior Criteria

1. *Exit Control.* The design of doors and door hardware (windows, handles, swings, color) can encourage or discourage residents from using them. The proper design of exit situations can reduce frustration or encourage the use of adjacent spaces.

2. *Walking Paths.* Dementia residents often continually move through spaces in search of meaning. Aimless wandering can be transformed into walking, which adds interest and purpose to a resident's life.

3. *Personal Places.* Retreat places that allow residents to get away from the 24/7 life of group housing give them a place to be alone and to be private. This is more difficult to achieve in a setting where residents are constantly being monitored.

4. *Social Spaces.* Residents spend most of their time during the day with one another. This should take place in a variety of common spaces that are very different from one another

5. *Healing Gardens.* Going outside can reduce frustration, add variety, and allow residents to recharge and renew. Secure spaces should be available nearby to accomplish this.

6. *Residential Features.* Residential elements like a fireplace, front porch, garden, and residential furniture establish a sense of connection with the environment that is comforting and deep-seated.

7. *Independence.* The environment should be designed with safe floor and wall materials, secure doors and windows, and accessible features like bathrooms. This allows residents who use the environment to do so with autonomy and independence.

8. *Sensory Comprehensibility.* The environment should be familiar and related to residential qualities that can be recognized. Familiar sights, sounds, and smells make a setting comfortable and reassuring.

Eight Individual-Organization Operational Criteria

1. *Personhood.* Dementia and aging are more likely to exacerbate differences than to create sameness. Every individual's differences and unique qualities should be identified and taken into consideration.

2. *Purpose.* Common goals, a facility statement of purpose, and clear principles allow the staff and family members to work together to achieve a highly satisfying life.

3. *Adaptability.* Caregivers need to work together as a team to respond to the differences an individual resident may exhibit from hour to hour or day to day. A team can provide a range of modalities representing the strengths of its members.

4. *Staff Suitability.* Staff members need to exhibit extreme patience, flexibility, self-assurance, and empathy. Special training is necessary to identify how reach resident reacts to the disease and how to best respond.

5. *Richness of Life.* A range of activities throughout the day structured in small and large groups contributes to the well-being of residents.

6. *Family Responsiveness.* Families are an integral part of the caregiving team. They need to be prepared

Residents' artwork is frequently used in corridors: This original artwork at the *De Brink* service house in Breda, the Netherlands, is typical of how public spaces are decorated in northern Europe by residents.

to deal with the inevitable changes in competence and communication ability that accompanies advanced dementia.

7. Real-Worldness. Connection to the world outside of the building, as well as everyday activities like reading a newspaper, keep residents involved in the community.

8. Responsibility. The caregiving organization owes the resident and his or her family a professional, well-managed residence that communicates any problems and provides high-quality support.

SPECIALIZED FRAMEWORKS

Home Quality Framework: Brummett's Concepts of Home

William Brummett's book on assisted living, *The Essence of Home* (1997), focuses on the concept of creating an environment that includes the basic aspects associated with a home. He identifies ten concepts that form the foundation of the social, organizational, and environmental norms we connect with the idea of home. Although this framework does not describe assisted living, there are many parallel ideas that connect the idea of home to our concepts of what assisted living should be. Concepts like choice, autonomy, privacy, and security, which are present in other concept lists, occur here simply as attributes of the home environment. It is no surprise that our definition of assisted living is intertwined with the factors that define a residential setting.

1. Self-Protection/Self-Symbol. Home is a place where we can express our identity, and it reflects how we expect to be perceived by others.

2. Vessel of Memory/Vessel of the Soul. Home contains the objects and symbols that represent our memories of our personal family life.

3. Connectedness/Belonging. Home is a place where we give and receive love and affection. It is a place for connecting with peers and friends.

4. Center/Origin. Home is a sacred place from which we travel to the profane world.

5. Familiarity/Order. Home is a place of comfort and relaxation that we know well. It is known and understood.

6. Stability/Predictability. Home is a place where relationships are known and change only when desired.

7. Privacy/Territory. Home accommodates solitude and reflection. It allows one to set clear boundaries and control them.

8. Security/Safety. Home provides sanctuary and shelter from the elements and from unwanted intrusion.

9. Control/Autonomy. Home is a place where you can exercise control over the environment.

10. Choice/Opportunity. Home provides a place for exploring your interests and a stage for engagement and interaction.

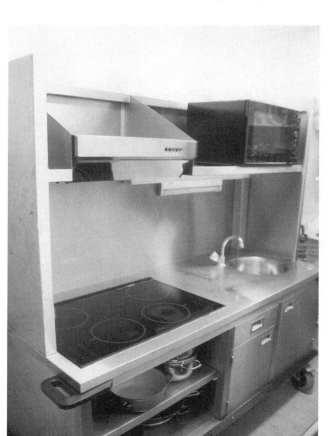

Portable stove is interesting to watch: This portable food preparation unit is used in a dining room at the *Hogeway* in Weesp, the Netherlands, that doesn't have a serving kitchen. It provides residents with something to watch as food is being prepared near their table.

Landscape Framework: Tysons's Landscape Therapeutic Goals

In *The Healing Landscape* (1998), Tyson addresses the place of landscape architecture and outdoor spaces in the overall milieu of the nursing home, the assisted living building, and the dementia facility. Using her own research as well as the work of others, she has identified 22 therapeutic goals in three categories: residents/patients, staff, and family/visitors. It is her contention that some of the most satisfying experiences are the most simple ones. This comprehensive list of goals reminds us

of the important role that the landscape can place in supporting the quality of residential life. Providing the additional category of visitor and family expands the scope and impact of the work to include a very important and often overlooked category.

Residents'/Patients' Therapeutic Goals

▲ Support abilities and compensate for losses.
▲ Instill a sense of belonging and usefulness.
▲ Provide opportunities to continue work, trades, or hobbies.
▲ Establish connections to the familiar.
▲ Establish a sense of personal pride or ownership.
▲ Maintain a sense of security in physical surroundings (including landmarks, predictable paths, and secure zones).
▲ Heighten awareness of nature, seasons, places, and time.
▲ Create places for physical exercise.
▲ Maximize a sense of independence and freedom (through unlocked doors to a secure garden).

Staff Therapeutic Goals

▲ Create a pleasant work environment.
▲ Provide desired amount of space for activities.
▲ Allow for complete surveillance of the area (inside and outside).
▲ Maintain flexibility to adapt to the environment (including furnishings that can change).
▲ Provide places for resident/patient respite (quiet places to take residents).
▲ Designate places for staff breaks and respite.
▲ Provide the ability to use space around the clock.
▲ Establish direct access to outdoor areas.

Families and Other Visitors' Therapeutic Goals

▲ Provide assurance that residents have quality care.
▲ Provide a familiar homelike living environment (attractive to the family/visitors).
▲ Offer social opportunities for residents/patients.
▲ Create a sense of privacy and comfort for visiting (quiet places for family/visitors).
▲ Encourage family/visitor involvement with the resident care program.

Jan van der Ploeg in Rotterdam, NE, overlooking the atrium.

PART II

100 CRITICAL DESIGN CONSIDERATIONS

It may be enough to realize that domestic comfort involves a range of attributes—convenience, efficiency, leisure, ease, pleasure, domesticity, intimacy and privacy—all of which contributes to the experience; common sense will do the rest.

—Rybczynski, 1986, p. 231

I n every design project, there are thousands of decisions and choices a designer will make from project inception to completion. Those decisions range from site planning to building configuration, plan development, material choices, and building esthetics. Conceptualizing the building from a functional perspective provides one set of inputs, while examining the architectural language of form and appearance informs the design process in another way. Within this process lie a number of critical junctures where the outcomes of decisions have a powerful impact on the success of a project. The following 100 critical design considerations has been assembled from 30 years of experience with the design of housing for the mentally and physically frail.

CRITICAL DECISIONS THAT MAKE A DIFFERENCE

In considering what is important and what is not, we assume that general architectural sensibilities are at work in developing a plan and an elevation. I have not spent a lot of time discussing solar access, wind patterns, site development strategies, fenestration details, or construction methods. I have ignored the commercial kitchen and the laundry, as well as a number of the back-of-the-house spaces that support the service component of assisted living. The 100 considerations to be discussed focus primarily on details that directly affect the quality of life of the resident or suggest strategies for making the building more attractive to family members and friends.

There is no "formula for success" in assisted living design. In fact, assisted living is likely to become more diverse rather than more homogeneous, defying any formulaic approach in the future. Buildings are likely to be more specific to the needs and desires of a selected group of older residents rather than following a one-size-fits-all pattern. Most of the successful projects I have evaluated over the years attribute their success to a cluster of specific qualities or attributes. Chapters 4 to 12 describe the 100 most powerful attributes I believe make a difference. They are not arrayed in a format that requires them to work together. In fact, some of them are likely to represent choices that are not compatible with one another. Therefore, one can probably not implement them all, but each attribute has a lesson to teach and can be useful to ponder in the search for how to optimize the best final design.

CARE MANAGEMENT IS EXTREMELY IMPORTANT TO SUCCESS

In a book about the environment, it is easy to overlook care and service considerations. The way the staff, management, and therapy come together to support the lifestyle of the resident defines the quality of life on a day-to-day basis. However, the environment is the vehicle for delivering service and becomes the symbolic representation of quality—especially for people who are seeking admission. The environment is a powerful force for motivating a move, but day-to-day service is what keeps people living there. Emphasis has been placed on themes such as social interaction and the creation of affect, which impact the social context of the environment. Although functional considerations are embedded in many of the categories, the focus is on design decisions that make a building more attractive to residents and family members. For example, lighting and carpet quality are mentioned in the context of safety and mobility rather than as a separate performance specification for an individual space.

4

NEIGHBORHOOD AND SITE ISSUES

The most important initial decision for any project is, where should it be located within a particular neighborhood? The old real estate adage that the three most important attributes of success are location, location, and location is also relevant here. Well-designed projects located on excellent sites are almost always successful.

An excellent site location has a combination of attributes including its visibility in the neighborhood, its land-use connection to the local community, and its sense of identification in the minds of residents and their family members. When a site has an off-site view, mature trees, good vehicle access, space for parking, and nearby destinations to visit, it often has enough to make it compelling and interesting.

1

A Site Within a Community's Cognitive Map

◄ *Seamless integration with the environment:* The *Gulkrögcentret* project in Vejle, Denmark, was designed to fit the surrounding street grid, sandwiched between the train station and a major hospital. The pedestrian streets that pass through the project are heavily used.

Selecting a good site for an assisted living project is one of the most important decisions a provider can make in ensuring the project's success. The following are a few important site attributes.

Mental Map Image

An excellent site is often one that people already know well enough to form a mental picture. It is within the "cognitive map" of residents living in the surrounding community (Lynch, 1960). It is a site that, by virtue of its physical relationship to other salient landmarks, is easy to identify and recall.

Community Connection

The best sites are not isolated but share a physical or associative connection with compatible community land uses. Some of these land uses include churches, day-care centers for children, retail stores and other shops, community parks, and elementary schools. When an assisted living building is part of a community, it is often associated with those land uses in a positive way. Urban housing for the elderly in northern Europe is often surrounded by shops and stores or located on floors above retail stores. These buildings often share a modest street entrance at grade level but are open to landscaped mid-block courtyards in the center of the site.

Well-Traveled Arterial or Memorable Intersection

A site location on a major road is likely to be seen more frequently and thus becomes familiar to more people. Major streets forming a grid are also the framework most people use to organize the mental image of a community. The perception of convenience to family members and friends may also relate to its placement on a major street. Marketing surveys often show that a high percentage of family members discover a facility as a result of driving by.

Proximity to Older Residents or Family Members

Family members want to live nearby so that they can easily visit. Older residents often feel more comfortable when an assisted living building is located near their home or within a neighborhood they know well. Having an adequate number of older people or convenient access to family members within the community is necessary for the success of a project.

Entitlement Permission

In metropolitan areas, land use approval is often contingent on a properly zoned or entitled site. Because assisted living is a blend of housing and services, multi-family residential, institutional, or commercially zoned properties are all potentially appropriate for assisted living. The character of the building, its scale and size, and its "fit" within the surrounding neighborhood are characteristics a zoning or planning board should closely examine.

Visible Connection to the Street

Once a site is selected, the building's placement and orientation should optimize visibility from the street. The ability to identify the entry from the street reduces ambiguity and makes the building less mysterious and easier to comprehend. A walkway that links the building entry to the public sidewalk is a symbolic welcoming gesture. On a well-designed site, the building's entry is neither too close to nor too far away from the street.

Friendly Inviting Appearance from the Street

An assisted living home should look friendly and be residential in character. Good curbside presence has as much to do with trees, flowers, shrubs, ground cover, grass, and other plant materials as it does with the architecture of the building. The building should exude street friendliness, making the windshield analyst curious about what lies inside.

Safety from Crime and Adverse Traffic

Site placement and building organization should mitigate any external threats from noise and adverse traffic. Safety from crime may require a surrounding fence or higher lighting levels in parking areas and public sidewalks. Most sponsors deal with security concerns by creating a single main entry to the building.

2

Reconciling Typography with Building Configuration

◄ *Ramp and stair combination:* Stairs are often easier for an older frail person to navigate, but a ramp is necessary for a wheelchair-dependent resident. Both should be available to overcome a substantial change in grade.

Site shape and topography are two of the most important factors in establishing the layout or organization of a building. Because so many older frail residents utilize canes, walkers, or wheelchairs to get around, flat, walkable surfaces are ideal. However, a good site location with a challenging topographic condition is often much better to work with than a poorly located site that is flat.

Elevators and a Compact Site Configuration

It is surprising how easily the design of a steeply sloping site can be managed with elevators and a site plan configuration that takes advantage of a site's natural grade. A multistory building circulation plan should rely on both elevators and a compact building configuration. Corridors should be no longer than 100 feet. Beyond that, many residents will have a difficult time walking from their unit to the dining room or elevator.

Exterior Site Conditions

Developing a flat, walkable pathway around the outside of the building is necessary to promote walking as a form of exercise. If a walkway is not available, it should be created. A pathway that has only ramps can be restrictive. Whenever possible, ramps should be planned in conjunction with stairs. In frost belt settings, ramps alone can be dangerous, especially for ambulatory residents who have balance control problems.

Ramps in Corridors

The designer should avoid the use of ramps within the building. Residents using canes and walkers can lose their balance, and residents in wheelchairs can easily lose control. Providers are often tempted to resort to this strategy when multistory buildings with high ceilings in common spaces are combined with dwelling units that have lower floor-to-floor height requirements.

3

Saving Trees and Other Significant Landscape Features

◄ *Weave a pathway through trees to create a glen:*   Trees from the rear edge of this site were protected and used to shade this walkway.

Older trees often give a building site a timeless quality, making it appear as if the building has existed for many years.

Assess the Existing Landscape

A tree survey should always be commissioned on a wooded site where there is the possibility of saving trees, although one needs to be realistic because some trees cannot be salvaged. A building configuration can also take direction from the placement of mature landscape elements. Open or enclosed courtyards are particularly well suited to the use of trees for shade or visual interest. Units with views through tree branches or toward a cluster of trees are often deemed more valuable because of the view.

4

Serving Older People in the Surrounding Neighborhood

◄ *Home care workers begin their morning:*   Ros Anders Gård (page 215) has an office on the third floor for home care and home health care workers who provide services to residents in the neighborhood.

Any building has the potential to serve residents in the surrounding neighborhood. Although this practice is not common in the United States, it is the cornerstone of organizational efforts to keep people independent in northern Europe.

European Service Houses

The European concepts of housing and home care are highly integrated. In addition to providing housing for older frail people, sponsors provide services to older people in the community in order to keep them in their own homes as long as possible. In fact, many successful "care and repair" programs provide home modifications in ad-

dition to care services in an effort to address both the physical environment and the service needs of older neighborhood residents. The *service house* is a mixed-use vehicle for accomplishing this purpose.

Local Neighborhood Connections

The vast majority of residents will have family or they themselves will have relocated from a dwelling unit that is less than 5 miles from the site. An assisted living building can be the site for the organization of neighborhood-based services to older frail people—just as it is in Europe. From zoning and land-use perspectives, our European neighbors have much more experience with mixed-use buildings. The need for parking space is also less of an issue in Europe. When a building in the United States provides its services to people in the community, it is often in spite of the regulations, not because of them.

Promise of Preassisted Living Services

This has been a long held traditional interest of some nonprofit elderly housing providers in the United States who often see their mission as tied to the fabric of the local neighborhood. However, for the most part, providers are hesitant to broaden their service delivery

approach to include the surrounding neighborhood. However, this situation is changing with access to the Internet and with a bigger commitment on the part of assisted living providers to help residents before they reach the condition that requires a move to assisted living. One of the benefits of this approach is that assisted living buildings would most likely be conceptualized differently by the community. They would be seen as a type of community center that helps older people to solve their problems, rather than only as a residential environment where older frail people go when they need personal care assistance.

5

Mixed Land-Use Models

◂ *Children's playground is interesting to watch:*   This gazebo at the front auto court entry provides a protected place for residents to view the children's day-care center playground at the *Heritage in Cleveland Circle,* Massachusetts. (Photo: Peter Vanderworker)

I n northern European urban neighborhoods, it is not uncommon for the first floor of a building to consist of retail shops, with housing above. With this arrangement, the street edge is activated with commercial uses, while the housing above benefits from a quieter, more secluded location. Mixed-use strategies can create a more seamless connection to the surrounding urban fabric.

Mixed Use Is Difficult to Implement in the United States

There is not much of a tradition of mixed use in the United States because of land-use and zoning restrictions. Often developers of senior housing get a break on the number of required parking spaces, but when other uses are added, this economic and spatial benefit is removed. However, some mixed-use projects (primarily in urban areas) have developed in spite of this restriction.

Mixed Use Must Have Civic and Economic Advantages to Survive in the United States

A good example is the *Heritage at Cleveland Circle* in Brighton, Massachusetts. In this project, 90 units of

housing are mixed with a 60-person preschool for children. Intergenerational programming benefits occur as a result of the juxtaposition of uses. In a newly constructed courtyard building, *Sunrise of Sheepshead Bay*, New York, zoning restrictions encouraged the placement of first-floor offices and retail stores by providing a density bonus. Valet parking on a slightly larger lot was allowed to overcome parking problems.

Benefits of Mixed Use

When a mixed-use scenario is developed, it often helps to connect a project with the surrounding community. It makes the building a part of the city rather than a single isolated entity. In Rotterdam, the Netherlands, the *Humanitas* project (page 158) is a good example of how compatible uses can be intertwined. In this large 195-unit redevelopment project, a grocery store was selected for the first-floor use. A corner of the site contains an escalator that moves residents from the street to a central community space where a mix of community-based services and activities are provided for seniors in the neighborhood and residents living in two adjacent towers.

Another excellent example is the *Flesseman Center* on the edge of Nieumarket Square in Amsterdam, the Netherlands. The perimeter of the building contains retail uses, while the courtyard has been dedicated to outdoor space use for residents living above the first floor (see color plates and page 55). In Helsinki, Finland, the *Brahenpuiston Asuintalo* project is on a sloping hillside site. The front of the building, located at street level, has a pharmacy, several retail stores, and a health center. The housing located above these stores on a higher portion of the site has grade access to a garden on the upslope side of the building.

6

Capturing Views

◄ *Porches with active off-site views are often popular:* Porches provide shade control, reduce the scale of the building, control breezes, and are convenient to the inside of the building.

Because many older residents typically spend more time indoors than outside, views of the surrounding neighborhood often take on greater significance. Two types of views are available for planning purposes. One is an *active view*—often toward a city—that overlooks the sidewalk, the streets, and the activity at the front entry. The other is a *passive view* of a garden, lawn, trees, a park, a lake, or a nearby creek.

Contrasting Active and Passive Views

Buildings often have both an active and a passive view available from different sides. Each view has its own character and rhythm, and residents benefit from access to both. Views of the street are hard, energetic, active, noisy, ever-changing, and stimulating. The garden provides a passive green landscape that is soft, soothing, subdued, slower in pace, and relaxing. Each view has its pros and cons. Activity begets stimulation and noise, while the passive landscape is often subdued—at times boring. Common spaces like porches and overlooks are better suited to active views, while the dining room benefits from the relaxed view of a lush, multicolored garden. Views from various common spaces should embrace the full range of view possibilities.

Near and Far Views

Views can be intimate, intermediate, or long distance. For example, a view of the surrounding neighborhood from several stories up is very different from the view of the front lawn available on the first floor. In some instances, the near view is preferable. For example, in a first-floor dementia garden, the immediate view stopped by a solid fence is almost always preferable to the view of what lies beyond through an open-spaced fence. In this case, the activity beyond the garden can cause confusion and agitation. On the other hand, hillside sites separated from the din of noisy activity provide marvelous opportunities for passive city or landscape views.

The Overlook Perch

One of the best views is one that captures both the neighborhood and the city. These views stir the imagination and lift the spirit. Units perched on an upper floor take full advantage of the surrounding environment. Views from a glazed, conditioned space are often more popular with older frail people than views from an open balcony, where drafty breezes and concerns about safety can cause problems. Both of these views are pleasurable but offer different sensations. Residents like a porch with sides that protect it from the wind, especially when it has access to both shade and sun to complement the climatic conditions of the day.

7

Places for Parking

◄ *Grasscrete creates a green parking lot:* Northern Europeans frequently utilize grasscrete in parking areas because it facilitates water run-off absorption and looks much more attractive than blacktop.

Locating places for parking is always controversial. Car drivers love to park as close as they can to the front door, but no one enjoys views that are occluded by a sea of parked cars. Because residents don't drive, we are only concerned about parking for family, friends, and staff. A parking ratio of 0.4 cars per unit is adequate for most sites. Urban settings where staff can walk or take public transportation require fewer spaces, while an isolated ex-urban site where every staff member drives might require more.

Preferential Parking for Family Members and Friends

Handicapped parking is normally required near the front entry. Spaces for family members and friends should be the most convenient. During weekdays their trips are normally of short duration, and convenient parking encourages them to visit more frequently. In all cases, the staff should fill the parking lot from the rear to the front, leaving the most convenient spaces for visitors, family, and friends.

Parking Lot Should Be Low Key and Landscaped

The parking lot should not dominate the entry of the building. The front of the building should be residential in character—not like the front of a shopping center. There should be no more than four parking spaces adjacent to one another without a tree well. Placing trees in the parking lot not only breaks up the view with landscape materials but also helps to reduce heat in the summer by providing shade and transpiration. In northern Europe, many hard surfaces are designed for both cars and pedestrians and are designed to be relatively narrow. Turf block is also more popular in Europe and is often the preferred surface material for large parking lots. When underground parking is required, not much changes except that the cars are more protected and the entry is often more convenient for staff, family, and friends.

8

Service for Logistics and Trash

◄ *Service vehicles are generally smaller today:* A 30-foot lay-by loading zone is usually large enough to accommodate 90 percent of the truck traffic one can expect at a 50- to 70-unit assisted living building.

Service areas are often overdesigned. Food trucks and waste disposal vehicles do not require huge areas to load and unload materials. Deliveries are generally modest in size and can normally be accommodated with a lay-by lane 25–30 feet in length that allows a delivery truck to pull out of the main traffic flow. Kitchens should be situated so as to make it easy to deliver supplies quickly and efficiently. Food delivery trucks are usually smaller vehicles that make trips to the site several times each week.

Trash and Refuse

Trash trucks can serve a building as frequently as once per day or as little as once or twice per week. Trash can be kept inside the building in a trash room or placed in an outside dumpster. Internal trash rooms are often complicated and expensive because they need to be cooled and ventilated in the summer. An unconditioned trash room can lead to quicker decomposition of organic materials, cause odors, and attract insects. Dumpsters solve this problem by storing the trash outside, some distance from the building, which reduces the odor problem.

Separate Elevator Access

In most stand-alone buildings of 100 units or less, furniture for resident move-ins and move-outs is delivered through the front door. In some buildings, a separate service elevator is used to reduce disruption from frequent move-ins. When this occurs, a separate service entrance is normally located on one side of the building.

9

A Porte Cochere to Shelter Residents Moving Between Vehicles and the Building

◄ *Porte cochere to shelter residents:* In frostbelt states or places that experience a lot of rain, a sheltered drop-off area is a very considerate feature. When it is organized with a parallel drive-by lane, clearance heights can often be kept to a more modest residential scale.

Many providers insist on creating a sheltered pathway between the car and the entrance to the building. This is especially helpful in frost-belt locations and in areas where heavy rainfall is common. It is surprising how a small inconvenience like walking 25–30 feet in inclement weather can discourage frail residents from participating in activities and outings. A porte cochere eliminates this problem.

Porte Cochere Height and Mass

Regulations often require clearance for emergency vehicles, even though most of them can be accommodated within 10 feet. Some fire departments insist on clearance heights as high as 12–13 feet. A porte cochere designed for this clearance is often very large and out of scale with the rest of the building. Designed to shelter one vehicle in a single one-way lane, a well-scaled porte cochere also creates an easy-to-recognize entry target from the street. In some localities like southern California, where weather is not a problem, a covered walkway from a dropoff zone to the building will suffice. In either case, the walkway to the building should be sheltered from the weather.

10

Retention and Detention Basins

◄ *Retention and absorption of run-off water:* Landscape treatments like dry river beds should allow run-off water to be absorbed naturally while it is being channeled to a fully landscaped retention basin.

One of the realities of designing in today's ecologically sensitive environment is the requirement to detain run-off water and discharge it back into the soil rather than channel it into the storm water system. Detention basins can be either an attractive amenity or a problem feature that is unsightly or requires a great deal of ongoing maintenance.

Basin Design Treatments

Surface basins can be as simple as a depression on the site to store water or as complex as a lavish wet pond replete with the appropriate landscape materials. Sometimes local restrictions will dictate the type of pond (wet or dry). Soil absorption calculations will often dictate the size or capacity needed. The size is normally calculated by a civil engineer who balances run-off with a large enough basin to hold a 50- to 100-year downpour. On small sites where a detention basin is not possible, underground storage tanks are often the only solution. Surface basins, depending on their size, depth, and the amount of permanent standing water, may require a fence around the perimeter. An unobtrusive, residential-style 3-foot fence designed with clusters of landscape will often reduce its perceived length.

Underground Water Storage for Quality and Flow Considerations

In some parts of the country, vertical well-shaped underground shaft enclosures are common. In others areas, the water is temporarily stored in a horizontal structure. If water quality rather than just run-off control is necessary, then the storage basin must be designed to discharge the water back into the ground.

11

Lighting at Night

◄ *Lighting at night should emanate from the building:* Indirect fixtures bathe the porch, providing a warm glow at night. Holiday lighting on the eves outlines the building. Both of these light sources are preferable to external lighting aimed at the building.

Lighting prominent landscape and garden features is one of the best ways to deal aesthetically with lighting at night. Elements like trees, hedges, garden areas, trellis structures, and gazebos located in the landscape are often visible from the street as well as from residents' units. In contrast to lighting the building, landscape effect lighting gives everyone something to look at after the sun goes down. Indirect lighting on porches and light emanating from interior windows gives the building a glow that is attractive from the street. This is always preferable to commercial lighting aimed at the building.

Walkway and Parking Lot Lighting at Night

Sidewalks that link the parking lot with the front entry should be well lighted at night for security purposes. It is most likely that parking lot and sidewalk lighting will benefit the staff during shift changes after dark, rather than residents, visitors, or family. Parking lot lighting at night should be at least 0.5 foot-candle throughout. The specification of attractive residential-scale light fixtures for both sidewalks and parking lots gives these areas a less commercial feeling. Pathway lighting around the site is handy for those who might want to take a walk after dinner, especially in the winter, when the sun goes down early.

12

Creating Courtyards to Capture Views and Ensure Privacy

◄ *Courtyards can provide variety:* When two courtyards are adjacent to one another, as at *Vigs Ängar*, Köpingbro, Sweden, it is often best to treat one as a hardscape patio and the other as a softscape garden.

Courtyard housing is a particularly good solution on tight urban sites that provide little opportunity to set the building in a parklike setting. A courtyard form uses the building's edge to define a protected space from the street. Outdoor courtyards accessible from common rooms are particularly attractive in group housing arrangements for older people. Seeing into spaces that are landscaped and outfitted with comfortable furniture makes these spaces more attractive and inviting.

Single- and Double-Loaded Corridors Around Courtyards

Courtyard designs are common in northern Europe because urban land is at a premium. Single-loaded corridors are commonly utilized in combination with double-loaded corridors because they allow a courtyard to be visible from part of the corridor. The *Postiljonen* (page 224) employs single-loaded corridors to daylight hallways and common spaces. These settings are often developed as clusters of 8–10 units in order reduce the distances the staff must walk.

Softscape and Hardscape Treatments for Courtyards

A well-designed courtyard should be balanced, with both hardscape and softscape. In a smaller courtyard, a balance of 40 percent hardscape and 60 percent softscape is a good ratio. In a larger courtyard, the percentage of softscape might be larger. In urban areas where courtyards are utilized for public purposes and circulation, the percentage of hardscape may also increase. When two courtyards are available, one can be designated for more active use, with a larger amount of hardscape, while the other can rely on more landscaping and serve as a controlled-view space. This adds to the character of both spaces—giving them more variety and uniqueness.

Southwestern Courtyard Tradition

Courtyards are also popular in western sunbelt communities because they provide opportunities for shade control. The old Spanish courtyards constructed from stucco-covered adobe and filled with fountains and trees were cool oases from the hot summer sun. It is important not to make a courtyard too narrow. It should never be narrower than the height of the building. A comfortable width for a two-story building is 40–60 feet.

Courtyard Orientation and Use Advantages

Often sheltered from the wind, courtyards are excellent places to sit as well as walk. They should be designed to be used as shortcuts from one side of the building to the other. When courtyards are surrounded by single-loaded corridors, the views into the courtyard help provide orientation and wayfinding. This configuration is also friendly because residents can see one another. Three-sided U-shaped courtyards are also popular because they create a view corridor, enhance the flow of gentle breezes, and connect the courtyard with the surrounding landscape.

5

THE OUTDOOR
LANDSCAPE

Typical assisted living residents are frail, do not drive, and have little need to visit a grocery store. Their "life space" is often limited to the building, the grounds, and the local shopping mall (by minibus). As a result, the outdoor space surrounding the building takes on special significance, substituting for frequent off-site excursions to shopping malls and work trips. The relationship to the landscape is also important. The work of Roger Ulrich (1984, 1995) and his colleagues at the University of Texas demonstrates how important views of the landscape can be for patients who are recovering from various surgical procedures.

One of the least appreciated and most poorly developed relationships is that between the inside and outside of the building. Porches, patios, and plazas can complement interior spaces. The site should be accessible from several places throughout the building, and a walkway should be available for exercise and for contemplation. A plant material palette with varied colors, textures, and scents can be stimulating and interesting. Places should be available for grandchildren to play and for family members to have a picnic or snack.

The site should be conceptualized as a series of outdoor rooms that are linked together by a circulation pathway.

13

The Controlled-View Window to the World

◀ *Corner windows capture views in two directions:*   These corner windows at *Virranranta* (page 206) have low sills and are quite large. A modest shelf placed over the radiator also provides a place for plants and other personal display items.

Because residents spend a lot of time in their own dwelling units, they are also likely to spend time looking out the window. When the view is of an active social space, residents are more likely to visit these spaces because they see others using them.

Large Windows are Preferable

The use of larger windows enhances the perception of space within the unit. A window 6 feet wide and 6 feet tall should be considered minimum. A sill height of 16–24 inches allows residents a view out of the window while lying in bed. A low sill height creates an extension of the unit into the garden rather than a separation from outside.

14

The European Erker

◀ *The European Erker window:*   This marvelous example at Flesseman in Nieumarket Square, Amsterdam, has glass windows on three sides, a French balcony with two glass doors that open, and a remote-control canvas awning for shade.

A common fenestration treatment in urban European projects is the Dutch erker, is an attached alcove window that resembles a square bay window. It projects 18–24 inches beyond the front face of the building, allowing light to enter the unit from three directions. The bay window became popular in the United States because it allowed more light to enter a room while providing a more enhanced viewing platform. The space created by the erker is at the edge of the unit and connects the inside with the outside.

The Visual and Experiential Attributes of the Erker Window

There are a number of different design treatments that can be labeled as an erker. One of the most handsome examples is at the *Flesseman* project in Nieumarket, the Netherlands. It has the following attributes. A three-sided balcony juts out about 18 inches into the right-of-way of the road below. In concept it is like a glazed balcony. The configuration makes it possible for residents to view activities up and down the street. It is large enough to accommodate a chair for viewing purposes. The floor is a tile material so that plant materials can safely be placed or hung there. A glass door faces the street, with a French balcony rail that allows the full width of the erker to be opened. Finally, the balcony is outfitted with a shading device that can be adjusted, depending on the time of day or the angle of the sun.

15

Gardens that Provide Continuity of Lifestyle

◄ *Exterior seating located near a central exit door is popular:* The courtyard in the *Sunrise at Hermosa Beach,* California, provides shade and wind control for this sheltered U-shaped courtyard, which is overlooked by a parlor.

The vast majority of older people have had experiences with gardening, either as a hobby, as a pastime, or simply as a homeowner. Thus, it is an activity that begins with previous experience and broad-based acceptance. Even though gardening is often carried out alone, it is an activity that can stimulate interaction with others. There is something about nurturing plant materials that is attractive to many older women. It is an activity that provides continuity in their lives from past to present. It also provides a way to interact with the natural ecology of the surrounding environment.

Resident Gardens

Raised gardens allow plant materials to be accessible to people in wheelchairs and also allow residents to garden without having to bend over. When raised 16 to 24 inches, gardens are closer to the eyes and the nose, making it easier for older people to sense and appreciate the plant materials. At the end of the growing season, resident gardens can look scruffy. They need to be managed as part of an activities program. Some residents may not use them because the work required is strenuous. Given their popularity and broad-based appeal, gardening programs should always be explored with residents in dementia and assisted living.

Practical Uses of Gardening

Some northern European projects have large resident garden areas. This is especially true of projects located in small towns and in the countryside. These gardens are popular because they support a hobby or a pattern of activity that has been present for a lifetime. In these gardens, food is grown that can be prepared in the kitchen and served to other residents. One of my strongest memories from an early trip was of a group of dementia residents from a small group home in central Sweden going fishing with an attendant. In the United States, this informal approach to securing food is often ignored. Sometimes health requirements complicate the situation. At other times, it is viewed as too complicated to implement. However, growing food provides one of the best opportunities to express self-sufficiency, allowing residents to feel engaged in the cycle of life.

Gardening Is Relatively Easy to Pursue Successfully

In Scandinavia, there is a strong desire to spend time outdoors in the summer. Gardening is a relatively easy activity to manage and provides a compelling reason for residents to spend time outside. Some plants, like flowers and tomatoes, don't require a highly developed green thumb. Gardening doesn't involve a major investment in time or money. Resident garden installations can vary in scale from a few pots to a large, raised planting bed surrounded by a fence, often with access to a water source and a small potting shed. The process of nurturing a garden is intrinsically satisfying to many people.

16

Shade Control

◄ *Trellis filters direct south-facing sun:*   At this small service house in *Halmstad*, Sweden, a trellis is used as a semitransparent porch enclosure. It provides some shade but also allows light to enter the porch and the adjacent activity spaces.

Most older people are interested in going outside on the nicest days. These are often days when the sun is brightest. When sitting outdoors, they want the option to sit in areas that offer sun, shade, or partial shade. Shade is particularly attractive in mid-summer, near the end of the day, or when the temperature is highest.

Shade Pavilions in the Landscape

Structures like gazebos, umbrellas, and garden trellises are interesting places to experience shade, as well as interesting objects that can be seen from indoors. A trellis provides partial shade, which allows an individual to select a location with both sun and shade. William Whyte (1980), in his book on New York City's pocket parks, discusses the importance of the choice between sun and shade, which often depends on the temperature. A bright, sunny summer afternoon is very different from a cool spring morning. Seasonal change as well as the time of day can affect the attractiveness of a particular spot. Also, if the day is hot or cool, one often feels differently about the desirability of direct sun. Sunbelt and frost belt settings also value sun and shade differently. In Miami and Southern California, a good shady spot is extremely valuable.

Shade Structures Attached to the Building

Awnings are perhaps the most common shade structure. These are easy to attach to a building and, if large enough, they can provide shade inside as well as outside. The Dutch have a tradition of using colorful, retractable awnings on their buildings. Those used for housing of the elderly are often controlled by a motor with a switch located inside the dwelling unit. Trellis shade structures attached to buildings can be designed as an extension of the fascia. When arranged this way, they appear more substantial. Over time, plant materials can be trained or shade cloth can be attached to a trellis to create a partial shade condition. If flowering plants are used, they may attract bees and insects. Air flow and breezes are also important considerations. Many residents find drafts unpleasant, which is why outdoor spaces next to the building are preferable. In addition to controlling airflow by using the mass of the building, they allow residents to be near entrance and exit doors. When all else fails, umbrella tables often work well. They are movable and can be adjusted to conform to sun angles. The major problem is their tendency to be overturned by wind gusts.

17

Accessorizing the Exterior

◄ *Respecting important historical fragments:* The *Kvarteret Karl XI* service house in Halmstad, Sweden, is built near the center of the city over sections of the battlements used in the old medieval city wall. These have been preserved as landscape features of the garden.

Like the interior of a building, outdoor "rooms" can benefit from accessories. Objects designed to be placed in a garden can have an aesthetic or a functional rationale. Rain gauges, thermometers, bird feeders, and wind sculptures serve a purpose as well as providing visual interest. Often the most interesting items are found in the local hardware, antique, or lawn and garden store. These are common items associated with residential settings. Their presence often reinforces the atmosphere of the place as a residential environment.

Objects That Are Compatible with Plant Materials

Objects placed in a garden can create contrast with plant materials. The object when combined with plant materials generates much more interest than it does alone. Familiar objects such as farm plows, antiques, cast stone figurines, wind sculptures, pots, and native stone can also connect residents with the past. At the *Sunrise of Westfield*, New Jersey, a large tree stump was removed, cut at the base, and placed on its side to reveal more than 100 annual growth rings. Utilizing local stone for rock placements in the garden provides another way to connect residents with the landscape. Objects can also be kinetic. They can move with the wind or they can attract birds and butterflies. Fountains and pools of water are very attractive to a range of wildlife. However, the noise of flowing water sometimes stimulates the urge to urinate in people with incontinence. Deep pools of water can sometimes pose a safety hazard. However, stones can be used to fill deeper pools, thus alleviating concerns about accidental drowning.

Dementia Gardens

For dementia residents, the *Hearthstone Alzheimer Care* at New Horizons in Marlborough, Massachusetts (Tyson, 1998), had good experiences utilizing cast concrete objects in the landscape. There is an element of surprise and whimsy that makes these objects interesting and sometimes amusing to residents. Another area of focus is the transition between inside and outside environments. Decorating the door and the adjoining porch with a knocker/bell, screen door, shoe scraper, mail slot, and decorative wreath can call attention to the door and cue residents to enter. In dementia gardens, experimentation with various objects is taking place. Old cars that can be sat in, bus stops, a garage with small tools, and a playhouse for children are installations that have been successfully mainstreamed into Alzheimers gardens.

Garden Design That Uses Historical Elements

In northern Europe, landscape designers often exploit historic elements of the site for design purposes. In the *Kvarteret Karl XI* project in Halmstad, Sweden, garden walls reflected the old battlements, which were originally part of the walled medieval city. In the *NZH Terrein Voorburg* project in Voorburg, the Netherlands, an old trolley maintenance barn was the site for a new project. A circular central courtyard was created in remembrance of the old roundhouse, and sections of train track were used in combination with landscape materials. The old patterns of use were thus reflected in a new design. Architects often use the history of the site as a point of departure for design elements they choose to retain. An old wellhead from the site of Queen Victoria's summer house was used to provide a focus for the dementia garden at the *Sunrise at Frognal House* in London, England. The European approach to utilizing found objects on site for design inspiration reflects the historic richness of older European cities and their respect for the past.

18

Interstitial Space Between the Inside and the Outside

◀ *Glazed lounge overlooks a pedestrian street:*   This glazed greenhouse enclosure at *Gulkrögcentret* in Vieje, Denmark, was designed to overlook an active pedestrian street that links the train station with a nearby hospital.

The edge between indoor and outdoor spaces has long been a fascinating area for architects and landscape designers. Residents like to be near the building edge and often avoid sitting in the center of a garden (Carstens, 1985; Regnier, 1985). Residents often arrange movable furniture to be near an entry or exit door because access to the building is important. The building provides a sense of security as well as access to facilities like restrooms. Covered porches in the front of a building that are oriented to the street and the building entry are also very popular.

Five Interstitial Zones and a Street Location

In the *Sunrise at Severna Park*, Maryland, five spaces have been placed between the building and the garden (see color insert). The first space starts indoors, with a fully air-conditioned and heated three-season/greenhouse space with floor-to-ceiling windows and skylights oriented toward the garden. The second space, which is connected to the greenhouse, is a screened porch. The screen wire protects this space from insects and blowing rain, making it possible to use a mixture of interior and exterior furniture. Adjacent to the screened porch is the third space, an open covered porch. The fourth space, located in front of the covered porch, is a trellis that provides partial shade. The last space is an open barbecue terrace adjacent to the trellis and screened porch Enclosed greenhouse spaces or covered porches oriented toward an active view are also very popular.

In Vieje, Denmark, the *Gulkrogcentret* project is situated along a street that links the train station to a nearby hospital. Residents favor several glass-enclosed, greenhouse-style lounge spaces that overlook the activity generated by this pedestrian pathway.

19

Connections to Friendly Neighbors

◀ *U-shaped building is oriented to an adjacent park:*   Northern European urban housing is often physically connected to adjacent land uses. This Swedish project opens onto an urban park across the street.

One of the most important ways to deinstitutionalize an assisted living building is to create public connections to adjacent compatible land uses. The optimum location for this is a neighborhood with friendly nearby land uses. Some of the best neighbors include churches, community centers, pedestrian-oriented retail stores, child-care centers, parks, post offices, restaurants, coffee bars, and ice cream/yogurt shops. In addition to being friendly next-door neighbors, these types of adjacent land use give residents and family members a nearby destination to walk to for exercise. The sidewalk system surrounding the building should always be extended to meet the public sidewalk. In many cases, the sidewalk will lead to a public transportation stop, making it easier for transit-dependent workers and visitors to arrive and depart.

Walkways and Gates Can Link Compatible Land Uses

Being located across the street from a friendly, compatible land use is not as good as being located next door. At the *Sunrise in Hunter Mill*, in Oakton, Virginia, a gate was installed at the edge of the site to the back parking lot of the shopping center next door. Residents have only a few steps to walk before they reach a sidewalk that leads to a coffee shop, supermarket, bookstore, and pet store. In the *Sunrise at Severna Park*, Maryland, the site is located adjacent to a church and a public library. The sidewalk system connects the building to the entrances of both of these places. In northern Europe, housing

projects often plan for several uses on one site. In the *Vanhainkoti-Parvakeskus Himmeli* in Pori, Finland, a day-care center for children is located on the same site and within a few steps of the front entry of the building. Residents are involved in a range of intergenerational activities next door and within the library of their own building.

Overlooks and Visual Connections

Because housing for the elderly and day-care centers for children often share the same zoning category, opportunities abound for overlooks between the building and children's play spaces. In many municipalities in northern Europe, child care and adult care are coordinated through the same government agency, so coordination efforts are less complex and bureaucratic. At the *Frederiksberg Aldrecenter* in Åarhus, Denmark, an adjacent day-care center has a playground located at the foot of a multistory service house for the elderly. Residents of nearby apartments have a great view of the play space from their balconies (see page 63).

20

The Healing Therapeutic Garden

◄ *Walking path loops around a babbling brook in this lush landscape:* The *Motion Picture Country House* dementia garden in Woodland Hills, California, uses conifers and deciduous trees in two different places to create variety and complexity in this garden.

A number of recently published books have touted the therapeutic benefits of gardens (Cooper-Marcus and Barnes, 1999; Cooper-Marcus and Francis, 1998; Tyson, 1998). There is empirical evidence (Ulrich, 1984, 1995) that exposure to garden views reduces the convalescence period of acute-care hospital patients. Others believe that the use of gardens for mental exercises like directed imagery in cancer therapy can have a positive impact on the effectiveness of various therapies. In addition, walking for physical exercise is clearly beneficial.

Gardens with Therapeutic Intentions

Dementia gardens are perhaps the most popular setting for the implementation of unusual, creative design ideas.

The gardens of *Sedgewood Commons* in Falmouth, Maine (Dannenmaier, 1995), explored different gardens for persons with differing levels of cognitive impairment. A program component accompanied each design, including items like a basketball hoop to build upper-body strength and personal garden plots for those who had the strength and focus to cultivate a garden.

Motion Picture Country House Dementia Garden

At the *Motion Picture Country House* in Woodland Hills, California, various landscape ideas have been explored in the design of the dementia garden. A formal civic area with a bench, an aviary, and a drinking fountain is located on a flat portion of the garden. Adjacent to this is a less formal area that includes a babbling brook located between pine trees adjacent to several secluded alcoves. A looped pathway links both of these garden spaces with the building and thus encourages walking. Both of these areas utilize different plant materials, thus creating interest and variety in the garden. Physical therapy can also take place in outdoor spaces. In the *Rygardcentret* in Gentofte, Denmark, one of the courtyards was specially designed with several different types of walking surfaces to simulate a range of walking conditions (see color insert).

Attributes of the Healing Garden

Clare Cooper-Marcus (1999) identify nine attributes of an effective healing garden: (1) homelike imagery, (2) places for privacy, (3) settings that stimulate mental alertness, (4) opportunities for social exchange, (5) places for family members to gather, (6) a large enough area for outside activities, (7) comfortable seating, (8) a feeling of security, and (9) accessibility to the handicapped. A garden that addresses all nine of these criteria is likely to be successful.

21

Selecting Appropriate Plant Materials: Color, Texture, Aroma, and Variety

◄ *An inviting garden pathway with bermed plant materials:*   A variety of perennials, conifers, and annuals make this pathway attractive.

Adding color, texture, and variety to the palette of plant materials gives the site design a unique and memorable look. Nowhere is this more important than at the front door. More people (guests and residents) will see the landscape located here than at any other place on the site. Older residents have difficult bending over, and given their poor eyesight and reduced sense of smell, flowers located near the ground are harder to appreciate. Elevating these materials through raised beds or pots enhances their color and aroma. Raising plant materials gets them closer to a resident's face; thus, eyes, nose, and fingers can more easily sense their beauty.

Adding Variety and Interest

A variety of plant types and species makes for a more stimulating landscape design. Variety means not just selecting both conifers and deciduous trees, but also insisting that different types of conifers and deciduous trees be present. Some of the most mundane landscape plans place plant materials in a mechanical fashion and rely on only a few species. This should be avoided. It goes without saying that poisonous species should be avoided. This is especially true for dementia gardens. However, poison control experts claim that older people are in little danger from eating plants like rhododendrons, which would require ingestion of a huge volume to endanger a person's life. Landscape color and variety are also important at the street entry and around the facility's sign.

22

A Visible, Attractive Sign

◀ *European buildings are often given a name:* The *Wilhelmiina* (page 163) is an example of this tradition. It has a low-key sign made of individual letters that hang below a steel portal that frames the main entrance facing the street.

An eye-catching sign is a very important element of the project design, especially in the United States, because so many people learn about a building by driving by. Signs are often limited by local ordinances that specify the available area. In general, the sign should be large enough to be identified and read from a moving car. A height of 6 to 8 feet above the road is adequate, and 20 SF of signage is probably enough to communicate what needs to be said. The sign is an important "symbolic calling card." If it appears unkempt, too massive, or unfriendly, it sends a subtle negative message about the nature of the building and the services provided.

Signage Strategies

The sign should be richly landscaped and perhaps placed on an earthern berm to give it additional height for visibility. A successful sign is one that appears to be emanating from the landscape rather than just stuck in the ground. It should be easy to read, with adequate figure/ground contrast. The sign should be dignified and should not call undue attention to itself. Commercial signs that look like they belong to a nearby pizza parlor give the wrong impression. The sign needs to be lighted at night, with at least two light sources for each viewing surface.

European Sign Strategies

In northern Europe, signs are very low-key. Often they are placed on the building rather than as a monument sign on the edge of the site. This is often because most buildings contain public spaces that are well known to people in the community. Signs here are used to name the building rather than to call attention to the sponsor. In England, buildings are often given names. These names are often sentimental and reflect the presence of a flower, tree, or natural site feature. The name often implies attributes that give the building personality. This is a wonderful tradition that speaks to the qualities of the place rather than just the sponsor's name.

23

Attracting Wildlife: Animals, Insects, and Birds

◄ *Squirrels as well as birds can be interesting to watch:*   There are a variety of squirrel feeders that challenge these creatures to work for a snack. These feeders increase the potential for placing wildlife activity near a window or patio.

Attracting wildlife is an inexpensive way of making the landscape more lively while maintaining the character and intimacy of a residential backyard. The aim is to create a garden similar to one you would experience in your own home. Some of the most interesting locations to view wildlife are near windows and porches, where residents can easily see activities.

Birds

Birds are the most sought-after wildlife species. They are friendly and very interesting to watch, especially in the winter. Bird feeders, bird baths, and bird houses are relatively easy to place and fascinating to watch. Hummingbird feeders can be attached to window frames for more intimate viewing. Many birds are territorial; thus, the number of functioning bird houses should be limited, given the size of the outdoor space available. Care should be taken if a resident house cat spends time out-

side. Cats have been known to attack birds, creating a less than pleasant outcome.

Butterflies and Squirrels

Squirrels are very lively animals that can be more entertaining than birds. There are a number of squirrel-feeding devices in bird and pet stores that require squirrels to do some work before they capture a meal. Squirrels can be a problem if bird watching is the primary activity. However, most bird-feeding devices have squirrel-proof features. Butterflies are fascinating and are easily attracted to annuals and perennials such as "Butterfly Bush." However, water is also needed to attract butterflies. There are numerous manufacturers of wildlife habitats. Woodlink offers an attractive line of rustic cedar and redwood wildlife feeding and sheltering devices. Other mammals, like rabbits, and ground squirrels can be kept in secured courtyards or cages, where they can be visited.

24

A Playground for Children

◄ *Day-care playground is visible from the service center:*   In northern Europe, day care for children is often colocated with elderly care centers. This playground at the Frederiksberg Aldrecenter in Åarhus, Denmark, is overlooked by residential units in adjoining towers.

Integrating the activities of preschool children with elder care has been a successful strategy for decades. There are numerous examples in the United States, especially in larger continuing care retirement commu-

nities, where facilities often provide day care for the children of staff as an employment incentive. In general, older residents enjoy watching children play. Small children are good at providing unconditional love and affection, which is very attractive to many older residents. The success of this strategy lies in how the two groups are mixed. These are two very different types of caregiving situations that require staff with different skill sets.

Changing the Image of Assisted Living in the Community

The most common complaint is that noise or commotion upsets an agitated resident but, when managed properly, the presence of children is magical. It can redefine the purpose of the building in the community. Instead of a place for older people to live out their last years, it can be conceptualized as a place where both older people and children are taken care of. The difference is sometimes subtle, but it helps break down the notion that the facility is only an old people's home.

Colocation Strategies

When separate buildings for older residents and child day care are located next to one another and share overlapping spaces, the management of that interaction is much less complicated. In playground spaces, seating needs to be located so that residents can have varying levels of visual connection with children. Seating that is close by (within 10–15 feet) should be provided, as well as seating that is 25 feet or more away. Some residents are bothered by the noise and the quick movements of young children but love to watch at a distance. One delightful example of a colocated project is the *Sternberga Servicehus* (Paulsson, 1997) (see page 257). Located near the small central Swedish town of Naverbyn, an old house serves as the children's day-care center. Adjacent to this house is the service house for the elderly. A small, fenced outdoor garden for residents is adjacent to the playground for children. This setting appears to work well because in this small rural town everyone knows one another.

More Modest Strategies

In most assisted living buildings, it is not possible to create a fully functioning children's playground, yet the grandchildren of residents should feel welcome. Even something as modest as a swing and slide provides the message that children are welcome. It should be located near the building rather than on the edge of the site or on the other side of the parking lot. A remote location is often too far away for residents to participate and can become an "attractive nuisance" if it is located too close to traffic.

25

A Looped Walking Pathway

◄ *Residents use this courtyard to exercise and socialize:* Tornhuset, on an urban site in Göteborg, Sweden, consists of several midrise towers facing a central courtyard. The large sociopetal garden contains a looped pathway, sitting areas, and a hardscape plaza.

One of the best ways to encourage residents to walk for exercise is to create a pathway around the perimeter of the building that starts and ends at the front entrance. If more exercise is desired, residents can do consecutive laps. The width of the pathway should be at least 5 feet, and it should have a nonglare surface. Dark gray or light brown concrete is the best solution. Blacktop is an acceptable material if it is prepared and laid properly. Darker colors will also subside into the green landscape of the lawn. Occasionally, decomposed granite is utilized around the base of trees, where water penetration and root disturbance are issues. However, in order to avoid erosion, the area needs to be carefully edged with wood or metal.

Plan for Benches and Rest Areas

In order for residents to feel comfortable walking, they need to have a place to sit, rest, and recharge every 100–125 feet. Benches should be positioned to take advantage of interesting views and should be at least 5 feet wide. Residents often walk with a friend or caregiver, and both need a place to sit down. Benches should be resilient and should have arm rests on both sides to make it easy to sit down and stand up. Teak is a popular material for bench construction. Benches should be placed on and secured to the pavement. Residents who have difficulty with ambulation often prefer to see the next bench before starting to walk again. This assures them that there is a predictable location where they can rest next.

Benches and Landscape Treatments

Landscaping around each bench location can be the basis for a very effective planning and planting strategy around the perimeter of the site. Because each bench is likely to attract residents, this landscaping approach places plant materials in areas that are heavily utilized. Some of these benches should provide diversions like views, wildlife feeders, accessories, or unique plant materials. When exposed to sun, these settings should have an adjacent tree or trellis to provide shade.

26

The Barbecue Plaza

◀ *Courtyard serves as a popular outdoor living room:* The central courtyard at *Postiljonen* (page 224) is surrounded by a single-loaded corridor. All major common spaces overlook the courtyard, making it omnipresent in the minds of residents and staff.

A large outside space of 300 to 500 SF should be available for social events. Holidays like Memorial Day, July 4th, and Labor Day are often planned as days for barbecues or picnics to which family members are invited. The most flexible large outdoor spaces usually extend from a major common space like a living room or dining room. However, a 2- to 5-foot landscape buffer should be considered between the interior room and the pavement. This will ensure that the view from the inside is of colorful plant materials rather than a stark concrete slab. The terrace should be sized to accommodate up to half of the resident population.

Logistics and Arrangements

The patio space should accommodate food service and should be easily expanded for special events. A storage area is useful for extra chairs, a barbecue grill, and an audio system for announcements and music. Power should be available, and night lighting should be sufficient. Part of the plaza should be shaded, and the floor should be made of a darker, nonglare material. If the project is shaped to create a courtyard like that of the *Postiljonen* (page 224), it will transform nicely into an easy-to-use patio space. The typical courtyard building often has a patio area adjacent to common spaces, which is visible from at least half of the units.

6

REFINING DESIGN
ATTRIBUTES

One of the most important factors in designing the building is to make it appear as different as possible from a nursing home. Residents and family members are seeking to avoid the look, the smell, the lack of control, and the bland atmosphere of the typical nursing home. A building with a residential appearance, much like that of the single-family home from which the older person is moving, minimizes transitional angst.

There are several attributes of nursing homes that are important to avoid. These include long, undifferentiated, double-loaded corridors, hard surface wall and floor coverings, vinyl-covered furniture, double-occupied dwelling units, dark interiors with a lack of natural light, and general lack of privacy.

Many nursing homes utilize inexpensive construction that results in a series of rooms and corridors. There is little hierarchy in room size, and few spaces open onto one another in an open-plan format. In short, these buildings often have ugly and undifferentiated spaces.

Assisted living should utilize the single-family house as the model for its measure of success. The more a building can be scaled to appear like a smaller, more intimate dwelling, the more cozy and attractive it will appear to residents and their families.

27

The Friendly, Approachable Building

◄ *The Goddard House (page 169) entry is friendly and approachable:*
The skillful composition of porches, gables, a small tower, and an entry pavilion reduces the perceived scale of the building when seen from the street. (Photo: Edward Jacoby Photography)

Increasing the approachability of a building involves taming the scale to make it appear smaller and more intimate. The view from the street establishes the first impression of a building. If it is narrow and deep, you are likely to have a different impression than if you view the building from its widest side. Subtle adjustments to the façade can make a big building appear smaller from the street. For example, adjustments at the base and the top of a building can change your impression of its height. Porches are often used to foreshorten height, be-cause your eye often reads the vertical exterior surface of the building, which starts 1½ stories up. The open first-floor porch doesn't appear to be massive. Using a roof dormer on the top of a building can reduce the height by as much as 5–7 feet by lowering the eve and gutter line. This often gives the impression that the building is about a half-story lower. These strategies, when applied properly, make the building appear more intimate and less overwhelming—more like a smaller residential dwelling.

28

The First Impression

◄ *The open stair creates an alcove for a concierge greeter:*   This two-story entry foyer links the upper floor with the main entry space at the *Sunrise at Bellevue*, Washington. (Photo: Robert Pisano)

First impressions are powerful and difficult to change. Although your first impression of a building is normally formed at the curbside, this feeling is modified by your experience of walking inside. Most providers strive to make this experience a positive one. A common strategy is to make the entry experience grand and elegant, like that of moving through a well-appointed mansion.

Because the front door is your first indication of what lies inside, it should be distinctive and friendly.

The Entry Experience

Creating a memorable first impression often involves a change in spatial hierarchy as you enter the building.

Frank Lloyd Wright was famous for his dramatic entries which usually involved moving from a very small to a very large space. Entering a two-story foyer does this while visually connecting the second floor with the ground floor. A staircase that links the first and second floors adds to the drama while creating a sense of connection to the upper floor. This arrangement is typical of the early-twentieth-century mansion in the United States. Having someone with a friendly face at a desk to greet and assist you when you enter reduces ambiguity and uncertainty. Skylights or clerestory lighting, when positioned properly, can increase the amount of natural light while reducing glare.

Connected Adjacent Spaces

The most viable social spaces are often those visually linked to the front entrance. Soft, comfortable living room furniture with a nearby fireplace is a friendly gesture. A place with tables where residents and family members can meet and perhaps have a light snack should also be nearby. In Europe, this area is sometimes a bar where alcohol or soft drinks are available. Also nearby, with some visibility from the front entrance, should be the dining room. In buildings that are relatively narrow, it is possible to connect the entrance visually to an outdoor garden at the rear of the building. Convenient see-through access to an outdoor sitting area is not only pleasant but makes the building easier to comprehend. An elevator in a multistory building should be nearby

but not necessarily visible from the front door. If the elevator is placed too close to the front door, the security of the building and its residential character can be compromised.

European Entry Ideas

When entering a service house like *Virranranta* (page 206), you enter the most public community spaces first. There is normally a vestibule due to the cold winter temperatures. Entering a service house is a lot like entering a senior community center. The public spaces lead to a more private housing component normally located the farthest distance from the public entry. Many buildings utilize features similar to those found in U.S. buildings, such as skylights, clerestories, dramatic stair connections, and changes in spatial hierarchy. However, these spaces have a public or civic purpose; they are not residential in character. In many of the most lively buildings, the first impression of space is provided by a large skylighted central atrium. This is either a finished indoor space or an indoor garden located below a multistory skylighted volume. Many of these European buildings are open to the public and thus are sited in conjunction with plazas, parks, and open spaces. In terms of spatial hierarchy, the building entry is often a low space with taller surrounding spaces (dining room, living room, and atrium). One reason for this is that these buildings are sized to accommodate not only the people who live there but also seniors who visit from the surrounding neighborhood.

29

The Sloping Roof, Front Door, Hearth, and Open Stairs

◄ *Fireplace anchors the corner of the parlor:* This comfortable, inviting space is adjacent to the two-story entry foyer in the *Sunrise at Alexandria*, Virginia. The fireplace is positioned to be visible from inside the entry door.

The architectural theorists Witold Rybczynski (1986) and Christopher Alexander and his colleagues (1977) have described four building attributes that cue the recognition of residential design for most individuals: the sloping roof, the front entry door, the fireplace, and the open stairs. These features also provide clues to the quality and

type of residential environment one is likely to experience. Interestingly, simple children's sketches of single-family houses often contain a front door surrounded by windows, topped with a sloping roof and flanked by a fireplace chimney. It is the basic connection with these attributes that creates residential identity.

Modernist Images

When modernists redefined the house in the 1920s, they started by simplifying its design. The flat roof was selected not only because it could accommodate a roof garden, but also because it was the opposite of the sloped, shingled roof. Some modernists also avoided the fireplace or redefined it as a contemporary metal fixture rather than a heavy masonry firebox.

30

Is It a House or an Apartment?

◄ *This mansion was transformed into a larger building:*   A turn-of-the-century Tudor mansion in Norwood, Massachusetts, was remodeled by sensitive additions to both sides of the original three-story house. (Photo: JH Putnam)

An assisted living building, depending on its size and configuration, can appear to be either a big house or an apartment building. Most sponsors prefer a building that appears as small and homelike as possible. Even though both can have residential references, the transition from one housing form to another is often dependent on the number of units to be accommodated. While 50 units in a three-story envelope can have the massing attributes of a house, 75 units in two stories are likely to appear as an apartment-style building. Such a building may use balconies to reduce the perceived length of the wings.

Corridor Lengths Are Long

Lengthy corridors can result from a low-scale building of over 75 units. As corridor lengths approach 100 feet,

they create problems for the most frail residents—although, as can be demonstrated in *Bellevue* (page 191), a 70-unit building in four stories can easily result in a centralized, compact footprint. In northern Europe, larger buildings are often decentralized, with smaller clusters of units around dining rooms, as in *Virranranta* (page 206). In other large buildings, like *Wilhelmiina* (page 163), the massing is broken up into smaller attached multistory structures that are accessible to one another from a common first floor. However, larger apartment buildings like *Humanitas* (page 158) also occur in northern Europe when a concept like "apartments for life" is promoted.

31

Making Big Spaces Smaller and Small Spaces Bigger

◀ *These corridors invite daylight and open the building to the courtyard view:* The glass window wall treatment creates a ground plane connection between the inside and outside, making the corridor feel like an extension of the outdoors.

The dining room is often the largest room in the building. If it is planned for a single seating, with 24 to 26 SF per person used as the standard for access, the room can be huge. On the other hand, narrow corridors and three-season porches can often benefit by techniques that make them seem wider and more spacious. Sitting down to dinner in a single monolithic room surrounded by a sea of gray-haired residents can be a little disconcerting.

Strategies to Make the Dining Room Appear Smaller

One of the most effective ways to break up a space is to select a form that contains several smaller alcoves and private dining room spaces. Half-walls are a common technique for defining rooms at the ground level while preserving open views at eye height. Half-walls can be modified in width and height by cabinets, screens, plants, and built-in furniture. Full and three-quarter wall segments that subdivide spaces often utilize windows or an art glass panel to create a semitransparent separation. Adjustments to the ceiling can include dropped soffits, raised recesses, heavy beams, and strapwork to break up the ceiling plane. *Sunrise of Richmond* (page 196 and color insert) uses several alcoves, ceiling strapwork, lowered "flying beams," and a central fireplace to subdivide the space. The *Goddard House* (page 169) subdivided its dining into three separate, more intimate, rooms, thus reducing the need to add additional ceiling height. Because the ambulatory status of many older residents requires a flat floor, ceilings are more likely to be used to express spatial variety. Whatever strategy is used, the outcome should be greater visual and auditory privacy within a space that is perceived as smaller and more intimate.

Changing Materials and Colors to Achieve Variety

Spatial variety can also be achieved by creating rooms that differ in size, color, material, and lighting. Using different types of floor coverings like carpet, wood, tile, or sheet vinyl can dramatically influence the character of different spaces. Another common strategy is to use different types of lighting to create spatial differentiation. For example, chandeliers, indirect lighting, pendant lighting, recessed lighting, and floor/table lamps can influence the perception of space. Chandeliers and pendant lighting often act to subdivide rooms because of their size and placement. When separate rooms are created, the use of wall coverings differentiated by color and type will create spaces of different character. A yellow wall in a space adjacent to a window that invites natural light is brighter in the morning. The same space, when combined with a tile floor and rattan chairs, seems more lively and appropriate for breakfast.

Furniture Changes That Break up Spaces

Another strategy to vary the configuration of a dining room is to utilize different table and seating arrangements. Creating a unique pattern with two-, three-, four-, and six-person tables with adjacent banquette seating can vary the overall look of a space. Natural room dividers like a fireplace with adjacent living room furniture can create a logical separation in a long, thin dining room space.

Strategies That Make Smaller Spaces Seem Larger

Spaces like corridors, offices, and porches are often perceived as too small. Small office spaces can greatly benefit from a window or a door with glass panels that link it to the corridor. Hold-openers for doors within one-hour fire-rated corridors also help mitigate the feeling of being cramped by allowing the door to be kept open. Dutch doors are also good because they allow separation but create connection. Edge condition spaces with windows benefit when low sill heights are used. A sill height of 4–12 inches and a header heights of 7 feet or more allow the room to connect with the outdoors and make it appear larger. Skylights and sloped ceilings also increase the perception of height.

Tricks of the Masters

The California modernist Richard Neutra (Hines, 1982) was known for his use of mirrors inside and outside buildings to expand spaces and to reflect views of outdoor gardens. He also utilized floor-to-ceiling windows and doors in an effort to connect the inside with the outside. Another of his strategies was to create a narrow corridor that was solid up to a 33- to 34-inch chair rail height and then opened with continuous glass above. In doing this, he created 36-inch-wide residential corridors that appeared to be much wider. Finally, he used large panes of movable glass, often 5 feet tall by 10–12 feet long, that could be fully opened. When designed this way, some rooms literally opened to the outside in good weather.

32

Corridors as Rooms/ Corridors with Character

◂ *Showcase windows display resident's important memorabilia:*   Created originally as a method to cue dementia residents to their rooms, each display creates a rich narrative about the life experiences of the people who live on the other side of these corridor walls at the dementia unit of *Hillcrest Homes*, in La Verne, California. (Photo: Irwin. Pancake Architects)

Long-term care facilities are dominated by corridors. When resident or social rooms open from a corridor, they are generally discrete spaces joined by a single door. This pattern of corridors and rooms lacks a hierarchy and is both boring and disorienting. Minimizing the impact of these long, narrow, dark passageways is necessary to achieve success in this type of building. One of the most effective ways to minimize the corridor is to make these spaces more like destinations (rooms) and less like narrow extrusions of space (passages).

Civilizing the Corridor

Corridors should vary in width rather than be one size. Corridors that are the same width for more than 35 to 40 feet begin to look monotonous. When a corridor grows to a width of 12 to 14 feet, it starts to look and feel like a room, not a hallway. The corridor width doesn't have to be equal or symmetrical on both sides. In fact, the more asymmetrical it is, the more informal it appears. A corridor that is 12–14 feet wide and 20–25 feet long can accommodate furniture and become a well-scaled, intimate sitting area like those planned for the *Sunrise of Mission Viejo* (page 181). Making part of the corridor a living room provides a convenient place for residents to sit on their way back and forth to their units, adding variety, interest, and the possibility of social exchange. Corridor heights, like corridor widths, should also vary.

Creating a Spine Circulation Connection

In *Virranranta* (page 206) and *Metsatahti* (page 229) tall, dramatic circulation spines were used to add special emphasis to the corridor. Clerestory windows or skylights add to the drama by introducing natural light. Nursing homes with a minimum corridor width of 8 feet are often uniform. Because regulations affecting the exiting of residents in gurneys allow little, if any, furniture to be placed in an 8-foot corridor, they often appear plain and monotonous. In assisted living, where this is not required, varying the corridor width from 6 feet to 12 feet can often be done without adding much additional space to the corridor.

Creating a Compact Footprint

Because older residents must go from their dwelling unit to the dining room, it is important that corridor distance be minimized. The maximum length from the portal of the furthest unit to the elevator should not be much more than 100 feet. If it is longer than this, frail residents with ambulatory difficulties will have a hard time maintaining their independence without assistance. In fact, the first residents who move to an elevator-assisted building often select rooms that are on the first floor or closest to the elevator. There should be a place with a bench or chair to rest every 35–40 feet. This gives a resident the chance to recharge as they walk to the elevator. Corridors should be no longer than 35–40 feet without an offset. The single-point perspective of a 100-foot-long corridor can be overwhelming.

Daylighting the Corridor

Another way of reducing the drabness of a corridor is by introducing light. *Postiljonen* (page 224) uses single-loaded corridors with glass window walls on one side to minimize the feeling of enclosure. In some buildings, single- and double-loaded corridors alternate, giving the user a periodic connection with a courtyard or an external view. Creating greenhouse-style glass enclosures along a corridor introduces natural light and provides an expanded view to the surrounding landscape. Single-loaded corridors also provide easy access to balconies or patios where residents can take in a breath of fresh air. In the Netherlands, exterior nonconditioned corridors are often faced with a three-quarter-height window wall that acts as a wind break but preserves the exterior nature of the corridor. Large 16- to 25-SF skylights are also wonderful sources of light in corridors. In a one- or two-story building, they can bring natural light into the darkest area of the building.

Corridors and Social Spaces

Opening a corridor to a social space with a view outside reduces the feeling of enclosure. Residential wood construction with one-hour fire-rated separations, which are common in western states like California, require Won doors or double doors on hold-opens to blend a corridor with an adjacent space. Asymmetrical corridor plans are more interesting than an orthogonal square courtyard and often aid orientation. Residents use corridors to walk for exercise in the winter and during cold weather. The system of corridors should be arranged to link pathways with destinations so that walking can be a more enjoyable experience. Seating in corridors allow residents to rest while providing opportunities for spontaneous conversations. Corridors should have handrails or, better yet, lean rails than are at least $3\frac{1}{2}$ inches deep to help steady residents. Lean rails have proven to be very effective in hundreds of installations and are far more attractive visually than handrails.

Decorating the Corridors

Artwork and wall-mounted accessories break up continuous wall surfaces and animate them with visually stimulating content. Furniture in corridors that still leaves a minimum of 5 feet for passage can add three-dimensional interest. Corridors can take on different characteristics by varying the wall coverings, artwork, furniture, and accessories. Baseboard trim and cove moldings add decorative interest, as do wallpaper borders. Some facilities develop themes that give each corridor a unique character. This adds interest, promotes wayfinding, and creates visual continuity that many residents find intriguing. Older frail residents often require a long time to get from their units to common spaces. Corridors with artwork and accessories make these long trips shorter by giving residents something to look at. Corridors that end with a painting or a piece of furniture can skillfully terminate the view down a corridor. In Europe, corridors are often used to display artwork that residents have collected. Decorated in this way, the corridor takes on a more personal and eclectic character.

33

Pools of Light

◄ *This compact bistro uses several sources of lighting:* A wood floor, tables, and a juke box allow this Arts and Crafts–style alcove at *Sunrise at Richmond* (page 196) to be used for special occasions and snacks during the day. (Photo: Jerry Staley Photography)

One of the most stereotypic features of a health care environment is its reliance on a relatively high level of uniform fluorescent lighting. For energy-saving purposes, this lighting is rarely mixed with other colors or types of lamps. The resulting appearance of the facility is often very institutional. Distribution patterns of light in institutions leave the faces of residents, the materials, and the colors of the rooms flat. The idea of pools of light is introduced by the "Pattern Language" of Alexander et al. (1977). The basic concept involves using shadow to add interest, depth, and variety. Because most older people need as much as three times more light as a younger person to see at the same level of visual acuity, it is important not to have lighting levels that are too low. Also, lighting levels in general need to be high enough for residents to exit the building safely during an emergency. The levels set by building codes for emergency exiting are characteristically at least 1 FC.

Range of Fixtures Needed

Attractive pools of light can best be created when a range of sources are utilized. These should include natural daylight, fluorescent and incandescent recessed lamps, sconce lighting, table and floor lamps, indirect cove lighting, and pendant fixtures. A variety of fixture types adds interest. When the color and texture of the lighting are varied, wall coverings, carpets and furniture are more animated. Living room lounges and dining rooms benefit most from pools of light. Fluorescent lighting comes in a range of colors from bluish-green to reddish-yellow. Colors that are oriented toward the warm range (2700 degrees Kelvin is a good standard) are more complimentary to skin tones.

Coordinating Other Influences

Light-colored walls that reflect light and maximize coverage should be used. Monofilament lights with clear glass surrounds should be avoided because they create glare. When these types of bulbs are necessary, a shade or frosted glass cover should be mounted over them to further diffuse the light. Rooms should respond to the need for varying levels of light. For example, an activity room should have 50–60 FC of light on the desk surface for reading cards, seeing crafts, and playing bingo (Brawley, 1997). A movie/entertainment room should be designed with several levels of lighting for watching videos, listening to music, or dancing.

34

Using an Open Plan to Create Definition and Ambiguity

◄ *Half-wall cabinets serve to break up as well as visually connect:* The dining room at the *Heritage at Newton*, Massachusetts, serves 100 residents. It has been visually subdivided by half-walls and ceiling treatments. (Photo: Bill Horsman)

An open plan has the advantage of defining the extent of a room in more than one way. It is the ambiguity of the extent of a space that often makes it interesting. Rooms that visually lead into one another provide opportunities for visual stimulation while also helping the older person preview the next space. The ability to link one room to another visually is even more valuable in a communal setting like assisted living, where opportunities to preview give residents a greater sense of control over the environment. When looking into an open-plan room, you perceive multiple layers of space. This is in stark contrast to the "what you see is what you get" dining room commonly used in nursing homes.

Defining the Extent of a Space

Changing floor material is a common approach to defining the spatial extent of a room. Older people have a downward gaze and, as a result, notice the floor more than they do the ceiling. However, even subtle changes in floor materials can cause level differences or surface friction differences that could lead to tripping. Ceiling treatments like soffits, recesses, and applied wood trim create spaces within larger volumes and thereby add to spatial variety. Windows in corridors and between rooms also allow natural light to penetrate these spaces as "borrowed" light. Dutch doors, which are popular in northern Europe, create a type of half-wall but also have the benefit of being movable. One minute, the door creates a passage; the next minute, a full or half wall separation.

Partial Walls and Columns

A half-wall is one of the most effective edge treatments available because it defines a space with a wall that meets the floor but is open above. This makes it possible to look into adjacent rooms while precisely defining the extent of each room at the baseboard. Half-walls can vary from counter height (30–42 inches) to slightly above eye level (60–72 inches). Higher wall heights define the extent of a space more precisely and connect to other spaces through a continuous ceiling plane. Half-walls are often accompanied by vertical columns that provide additional cues to the extent of a room. Walls formed by materials that provide a partial view into an adjacent space create another effect. These materials can be patterned glass, wood grids, horizontal slats, fixed window panels, glass block, or metal screens. Base cabinets utilized as a wall are also very effective in creating separations but have a continuous top surface that connects one room to another. The benefit of a cabinet is the wider separation it creates. Plants are often placed above half-walls, and plant fronds and leaves together create a partially blocked view. Another form of plant coverage is found in European atriums, where plant materials are trained on wire and tubular grids. When mature, these plants, in combination with their metal supports, create a visual, semitransparent separation. All of these ideas could also be applied outdoors with a wood or metal trellis and with various types of plant materials. Hildebrand (1991) in his analysis of the architecture of Frank Lloyd Wright likens the semioccluded views of columns, half-walls, and art glass placed on the edges of spaces to the primal instincts of man. Using the research of Steven Kaplan (1987), he argues that the mystery and uncertainty provided by this condition is a stimulating and provoking experience.

35

Personalization at the Unit Edge

◄ *Inside-out and outside-in:*   The Dutch door, window, light, and alcove at the *Captain Eldridge Congregate House* at Hyannis, Massachusetts, create an interface between the private unit and the semiprivate atrium corridor. The window also allows borrowed sunlight from the atrium to enter through the kitchen window.

Personalizing the area adjacent to the entrance to one's unit is a common strategy. It is often done with artwork or a shadow box to help a resident identify his or her room and to serve as a device for introducing the staff and family members to the person's background and life experiences. There is not much empirical evidence that personal items placed here help in identification or orientation, despite an early experiment at the Corrine Dolan Center (Calkins, 1995). However, despite the fact that the results were not definitive, shadow boxes and cases have become a common feature in most assisted living and dementia units.

Wayfinding

Items that are unusual in size, shape, and color are likely to attract more attention and be more effective as wayfinding devices. For example, a wreath on one door, twinkle lights on another, and a window box (see page 139) with plants on a third are more likely to be effective orientation devices because they are very different from one another. Large, differentiated, and distinct items often appear to be the most effective. Shadow boxes filled with meaningful memorabilia, although they may not be effective as orientation devices, serve to decorate the hall-

way. They also help to make the corridor much more personal and expressive.

Personalizing Corridors

In northern Europe, it is not uncommon for residents to hang personal photographs and paintings on the corridor walls adjacent to their units. This makes the corridor more interesting, because it reflects the lifestyles, tastes, and interests of residents. The items utilized to personalize an entry can include but not be limited to (1) a plant or package shelf for display items, (2) a door knocker, (3) a mailbox, (4) a window to the corridor, (5) a custom-made decorative door, (6) a sconce or can light mounted near the door, (7) a name tag, (8) a room number, and (9) a shadow box. These are just a few of the items that can be combined to create a unique and personal statement at each door. Corridors that do not utilize any of these ideas often appear to be undifferentiated and dull. One of the more effective features is an internal window that connects the unit with the corridor. This is often identified by residents and family members as a device that can provide staff with an early warning of an impending problem.

Key

1.   Kitchen with windows on two sides
2.   Personalized alcove
3.   Location for previewing activity below

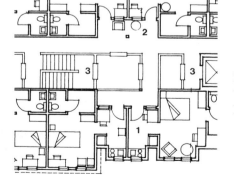

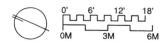

Corridor alcove plan: This plan of the alcove portrayed above shows the relationship between the alcove, unit window and door and the central light filled atrium.

7

STIMULATING SOCIAL INTERACTION

The main reason for bringing older people together in age-restricted housing (other than to share logistical tasks) is to stimulate social interaction and the formation of friendships. Residents who stay at home may be satisfied with their housing, but they often lead a socially isolated life. In a group living arrangement, they have the potential to be stimulated through interactions with others.

Providing residents with opportunities for social interaction and control over their interactions with others is a key element in successful design. Creating places and situations that attract residents to interact directly with others is stimulating. Inviting family members and friends by making them feel welcome is also extremely important. Planned activities can create lively, predictable social exchanges, but of equal importance are extemporaneous social exchanges.

The building should be designed to be friendly. Circulation pathways that overlook and connect, opportunities for triangulation, and places for previewing should be laced together in an effort to create a setting that encourages residents to establish friendships with one another.

36

100 Percent Corner

◀ *A 100 percent corner is visually connected to surrounding spaces:*   This table at the *Heritage at Newton*, Massachusetts, overlooks or is connected to the parking lot, concierge desk, library, dining room, country kitchen, activity room, mailbox area, entry, and porch, making it a popular place for residents to visit. (Photo: Bill Horsman)

There is often one place within a building where the opportunity exists to create a powerful social nexus. This is a place that, because of its unique physical connection to views and activity, naturally attracts residents. A successful 100 percent corner often embodies a combination of the following: external and internal views of interesting activities, access to food or snacks, proximity to a major circulation pathway, and comfortable seating for sitting and talking. A 100 percent corner can be created by design or it can occur naturally. It usually results from a unique cluster of attributes and activities. Every building should contain interesting and engaging places where residents can interact with one another or use passively by themselves. Having a 100 percent corner facilitates meaningful activity as well as social exchange.

When and How the 100 Percent Corner Is Used

The activities in this space can vary from hour to hour. Different groups might use it for reading the morning paper, taking a midmorning snack, waiting for mail delivery, playing cards, or socializing after dinner. There can be more than one of these places in a building, but a single setting is likely to be more heavily used. If the 100 percent corner is constituted properly, it needs no

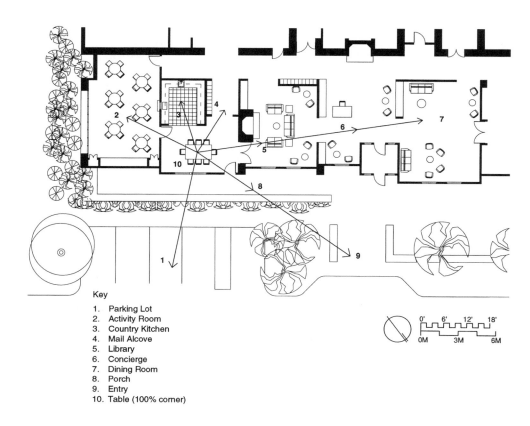

Key

1. Parking Lot
2. Activity Room
3. Country Kitchen
4. Mail Alcove
5. Library
6. Concierge
7. Dining Room
8. Porch
9. Entry
10. Table (100% corner)

assistance from an activity director to work. It becomes a naturally occurring place of interest to interact with or to observe others. The most likely furniture configuration for a 100 percent corner is a table with six to eight chairs.

Attributes of A Successful 100 Percent Corner

The creation of this type of place involves physical and visual linkages to other people and other places in the building. The following factors enhance the success of a 100 percent corner:

▲ *View to the outside*: This preferably is of an entry porch, the parking lot, or an active area of the site.

▲ *View to an major circulation pathway*: This should be a heavily trafficked pathway like the circulation route from the front door to the elevator or from the elevator to the dining room.

▲ *Access to a public restroom*: A restroom should be located within 25–35 feet.

▲ *Access to snacks*: This includes informally provided food and drink.

▲ *Visual/physical access to mailboxes*: Some residents want a place to sit in anticipation of the mailman's arrival.

▲ *Good lighting*: Lighting should be adequate for reading and card playing.

▲ *View of staff activities*: Watching the staff do their work includes the activities of nurses, caregivers, the activity director, and the executive administrative staff.

▲ *View of any internal resident activity*: These can include activities like those at the building's entrance, activity room, library/lounge, or outdoors.

▲ *Several comfortable chairs around a table*: This should be a space that is large enough to support a six- to eight-person table.

▲ *Access to storage and supplies*: A nearby storage cabinet should contain cards, table games, puzzles, and other amusements.

37
The Retreat

◀ *Retreats located away from but still visible from major pathways:* This retreat at the *Sunrise at Severna Park*, Maryland, is placed in a wooded enclave that overlooks an adjacent highway about 50 feet from the edge of the building.

A retreat is a private place for residents to go on their own or perhaps with a friend or a family member. It is a place where a resident can get away from everyone else. Conceptually, it is the opposite of the 100 percent corner. It can be located either inside or outside; outside settings are often more popular. Residents can always go to their rooms, but a retreat gives them another place to go. A retreat is usually a destination and can provide meaning and purpose to a walk. It should also reward the resident with an interesting view, a special fragrant plant, the chance to see wildlife, or a quiet solitary setting.

Defining the Retreat

A constructed object that defines the setting can make it more identifiable and memorable. This could include a trellis, gazebo, or simple platform. It could also be as simple as a change in paving material or a shift in orientation or direction. A retreat often overlooks an active or passive view. It might be a view of a children's playground, a babbling brook, an adjacent park, a heavily trafficked street, or an adjacent shopping street. Some residents choose to meditate, pray, or just contemplate the world around them. Therefore, retreats that are quiet and retreats that are a little more lively can both serve a purpose. Locating a retreat too far from the security of the building can discourage some residents from visiting it.

Attributes of a Successful Outdoor Retreat

An exterior retreat is more likely to be successful when it has some of the following attributes:

▲ Located in a secluded setting away from the beaten path

▲ Having a compelling near or far view that changes over time and is interesting to watch

▲ Sheltered from the sun

▲ Attractive to birds and wildlife

▲ Comfortable for two or more persons to sit and interact

▲ Relatively peaceful and quiet

38

Familiar Behavior Settings That Stimulate Improvisational Use

◄ *Entry lounge is a lively setting for residents and visitors:* The *Nybodergaården* (Regnier, 1994, page 146) in Copenhagen, Denmark, has a bar, piano, and table clustered at the front door. The space is popular, especially at the end of the week for "thank God it's Friday" celebrations.

One of the best ways to develop a successful social space is to tie it to an important ritual or behavior. In northern Europe, taking morning and afternoon coffee is such a behavior. The interior atrium at the *Rosenborg Centret* in Copenhagen, Denmark, is a space filled with plants, tables, and chairs that is used in the morning, in the afternoon, and after dinner for this social ritual (see color insert). When an important activity can be staged in an environment that reinforces its meaning, everything about the activity becomes more vivid. Places that are attractive, comfortable, and memorable are also very evocative. The spaces themselves suggest to the staff imaginative ways in which they can be used. Ordinary places that do not evoke feelings about how they can be utilized are less likely to be creatively employed.

Examples of Behaviorally Evocative Spaces

The snack bar in the *De Drie Hoven* building in Amsterdam, the Netherlands, is designed to resemble a tradi-

tional Dutch brown café. The brown café is a friendly neighborhood meeting place in the Netherlands where food, drink, and social interaction are available. In the *Nybodergaården* (Regnier, 1994, page 146) nursing home in Copenhagen, a Danish version of the American "thank God it's Friday" ritual is carried out in their multistory central atrium (see color insert) every Friday afternoon. The screened porch in an Alzheimer's unit is a popular place for summer afternoon events including ice cream socials, lemonade and cookies, or a watermelon feast. Finally, at the *Sunrise of Falls Church*, Virginia, an ice cream parlor was designed to be open to the community, as well as to family members. In addition to being a place for enjoying ice cream, it is used for taking snacks, for exercising, and for Sunday religious services. In all of these examples, evocative spaces were employed to make experiences more memorable and upbeat.

39

Sociopetal Space and Sociopetal Furniture

◄ *Ottoman is a very effective sociopetal furniture piece:* This 48-inch ottoman creates a rationale for clustering chairs around it. It is used as a place for newspapers and magazines, as well as a resting place for the feet of residents who converse with one another here.

A sociopetal space is an inwardly oriented shared area that is accessible from surrounding perimeter rooms. Any space can be a sociopetal space if it attracts residents, who use it to interact with one another. Because one of the main purposes of group housing is to stimulate social exchange, sociopetal spaces play an important role in connecting individuals with one another. In many buildings designed with clusters of units, residents' unit doors open onto a furnished living room. This shared space allows residents to become acquainted with one another. Furniture arranged to optimize interaction can also encourage residents to come together and interact.

Examples of Sociopetal Space

The main central area at the Philadelphia Geriatric Center's Weiss pavilion is a classic sociopetal setting. Because every resident room has a door that opens onto this large central space, a range of social and therapeutic activities including dining, exercise and social interaction are regularly staged here. The living room lounge in the *Sunrise at Findley*, Ohio, is also such a space. Eight to ten resident units open onto this lounge, which is subdivided by a fireplace (see page 84). One side has hard surface flooring with tables, while the other has soft seating including a couch and easy chair. Atrium and mews-style enclosed streets like the one at the *Sandvejen* at Silkeborg, Denmark, attract residents, who socialize with one another as they walk through these centrally located spaces.

Sociopetal Furniture

Overstuffed chairs located around a 48-inch circular ottoman is an example of a sociopetal furniture arrangement. When older residents sit around this space, they place their feet on the ottoman, relax, and converse with one another. Social interaction is stimulated by the physical closeness of the setting and by the fact that they can speak privately to one another in a relaxed atmosphere. In Denmark, an eight-person family-style table used for meals has sociopetal characteristics. The table stimulates conversations between the two caregivers and the six residents who take meals there.

40
Previewing

◄ *Stair landing works as a great previewing space:*   The central stairs at the *Captain Eldridge Congregate House* at Hyannis, Massachusetts, allow residents to look over and check out the dining room before they make a commitment to enter that space. (See page 75 for plan.)

The term *"previewing,"* from the work of John Zeisel (1981) and Sandra Howell (1980), refers to a spatial condition that allows residents to look into a shared space before they make a commitment to enter that space. This is important in group living environments, where residents want to maintain as much control as possible over social interactions with others. In a group living arrangement there are always people residents like to encounter and others they would rather avoid.

Examples of Previewing

One of the best examples of previewing is at the *Captain Eldridge Congregate House* in Hyannis, Massachusetts. In this building, Zeisel and his colleagues placed the elevator lobby and a stair landing in the center of the building overlooking the dining room. Residents moving from one floor to the next have ample opportunity to preview community spaces on the stair landing before entering them. Waiting for the elevator also provides residents with time and an excuse to preview the floor below. Zeisel also placed windows adjacent to unit entry doors, allowing residents to preview the adjoining corridor before leaving their dwelling units (Regnier, 1994).

Facilitating Previewing

One common approach to facilitating previewing of a shared space is with a half-wall, a window, or a door with a window. This makes it possible for a resident standing in the hallway or an adjacent space to see into the room without having to open the door. Thick walls that separate rooms can create a small vestibule 2–3 feet in depth. This type of entry space can also be used for previewing purposes. Another way to achieve previewing is to pass through a common space on the way to another destination. A resident can walk through the space and be fully apprised of the existing social context without having to make a commitment to socialize with anyone in the room.

41
Dyads for Intimacy

◄ *Corner alcove is perfect as a cozy conversation area:*　This one at the *Hoyås*
building in Oslo, Norway, is relatively private but is still in the middle of the action,
allowing views both inside and outside.

One of the most popular patterns for social interaction is two chairs placed next to one another. These chairs are often separated by a low table or a floor lamp. Rudolph Moos and his colleagues (1987) found this to be the most heavily used furniture configuration in their early analyses of service-based housing. Designers often create larger groupings that accommodate four to six people, but the use of groupings this large is rare in most buildings. Designers in general should specify more two-person spaces. Alcoves work well for two people, as do small, intimate inside corners. Keep in mind that privacy and intimacy are important characteristics of two-person spaces.

42
Dining Experience That Is Pleasant and Satisfying

◄ *Edge location allows the dining room to take on a different character:*
The dining room at the *Heritage at Framington*, Massachusetts, has been divided into several different spaces through the use of different floor and wall coverings. This space, next to a garden view, is more informal than the adjacent dining room.
(Photo: Bill Horsman)

The dining room is the most heavily used common space in the building. Residents take three meals per day here and probably spend more time in this room than they do in any other space, with the exception of their own dwelling units. Furthermore, dining is one of the most pleasurable, sensuous experiences residents have on a daily basis. They look forward to the dining experience and are often critical when it doesn't meet their expectations. Often residents gather before dinner for conversation or for a drink. Having an adjacent living room or lounge can facilitate this pattern of activity.

Sound, Light, and Views

Simple things like lowering the ceiling to a 9- to 11-foot height, using padded seats and backs on chairs, and pro-

viding carpet make it much easier for residents with impaired hearing to socialize. Lighting is also important. Pools of light that bathe the dining room make it easier for residents to see their food and one another. Many older people with hearing loss partially compensate by paying attention to lip movements to better "see" a conversation (Hiatt, 1987). Therefore, helping residents hear better often requires increasing the light level so that they can see better. Lighting often includes a combination of sources including sconces, chandeliers, down lights, indirect lighting, and skylights. Glare is another concern, especially with sconces and chandeliers, which should be covered with shades to diffuse the light. Views from the dining room to the outdoors are also important. It is hoped that the primary view will be of landscape materials rather than a black-top parking lot. Although most residents don't find it very appealing, the option to take a meal outside is appreciated on special occasions.

Environmental Determinants of Seating

A centrally located dining room that minimizes the distance from each resident's room is important, especially for those with mobility difficulties. In some buildings, several dining rooms are located throughout the building to minimize distance. A good rule of thumb for a comfortable, spacious dining room is to allow 24–26 SF per resident. This provides enough space for residents who use wheelchairs and walkers. Designing a room large enough to seat all of the residents at a single seating is common in smaller buildings that utilize universal workers for caregiving and food service. In larger buildings, the dining room can be smaller, taking one and a half to two seatings. Even though most residents want to take a meal during the first seating, the idea of longer dining hours is appealing to others. Music at dinner is sometimes highly appreciated. However, background music can make it harder for the members of a lively social group to hear one another.

Seating and Service

A variety of table sizes should be provided, including those for two, four, and six persons. However, the most efficient arrangement for planning purposes is the four seater. A table that seats four can vary in size from 36 to 42 inches. Round and square tables are both popular. Round tables are easier to navigate around, while square tables make it possible to group tables together. About a quarter of the tables should be high enough to accommodate residents in wheelchairs (Rascho, 1982).

As a project ages, it is not uncommon for as many as 20–25 percent of the chairs to be removed for residents in wheelchairs. A salad bar is a popular feature at many facilities. It should be located relatively close to the kitchen, with access to the entire dining room. A choice of entrée is important to most residents. In addition, a display of food near the front entrance to the dining room makes it easier for residents to see the choices that evening before they order. Devising a compelling menu of choices is not an easy task. Resident committees, sampling parties, and the use of residents' favorite recipes are strategies that allow residents to participate in suggesting menu items.

The Northern European Dining Experience

In northern Europe, the decentralized system of small unit clusters in housing for the frail generally leads to smaller family-style dining spaces that accommodate groups of six to eight residents. *Wilhelmiina* (page 163), *Virranranta* (page 206), *Humlehusene* (page 220), and *Postiljonen* (page 224) utilize small-scale dining arrangements. These intimate settings are very much like that of dining at home. The main meal is lunch in these settings. Breakfast and dinner are smaller, more modest meals that are sometimes served cold. Northern European service houses normally rely on a buffet serving line in a large dining room for the main luncheon meal. Frail residents are assisted with their plates by caregivers or have the option of taking a meal in their own dwelling units. In these service houses, residents take meals with other residents and with people from the surrounding neighborhood. Residents who take meals in their dwelling units have access to microwave ovens. Luncheon meals are delivered hot, with a dinner meal that can be heated later that evening.

43

Vicarious and Unobtrusive Observation

◄ *Seating near atrium edge overlooks the action below:* The *Nybodergaården* (Regnier, 1994, page 146) nursing home in Copenhagen, Denmark, has 8-foot-wide, single-loaded corridors that wrap a central skylight atrium. Umbrellas are used to shelter these popular sitting spaces from direct sun (see color insert).

One of the most popular pastimes for residents is to watch other people. This occurs throughout common spaces as residents take in the movements of staff, family, and visitors. Some of the most popular sitting areas are near windows that overlook active views. Shaded exterior and conditioned interior porches are also very popular. Another place for watching people is near the front door, with views of people and vehicles entering and exiting the building. One of the great architectural challenges is to support the pleasure behind this activity without making it a negative experience for visitors entering and exiting the building. Seating should be located so that there is a comfortable distance between res-

idents who are watching and visitors who are being watched.

Lively Contexts in Northern Europe

Another difference between northern Europe and the United States is the amount of activity associated with the surrounding neighborhood. Many northern European buildings are located on heavily trafficked streets in urban areas with views to parks, street traffic, and retail activities next door. Such a location provides many choices for residents who wish to experience the simple pleasure of watching a range of activities.

44

Unit Clusters That Encourage Social Exchange

◄ *Ten dwelling units are clustered around this living room:* The *Sunrise of Findlay*, Ohio, has a large shared lounge space that has been split in half by a fireplace. One side has living room furniture, while the other side contains a wood floor and tables for games and snacks.

Clustering units around a common space is normally employed to reduce the perceived length of a corridor and to create opportunities for social interaction and friendship formation. Clusters occur in different configurations that depend on the number of units grouped together. The simplest approach is to locate two doors next to one another or four doors that all open onto a corridor alcove. This simple juxtaposition can create

many opportunities for social exchange. Propinquity strongly influences friendship formation. The chances are that at least two of the four residents will develop an informal friendship or a deeper, more substantive bond. The bigger question is, how many units make a good cluster? Usually no more than eight to ten rooms can be comfortably situated around a corridor lounge.

Components of Unit Clusters

When clustering units together, the nature of the connection between the unit and the corridor is a key to its social success. The following techniques can be utilized to better connect a unit with the corridor and the entry doors of surrounding neighbors:

- ▲ *A window*: Privacy can be ensured by curtains that can be opened or closed by residents when they want to socialize or be alone.
- ▲ *Dutch doors*: Opening the upper half of a barn-style door to the corridor is a friendly gesture common in northern Europe.
- ▲ *Display shelf*: A space outside the door for displaying items can make the unit appear more friendly and personal from the corridor.
- ▲ *Alcove*: An entry alcove off the corridor creates a buffer space where personalization can take place.
- ▲ *Furniture or artwork Item*: A flower pot, painting, wreath, or artwork accessory located next to the door can make the setting unique.
- ▲ *A light fixture*: This can extend the idea of the front stoop and act as an informal signal to others about the resident's interest in socializing.

A window provides a powerful connection between the unit and the corridor. It also allows the unit to be daylighted on the corridor side if a skylight or window introduces natural light into the cluster. In one-hour, fire-rated corridors, the window glass may be reduced in size or may need to be rated. Dutch doors also make this kind of social connection more viable because residents can choose to leave them partially open. Dutch doors are common in northern Europe and have been used in *Copper Ridge* (page 201).

Corridor Clusters Conducive to Socializing

The *Kvarteret Karl XI* in Halmstad, Sweden, has an interesting corridor arrangement. Here a single-loaded corridor with an exterior window wall on one side has been sculpted into separate bay window alcoves (see page 88). A bay window is located opposite each entry door. Residents have claimed these corridor alcoves as small, glass-enclosed sitting areas. Some have decorated the space with plants and have placed chairs there to overlook an interesting view of the adjacent central city. Residents greet one another as they walk by each of these ad hoc balcony spaces. This is a much more socially stimulating arrangement than a conventional balcony that is isolated from the corridor.

Northern European Cluster Arrangements

In northern Europe, residents' rooms in decentralized clusters often open onto common spaces. At *Virranranta* (page 206), eight units clustered in a V configuration have entry doors that open onto a dining room table. Skylights and an adjacent outdoor sitting area invite natural light into this shared space. In the *Humlehusene* project (page 220), units are arrayed on one side of the corridor, while the other side is subdivided into a kitchen, a dining room, a living room, and an activity space. The units open onto an open corridor that links residents to these activities and provides a view through the common space to a courtyard.

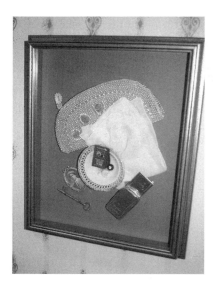

45

Triangulation

◄ *Shadow box tells a story that can be shared:* This shadow box is entitled "Night at the Opera." It contains the elements of a narrative that can serve to stimulate a memory or be the basis of a story that can be shared with others.

The concept of *triangulation*, from the observations of William Whyte (1980), involves two people striking up a conversation about a third subject. His observations come from street performers and the opportunity that their performance provides strangers in the audience for social interaction. The same thing can occur in housing when a thought-provoking work of art or an accessory triggers conversations between two individuals. Triangulation can take place between staff and residents, residents and visitors, and staff and visitors. It can spark conversations that might lead to a friendly encounter or a longer-term relationship.

Shadow Boxes and Antiques

Typically, antique items that are familiar to older residents provoke the most curiosity. A shadow box with personal items that tell a story or explain a situation are often the most intriguing. In many cases, the items are foreign to younger people but salient to older ones. Discussing the item creates an opportunity for intergenerational exchange by giving the older resident something to talk about that is unique to his or her recollections and past experiences. In one shadow box in a Virginia home, smoking paraphernalia including matches, a snuff box, a pipe, and a tobacco pouch from the 1920s was displayed. Another shadow box, entitled "Night at the Opera," included tickets, glasses, gloves, and a program from a turn-of-the-century performance. Antique items like these also add intrinsic value to a setting by introducing unique and unusual items that are imbued with special meaning.

46

Staff Offices That Invite Interaction with Residents and Family

◄ *Office should accommodate connection as well as privacy:* This office alcove at the *Sunrise of Severna Park*, Maryland, has an open half-wall and a Dutch door at one end and a quieter fixed-sash window at the other end.

Staff members have difficult jobs that involve balancing the daily routine of medications, meals, personal care, and social interaction with their responsibilities to regulatory agencies, doctors, and family members. The staff office must provide space for work to be completed while appearing to be a friendly and inviting place for family and visitors. One way to make the staff office look friendly and inviting is to create an alcove arrangement that relies on windows, half-walls, and Dutch doors. The traditional 42- to 48-inch nurse's station counter is not very friendly and doesn't make residents or visitors feel welcome. Ironically, it also doesn't do a very good job of providing private space for phone conversations and note taking.

Staff Office Location and Design

Staff offices should be situated in convenient, accessible, locations that are easy for residents and family members to visit. Office spaces should be accessible, but they shouldn't dominate the entry of a building. Opening up a staff office can involve the creation of a 30- to 42-inch counter height in combination with a door, a cased opening, or a window. The combination of these elements gives nurses and caregivers privacy but also connects them more effectively to visitors and family members. Dutch doors are also very attractive, because the top of the door can be open while the bottom is closed, topped by a 6-inch shelf (see page 141). This provides a convenient place for visitors to stop and converse with staff.

Small Offices in the Middle of Activity

Staff need offices to make phone calls, meet with others, and fill out paperwork. Beyond that, there is little

need for offices. In a perfect world, staff would be spending most of their time with residents rather than in an office. The same is true for the activity director. He or she should have a desk or an alcove in the activity room rather than work in an isolated office. This makes the activity director part of the action rather than being isolated. Conference rooms can facilitate meetings and discussions between several people, allowing offices to be relatively small.

Northern European Nurse's Office Designs

Nurse's stations in northern Europe are unlike their American counterparts. Alcoves are very popular, with tables that generally provide a place for residents and staff to meet and talk with one another (see page 135). Often the nurse's station is integrated with the serving kitchen. A few cabinets within this kitchen are dedicated to medicine storage and resident care books, along with a small note-taking desk with a telephone. In *Virranranta* (page 206) and *Ros Anders Gård* (page 215), the serving kitchen has a place where medications are stored and distributed, charting notations are made, and crossover discussions take place. This design treatment places staff in the middle of the action and in better contact with residents.

47
Friendly Face Greeter

◀ *A concierge greets visitors as they enter the Heritage at Newton, Massachusetts:* The room to the left is a library that is centered around a fireplace, while the room to the right (behind the photographer) is the dining room (see page 77 for plan). (Photo: Bill Horsman)

When someone enters an assisted living building for the first time, it is not uncommon to experience some apprehension. A greeter with a friendly smile replaces uncertainty with a sense of welcome. This person also clearly communicates to the visitor that the staff is there to help them.

Desk and Position of Greeter

The most effective way for the greeter to carry out his or her duties is behind a conventional desk located about

15–25 feet from the front entry door. A greeter often doubles as a receptionist and has other duties. A movable desk is more friendly than a built-in counter. Some of the most formal organizations, like banks, have learned how important it is to make people who enter the building feel welcome. The old bank pattern of a teller behind a glass window is almost impossible to find today. In order to increase productivity, this person should have easy access to a workroom, as well as a workstation with a computer and telephone.

48

Social Exchange and Friendship Formation

◀ *Socially stimulating single loaded corridor alcove:* In the *Kvarteret Karl XI* service house in Halmstad, Sweden, residents have placed furniture in the bay window alcove of the corridor, using them as ad hoc interior balconies.

The main reason for creating a group living situation, other than taking advantage of caregiving economies of scale, is to bring residents together so that they can gain the benefits of social interaction. Social exchange is important in maintaining strong feelings of life satisfaction and self-worth. The publication *Successful Aging* (Rowe and Kahn, 1998) devotes a chapter to the effects of social interaction on longevity and quality of life. Most well-designed assisted living buildings have social interaction in mind as a major determinant of plan organization and furniture arrangements.

The Friendly Building

The building should be designed to encourage casual social encounters, social exchange, friendship formation, and the development of informal helping networks among residents. Propinquity, which creates opportunities for chance encounters comparable to bumping into a neighboring resident, can lead to deeper friendships (Zeisel, 1981). In northern Europe, the service house is by definition a social setting that provides opportunities for shared social activities like taking a meal. The idea that older people will come together to interact with one another is assumed. Numerous techniques described in more detail in other parts of this book lead to a friendly building design. Some of the most effective techniques include: (1) the creation of sociopetal arrangements of space and furniture, (2) the clustering of dwelling units around a common shared space, (3) the arrangement of spaces to provide opportunities for previewing, (4) the dedication of spaces for specific social activities, and (5) the treatment of major corridors and pathways as activity generators.

49

Encouraging Informal Helping Networks

◄ *Winter garden space for cohousing unit:* This attached greenhouse space extends the living room into the landscape for the six residents who share this cohousing unit at *Gyngemosegård* (page 174) in Herlev, Denmark.

When older residents feel the satisfaction of helping one another, a deep sense of independence and self-worth is created. In addition, helping one another nurtures the feeling of fellowship and caring. Involving older residents in various work-related roles around the building can be helpful, especially for men, who often feel more comfortable in this role. Activities like watering plants, delivering mail, raising and lowering the flag, and helping with volunteer activities are possibilities. Intergenerational programs have also recruited resident volunteers to tell stories and read to children.

Sharing of Residents' Expertise

The continuing care retirement communities sponsored by the Friends community in and around the Philadelphia area are well known for their approach to social participation. Residents feel an obligation to share their talents and passions with one another. The exchanging and sharing of expertise make these settings socially cohesive places to live. The strong demand created by residents who want to move to *Havenbogen* in Schiedam, the Netherlands, has encouraged them to implement a program heavily dependent on volunteerism. The building is a five-story, curved, single-loaded corridor apartment building that is open to three age cohorts (55–65, 65–75, and 75+) (see page 247). The youngest residents are encouraged to provide volunteer services to older ones who need more support. Younger residents participate in a range of programs including meals-on-wheels, where they help the staff to deliver meals. In Denmark, co-housing buildings for seniors are created around a set of policies (Boligtrivsel I Centrum, 1993) that describe how residents will help one another and jointly carry out the responsibility for managing a collective household. Although few if any of these buildings have dealt with tough issues like sharing the responsibility for personal-care needs, residents do help one another. The result is a safer, more socially satisfying collective lifestyle.

50

Places for Families

◄ *Family center is oriented toward training and counseling:* The *Harbour House* (page 211) in Greendale, Wisconsin, has created a pavilion for family counseling, staff training, and community outreach. (Photo: Skot Wiedemann Photography)

One of the most important qualities that differentiates assisted living from conventional long-term care is the commitment to inviting family members to participate in the life of the place. The recent research (NIC, 1998) reviewed in Chapter 2 shows how influential family visiting is in residents' assessments of housing satisfaction. Families play an important role that staff members can never duplicate, regardless of how well intentioned they are.

Family Participation

Family get-togethers are common in assisted living buildings. When a highly motivated group of families is involved, group events can be hosted as frequently as once a month. Most facilities host four to six major events per year. Outside of group events, one of the most popular activities is taking a meal with a family member. Subsidizing the meal or providing it for cost to family members can create an added incentive. However, many family members prefer taking their relatives out of the building for a ride or for a meal. Making it easy to pick up and drop off a resident facilitates the process of going out. This is especially true for those who use a wheelchair or walker. A covered drop-off space is necessary in a location that is subject to inclement weather (see page 50).

Meeting Spaces

When families come to visit, they usually seek a private area to meet residents. Edge spaces located away from the central core of the building are often the most popular. Conversational seating for groups in a living room or parlor should be designed to support visitors and family members. During the summer, porches, trellises, gazebos, patios, retreats, and other outdoor sitting areas are also popular. Many ad hoc picnics with sodas and sandwiches take place outside in the summer.

51

Cohousing and the Possibilities of Sharing

◄ *An atrium for residents of cohousing:*   Mølleparken in Brabend, Denmark, is an all-seniors cohousing arrangement that has created a socially successful enclosed, nonconditioned but ventilated glass atrium between two rows of housing units.

Cohousing is a very popular housing alternative in Denmark (McCamant and Durrett, 1988). Projects are either age-integrated or labeled as senior cohousing. Senior cohousing projects typically vary in size from small clusters of 5–7 people to larger buildings with 35–50 residents. Almost all have a dedicated space for a shared room, a dining area, and a television lounge. Compared to residents in age-integrated schemes, senior cohousing residents rarely take meals together on a regular basis In general, residents feel an increased sense of security, and 60 percent value the sense of togetherness that senior cohousing provides. Shopping organized in an informal way seems to be quite popular (Hansen, Dahl, et al., 2000). The best thing about cohousing is how the process of reciprocal helping is facilitated. Although being a good neighbor is normal in group housing, cohousing goes further by establishing rules and procedures that allow residents to share duties for common area maintenance. It also creates a frame of mind that emphasizes interdependence and sharing with one another. These qualities make the building a very socially cohesive setting. Someone who is sick temporarily gains the benefit of this compassionate context. However, there is a firm principle in cohousing groups that residents should not provide home care assistance for each other.

Design Ideas

The *Molleparken* project in Brabend, Denmark, is a two-story, L-shaped apartment block that contains a glass-covered atrium between the two rows of units. This mewslike covered space has places for residents to socialize during the day. Most cohousing arrangements operate around several shared spaces where joint activities are carried out. *Gyngemosegård* (page 174) has two smaller cohousing groups that accommodate six to eight people each (see page 178 for plan). One group is far more successful than the other in maintaining shared patterns of assistance and socialization. In order for cohousing to be successful, all participants must feel an obligation to contribute to the collective effort.

Caregiving Issues

Personal care assistance in cohousing is provided by home care personnel, as it is to all Danish people who are living independently in the community. Residents of cohousing often provide temporary help by running errands for one another. Cohousing arrangements designed around a mix of ages seem to be less advantageous to older people then age-segregated ones. Older people in age-mixed settings can be saddled with duties and responsibilities because they have discretionary time, but they rarely have the assurance that they will be the center of attention as they become increasingly frail.

52

The Hard or Soft Atrium: A Place to Overlook and Meet People

◄ *Atrium nurtures a lush tropical garden:* The fully conditioned four-story atrium at the *Kuuselan Pavelukoti* (Regnier, 1994, page 141) in Tampere, Finland, has a single-loaded corridor that wraps around the perimeter. Lounges hung off the corridor overlook activities below.

The use of a conditioned or unconditioned but ventilated central atrium is a common solution in northern Europe. The *Humanitas* (page 158) and *Gyngemosegård* (page 174) both have atrium spaces. The most common method is to build two parallel wings of housing, enclose the two ends, and cover the space between them with a glass roof. Roof ventilators are installed at the highest points of the roof to allow hot air to escape. These are triggered to open by thermostats that activate when temperatures in the atrium rise above a comfortable level. Makeup air is provided on the first floor, usually through vents at the lower floor at the ends of the building. The nonconditioned design is the most common because it is less expensive to operate but still provides excellent protection in the winter. Dutch weather is characterized by strong, cold winds from the North Sea. The glass enclosure allows residents to be partially protected when going from one space to another. When the sun shines, solar energy quickly heats the atrium.

Hard, Soft, and Combination Atriums

There are generally three types of atriums:

1. *Hard surface*: Hard-floor atriums are often enclosed buildings with common spaces in the center. These are designed for specific purposes and often contain common spaces. They are often fully conditioned interior spaces with landscape materials in pots or planters.
2. *Soft surface*: Soft-surface atriums are central atriums with large gardens that contain trees and tropical plants. Hard flooring, when installed, consists of pathways around the perimeter and across the cen-

ter. Hard surfaces in the center of the atrium are often gravel or bricks set in sand. These are often nonconditioned, naturally ventilated spaces with auxiliary heaters for cold, overcast winter days.
3. *Combination of hard and soft surfaces*: These atriums have an equal balance of hard and soft spaces but can vary from 40 to 60 percent of either hard or soft material. Residents walk through these spaces surrounded by mature, colorful plant materials. These are often the most carefully designed and may be limited in size. Both conditioned and nonconditioned examples are common.

Use Patterns and Characteristics of Atriums

Atriums are great places for exercise, particularly in the winter. Walking in these spaces is comfortable and stimulating. The atrium is also an excellent place for special events and social gatherings. Some are flexible, supporting a large group or only a few individuals. In almost all cases the surrounding dwelling units are single-loaded, with an interior walkway that faces the center atrium. This looped corridor configuration creates a socially conducive central space. When walking to and from their units, residents are always overlooking and aware of the central atrium. A typical two- to three-story northern European building has between 40 and 60 units. Atrium designs are used in assisted living buildings but are even more popular with independent older residents. There are very few atrium-style buildings for the elderly in the United States. Most of our experience with this building type has come from hotels like Embassy Suites and the Hyatt.

53

Ententainment Tonight

◄ *Large-screen format televisions are very popular:* These are often used for movies, but they can also be used to cue stretching and chair exercises. Most systems also feature surround-sound audio for concert-quality music.

With the continuing popularity and declining prices of large-screen and projected image televisions sets, a dedicated or shared space for a movie theatre has become more popular. Movie night once involved a dozen residents clustered around a 25-inch television watching a videotaped feature film in the living room. Today, external projection or "big box," self-contained home entertainment units are outfitted with sophisticated sound systems with satellite dish feeds, VCRs, and DVD-quality images. Surround-sound systems, with five speakers placed in strategic locations in the ceiling and walls are often complemented by auxiliary base speakers. This level of audiovisual sophistication makes movies more spectacular and concert music more vivid. Watching movies while sharing freshly popped popcorn is a very popular pastime that many residents enjoy.

Large-Screen Television Uses

This emerging technology is likely to be one of the most highly appreciated amenities because residents did not have one in their own home or apartment. With today's increasing digital technology, the image, sound, and detail associated with films and music are far better than in the past. This is particularly appreciated by individuals who are experiencing visual and auditory loss. Residents often remark how they can "feel" the music when large woofer speakers are employed. A spirited song or a dynamic movie scene that is highly dependent on sound for its dramatic content is made more vivid and powerful. Playing music in the afternoon as a prelude to dinner is a great way to introduce classical music or more lively show tunes. Finally, a large-format television mounted on a small 10- to 12-inch platform can also be used for stretching, stand-up, or sit-down chair exercises. When used in a resilient carpeted room, exercise videos are more comfortable and effective.

54

Clubs and Activities

◄ *Activities can be custom-fitted to small groups and individuals:*　This resident's favorite pastime is assembling puzzles. His family frames and mounts each puzzle he completes as a record of his accomplishment.

Most facilities hire a professional activity director to manage and organize activities within the building, as well as trips to places and events in the community. Activities are often the catalyst that establishes social connections between residents. Activity rooms are usually busy places that can be messy. As a result, they are usually located away from the front entry, where the more elegant dining and living rooms are usually placed. In a multistory building, second- and third-floor locations with adjoining outdoor balconies are common places for an activity room.

Individualized Interests

It is important that activity programs focus on the individual interests of residents rather than taking a one-size-fits-all approach to program development. A relatively small building rarely has the luxury of special places for particular activities. However, rooms can be subdivided into hard and soft flooring surfaces, loud and quiet areas, messy and clean precincts, dark and light places, and soft couch or hard table spaces. Thinking about the range and types of activities is one of the most helpful ways to determine an appropriate context. Art programs, for example, can be very successful for two to three residents in a small alcove with a window, a storage cabinet, and a sink. One doesn't need a dedicated art room to implement a successful art program. Activity rooms should have a door that can be closed to control noise and increase security.

Activity Programs Related to Lifestyle

The *Hogeway* building in Weesp, the Netherlands, is a dementia facility with a unique program. There are 160 residents in this building, but they are separated into 15 different lifestyle groups. Each small-group cluster consists of 10 to 11 people. Residents live together and take their meals in small, self-contained clusters of dwelling units. Each resident cluster is centered on a shared interest or targeted to residents with similar backgrounds. There are small-group clusters with a focus on religion and music, as well as ones that are oriented to city dwellers, the upper middle class, and people who work with their hands (see page 287). The idea of clustering residents based on lifestyle is interesting, but what they do that is even more amazing involves club participation. Each resident is also encouraged to join two or three different clubs. Over 50 clubs are available. They vary from those oriented to singing, card playing, and poetry reading to others like a Bach and Mozart appreciation group and a beauty and makeup group.

Hogeway Clubs Cut Across Lifestyle Clusters

Because each club draws from the whole building, the clubs attract a unique and motivated cluster of individuals from the universe of 150 residents. Club memberships give residents a chance to interact with people from other residential clusters who have similar interests. A resident can make friends among lifestyle peers, as well as with those who share a similar club interest. Residents live in clusters with their lifestyle neighbors and move throughout the building during the day to rooms where club activities are planned. Clubs targeted to the specific interests of residents can be a highly effective strategy for involving residents in socially stimulating circumstances.

55
Vacations for the Residents and Staff

◄ *The Danes have vacation resorts for older frail people:*   The *Dronningens Ferieby*, located along the east coast of Jutland, consists of specially designed resort houses for handicapped older people and their caregivers.

One unique aspect of the northern European program of long-term care is the serious attitude they take toward the summer holidays. Throughout the year, Scandinavians look forward to their four weeks of paid vacation in July and August. Many people, including modestly paid middle-class workers, have summer houses or cabins on the water where they go when the weather is pleasant. This tradition of celebrating the warm summer days is deeply ingrained in the lifestyle and psyche of the Scandinavian people. Understanding this cultural pattern makes it less surprising that many buildings take residents on vacations. These vacations can range from a weekend stay at a nearby coastal resort to a ten-day vacation in Greece. Residents are often offered a vacation regardless of their level of chronic disability. It is the older person who makes the decision, not the person's situation. Because many residents who take a vacation are highly impaired, they must travel with attendants or family members. The costs are normally paid by the facility, which often has a line item budget for this expense.

Danish Resorts

Many vacation resorts have been established solely for the elderly and the developmentally disabled. One of the best know is the *Dronningens Ferieby* holiday town. Located in Åarhus County near the small coastal town of Grenna, it consists of 44 small one-story houses that accommodate five residents each. Each house is about 75 square meters in size and is designed to be totally handicapped accessible. The resort is located parallel to the sea and has a special pier for wheelchair users. The houses are clustered behind sand dunes and naturally occurring seaside landscapes in a configuration that maximizes privacy. These houses are open during the year to handicapped children, as well as to older people who are participants in home care programs. In Denmark, residents are encouraged to participate regardless of their level of frailty. Although these houses are available to residents in other countries, the Danes are clearly more committed to the concept of a normal lifestyle for the frail elderly that involves the possibility of a yearly summer vacation.

8

EXTENDING INDEPENDENCE

One of the great advantages of assisted living over traditional skilled nursing care is that residents can be reached before they become so weak and frail that no independence-inducing intervention will work. Residents who enter assisted living are generally in better physical shape than nursing home residents, so interventions like exercise and physical therapy are more likely to help them.

Furthermore, assisted living provides services at the margin of need that allow residents to stay in a private, self-contained apartment rather than a nursing home bed. Programs that encourage residents to walk around the building for exercise, engage in a group exercise program, or walk along the corridors inside the building can build strength or at least maintain their current abilities. Various communication technologies hold the promise of allowing residents to be more independent by calling on services only when they need them.

The staff should encourage residents to be as independent as possible, and the environment should provide opportunities to exercise independence.

56

Encouraging Aging in Place

◀ *Double-leaf doors accommodate bedridden residents:*   This feature in the *Postiljonen* nursing home (page 224) allows a 36-inch and a 10-inch door to be open so that residents confined to bed can be easily moved without a complicated transfer.

One of the most appealing aspects of the northern European system of elder care is the desire to keep older people in settings that encourage maximum independence. This begins with the provision of home care to older people in their own home or apartment. In general, most older people, not surprisingly, prefer to stay at home as long as possible. As they age in place, become more frail, and experience the insecurity of living alone, older people often make the decision to move to a group housing arrangement where staff support is nearby.

If an older person wants to move to a service apartment, they can do so if their medical and personal care needs require that level of support. Home care services are delivered in a variety of ways in apartment buildings and service houses. Northern European building codes and licensing laws are exceedingly flexible when it comes to the concept of aging in place. Building codes rarely if ever govern moves as residents become more frail. Unlike the United States, there are no traditions or legal concerns that require older people to move from place to place as they become sicker and more impaired (AARP, 1993).

Care and Repair Programs

Caregiving and environmental modifications to a dwelling unit are often tied together through *care and repair* programs. These programs, which often emanate from a neighborhood-based service house, can involve outfitting the dwelling unit with better security hardware, communications technology, or environmental modifications. The most common modifications to dwelling units include grab bars and handrails that reduce the probability of falling. Some adjustments make tasks more convenient or easy to carry out. Overcoming the chronic pain of arthritis, for example, is the main reason for using lever knob turners for the stove, sink, and entry door. Other changes are designed to increase the ability of residents to handle tasks like toileting, bathing, dressing, cooking, laundry, and cleaning more effectively.

Apartments for Life

The *Humanitas* (page 158) program in Rotterdam, the Netherlands, has a unique approach to aging in place. It allows residents who are in need of nursing care or personal care assistance to stay in a specially designed studio or one-bedroom apartment for as long as they live. This is a radical approach to the idea of aging in place Dwelling units have dozens of features that can be adjusted or added, along with numerous design modifications including the following:

▲ A toilet room large enough to accommodate a stretcher bather

▲ An absence of thresholds

▲ A double-leaf front entry door that opens to accommodate a bedridden resident

▲ Specially designed toilets and sinks adaptable to wheelchair use

▲ A kitchen counter that can be adjusted in height to accommodate individuals with differing disabilities

Humanitas Residents Selected by Age Cohort

Residents are supported by services delivered to their apartments until their death. In general, about one-third of the residents are independent (age 55 is the lower age limit), one-third need personal care services (assisted living), and one-third are medically dependent (nursing home). Extensive personal and medical care services are delivered to their individual dwelling unit if necessary.

Rehabilitation services are located on a lower floor only an elevator ride away from most residents' apartments. Staff are assigned to care for residents, but they do so by giving them greater autonomy and independence. Although this approach has a greater inherent risk, the residents who have moved here are happy to make that trade-off. The result is a noninstitutional setting that cares for a range of individuals up to and including bedridden patients who require nursing.

Other Ideas for Aging in Place

Many other northern European buildings are designed with the idea that the building will be modified as the population ages in place. These buildings are planned from the beginning for added services and office space. The *Bergzicht* building in Breda, the Netherlands, is a good example. This building was one of ten case studies reviewed in earlier work by Regnier (1994, page 136). In the last 5 years, a portion of the bicycle storage area has been remodeled into a home care agency that provides services to residents. Meals have always been provided in a first-floor multipurpose room, but the number of meals taken by residents has increased in the last decade.

Norway's Caring Home Initiative

The *Smedstuveien* building in Trondheim, Norway, is a new 33-unit, three-story, equity-based, cooperative building. It has an interesting plan for anticipated changes as the building and its population age. The city has purchased several of the units in a cluster from the private developer who created the project. They are currently renting these units to people from the surrounding neighborhood, but they have retained the right to remodel these units in the future. If they want to add a meals program or a home care office (for this building or for the neighborhood), they have the right to make this adjustment in the future as well.

57

Helping by "Keeping Your Hands in Your Pockets" or "Keeping Your Hands Behind Your Back"

◄ *Exercise therapy program is developed and monitored for each resident:* In Denmark, a "use it or lose it" attitude encourages residents to stay physically fit. At the Frederiksberg Aldrecenter in Åarhus, Denmark, exercise and physical therapy are mainstreamed.

The attitude in northern Europe toward providing caregiving assistance is often described by reference to these two phrases, which refer to the desire to give older residents control over activities by having them do as much as they can for themselves. In the United States, *learned helplessness* (Seligman, 1975) is the term used to describe the process of residents abandoning their responsibilities to the staff, who gradually do everything for them. The northern Europeans believe that residents must do as much as they can for themselves. When a well-meaning staff person does something for residents that they can do for themselves, it erodes their spirit, self-confidence, and competency.

It's Harder to Encourage Residents to Help Themselves

It often takes more time and is much more frustrating for caregivers to help residents do things for themselves. For example, a resident may need help into and out of the shower but, once situated, is able to wash herself. A resident may need someone to hand her a towel but may be able to dry herself without assistance. In general, this philosophy means that each resident is expected to perform at his or her maximum level of ability. Aid and support are provided only when needed.

58

Technology That Supports as Well as Extends Independence and Privacy

◄ *Computer-based technology cues residents with memory loss:*   In Finland, computer programs that combine images with traditional folk songs are used to stimulate recall and reminiscence with older residents.

Communication technology has great potential to enhance the quality of life in assisted living environments. This technology currently provides voice-to-voice connections between residents and staff for emergency needs. Systems like Lifeline, Protec, Guardian, and Telealarm are used for emergency response but also have the capability of voice-to-voice communications. Such two-way systems allow residents to feel secure, knowing that if a problem arises, they can call for help quickly.

Dementia Care Technology

Systems that trigger an alarm if a resident with dementia exits a secured area are also common. In the near future, advances in these systems are likely to provide more freedom to track residents by using global positioning technology. When this technology becomes widespread, it will be possible to track every individual in a dementia unit.

Computer-based technologies in northern Europe are also being utilized for therapeutic and diagnostic purposes. Visual displays of old tools, crafts, and objects, as well as a range of familiar music keyed to salient periods in the lives of residents, are devices commonly used to trigger recall. Advanced computer technology is making this type of programming easier to utilize and share. In Finland, programs are produced by a central government agency and then downloaded to service houses and facilities throughout the country.

Management Technology

Computers and systems applications for the provision of medications, food, and other materials are becoming more advanced. On-line ordering of food and supplies is much more widespread, and computerization of management and logistical tasks for staff is more common. Documentation of care provision and the communication of problems to other staff and to medical personnel are increasingly tied to computer-based technologies.

Home Care Technology

Some of the most interesting computer and communication technologies are likely to occur in the home care arena as simple emergency response equipment is replaced with technology that enhances communication and diagnostic analyses. A few years ago, it was impossible to find assisted living environments that had computers for residents' use. Now it is frequently common to have computers for e-mail and Internet access in an activity room. Most older frail people are leery of computer-based technology. However, as these systems are made increasingly more user friendly through telephone and television applications, they will become less foreign and more familiar. Programs that read and transmit vital signs are now common. In the future, blood readings and other diagnostic analyses will be available from remote locations.

Lifting Devices and Robotics

In northern Europe, the last five to ten years have seen a proliferation of lifting and transfer devices. Many of these are attached to ceiling-mounted tracks that link a bed location with the bathroom (toilet and shower). These have become more common in Europe because professional caregivers who develop back problems can easily apply for government disability. Because most caregiver employees are government workers, local municipalities have been careful to pursue technologies that can avoid this costly side effect. In the United States and northern Europe, there have been few advances in the area of robotics in the last ten years. As these devices become more sophisticated and are more able to operate in unstructured environments, their utility will increase. Researchers in this area expect to achieve great advances in the next 10 years, probably just in time for the boomer generation, which has grown up with *Star Wars* and science fiction.

59

Therapy with a Lowercase *t*: Building Resident Competence in a "Therapeutic Environment"

◀ *Easy Street installations reproduce environmental challenges:*   At the Youville Hospital's rehabilitation center in Cambridge, Massachusetts, a car located adjacent to a sidewalk simulates the challenge of transferring to the front or back seat of a compact car.

Every assisted living building should be conceptualized in a broad therapeutic context. Each building design has the capability of increasing residents' independence, life satisfaction, self-worth, and physical competence. Often we view a building as a dwelling unit when in reality it is a much more encompassing environment where 90–95 percent of a resident's time is spent. The word *therapeutic* often conjures up the image of a physical therapy room, which is a very narrow way of defining it. Therapy should be conceptualized with a lowercase t. Almost everything in the building that allows residents to increase their cognitive or physical ability has therapeutic potential. In previous work (Regnier, 1997b), these potential therapeutic benefits were subdivided into three categories: physical activities, social, emotional, and spiritual activities; and stimulation/affective activities. In northern Europe, much more emphasis is placed on the obligation residents have to stay as physically fit as possible.

The following list presents 15 lowercase t therapies that can be accommodated in a building's design:

▲ *Walking therapy:* A corridor system with seating every 35–40 feet connecting interesting destinations.

▲ *Outdoor exercise therapy:* An exterior walkway with benches every 100–125 feet that loops the building, with comfortable places to sit and rest

▲ *Access to the surrounding community:* A sidewalk that leads residents to pathways in the neighborhood or to nearby neighborhood destinations

▲ *Stretching therapy:* An activity or entertainment room with comfortable seating where chair exercises can be carried out every day

▲ *Access to physical therapy equipment:* Access to exercise and physical therapy equipment that can help develop muscle strength, bone density, and aerobic capacity

▲ *Swimming therapy:* Access to a heated pool where upper- and lower-body muscle groups can experience resistive exercise

▲ *Weight therapies:* Access to equipment designed to build muscle strength, especially for upper-body muscle groups in women

▲ *Social exchange and friendship formation:* A building design and a social program that incorporates unit clustering and common space design principles to encourage residents to meet and develop friendships

▲ *IADL/ADL therapies:* Therapies in a dementia unit or facility that encourage residents to do things for themselves, like meal preparation and grooming

▲ *Occupational or ergo-therapy:* Hard surface flooring spaces that encourage residents to continue small muscle group manipulations and coordination exercises like weaving and craft making

▲ *Sensory stimulation therapy:* Aromatherapy, touch therapy, and music therapy, all of which operate on the senses and are particularly effective for people with dementia

▲ *Reading/intellectually stimulating therapies:* Quiet places for reading out loud and for intellectually challenging activities like games and puzzles

▲ *Plant therapy:* Places either inside or outside where residents can work with their hands and nurture plants

▲ *Pet and intergenerational therapy:* Policies and places that encourage visiting pet programs and visiting grandchildren

▲ *Religious/spiritual therapy:* A place where residents can meditate, pray, and listen to religious services, as well as transportation to churches and synagogues in the community

60

Blurring the Line Between Exercise and Physical Therapy

◄ *Swimming is one of the best forms of exercise:*   This pool at the *Wilhelmiina* (page 163) is shared with older people living in the neighborhood who come to the service center for therapeutic treatments.

Although exercise and physical therapy have clearly different purposes, in northern Europe a new generation of physiotherapists is emerging who use traditional physical therapy in conjunction with exercise physiology. A customized program of physical exercise and therapy has resulted from their work with older people. Exercise and physical therapy areas should be located adjacent to one another so that equipment can be shared in response to specific problems. In essence, physical therapy and exercise are increasingly being seen within a single context.

Danish Exercise Strategies

Denmark is one of the northern European countries most dedicated to the development of a strong physical therapy and exercise program. The service house at *Gyngamosegård* (page 174) is an excellent example. Three rooms on the upper floor of the common service building deal with physical therapy, exercise, and occupational therapy. These large, open rooms are connected to one another. This open plan is complemented by ceiling heights that vary. One side of the exercise and therapy space has a transparent window wall that overlooks a garden in the center of the complex. Occupational therapy equipment focuses primarily on coordination and small-muscle manipulation. The occupational therapy program centers on a training kitchen that is used by individuals to relearn basic food preparation and independence skills. The participants are usually community residents who have experienced an acute debilitating episode like a stroke or a broken hip. In this project, as in others, all residents are encouraged to walk for exercise.

Finnish Exercise Strategies

Finnish service house facilities almost always include a swimming pool and a sauna. Historically, saunas predate bathing facilities within homes and are an important cultural amenity for older people. Every facility I visited, including small projects with fewer than 15 units, had a dedicated sauna. Indoor swimming pools are used in conjunction with a sauna but are also used independently because they provide opportunities for exercise. The inclusion of a swimming pool in facility design is such a high priority that many service houses share a swimming pool with other community groups to offset operation and maintenance costs. Seventeen of the 20 buildings I visited in Finland contained a swimming pool or had access to one next door.

Muscle-Building Strategies

In the last ten years, considerable research has been devoted to the benefits of strength training. Researchers like Spirduso and Gilliam-MacRae (1991) and Fiatarone (1994) have produced extraordinary results through concentrated weight-bearing exercise programs. Spirduso and Gilliam-MacRae's story of an older frail woman who went from being confined to a wheelchair to running in the Senior Olympics is heartwarming and filled with hope. Equipment that appears to be the most useful includes upper- and lower-body weight machines, treadmills, and recombinant bicycles. Lately, hospitals have been examining ways in which they can combine rehabilitation therapies with assisted living. In a joint venture with Sunrise Assisted Living, the Innova Hospital Corporation in Fairfax County, Virginia, is building assisted living projects on their hospital campuses. *Sunrise at Fair Oaks*, Virginia, is a recent example. These buildings have an extensive rehabilitation center as well as a short-stay unit cluster. This cluster serves older residents as well as younger patients, accommodating three- to five-day stays for people convalescing after surgery or completing a rehabilitation program.

Aquatherapy

This is considered to be one of the best forms of exercise, especially for people who suffer from connective tissue problems, joint disorders, or arthritis. In the United States, only continuing care retirement communities with relatively large budgets for common space can afford the development, operation, and maintenance costs of an enclosed pool. In the United States, it is very difficult to find assisted living buildings that have a pool. Some have working agreements with rehabilitation centers that may have a pool available for residents' use. In northern Europe, there is a strong commitment to design service houses that include a swimming pool for exercise.

Stretching and Movement Exercises

Probably the most common form of exercise in assisted living facilities consists of chair exercises that stress

stretching and aerobics. In most buildings, exercises take place in the morning or the early afternoon. Often they are conducted by the activity director, who may use a large-screen video as an accompaniment. A large-screen television should be elevated 10–12 inches so that residents can clearly see the images while standing up. The room should be large enough to accommodate 15–20 people with chairs. A carpeted floor with a resilient aerobic pad is a good surface, particularly if aerobics or calisthenics are contemplated.

61

Encouraging Walking

◄ *Bench on stair landing encourages use:* The *Elder Homestead Program* in Minnetonka, Minnesota, has a landing with a bench for residents, who can rest when they climb the stairs for exercise.

One of the most important forms of exercise for assisted living residents is walking. Because many residents experience mobility challenges, walking around the building once or twice can be a major workout. Residents should be encouraged to walk, and the site should be designed to encourage walking. The corridor system should be conceptualized as a series of paths and destinations so that residents will find it interesting to walk from one place to another. The walking-for-exercise pathway system should be thought of as having three parts: (1) interior corridors, (2) exterior on-site pathways, and (3) off-site excursions into the neighborhood and adjacent properties.

Walking Inside the Building

It is important to encourage residents to walk as much as possible rather than rely on a wheelchair. A walker or cane is helpful for residents who need periodic balance control support. Benches or places to rest in building corridors should occur every 35–40 feet so that residents will be able to rest periodically on their way to and from the dining room. Locating a bench on a stair landing can also encourage residents to use the stairs for exercise. Generally, it is safer for residents to walk upstairs rather than down. In northern Europe, it is common for the corridors to be single-loaded. These are often designed with small alcoves where seating can be located.

62

Considerate Design Features That Are Universal

◄ *Plywood surround allows grab bars to be flexibly located:* This ¾-inch plywood backing allows grab bars to be located in the best position to facilitate entry to and exit from the toilet. The grab bar location varies, depending on the size and muscle strength capabilities of each resident.

The universal design movement has evolved as advocacy efforts for handicapped people have pointed to solutions that benefit all populations, not just the handicapped or the elderly. Numerous publications, reports, and handbooks have addressed this new way of thinking about design (Liebrock, 1999; Leibrock and Terry, 1997; Mace, 1991; Mueller, 1997; Peterson, 1995, 1996; Story, Mueller, et al., 1997; Welch, 1995). However, the majority of the literature on universal design focuses on appliances, objects, and tools (NAHB, 2000; Pirkl, 1994) rather than on architecture because these often cause the most frustration. In assisted living housing, accessibility issues generally center on the design of the dwelling unit, common space, site design, and the building's entry. Older people are clearly the largest single group that benefits from universal design applications. However, their physiological deficits make it difficult to use grab bars and supports that are strategically placed for younger disabled people.

Toilet Transfer: A Case Study

When grab bar locations are positioned for younger handicapped people, they are often not very useful to older people. For example, grab bar locations for toilet transfers often assume the wheelchair transferee has good upper-body strength. This is clearly not the case with many older people (especially woman), who, due to normal aging, experience major losses in muscle mass. Given their own physiology, these residents can find the grab bar location too high or too low. The best way to deal with this problem is to back the wall adjacent to the toilet with ¾-inch plywood so that grab bars can be located in different places according to the wishes of each resident. Some might prefer a low horizontal bar to push from, while others would do better with a sloping bar that allows them to pull up from several different locations. Occupational therapists who study these details can locate a grab bar to match the physiology of the resident. The plywood backing allows the bar to be moved

when another resident moves into the unit. The average size shoe doesn't fit everyone, just as the standard handicapped grab bar location doesn't fit everyone.

Six Simplified Guidelines

The following simplified list is adapted from the *Fair Housing Act Design Manual* (Young, Mace, et al., 1996):

▲ *Ramps:* Although an 8.33 percent slope is allowed, 5 percent, or 1 in 20, is preferred for older people. Landings should occur every 30 feet at the maximum, with a maximum 1/20 cross-slope. The minimum width is 4 feet, but a 5-foot width will allow two-way wheelchair traffic. Handrails should be mounted 32 inches above the ground.

▲ *Handicapped bathroom:* The bathroom should accommodate a 5-foot distance between fixtures, with a door that swings out. Specify a shower (3 × 3, 3 × 4, or 2.6 × 5 feet) with a lip that is less than ½ inch. Typically, less than 5 percent of units require a standard handicapped bathroom. However, all public bathrooms must conform to this standard.

▲ *Adaptable bathroom design:* Each unit bathroom should accommodate T and K turns based on the fair housing requirements. The door to the bathroom should swing out or should be a pocket/barn door. There should be a 30 × 48-inch area in front of the lavatory (side approach) and a 30 × 48-inch clear area in front of the bathtub/shower. The toilet should be placed in a space that is 48 inches wide and 66 inches deep.

▲ *Showers:* The 3 × 3-foot and 2.5 × 5-foot shower are the two sizes recommended in California to meet accessibility/adaptability standards. A 3 × 5 or 3 × 4-foot shower (with the capability of being retrofitted to 3 × 3 feet) are preferred sizes. The dam at the base of the shower should be removable or it should be a flexible rubber material that can be crushed and thus reduced in height for wheelchair passage.

▲ *Kitchens:* There should be adequate space in front of kitchen fixtures for a 30 × 48-inch side approach. A removable base cabinet with a clear height of 27 inches and a clear width of 30 inches is recommended for wheelchair access.

▲ *Doors:* A 36-inch minimum size (a minimum clear opening of 32 inches) with 18-inch minimum latch side clearance is required. Sliding barn doors or pocket doors are preferred inside the unit. When bathroom sliding doors are larger than 36 inches—that is, 40–42 inches—they facilitate the transfer of residents by providing space borrowed from the adjoining corridor.

Home Modifications

In the research on the home modification needs of older people, Pynoos (1998, 2000) projects that more than a quarter of the population aged 75–84 experience difficulty performing ADLs. This figure increases to 50 percent for the 85+ population. While 23 percent of the housing stock older people live in have grab bars today, only 9 percent have wheelchair adaptations, 5–8 percent have call devices, 8 percent have railings, and 5 percent have ramps at the street. The bathroom, the kitchen, and the stairs between floors (in a multistory building) are considered the most hazardous places in a typical single-family home.

9

STIMULATING
THE SENSES

With normal aging, older people lose ability to hear, see, touch, and smell. This sensory loss is often experienced as a muting of the senses that reduces its powerful effects. The senses are important for understanding the environment—to differentiate between inputs, to assess quality, and to formulate a response to the environment.

Glasses, hearing aids, and certain surgical procedures can overcome some of the loss, but little else is available to compensate for lost abilities. Sensory losses often lead to other problems. For example, glare becomes a bigger problem, competing background noises can disturb speech recognition, and food may not look or taste as good as it once did. In nursing homes, adverse stimulation from noise and odors can make the experience a noxious one. The idea of creating more pleasurable experiences for older residents is woefully underexplored, especially in long-term care facilities. Massage therapy, aromatherapy, and spa baths are good examples of attractive possibilities.

Every design decision should be examined to assess its potential impact on human sensory modalities. Does the intervention make the environment easier to comprehend and more pleasurable to experience?

63

Colors and Patterns

◄ *Strong patterns in carpeting and fabrics:* *Goddard House* (page 169) has used patterned carpeting and fabric, in contrast with strong, deep wall colors and simple, elegant drapes.

Selecting colors and patterns for the interior applications of assisted living environments is influenced by taste and physiology. Physiologically, during normal aging, the lens of the eye yellows, and the eye requires more light and greater contrast for visual clarity. Creating contrast is one of the easiest things a designer can do to enhance visual function. In general, lighter colors make a room appear larger, while darker colors make it appear smaller. Light-colored letters on a dark background are generally the easiest to read.

Colors Make a Difference That Is Different for Everyone

Keep in mind that everyone perceives colors differently, not just because of their age, but also because of their culture and background. Color and pattern have symbolic and cultural meanings that differ for everyone. Generally, warm colors in the red/orange/yellow range energize a space, while cool colors in the blue/turquoise/green range are more soothing. Cool colors are often associated with tranquility and contentment. The yellowing of the cornea turns blues into grays and whites to yellow. Purple also appears grayer, and blue and green often become less distinctive and run together. Pastels are frequently harder to read, especially blues, lavenders, and pinks; therefore, brighter colors are sometimes best. The easiest colors to read are red, orange,

and yellow. Color perception is also affected by the color of lighting. Under incandescent light, fabrics appear more yellow. This is generally preferable to fluorescent light, which often has a blue-green cast. However, full-spectrum fluorescent lighting creates a reflection that is more like incandescent and natural light. Another way to create contrast is to select colors from the opposite sides of the color wheel. The designer who selects a green carpet might likely select furniture or fabrics with a red coloration. Ceilings should have high reflectance, in the 70–90 percent range. Walls should be on the light side, varying from 40 to 60 percent reflectance, while floors can be darker, in the 30 to 50 percent range, which is the density of light wood.

Patterns

Patterned fabrics and wall coverings can add variety to an otherwise bland environment, but they can also be overwhelming. Subtle patterns in wall coverings with colors in the lighter pastel yellow to light brown range are usually safe. Fabric patterns should be rich and should match the scale of a room. A large pattern for a chair back might do well in a large dining room but would be less successful in a small office space. There is no current literature that advocates one type of pattern over another. This still appears to be a matter of taste and preference.

64

Enhancing Appealing Textures, Scents, and Sounds

◄ *Accessories soften the furniture in this dementia unit:*   The fabric used here is woven Krypton. In order to add softness to this couch, Martha Child Interiors utilized stuffed animals that could be cleaned separately.

One of the problems in health care environments is the lack of variety. These settings are often very bland and boring. The color palettes, material choices, and general ambiance have few residential references. Smells, sounds, and scents that contain references to positive places and experiences can transform a place.

Textures

In general, a variety of textures are usually good. People who are blind or partially sighted often use texture to differentiate and identify spaces they are entering. In the United States, some textures, like stone or brick, might be considered too abrasive for interior applications, but in northern Europe, exterior textures like brick and stucco are often used for interior wall surfaces.

Scents

Some of the most pleasant smells are those associated with food. Smells like that of baking bread can be very evocative. They remind people of home and are frequently used in dementia units for reminiscence purposes. Cookie smells are often used in the afternoon to signal an afternoon snack. Aromatherapy is becoming more popular, especially in Europe, where it is often a part of the bathing process. Spaces that are connected to the outdoors, like porches and balconies, also introduce smells that are associated with different seasons and different weather conditions.

Sounds

Although music blindly playing over an intercom has a strong institutional reference, properly presented music can be very stimulating and memory-provoking. Homes often have a carpeted room where various forms of music can be played in the evening or before dinner. Experiences utilizing a juke box in an activity or living room have also been generally positive. As long as selections are made by residents and fit the general group preferences, they are well liked. Sometimes staff will play music they enjoy that doesn't always mesh with the preferences of residents. Sounds can be used to add flavor and sometimes create a wacky, off-the-wall experience. In the *Hogeway* dementia facility in Weesp, the Netherlands, birds chirping, wave sounds, and recorded hula music have been used in a corridor alcove to transform the place into a South Sea island retreat (see page 274). When residents enter the alcove, the sounds are triggered by a motion detector. The furniture and a wall mural add to the illusion. Aviaries have also been used in many settings to add the pleasant sounds of birds nesting, chirping, and flying about.

65

Reducing Obnoxious Noise and Smells

◄ *Nursing home corridors are noisy, with a lot of glare from shiny surfaces:* Carpets, wall coverings, artwork, and acoustical ceiling treatments can absorb noise and add variety and interest to the bleakest corridors.

In most traditional skilled nursing environments, the two most common complaints of family members concern obnoxious odors and noise. The smell of urine is the greatest problem. Today there are a number of new products and practices that reduce this problem. Krypton fabrics for chairs and sofas, as well as the moisture-proofing protocols and products available today, keep urine from soaking into furniture coverings. Antimicrobial carpets with attached resilient backing and concrete sealing protocols also make carpet absorption less problematic. Finally, the ventilation systems used today introduce continuous fresh air under positive pressure to common spaces and corridors. This air migrates through the units, exiting the building via ventilation shafts in the bathroom. When the system is designed this way, it constantly moves foul air away from common areas, where it is most likely to be noticed by guests. Various personal incontinence products have also reduced the problem of urine spillage.

Noise Problems

The other major complaint about institutional environments is the high noise level. This is often related to the large amount of hard surface material that is often used for easy cleaning. Walls, floors, and ceiling are often hard and are frequently coated with reflective semigloss paint. In some rooms, there is very little soft material for sound absorption. Vinyl flooring is often mistakenly used in place of carpeting because it is considered more sanitary. A high-quality loop or cut-pile carpet with an integrated pad remains the cheapest and most effective way of reducing noise in a building. In addition to reducing noise, carpets are softer surfaces that cushion falls more effectively than a hard-surface floor covering. Some noise sources can be avoided. For example, the use of a public address system, common in older nursing facilities, is an obnoxious, unwanted sound. Finally, furniture fabrics are also helpful. In a dining room where chairs require vinyl seats, chair backs can be padded and heavy window fabrics can be used to absorb noise.

66

Using Resilient Materials

◄ *Carpeting in the corridor is a safer alternative for residents with balance control problems:*   In the *Hearthstone* at New Horizons dementia residence in Marlborough, Massachusetts, corridors with half-walls and openings invite residents to enter rooms arrayed on both sides.

Because of the safety that carpeting provides, it is commonly used throughout a facility as the dominant floor material. In dining areas and entry vestibules, where food spills and dirt can cause problems, a loop carpet is often a better solution than a cut-pile carpet because it is sturdier and somewhat easier to clean. In some dining areas, like those used by memory-impaired residents, a hard surface is sometimes a better choice. Sheet vinyl with a resilient backing is available in a number of attractive patterns. Wood grain patterns are among the most interesting because they are realistic and come in a variety of colors and patterns.

Reducing Injuries from Falls

Bathrooms floors should also be covered with nonslip sheet vinyl for easy cleaning. Numerous tile patterns are available today that resemble residential applications. Smoking rooms and elevator floors often benefit from something other than carpet. Fire stairs are often overlooked, but staff often use them to rush to a resident's room. For safety purposes, carpeting makes great sense here because of the risk of falling. Another possible risk associated with falling is injury from sharp edges and corners. All counters and casework should be rounded, and hard edged surfaces like glass and metal table tops avoided.

67

Taking a Sensuous Bath

◄ *A sensuous bathing experience is rare in long-term care:*   The *Harbour House* (page 211) dementia unit created an attractive bathing environment with a whirlpool tub, adjustable lighting levels, heat lamps, music, bubble baths, and candles. (Photo: Skot Wiedemann Photography)

One of the most disappointing aspects of traditional skilled nursing environments is the treatment of bathing. Sensuous experiences are relatively rare for older frail people who have lowered sensitivity to tastes, aromas, and touch. Bathing, which is traditionally a relaxing, positive experience for many people, is often a disturbing and unhappy experience in many nursing homes. Some residents with dementia often display an aversion to water and the process of bathing. Some even consider it frightening. However, most bathing rooms are not designed to reassure residents or make them feel comfortable. The typical institutional bathing room has a stall shower, a tub with a hydraulic lift, a toilet, a sink, and equipment storage. The space is usually a very large, hard, cold, and noisy ceramic-tiled space that rarely has the benefit of any natural light.

Noisy, Cold Bathrooms

Heat can be very effectively introduced through the use of heat lamps or supplemental wall-mounted radiant heating devices. White-colored (rather than red infrared), 250-watt heat lamps allow the room to be quickly warmed. These fixtures also add a tremendous amount of light to the room, which can add in the inspection of skin contusions and abrasions. The bathing process provides an excellent opportunity to inspect a resident's general skin condition and to check progress in problem areas. Noise and reverberation are often problems because the room is covered with hard surfaces and has very few soft, absorbent materials. Because the bathroom is one of the loudest rooms in the building, it should be designed to mitigate noise. Using a moisture-repellant but sound-absorptive ceiling material like tectum or heavy drapes can help. Towels for residents stacked on decorative open shelving are also effective. Side transfer tubs that are excellent for an assisted living application can also cause a lot of noise. The collapsible side wall design requires the resident to sit in the tub while it is being filled. When the high-volume, laminar flow of water filling the tub makes contact with the fiberglass shell, it often creates a lot of noise.

Soft Music and Aromatherapy

Beyond making the room warmer and quieter, other treatments can make the bathing experience more memorable. Bath oils or scents generated by portable aromatic devices are often very relaxing. Some bathing equipment, especially tubs with whirlpool features, is not compatible with bubble bath or oil additives. Another soothing experience is to play soft, relaxing music. Residents may have strong preferences for favorite pieces of music. Dimming the lights or lighting candles can also make the experience more relaxing. Many older women are accustomed to taking a bath and appreciate it when it is treated as a sensuous, restful experience. Although a spa massage makes great sense at a resort, long-term care facilities rarely see this as the pleasurable experience it can be for residents.

Fantasy and Whimsy

The bathing experience can also be made magical and fun. A ceiling painted light blue, with cloud patterns to resemble a blue sky, or a wall covering or photo mural that transforms one wall into a garden scene, gives the bathing room the feeling that it is outdoors. Even large artwork images of comfortable, cozy indoor and outdoor scenes can be very effective. Although they may appear childlike, bath toys can also be an effective distraction for dementia residents who are frightened or disturbed by the bathing process. A glass of wine with a bubble bath may not be right for everyone, but it is important to recognize the potential for making this experience a unique one for each resident. Making the experience a fanciful, sensuous one is far better than the reality of a cold concrete or ceramic-tiled space where residents are hosed down.

Snoezelen Bathing

In the Netherlands, some facilities, like the *Hogeway* in Weesp and the *de Landrijt* in Eindhoven, have taken the idea of *snoezelen* into the bathing room (see page 147). They have produced settings with soft lighting, soothing music, and cozy furniture designed to make the bathing experience less threatening and more enjoyable.

68

Reducing Glare

◀ *Skylights flood interior lounge spaces with light:*   Windows from dwelling units to the central lounge allow borrowed light to penetrate the unit from the corridor/lounge side. Natural light adds to the ambient light level, reducing the contrast and thus the possibility of experiencing glare.

Glare, especially from clear bulbs with visible filaments, is particularly troublesome. A frosted globe or shade reduces glare by spreading the intensity of light to a larger surface, thus reducing contrast. The aging eye is more susceptible to glare because of changes associated with the hardening and yellowing of the cornea. Cataracts, which are common in old age, also exacerbate problems with glare. Glare can often result from a contrast in light level from one room to another or from a dark wall color against a window wall. Increasing the amount of light inside a room or lightening the color of the wall covering can reduce glare by balancing the light more effectively. Skylights located in the darkest portion of a room can introduce a large amount of light that "balances" an exterior window wall.

Glare Reduction Techniques

Utilizing a covered porch or canopy can help to reduce the light level differences in a dining room or entry lounge, where residents are likely to experience problems in shifting from one light level to another. A bright window at the end of a corridor can also create glare, which results from the contrast between the dark walls of the corridor and the sunlit end condition. Placing a window on the side of the corridor rather than at the end can often introduce reflected natural light without causing glare. Light from high clerestory or transom windows allows light to penetrate deeper into a space, sometimes reducing glare. Indirect lighting sources are one of the best ways to avoid glare. Pendant lamps that provide direct light but also bounce light off a ceiling or wall are popular because they represent a good compromise between quality and cost.

10

CREATING AFFECT

Happiness is often in short supply in nursing homes and institutions. However, humor, whimsy, and positive feelings are exactly what is needed to cheer up residents, who traditionally have chronic problems with depression.

The more the building can take on the cozy, affect-laden qualities of home, the more positive the feelings of residents will be. Most of them are extremely homesick. In many cases, their homes have been the setting for a lifetime of experiences. The front stoop where the dog slept, the backyard barbecue, the antique chest of drawers inherited from one's mother, and the apple tree planted 25 years ago are all imbued with memories. The more a building can gently recall elements that are similar to the home that was left, the more satisfying it can be. Pets, plants, and children have the potential to provide uplifting experiences. Artwork can trigger positive thoughts or recollect salient moments from the past.

Joy, laughter, amusement, surprise, whimsy, and delight are the kinds of emotions that should be triggered by the building, the furnishings, the staff, other residents, and visitors. The more the environment can support uplifting experiences, the happier residents will be.

Courtyard contains exercise challenges: The courtyard at the Rygårdscentret in Hellerup, Denmark, is designed with different paving materials to create an outdoor physical therapy space for residents.

Inward-oriented pensive courtyard attracts residents: The Flesseman Center in the historic Nieumarket district of Amsterdam is a peaceful oasis filled with plant materials, flowers, and a reflecting pond.

Covered porch creates a small but pleasant outdoor sitting area: This "back porch" at Raufosstun in Raufoss, Norway, opens onto a small stand of birch trees in the middle of an intimate courtyard that Norwegians often refer to as a *tun*.

A small garden for everyone: This small, raised garden is a feature found in every patio of the Vickelbygården nursing home in Skärblacka, Sweden. Every unit has an exterior door that leads to a private or semi-private garden, a feature one would rarely find in a U.S. nursing home.

Screened and covered porch: Spaces sandwiched between the indoors and the outdoors are often popular places for socializing in the summer.

Edge spaces attract residents in this dementia facility: Similar in concept to *Sunrise at Mission Viejo* (page 181), this garden in Severna Park, Maryland, has five different types of spaces sandwiched between the inside and outside. These include a skylighted three-season porch, a screened porch, a covered porch, a trellis, and an open barbecue plaza. (Photo: Eric Taylor)

Winter-garden is oriented toward a view of the adjoining lake: This space at Virranranta (page 206) is popular when the site is surrounded with snow. The unusual volume with a sloping roof makes this totally transparent enclosure an interesting place to sit and take in nature.

This balcony grill and trellis is designed to protect dementia residents: The balcony has some sections that are open to promote air circulation and some glass panels that facilitate viewing. Note the low sill heights and plant materials that are trained to climb the inside edge of the grillwork. (Photo: Eric Taylor)

The Danes are strong believers in creating informal opportunities for exercise: This glass-enclosed greenhouse space along a corridor in the Omsorgscentret Egegården in Søborg, Denmark, provides an ad hoc space for physical therapy and exercise.

Dining room square bay window alcove is oriented to an adjacent garden view: This feature at the *Sunrise of Richmond* (page 196) also benefits from Arts and Crafts detailing. Note the "flying beams" that create a decorative portal. (Photo: Jerry Staley Photography)

Three-season porch takes advantage of views to the garden: Internal skylights supplement the sunlight that enters this space from a window wall at the Sunrise at Richmond (page 196). The sloped ceiling conforms to the shape of a one-story porch addition. (Photo: Jerry Staley Photography)

Fire stairs in northern European homes are often used to daylight interior spaces: This stair at the de Overloop project in Almere, the Netherlands, takes in a panoramic view of the courtyard, including an attractive water feature. "Lean-to" housing units can be spotted at the rear of the site.

Atrium garden is a popular behavioral setting for morning and afternoon coffee: The Rosenborg Centret, in Copenhagen, Denmark, uses this magnificent space for the ritual of taking coffee, a Scandinavian cultural tradition.

Softscape atrium destination for residents: In the Moerwijk project in Den Haag, the Netherlands, a sloped glass atrium surrounded on two sides by units has become a popular retreat place for residents. At other times, the space is used for ad hoc activities like a flea market.

This hardscape and softscape atrium provides a range of different places for residents: A pool and a central landscape feature give this polygonal atrium at the Egely project in Ballerup, Denmark, a focal point.

This atrium terraces down a hill by the sea in Trondheim, Norway: The Hasselbakken clusters have ten units on each side of this atrium that steps down three stories while framing an extraordinary view of the Atlantic Ocean.

The first floor in this atrium is used for meals and social activities in this nursing home: The Nybodergaården (Regnier, 1994, p. 146) in Copenhagen, Denmark, takes its long linear form from the surrounding sixteenth-century housing for maritime workers.

Swimming pools are common in Finland: This pool at Helmiranta in Kauhava, Finland, has a window wall on one side and a ramp on the other. It is also open to special groups like developmentally disabled children and young babies.

Life skills vanity table and vintage clothing: The vanity table at *Sunrise at Bellevue* (page 191) can be used by residents for basic grooming or for putting on makeup and primping. This is a great way to involve family members in an activity that is pleasurable for everyone. (Photo: Jerry Staley Photography)

Family dining experience: The Danes and the Swedes value intimate dining arrangements involving six to eight residents in family-style meals. They believe this is particularly reassuring for memory-impaired residents.

Dutch Hofje housing benefits from the patina of age: The Hofje van staats in Harlem, the Netherlands, was originally constructed in 1730. The units have tall ceilings and traditional tall windows. The fireplace was originally the only source of heat in the unit.

The farmhouse vernacular of Elder Homestead is cozy: This building in Minnetonka, Minnesota, designed by the late Arvid Elness, FAIA, established a residential precedent that influenced subsequent assisted living buildings throughout the country.

De Overloop is a modern building with traditional features: The building wraps around a courtyard, creating views from the unit into this landscaped space. The all-glass balconies are elegant but don't appear to be heavily utilized. (Photo: Viotto Niemelä)

The dining room at Wilhelmiina (page 163) is beautiful at night and during the day: A curved alley at the back of this project was used to generate the exterior form of this space. The lath house is an outdoor dining terrace.

69

Pets, Plants, and Children

◀ *Children are usually a delight to have around:*   Metsätähti (page 229) combines children and older people in one integrated plan. Here the residents and children are helping to prepare dinner rolls that will be consumed at the noon meal.

One of the lessons we have learned from the successful Eden Alternative (Thomas, 1996) is the powerful contribution that these three simple features can make in a traditional long-term care setting. Pets, plants, and children add to the level of normality while adding joy and affect to the environment.

Adding Children to the Mix

For many older people, the view of children at play and the opportunity to interact with children have an unexplainable fascination. Intergenerational programming is an idea that has been around for decades and appears to be successful in most places where it has been thoughtfully implemented. Wheelock College in Boston, Massachusetts, has attracted attention because of the training program in intergenerational studies it has developed in conjunction with the *Stride Rite Intergenerational Center* in Cambridge, Massachusetts. The children and grandparents of employees are served through this innovative corporate program, which provides child care and adult day care to Stride Rite employees. Early childhood education programs that involve older people in direct participation are not as common as settings that simply provide an opportunity to observe children playing. In the Stride Rite setting, one major space is available for children and older participants to mix. Children, however, spend most of the day in their own classrooms at one end of the building.

Giving the Older Person Control

One factor that affects the implementation of intergenerational programming is the amount of control the older person has over the interaction. When the older person has some control, the program is almost always more successful. Structuring interaction can be as simple as creating environmental situations where residents can stage their interaction, from passively watching children at play to more active participation. Seating located at varying distances from play activity allow residents to retreat from a front-line location to one where they can be protected by distance. Problems like disorder and noise can be mitigated by distance, fences, and landscape treatments. Facilities can also set aside a place in the building where children are welcome. A toy box and children's furniture in combination with adult furniture can make it a special place for play and interaction. Locations should be selected where the noise and activity of children do not disturb sensitive residents.

Overlapping Uses

Day-care facilities for children and assisted living buildings are often located adjacent to one another because the same zoning category applies to both land uses. When facilities are colocated, each has a separate and distinct identity. Interaction occurs when residents host the children or the children host the residents in their respective buildings. There is also the possibility of sharing a space, which facilitates opportunities for interaction. The *Heritage at Cleveland Circle*, Massachusetts has a special room that was created between the assisted living and child-care entry spaces. It is a setting where glass panels and convenient doors make it easy for older and younger people to interact on a planned or casual basis. The *Sunrise of Fairfax*, Virginia (Regnier, 1994, p. 151), shares its campus with Merritt Academy, a private K–8 school. Most of the intergenerational programming occurs in the assisted living building, but residents are also invited to participate in events at the school. Because both the building and the school are affiliated with the Sunrise Corporation, programming efforts are more consistent. Each grade has an activity that is traditionally carried out with older residents.

European Examples of Intergenerational Contact

In Europe, there are many opportunities for intergenerational contact because the same agencies that monitor older people often take responsibility for children and see both activities as compatible. Many buildings are designed to be child friendly. Older service houses in rural areas might take on child-care responsibilities in the community because space is available in the building and access to food and other logistical supports can be offered. At *Metsatahti* (page 229), 21 children and 14 older people share the same building. Elderly residential units are located on one side of the building and the day-care center on the opposite side. Support facilities like the kitchen, laundry, and office space are shared. The children have their own play spaces and resting rooms but share the dining room with older residents. Activities that involve both children and adults occur throughout the building on both sides. The small scale and relaxed atmosphere of this rural town, where everyone knows everyone else, adds to the ease of operation and the mixing of the two populations.

Pets

Animals fascinate us. This is one of the reasons zoos are popular places for children and older people to visit. In assisted living, pet cats and dogs provide unconditional affection, which is very attractive to many older people who, by virtue of their living arrangement, may receive less physical and emotional support from family members or friends. Cats and dogs are familiar warm-blooded animals that appear to be among the most successful community pets. However, the original Eden experiment was also successful in utilizing parakeets, for which individual residents took responsibility (Thomas, 1996). A community dog or cat also needs to have a place to drink, eat, sleep, play, exercise, and urinate/defecate.

A Place for the Pet

The *Argyle* assisted living residence in Denver, Colorado, utilizes a wheelchair alcove as a place for their pet cat to sleep. Birds have also become popular with the advent of services that maintain and stock portable aviaries. Some facilities have courtyards or fenced-in gardens where rabbits can be contained. Finally, buildings that cannot agree on a policy for keeping a pet can host them on an occasional basis. Various organizations visit buildings and hospitals on a regular basis to share with residents the affection and positive feelings that animals can provide to residents.

Plants

Plant materials humanize a setting while providing an opportunity for residents to nurture and care for something that is alive. As with pets, there is a component of responsibility. Although a plant doesn't respond to nurturance as effusively as a dog, without care and attention a plant will die. Older people often nurture plants as a hobby. As they reduce their scope of activities and find it difficult to garden outdoors, it is not uncommon for them to collect potted house plants. Rodin and Langer (1977), in their now classic nursing home social psychology experiment, used a plant to give nursing home residents a sense of responsibility and control. The outcome demonstrated how powerful an intervention like this could be, as major differences in quality of life resulted between the experimental and control groups. The responsibility for tending plants has also been used, with powerful humanizing effects, in Eden Alternative research (Thomas, 1996).

Decorative Impacts

Plant materials located throughout the facility in the form of small trees, midsize bushes, and hanging plants are attractive and represent the beauty of nature. Plants can also be used as visual separation devices, creating more intimate and private areas within a large space like a dining room. Plants are partially transparent, allowing one to see them and see through them. Many assisted living buildings in the United States utilize artificial plant materials because they don't have enough natural light to keep plants alive or they don't have the resources to recycle, water, and maintain real plants. Even artificial plants are attractive and provide viewing satisfaction.

European Planting Approaches

The atria in European facilities are prime places for the placement of larger plants and trees. Many of these spaces have glass roofs and transmit enough light for plants to grow. In most facilities, protection from large swings in temperature allows unusual tropical species to grow. Scandinavian cultures value natural contexts and often utilize indoor plants as a way of paying homage to the natural world during their long, dark, severe winters.

70

Affect-Laden Interiors

◀ *Norman Rockwell's paintings are funny and poignant:*   They are particularly effective in assisted living environments because they represent a form of humor related to behaviors and situations common in the early to middle twentieth century, when many residents were growing up.

The institutional character of a nursing home is often reinforced by a lack of human-interest artwork. If artwork is present in abundance, which is often not the case, the content usually does not evoke much connection with human experience. Artwork in many settings focuses on inanimate objects, landscape scenes, or abstract graphics. These create visual interest but rarely connect with the older resident emotionally. Finding an image that is visually interesting and has genuine emotional content is often very difficult. Some of the most emotionally laden subjects are children, intergenerational scenes, animals, and humor.

Images That Evoke Meaningful Memories

Images of (grand)children and pets may not be as powerful as the real thing but nonetheless provoke powerful memories and recollections. Residents may smile or tell a story about a drawing, painting, or photograph that evokes a strong emotional message. Abstract art often requires more intellectual investment and often doesn't connect with the older person emotionally. Art that is disturbing or violent can be worse than no art at all, especially for residents with dementia. Antiques and craft materials can also be very effective in stimulating warm pleasant memories. *Woodside Place* in Oakmont, Pennsylvania (Regnier, 1994, page 156), used large handmade quilts for color coding and orientation purposes. These domestic objects add interest and warmth to living rooms and public common spaces. Accessory items like baby animals, stuffed animals, baby dolls, chipmunks, and bunnies push emotional buttons for many older residents, introducing a softness and a lighthearted quality to the place that makes it seem less threatening. These items are considered "cute" by most residents, the majority of whom are female.

71

Creating Humor and Whimsy

◄ *Humor is often in short supply:* This very realistic dog with a hat looks silly but is guaranteed to get a smile from almost anyone who walks by. Creating humorous situations adds levity to the setting for both residents and staff.

Photos, artwork, and accessories that often add joy to a setting are also curiously missing from most long-term care environments. Given the healing power of laughter and positive thinking, as advocated by authors like Norman Vincent Peale and films like *Patch Adams*, it may seem very unusual for this seemingly positive influence to be so absent. Humor is unlikely to do harm and may have some benefit in these settings. Like other affect-laden artwork, humor can be represented in many different forms.

The Importance of Humor in Artwork and Photographs

The artist Norman Rockwell often represented the humor of small-town life in early- to mid-twentieth-century America. His work not only presents humorous scenes, but also connects residents with memories of their youth and situations with which they can identify. Scenes from the past that are typical of what people in their 80s might have experienced as children or young adults are uniquely meaningful and evocative.

Creating a Humor-Filled Environment

Cartoons representing humorous situations can be used to evoke a smile or a laugh. Designating a public space for cartoons, jokes, funny experiences, and anecdotes can enliven a common space or corridor. Interesting accessories placed in a funny situation can also be amusing. *Sunrise at Mission Viejo* (page 181) has a brightly colored collection of insects and animals made from short lengths of reinforced steel that are used as garden ornaments. They are curiosity-provoking objects that are not easy to recognize and, once understood, can be amusing. Children, whose sense of discovery can bring joy to residents, love to find something wrong or silly in a drawing. Watching dogs smoke cigars and play cards, for example, is something they would likely find very amusing.

Performance Comedy

Videos, tapes, and photographs of comics and humorists can bring back memories of antics and comedic moments from the past. Comedians like Lucille Ball, the Three Stooges, the "Our Gang" children, Charlie Chaplin, George Burns, Jack Benny, Bob Hope, and Johnny Carson represented what was funny in life situations decades ago. Some of the jokes and situations are still hilarious, but many, when told or shown today, are not as meaningful to a contemporary audience because times and circumstances have changed. Comedies shown on movie night might make more of an impact if they emanate from the 1950s and 1960s rather than consisting of the most recent summer blockbusters.

72

Reminiscence and Life Review

◄ *Vintage clothing is used for reminiscence:*   The vanity table is used by staff and family members to comb hair, apply makeup and nail polish, and dab on perfume. Making people feel better about themselves by increasing their attractiveness is likely to be even more important in the future. (Photo: Jerry Staley Photography)

The use of old objects, photographs, and antiques to create an engaging interior design has been the source of inspiration for many projects. The use of validation therapy (Feil, 1993) in dementia units has greatly expanded reminiscence strategies that use objects and photos that trigger memories from the past. Antique items from everyday life are some of the most stimulating and effective items that can be mounted on walls, used in the building as props, or formally displayed. In some units, antique items are also kept in boxes and brought out for discussion purposes. Residents with dementia are more likely to see and use these items if they are mounted in a visible location or can be touched and manipulated.

Photos That Trigger Memories

Photos showing different life situations (graduations, military service, weddings, birth of children, etc.) or from important events in the life of an older person (VE Day, the Hiroshima bombing, the *Lunar* manned landing, etc.) can be very effective. Historic photographs from the surrounding community or the neighborhood are also interesting because they show places with which everyone in the building can identify. A local country club, a major employer, a busy intersection, an old store, a local hero, and important historic civic leaders are just a few of the possibilities for images. Local museums, universities, and the chamber of commerce often have archives that can be tapped.

11

PLANNING THE DWELLING UNIT

The dwelling unit is the major private space for residents. It is the place where they spend most of their time and can display items that mean a lot to them. Furniture can also trigger the recollection of many positive memories, so it is important that residents have the option of bringing things from their previous dwelling unit.

Safety is one of the most important aspects of unit design. The bathroom can be a hazardous place that should be carefully designed. Grab bars placed in the right location, access to the toilet and shower, and a slip-resistant, resilient floor covering are only a few of the many important factors to consider. Allowing residents control over natural and artificial light, ventilation, and conditioned air is also extremely important. Designing the unit so that it supports independent behaviors and privacy but has easy access to common activities allows residents to access the best of both worlds.

The dwelling unit is a key component of resident satisfaction. It should be large enough to contain possessions that are salient to the older person, with a full bathroom and at least a small tea kitchen. Space for an overnight visitor is also beneficial.

73

Intramural or Extramural Housing: Ongoing or Intermittent Support?

◄ *Extramural housing usually has a full kitchen:* This kitchen from the *Frederiksberg Aldrecenter* project in Åarhus, Denmark, is typical. Residents are often encouraged to cook their own meals or heat up prepared meals, or home care workers use the kitchen to cook a meal for residents.

In the Netherlands, a debate has developed regarding the nature of housing for frail older people. The sharpest divisions appear to center on how autonomy and freedom are provided. The Dutch have been concerned about whether housing policy should encourage the production of independent housing with access to services (extramural housing) or service-supported housing with meals, personal care, and other services provided as part of the setting (intramural housing). In American terms, this is similar to debating the benefits of licensed assisted living versus a housing and services model.

Independence versus Supportiveness

Both settings are available to residents. The debate centers on the intrinsic value of one philosophy over another. Both types of housing are being pursued with slightly different populations. An integrated service model is attractive to the most frail and to people with dementia, while the housing and service model attracts couples and residents who hope to age in place. The home care system in northern Europe is so well organized and financed that a housing and service model for the frail elderly seems to work very well. In the United States, the home care delivery system isn't robust enough to serve this population on an ongoing basis. However, many older people prefer this approach. Units are also getting larger. In the last ten years, unit sizes for independent elderly people have grown by an average of 100 SF. Housing that supports an aging in place philosophy needs bathroom spaces sized to accommodate helpers who assist residents with bathing and toileting (Steinfeld and Danford, 1999).

The Danish Model

Over the last 10–15 years, the Danes have used larger, more independent units, with options for home-delivered meals, home services, and unit designs similar to those of *Humanitas* (page 158) project. Units in most service houses are approximately 550 to 650 SF, with full kitchens and separate bedrooms. The link to the service center allows care, food, and activities to be conveniently located in an adjacent building. However, when visiting many of these service house projects in 1991 and 1999, administrative personnel often complained about how frail the residents were in comparison to what they thought would work best in this type of housing. In a number of new projects (*Ros Anders Gård* [page 215] and *Virranranta* [page 206]), emphasis was placed on serving the frailest of the frail. Dementia dwelling units 250- to 320-SF were linked to generous common spaces.

Pelgromhof Case Study

The *Pelgromhof* building has an interesting arrangement, containing both types of housing. The 169 independent housing units here average 650–700 SF, with full kitchens and bathrooms. Lunch is provided in a centralized dining room. A cluster of 46 units with a more traditional three-meal-per-day program is also available. These units average 350 SF. Interestingly, residents were relocated from an existing older building where the units were less than 200 SF. When the relocated residents were given a choice, equal numbers were attracted to the larger, independent units and the smaller, more service-intensive units. The sponsors speculated that the residents who were more risk averse selected the larger units, while the others opted for the convenience and support of the service-intensive units. Both populations were the same in terms of average age and competence level.

74

The Entry Experience

◄ *Nursing home units typically have a tea kitchen:* Personalization is important in making *Postiljonen* (page 224) a positive, warm experience. The larger unit size allows residents to bring a number of important furniture items from home.

Utilizing a slightly lower ceiling height at an inside entry is one strategy for making the unit appear more intimate. Placing a recessed can light or a sconce just inside the door creates a pool of light that illuminates the resident's face and the face of the visitor. Changing floor materials at the entry also marks the transition from the outside corridor (a public place) to the inside (a private place). In many facilities, an alcove is situated near the front door so that an important item or a personalized piece of artwork, furniture can be placed there. The entry to the unit is a "first impressions" space that can benefit from built-in shelving where knicknacks, books or family photographs can be displayed. Also, the view from the entry provides an opportunity to preview the rest of the unit. Bigger units generally have a larger entry place for galoshes, umbrellas, a raincoat, a clothes tree, or a clothes closet.

Entry Rooms

When a resident's unit contains a window or a side light near the door, this further defines the entry space. At the *Captain Eldridge Congregate House* in Hyannis, Massachusetts (see page 75), a window, Dutch door, and entry alcove open into the kitchen, where residents can invite others to sit. The adjacent bedroom are bathroom were defined as private spaces. At the *De Overloop* project in Almere, the Netherlands, the same elements (window, Dutch door and alcove) adjacent to a small kitchen create a more public zone next to the corridor. A three-quarter-height cabinet separate the resident's sleeping area and the kitchen. In northern Europe, it is common for the entry space to be an enclosed vestibule, with doors on all sides. This cultural pattern is common in most houses and is encouraged by codes and residents' housing preferences. Privacy, noise isolation, and temperature control are the reasons given for this unusual entry pattern.

75

Making Your Room Your Own

◄ *Woodside Place dwelling unit has an attractive residential feeling:*
Effective humanizing elements include the plate shelf with a wallpaper border, the
wood grain vinyl flooring, the suspended pendant light fixture, and residential furniture
and accessories.

Personalization is the key to making the residents, their friends, and the staff feel that a room is a home to live in and not just a bed to sleep in. The most effective way to personalize a dwelling unit is to bring one's own furniture and personal items. The act of making a room one's own makes it a personal expression. However, the room should start with wall coverings, floor coverings, light fixtures, kitchen cabinets, and windows that look residential in character. Personalization can start on the outside of the unit at the alcove entry. There a package shelf or a recessed space next to the door can display an interesting accessory. A small corkboard near the unit entry is a good place for a funny saying, a joke, or a cartoon each week. A small showcase can have photos and personal memorabilia that introduce the resident to the staff and to other residents. Sometimes the space outside a unit entry can be captured and made into a personal entry area with a few pieces of furniture or artwork.

Required Dwelling Unit Furnishings

Some antiquated licensing requirements still require "standard" furniture items like a bed, a nightstand, and an over-the-bed table. Although many more residential-style choices are available, it is unfortunate when standard institutional furniture determines the character of a room. The bed is the one piece of furniture that may need to be specified. The flexibility needed to lower or raise a bed for therapy or for resident transfer makes a hospital bed necessary in some instances. With the range of bed covers and decorative materials available, hospital beds can be relatively easy to camouflage.

Woodside Place—An Important Case Study

The small 150-SF rooms at *Woodside Place* in Oakmont, Pennsylvania (Regnier, 1994, page 156) are a fine example of how a small room can be made to appear more cozy. The floor material selected is a wood-grained vinyl sheet product. This gives the appearance of a wood floor while maintaining the protection of vinyl. A simple Shaker-inspired plate shelf is used around the perimeter of the room on two walls. Flanked by a wallpaper border above, the 3.5-inch shelf, in combination with pegs mounted every 9 inches, allows small objects to be displayed and clothing to be hung. The pendant light fixture selected has a residential appearance and provides both direct and reflected light. Windows with relatively low sills and traditional mullion treatment are residential in character. Simple stained wood trim around doors and windows also reinforces the residential feeling.

Northern European Dwelling Unit Ideas

Europeans are great believers in the power of residential materials. Although exterior design treatments lean toward a nonresidential modern vocabulary of stucco, brick, and glass, interiors clearly are designed for residents to display their most cherished possessions. Because rental leases are for longer periods of time in Europe than in the United States, its not uncommon for wall and floor coverings to be completely changed when a new resident moves in. Another unusual feature is that older residents almost always bring with them light fixtures that have been in their families for decades. Because these fixtures contain a light source, they are often the most eye-catching accessories in the dwelling unit. Traditional furniture items like the Swedish kitchen bench go back to the turn of the twentieth century, when many Swedes used them as quasi-daybeds in what was then the warmest room in the house (see page 243). Although the northern Europeans don't believe in carpets, the use of wood-grained vinyl and wood-grained plastic laminants, like Pergo, is common. Because European dwelling units are often a little larger, furniture and custom casework are more common than in U.S. units. Armoires and built-in closets are used almost exclusively throughout northern Europe in place of closets.

76

A Safe Bathroom

◄ *Roll-in shower design makes European bathrooms more accessible:*
The *Ros Anders Gård* (page 215) bathroom has a corner shower with a window
for natural light. Notice the ceiling track available for residents who need a lift device
to transfer.

One of the most important spaces to design properly is the bathroom. This room clearly requires the most rigorous workout for residents, who must rotate, stand up, sit down, bend over, and transfer in this room. For this reason, the bathroom is often the most dangerous space in the dwelling unit (Steinfeld and Danford, 1999). Falls can be devastating, and residents using toilets and showers can easily lose their balance. The majority of residents are not wheelchair bound, but as many as 40 percent of an older, high-acuity population may be dependent on a walker, a four-pronged cane, or a wheelchair to get around. At least 10 percent of the units should be designed to meet accessible bathroom standards, and all bathrooms should be designed to be adaptable.

Adaptable Design

An *adaptable* bathroom is one that can be adjusted to the needs of a handicapped person. In an adaptable design, wide doors, knee space, switch locations, and grab bar reinforcement are built in. Other items can be added or changed if necessary. For example, grab bars can be omitted and installed when needed, knee spaces can be concealed by a removable base cabinet, and countertops and closet rods can be installed on adjustable supports.

Accessible Design

An *accessible* bathroom is one that meets the requirements for accessible design. Some of its main features include wide doors, a clear space for wheelchair turnaround, lower countertops, lever, and loop handles, seats at bathing fixtures, grab bars, knee space under counters, audible and visual signals, and easy-to-reach switches

and controls. These rooms are often excessive in size. They are based on the requirements established for younger disabled people with excellent upper body strength who need more space for wheelchair manipulation. However, older residents often have caregivers in the same room assisting them. In some states, 50 percent of resident bathrooms are required to be accessible.

Bathroom Door

European bathrooms are almost always designed with either a 1-meter-wide sliding barn door or a sliding pocket door. Their research has identified these as the easiest doors for a handicapped person to manipulate. They are often outfitted with leather strap handles that further facilitate opening and closing. In the United States, 36-inch swing doors are the norm. However, for safety purposes, the door should swing out of the bathroom. Residents have been known to fall in front of a in-swinging door, making it almost impossible for emergency medical personal to enter the bathroom. Although swing doors are less expensive, a strong argument could be made in many situations for a sliding door. In smaller units, a number of large doors opening onto one another can be very disruptive. A 36-inch width is the common minimum size, but some architects prefer 42-inch sliders because they open the room up more to the corridor, facilitating two-person transfers from a wheelchair. A swing door should also move in a direction that minimizes views from the front door into the bathroom or bathroom mirror. A hook on a swing door or a small line of pegs on one wall can be useful for hanging clothing in the room. Finally, motion detectors have proved to be very useful. They turn on the bathroom light as the memory-impaired older person walks by, cueing the person to enter and use the commode.

Toilet Design

The toilet should be between 17–18 inches in height. A thicker raised seat can provide additional height if necessary. The taller seat makes it easier for residents to get on and off of the toilet. The greatest problem with a toilet seat that is too high is that the legs of a shorter person dangle. When the legs are pressed against the edge of the toilet seat, the resident can lose circulation in the legs and may slip and fall when attempting to stand up. The toilet should always be located against at least one solid wall so that a grab bar can be firmly mounted. Locations away from a wall may require drop-down bars, which are bulky and more difficult to manipulate. The toilet paper dispenser should be relatively easy to grasp and should not be behind the person. Finally, emergency call hardware should be located close to the toilet and to the shower (ideally, between them). Many older people who are experiencing a heart attack may also have the sensation of incontinence and may sit on the toilet to recover. Also, residents who slip in the shower may need to access the call hardware from the floor near the shower. Some dementia units have had excellent results in cueing residents to use the toilet by making it visible from the bed.

Lavatory Design

The lavatory should be easy to reach, and fixtures should be easy to manipulate. If a side entry position is specified, there is no need to have kick space below for a wheelchair. In front-mounted designs, the cabinet face should be designed to be removed if necessary. In northern Europe, there is a tendency to make the bathroom cabinetry flexible so that it can be disassembled if someone in a wheelchair lives in the unit permanently. There should be storage for towels and enough storage for personal hygiene supplies and medications. A 30- to 36-inch-wide three-part recessed medicine cabinet is a good investment because it provides extra medicine storage space, and the mirrors can be manipulated to make it easier to see other parts of the head for grooming. An attached magnified mirror on an extendable support also provides help for shaving or putting on makeup.

Shower Sizes

Minimum shower sizes to meet adaptability requirements vary from state to state. In my experience, the best size is a 3 × 4 feet. Some laws suggest that a 3 × 3-foot shower is adequate. However, this small platform size can be crowded and awkward, especially when the resident is assisted by an attendant. The 30 × 60-inch size, which is mandated by some state governments, is also problematic. The 30-inch width is too narrow and can generate considerable overspray on the floor, creating a slip hazard. A 60-inch width is very large. Grab bars in a space this large are located farther away, and the compartment is often big and cold. Grab bars in the shower should reflect state requirements. At a minimum, they should include a vertical edge bar near the control wall and a horizontal bar at the back wall. Hand-held sprayers are most popular and most flexible for many residents, who may sit for part of the time. Although drop-down seats work well, a separate movable chair can be adjusted to the resident's height and moved to the best location for the bathing process. Molded seats are rarely located in the right place for the right person. Temperature control regulators should be placed on the shower supply or a maximum temperature of 110 degrees Fahrenheit should be employed to avoid the danger of scalding.

Northern European Roll-in Showers

Shower designs in all of the European case studies call for a roll-in shower in the corner of the bathroom. In these designs, the whole bathroom floor is waterproofed and drains into the shower. This works very well, especially with residents who are wheelchair bound. This design can be replicated in the United States but often at more expense because an integrated shower design is necessary. Finally, little has been said about the use of a bathtub. For safety reasons, it is rarely specified in today's housing for frail adults. However, an excellent bathtub manufactured by Fiberglass Systems in Boise, Idaho, with a shallow depth and a generous transfer edge, works very well and is also economical. This design was used at the *Sunrise of Frognal House* in London, England, to appeal to a consumer demand for tubs rather than showers in assisted living dwelling units.

Other Dwelling Unit Requirements

Flooring should be slip resistant and should utilize a familiar residential pattern. Ambient lighting should be adequate, which normally requires a minimum of three fixtures. One fixture should be mounted over the sink, the second placed in the middle of the room, and the third located over the shower enclosure. An additional 250-watt heat lamp on a timer can provide extra light for checking skin problems as well as extra heat on a cool or chilly morning. In dementia units, wall colors have been selected that create contrast with fixtures so that residents will be able to identify them more effectively. Wallpaper borders can be effective in bathrooms, which may suffer from lack of variety in color and texture.

77

The Tea Kitchen and the Quest for a Complete Unit

◄ *Complete kitchen is common in northern Europe:* Standards require that even small dwelling units contain a full kitchen with a cooking source. This is a compact kitchen in the *Metsätähti* (page 229) dwelling unit.

Specifying a small tea kitchen has both a symbolic and functional rationale. The presence of this feature underscores the definition of the setting as a dwelling unit rather than just a room with a bed. It further separates assisted living from the traditional nursing home or hospital room. Having the capability for food storage and limited food preparation provides choices for residents. It also facilitates entertaining guests and provides a place for snacks. Residents might bring back a piece of fruit or part of a sandwich to snack on later or keep ice cream in the freezer. In the United States, a small tea kitchen 5 to 8 feet in length with a sink, a refrigerator, a microwave oven, and lower and upper cabinet storage is standard. The northern European sensitivity to aging in place has led to an emphasis on larger kitchens. In the United States, the provision of three meals and two snacks, mandated by license in many states, discourages residents from using basic food preparation skills. They might use the refrigerator, the sink, and occasionally the microwave oven to heat something, but meals are usually not prepared or served there.

Northern European Kitchens Designs

In general, the attitude toward aging in place and access to a highly evolved home care system have mandated a larger, more complete kitchen. In some units, home care workers regularly prepare a small breakfast for older residents. The kitchen also provides a reference to a normal lifestyle. Its presence encourages residents to prepare some meals and to maintain their independence as long as possible. As the size of apartments increase, so does kitchen space and equipment. A recent move to create specialized units for people with dementia has led to smaller kitchen installations. However, even in these units, cooktops or microwave ovens are still regularly specified.

Kitchen Upgrades

In the United States, there is still a debate about what food preparation features should be borrowed from congregate housing. In a working kitchen, light is very important. Under-the-cabinet lighting provides good ambient and task lighting. Roll-out shelving for food storage is also an important feature because it eliminates stooping and bending. Shelves between the counter and upper cabinets are also popular for items that are used every day. The carefully designed General Electric "Real Life Design" kitchen contains features like a roll-out stool at the sink, deep pantry storage, lateral placement for the storage of pots and pans, and eye-level appliances. This kitchen is designed to match the needs of the user with special design features.

78

Big Windows and Low Sills

◄ *Large windows with low sills:* Windows like this one at *Gyngemosegård* (page 174) allow more light to enter the unit while taking in a better view of the surrounding landscape. Radiant heaters are normally located below windows.

Assisted living studio units of 300–325 SF (ALFA, 2000; NIC, 1998) are relatively small spaces. Residents who normally come from much larger dwellings and often bring a lot of furniture with them can have a difficult time adapting to such small spaces. One strategy for making a small unit appear larger and more spacious is to specify large windows with low sill heights and to increase the ceiling height to 9 or 10 feet. Sill heights of 14 to 24 inches are common in the United States and in northern Europe. Low sill heights also make it easier for residents in bed to see activities and landscape features outside. Building codes may require tempered glass in situations where sill heights are lower than 18 inches. Window sizes of approximately 6 feet by 6 feet (36 SF) should be considered the minimum. In rooms with higher ceilings, a 12-inch clerestory window band can bring additional daylight deep into the unit.

Window Types and Styles

Windows in the United States have increasingly been outfitted with devices to keep residents from opening them all the way. This practice is grounded in the fear that confused residents may try to "escape" from a unit by crawling out of the window. In some buildings, this constraint is placed only on the windows of dementia residents. There is no strong preference for either horizontal or vertical sliding windows. However, casement windows appear to be a bit less popular. Regardless of the window type selected, it is important to make certain that windows are easy to open.

European Window Treatments

Balconies and patios are a little more common in northern Europe than in the United States even in facilities for people with dementia. In some urban areas, French balconies and Dutch erkers are very popular. In the Netherlands, exterior canvas awnings are often used to block the sun when necessary. These are usually controlled from the inside by a switch leading to an electronic motor that opens or closes the awning.

79

Unit Size: Sleeping and Living in One Room or Two?

◄ *Studio design creates a bed alcove and a small kitchen space:* The studio unit design from the *Sunrise of Mission Viejo* (page 181) uses a wide alcove at the entrance for a small table/kitchen area. (Photo: Jerry Staley Photography)

Assisted living units are available in sizes that normally range between 275 and 600 SF. In a typical housing environment, 50–60 percent of the units are studios. There is considerable debate over what size makes sense for the majority of residents. Larger units are consistent with the preferences of the newest cohort of older people. Creating one room for sleeping and another for living can make the unit more private by allowing the bedroom to be a sanctuary for personal photos and artifacts. Another major difference in the housing stock of northern Europe is the preference for one-bedroom units and the desire to keep all units (including nursing home units) single occupied.

European Dwelling Unit Sizes

The typical northern European service house dwelling unit, as in the *Humanitas* (page 158) project, is in the range of 550 to 650 SF and has one bedroom. Because many northern European projects start with the assumption that housing and services are delivered separately, housing units are often larger and have full kitchens. Today, it is not uncommon to find a 750-SF one bedroom unit. Northern European residents prefer to have enough space for an overnight guest like a family member or a caregiver. Units for mentally and physically frail residents range from 225 to 300 SF. When a studio is specified, it is often configured with an alcove so that residents can have a separate area for their bed and additional space for living room furniture. In smaller units with less that 300 SF, this is often difficult to achieve.

80

Controlling Air Temperatures

◄ *Ventilators are commonly used to control temperatures in atriums:* This nonconditioned atrium at *Hasselbakken* in Trondheim, Norway, has ventilators that open automatically when the temperature becomes uncomfortably warm.

One of the most frustrating environmental issues is a resident room with poor temperature control. This can not only make life miserable but can also lead to chills and ultimately to health problems. Most projects today opt for individual systems in each unit rather than a centralized commercial boiler and chiller that serves residential units through a two- or four-pipe system. These systems should be controlled by an external thermostat placed in a central location. A separate external thermostat is an important feature, because built-in thermostats are often poorly calibrated and difficult for residents to read and manipulate.

Complications with Temperature Control

Temperature control is sometimes difficult to manage in nursing homes where two people share the same room.

For example, in a side-by-side bed arrangement, the resident next to the window may not experience the same ambient temperature as the person closer to the corridor. In many units where airflow exits through the bathroom, a continuous flow of cool air is present. Therefore, an auxiliary heater or heat lamp in the bathroom is important, especially if the bathroom has an exterior window. Although fresh air is normally provided through the ventilation system, it is important to have windows that are easily operable. In Europe, where perimeter radiators are a common source of heat in the winter, dwelling units are outfitted with *trickle vents* that allow natural air movement to occur through the window sash. These vents can be closed or partially closed in the winter.

81

Moving Residents Who are Highly Impaired

◄ *Ceiling track links the bed with the bathroom:* At the *Postiljonen* (page 224) nursing home, a ceiling-mounted track allows residents to be transferred from the bed to the bathroom using a electric lift device.

Residents with impairments so severe that it is impossible for them to walk need to be lifted into and out of bed. Normally, U.S. residents with this level of impairment are placed in a nursing home. However, as residents with higher levels of impairment seek to stay in assisted living, new ways to transfer them will be necessary. About five to ten years ago, facilities in Europe started to phase in different types of lift devices that are just now becoming more common in the United States.

Portable and Built-in Lifting Devices

The portable lifting devices manufactured by medical equipment suppliers are U-shaped and contain wheels and a hoyer-style hydraulic or electric lift. The major requirement for their use is a relatively large bathroom and bedroom area so that the resident can be easily moved to the commode. These portable devices are bulky and slow. The most common lift technology used in northern Europe today consists of devices that are attached to a ceiling track. They utilize a similar electric power plant that, in combination with a canvas support, lifts the resident from the bed. The overhead rails are designed as either single- or multidirectional. Single-directional models link the bed to the bathroom. They can be used to transfer a resident to a wheelchair or carry the person directly to the commode or the shower. Lifts also allow residents to be transferred to a chair or a wheelchair so that they can be out of bed for part of the day.

82

Room for Storage

◄ *Graduated dressing armoire for dementia residents:*   Designed for the dementia unit at *Hillcrest Homes* in LaVerne, California, it consists of two compartments. One contains clothing to be worn that day, arranged in reverse order. The other is for clothing storage. Casters allow the armoire to be moved to the rooms of residents who respond to this approach. (Photo: Irwin. Pancake Architects)

Dwelling unit storage is highly appreciated by residents and family members. It seems that there can never be too much storage for most residents. To work well, storage space should be spread throughout the unit wherever it is most useful. It should also be well organized and efficiently laid out. Storage should be located in the kitchen, in the bathroom for towels and medications, in the bedroom for clothes, and near the front door for coats and other bulkier items. A second closet in the dwelling unit is also highly appreciated. Residents often bring with them furniture items like breakfronts that are used to display important personal mementos (Rowles, 2001). However, there is a limit to the amount of storage space that can be provided. When people move into assisted living, they often must dispose of many important personal items they have collected over a lifetime. Someone who needs a lot of storage usually is not a good candidate for assisted living.

Storage Considerations

A remote resident storage cubicle of 27–64 cubic feet is often available somewhere in the building However, too much storage space becomes an excuse for saving items that could best be given away or sold. Resident storage space is expensive space to build, condition, and maintain. In Europe, storage also is very popular. However, full-sized closets are rarely constructed. A hall or entry closet is often constructed as a cabinet. Armoires in the bedroom are also popular.

83

To Double-Occupy or Not?

◄ *Design for double occupancy:*   Occasionally a couple, two sisters, or two older friends want to live together. Dwelling units that facilitate this option should be available. In the United States, double occupancy is a common strategy for reducing the price.

A debate has been raging during the last few years about the desirability or inappropriateness of double-occupancy dwelling units. The major fear is that if double-occupancy units are widely sanctioned, when federal reimbursement is extended to assisted living, double occupancy will be the standard, as it is currently in skilled nursing facilities. It is probably best to allow double occupancy because it is popular for a small minority of residents. ALFA's (2000) assisted living overview reported that 12.6 percent of the assisted living units surveyed in 1999 were double-occupied. Some residents share a unit for social purposes. They genuinely appreciate having a roommate for security and companionship. Others need or want to take advantage of the 25–35 percent cost savings that is normally associated with a double-occupancy unit.

Designing for Double Occupancy

Although double-occupancy or semiprivate units will never be a major segment of a building's dwelling unit inventory, 15–20 percent of units should be available for two people to share. For flexibility, these units should also be designed for single occupancy. One of the worse double-occupancy designs is the traditional side-by-side bed arrangement. Unfortunately, it is one of the most common layouts in skilled nursing facilities. A better strategy is to adapt a one-bedroom unit to double occupancy. This is done by transforming the living room into a second bedroom. If the door to this second bedroom is a 15 light French door, then borrowed light can enter the central portion of the unit (kitchen/bathroom). The number of double occupancies is likely to grow as a project ages and residents become more frail. As residents age in place, they are likely to run short of money at the very time when their need for services increases. They may consider trading off space and privacy for more help and assistance. In Europe, double-occupancy units are not common. In fact, when two married people move into a building, they are often accommodated in two units located next to one another.

84
Experiencing the Outdoors from the Unit

◄ *Corner window opens the unit up to a view and to the patio:* In *Hasselbakken* in Trondheim, Norway, this full-height corner window is used to connect the unit with the outdoors.

Opening the unit to a balcony or patio is somewhat unusual in assisted living. Balconies are far more common in the West, where better climatic conditions have led to a stronger tradition of outside living. The placement of balconies on an exterior elevation often improves the elevation of the building by adding an interesting massing feature. Access to narrow balconies by residents with wheelchairs is always a problem. Balconies should be a minimum of 5 to 7 feet deep. Also, the sill transition from inside to outside needs to be flush for wheelchairs but sloped enough to keep water from entering the unit. First-floor patios have more utility because they allow residents to come in contact with nature in a more direct way. Balconies and patios are almost never provided in U.S. nursing homes. However, access to a shared outdoor space from a public living room or dining room is common, especially in sunbelt climates.

European Gardens and Balconies

Small private garden spaces that open directly from dwelling units are common in Danish nursing homes. The Danes believe that access to the outdoors is healthy, and they are less concerned about security than Americans. In the *Raufosstun Eldresenter* in Raufoss, Norway, each unit has access to a small covered patio with a built-in bench and a shelf for potted plants (see color insert). The units are clustered around a secured courtyard with a central stand of birch trees. The view and the connection to the outside is beautiful and inviting in both winter and summer. Each dwelling unit in the one-story *Humelhusene* (page 220) dementia unit in Albertslund, Denmark, has an outdoor patio.

85

The French Balcony

◄ *French balcony opens up a small unit:*   French balconies like the one at *Ros Anders Gård* (page 215) allow access to fresh air without the awkward threshold transition that most balconies require. Unit square footages are normally enhanced by half the size of an exterior balcony when a French balcony is used instead.

A French balcony is a wonderful compromise. It provides a window wall that can be opened to the outside without having to physically move outside over a bulky threshold. Furthermore, the savings in the cost of the balcony can be reinvested in a larger living room or bedroom. Balconies attached to a building are often too narrow to be useful. They can also end up as unsightly storage space for items that do not fit inside the dwelling unit. A French balcony also allows a screen door to be used, so it can ward off insects at night. Finally, it creates a place to sit in the shade. South- and west-facing balconies without shade control are not very usable in the middle of summer.

European Examples of French Balconies

There are numerous European examples of nursing homes, dementia units, and assisted living in northern Europe that use the French balcony to advantage. The *Sondre Nordstrand* (see page 264) in Oslo, Norway, the *Villa Viklo* in Oulu, Finland, and the *Ros Anders Gård* (page 215) are dementia facilities that have successfully utilized the French balcony. In all of these applications large windows were also provided to increase the amount of daylight reaching each dwelling unit.

12

ENGAGING THE STAFF

One advantage of an attractive environment is that staff members also have a wonderful environment in which to work. Helping the caregiving staff to feel positive about their work and the people they are helping is paramount. If they are happy, the residents will probably also be happy.

Caregivers work hard at a job that doesn't pay very well and often requires a large emotional and physical investment. They deserve enormous respect for the hard work they do and the care they provide. Like teachers, they often get little more than intrinsic satisfaction from their job. However, the work they do is the measure of how compassionate our society is toward those who must depend on others. Some of the best caregivers extend themselves to residents through personal friendship. Caregivers should be designated for each resident so that any changes in the resident's health or personal status will be quickly noted.

Staff turnover is a major problem in the long-term care industry. The greater the staff continuity, the better it is for residents, who often develop personal relationships with the people they depend on.

86

An Approachable, Knowledgeable Staff

◄ *Resident participation encourages a sense of control:*   At the *Dronning Anne-Marie Centret* in Frederiksberg, Denmark, residents living in 12- to 15-unit clusters meet with staff twice a month to discuss hiring issues and management policies.

Staff offices should be located near major circulation pathways and the elevator in a multistory building. Visual and physical accessibility is important for families and residents because it encourages informal exchanges. A central staff location creates a single point of contact and facilitates staff communication and ease of movement throughout the building. Because many staff members spend much of their time outside of their office, these spaces can be relatively small. However, they should afford privacy for phone calls and paperwork. Interior windows are very useful when placed in locations that allow staff to make visual contact with family members and residents. When trimmed with lace curtains or window treatments, they can create a veil of privacy between the staff and the public (see page 86 and 272). Visibility enhances the perception of accessibility, leading to a generally more friendly environment. A centrally located conference room is most useful for meetings between staff and families.

Identifying Each Resident

When the number of residents ranges from 60 to 70, they can be identified by name and addressed in a personal way. Staff should be organized so that at least one person has specific knowledge about each resident. The northern Europeans assign a primary and a secondary *contact person* to each resident. These are staff members who have detailed knowledge of a resident's likes and dislikes, as well as his or her health and personal care needs. If the primary contact person is not around, the secondary one is likely to be available for consultation. Good communications between the staff, the resident, and the family can capture important insights about the habits and preferences of each resident. Many personal aspects of the life experiences of a resident can be noted when this relationship exists. Formal monthly or bimonthly meetings between the staff and the family should be carried out to review and update the caregiving plan.

87

Encouraging Improvisational Activities

◀ *Spontaneous improvisational activity should be encouraged:* Long corridors make great bowling alleys at the *Hearthstone at New Horizons* dementia center in Marlborough, Massachusetts. Bowling is a good exercise for maintaining upper body strength.

The building is an environmental stage on which a wide range of activities can be pursued. The staff should be encouraged to use the building and its many different spaces creatively. Some of the most popular spaces are on the exterior edge of the building, including porches, patios, and gardens. Birthday parties, impromptu sing-alongs, ice cream socials, lemonade and tea breaks, reading funny stories, telling jokes, and celebrating occasions can work well in a variety of spaces. Sometimes, when carried out in a larger, more public space, activities can attract spectators who may become participants in the future.

The Palmcrest Cruise

For many years, the *Palmcrest Nursing Center* in Long Beach, California, has taken an imaginary "cruise" in the summer to different exotic locations. Staff members wearing costumes present skits and special performances at mealtimes representing the people and the cultural attributes of the place they "visit." France, Jamaica, and the South Seas have been popular imaginary destinations. Events like this can attract family members as observers or participants, stimulating a different kind of family-centered interaction.

Impromptu Events

In June of 2001, I walked into a dementia facility in the middle of a hula hoop contest. Staff members were competing with stopwatch accuracy, and residents were cheering for their favorite participant. Impromtu activities such as this are novel and effective methods of stimulating excitement and interaction. When staff members wear vintage hats for the day, it adds novelty, whimsy, and unpredictability. Almost every week, there is some holiday one can celebrate with decorations and music. In Los Angeles, Cinco de Mayo (Mexico's Independence Day) is a holiday that staff members can celebrate by sharing aspects of their culture and history with residents. The visits of pets and children can also add surprise, joy, and unpredictability. Impromptu ice cream socials, sipping lemonade in the afternoon on the back porch, and slicing a watermelon as a snack before dinner on the screened porch are all easy-to-implement events that remind residents of past experiences. Events, when staged or carried out in this way, are memorable, interesting, and fun for everyone.

Decorating Spaces to Celebrate

Decorating spaces for festive occasions is a great way to transform the environment and to change the mood of the residents in these settings, if only for a few hours. Creating a spontaneous and amusing afternoon or morning event can add excitement, interest, and richness to the day. Decorating the front entrance and drop-off area of the building for holidays like Thanksgiving, Halloween, Christmas, Hanukkah, Easter, July 4th, and Memorial Day helps to mark time and to make that week and the week preceding it a special and memorable period.

88

Treating the Staff Right

◄ *This Danish nurse's station is a simple table in an alcove:*   Compared with U.S. nurse's stations, northern European versions are always more approachable. Many are part of the serving kitchen, while others are simple desks, tables, or alcoves that encourage residents' interaction.

The caregiving staff are the unsung heroes in the daily life of a facility. When they are motivated and excited about what they can achieve, they exert a powerful influence on the life of the place. A well-designed staff lounge should be available so that they can take a break and get away from their jobs for a few minutes. The lounge should have lockers, a place to prepare and store food, space for vending machines, a restroom, and a table for eating a meal or a snack. A window to the outside provides natural light and a view of the surrounding landscape. A small outdoor patio should be available for use during good weather; it also provides a place for staff to smoke. Staff lounges are best located near the kitchen but should be convenient for the caregiving staff as well.

European Safety Considerations

In Europe, the staff often have more extensive facilities, including showers and lockers. In some decentralized facilities, small staff rooms with a couch and a desk are available for staff to get away and take notes or relax for a few minutes. A few northern European facilities have access to exercise equipment that is either dedicated to staff use or shared with residents. Occupational health is a priority in these countries. Access to exercise equipment is one way providers can support staff health proactively by minimizing the potential for back injuries.

13

DESIGNING FOR DEMENTIA

Most surveys show that the percentage of residents in assisted living facilities with memory impairment is about 40–50 percent. Therefore, if you are providing assisted living services, you are also caring for residents with dementia. Managing a dementia population requires sensitivity to several key design issues (Brawley, 1997; Day, Carreon, et al., 2000).

Securing the exits, providing access to the outdoors, and allowing residents to wander freely are important characteristics of a well-developed plan. Relating the pro-gram to ADLs allows residents to live in the facility as they would at home. Most of these programs focus on helping with meals, doing the laundry, cleaning up, and socializing. Residents in dementia units are far more likely to spend time with one another than to stay by themselves in their rooms.

Separating residents with dementia from other physically frail residents who are mentally intact is generally a good strategy. It allows special staff training efforts, lifestyle programming, and therapeutic interventions for people with dementia to be more effectively implemented.

89

Small-Group Clusters of Units

◄ *Woodside Place clustered residents into three small bungalows:* Using separate "houses" to define clusters worked well here. *Copper Ridge* (page 201) increased the cluster size from 12 to 20 residents to make it more staff efficient (see page 138 for plan).

Clustering units together to form small social groups of individuals who take meals and spend the day together is becoming the most popular approach to the design of housing for people with dementia. One reason this appears to work so well is that residents with dementia spend much of the day outside of their dwelling units, hanging out in common spaces and participating in various group activities. They often treat their dwelling unit as a place to sleep and rest rather than as a place to spend the day. This pattern of behavior has led many designers in the United States and abroad to conceptualize these units as a home within a home. The units vary in size, but in the United States it is not uncommon to find 10–15 residents clustered together in one group living arrangement. The *Harbor House* (page 211) is a good example of this approach. In Europe, the numbers are considerably smaller. The Danes believe that six to eight is the optimum cluster size. The *Humlehusene* (page 220) and *Postiljonen* (page 224) are both good examples of this philosophy. Each cluster of units is typically equipped with a living room, kitchen, dining room, activity (family) room, and a balcony, garden, patio, or porch located outside. Resident dwelling units may be smaller, with more space allocated to common spaces where residents spend most of the day.

Hierarchy Concerns in Unit Clusters

The major problem with the small northern European cluster is that it often doesn't provide much hierarchy for individuals in terms of additional places to go or activities to experience. This approach is also considered more costly by many U.S. providers because the clusters are smaller and the staff ratios are higher. The larger U.S. clusters of 12–15 residents generally have more spaces to visit and a wider range of activities and distractions. However, they often lack the intimacy and the family feeling of the smaller northern European clusters. In these small clusters, everyone can be easily accommodated around a single family-style table for meals and activities (see color insert). The centerpiece for the small-group unit is often the kitchen, which serves as a nurse's station, life skills center, and food-serving space. In the United States, food is almost always prepared in a separate commercial kitchen and then moved on carts to servery kitchens in the dementia unit cluster. In many northern European project like the *Ros Anders Gård* (page 215) the preparation of food from raw foodstuffs is considered an important major activity of the day.

Northern European Unit Cluster Philosophy

A dementia facility in northern European typically groups four to six clusters of units. Each unit cluster contains 6 to 8 residents; therefore, a building might have as few as 24 or as many as 48 residents. There is a tradition of preparing meals as a group, as well as having food delivered from a central kitchen. The noon meal is likely to be prepared off-site and delivered in bulk. However, breakfast and dinner meals, which are more modest, are cooked and prepared in the kitchen. In the *Hogeway* project, in Weesp, the Netherlands, one unit cluster has its meals provided through a large stainless steel portable kitchen that is rolled to the unit (see page 39). The process of food preparation occurs in front of residents, as in an upscale restaurant. In other Hogeway unit clusters, residents shop for food in the basement of the building, where a full-sized supermarket has been established. Caregivers shop with residents for food and then take it upstairs to prepare meals in a kitchen in each unit cluster (see page 268). The menu and the approach to satisfying each resident's food preferences is handled in an individual way.

Cluster Shapes and Configurations

The configuration of a unit cluster can vary greatly, often depending on the shape of the site and the strategy the architect has used to group the units together. U-shaped configurations like that of *Copper Ridge* (page 201) are fairly common, with shared space placed between the two residential wings. *Humlehusene* (page 220) has a central corridor spine with units on one side and an open area for common shared spaces on the other. In this design, the kitchen, living room, and dining room are located next to one another in an open plan. The dementia small-group cluster of eight units in *Virranranta* (page 206) has dwelling units on both sides of a central dining room space.

90

Social Wandering

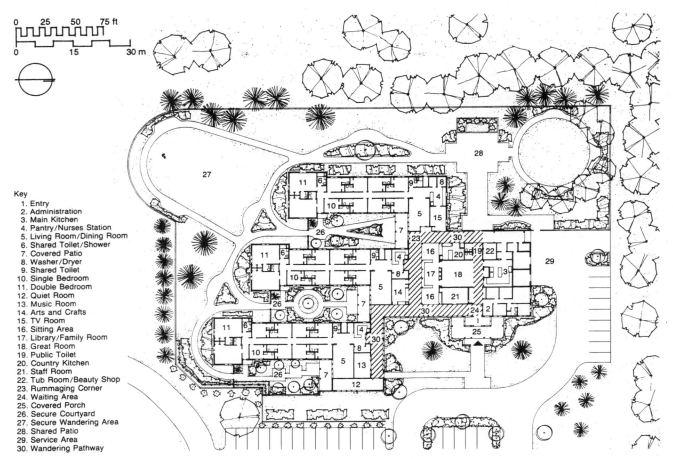

Key
1. Entry
2. Administration
3. Main Kitchen
4. Pantry/Nurses Station
5. Living Room/Dining Room
6. Shared Toilet/Shower
7. Covered Patio
8. Washer/Dryer
9. Shared Toilet
10. Single Bedroom
11. Double Bedroom
12. Quiet Room
13. Music Room
14. Arts and Crafts
15. TV Room
16. Sitting Area
17. Library/Family Room
18. Great Room
19. Public Toilet
20. Country Kitchen
21. Staff Room
22. Tub Room/Beauty Shop
23. Rummaging Corner
24. Waiting Area
25. Covered Porch
26. Secure Courtyard
27. Secure Wandering Area
28. Shared Patio
29. Service Area
30. Wandering Pathway

Woodside plan allows for social wandering: The looped pathway at *Woodside* (Regnier, 1994, page 156) creates a way for agitated residents to walk without getting lost. Common spaces including a living room, country kitchen, activity room, and great room are located along the corridor.

A common behavior of many dementia residents is incessant wandering from one place to another in the building. Although it is not entirely clear what triggers this response, residents appear to feel lost and are trying to find a place they recognize as home. A looped pathway that allows wanderers to walk around and arrive at the same place from which they departed is reassuring. A circulation pathway like this also promotes walking as a form of exercise. *Social wandering* is a term coined by David Hoglund (Hoglund and Ledewitz, 1999) that describes movement through a more purposeful sequence of spaces that can be designed to increase the quality of that experience. For most dementia residents, wandering is a behavior that is carried out without a lot of thought. For others, the search for something they cannot find may be frustrating and disturbing. Social wandering combines the looped route with a series of interesting destinations. These destinations may involve social interaction, resting, watching, rummaging, or various planned activities.

Five Social Wandering Solutions

The wandering loop that links each of the three bungalows with the great room, fireplace, country kitchen, activity room, and entry veranda at *Woodside Place* in Oakmont, Pennsylvania (Regnier, 1994, page 156) is one of the first recognized applications of this idea. In *Copper Ridge* (page 201), a single-loaded corridor around the central atrium connects the three houses here with activity rooms, window seats, a living room lounge, and access doors to the central atrium. In the *Minna Murra Lodge* in Toowoomba Garden, Queensland Australia, a relatively small building complex of 15 units uses a looped corridor to connect units, dining tables, and residents' rooms to two garden areas (Cohen and Day, 1993). The

Anton Pieckhofje in Haarlem, the Netherlands, has a simple hexagonal donut plan. A single-loaded corridor separates the interior courtyard from the entry doors of each of the six houses there. The looped connecting corridor link several alcoves and a small sitting room that overlooks the central garden. The second floor is family rental housing. *Sunrise of Gahanna*, Ohio, is a 50-unit project with a walking loop that links four separate houses. Like *Copper Ridge* (page 201), it loops an exterior courtyard with attractive glass-covered arcades that overlook the central garden. The walking loop here goes by a ice cream parlor and several activity spaces including access doors to three secured outdoor garden spaces.

Wandering Behavior

For some wanderers, coming to the end of a corridor is confusing. They literally don't know what to do, nor do they understand that turning around would solve the problem. Destination rooms that help them to turn around can continue the pattern back and forth. It is also important to allow residents to wander inside and outside. This is easier to achieve in sunbelt locations but is also a central feature of the *Woodside Place* (Regnier, 1994, page 156) program in the frost belt city of Oakmont, Pennsylvania. *Sundowners syndrome*, a form of agitation that occurs toward the end of the day, may also stimulate the urge to wander.

91
Facilitating Orientation

◄ *Architectural differentiation is most helpful in guiding orientation:* Color coding has limited impact, but selecting an unusual feature like this window box creates a landmark that residents and staff notice and remember. The secret is to use a feature like this only once.

Kevin Lynch, in his book *Image of the City* (1960), talks about the forlorn feeling one experiences when hopelessly lost in an urban context one cannot identify. This is a feeling dementia residents experience every day of their lives. The challenge is how to best keep residents from feeling lost. One of the most useful tools in wayfinding is *architectural differentiation* (Weisman,

1987), which involves the use of a unique object or an eye-catching architectural treatment in a salient location. Cohen and Weisman (1991) illustrate this concept with a large swordfish mounted on a wall that serves as an orientation device in a facility they evaluated. As discussed earlier, a looped pathway can bring order to a facility by linking together salient destinations. A looped pathway doesn't necessarily help residents find their way, but it does keep them from getting lost. The Magic Kingdom at Disneyland has four looped pathways that connect the center of the park with each of the four major park segments (Frontierland, etc.). If you walk long enough, you are bound to find yourself back in a familiar location in the middle of the park in front of Sleeping Beauty's Castle. Some wayfinding techniques, like color coding, are ineffective. The main reason color coding works poorly is its subtlety. Changing one small item like the color of a floor or wall is often not sufficient to call attention to the change.

Orientation Devices Must Not Be Subtle

One of the most important orientation tasks is to make certain that residents know which room belongs to them. Marking a unit entrance cannot rely on the same design with a different color. Each entry door should have something unique that marks it. This problem is often best handled when an attached object or a treatment is salient to the resident. In one Swedish facility, the staff placed a model of a summer house at the end of a hallway to mark a resident's room. The resident had constructed the model, and when he saw it at the end of the corridor, he knew which room belonged to him.

92

Disguising the Exit, Elopement, and Exit Control

◄ *Disguising dementia exit doors:* One effective strategy is to continue the wall covering and chair rail across the exit door. This allows the door to blend in with its surroundings. Locating the door at the rear of the unit, where it is not expected, also helps to maintain its anonymity. ▼

Some dementia residents have a desire to elope from the facility. This problem behavior often dissipates as the resident grows accustomed to life in the new environment. When first relocated, some residents think that their placement is a temporary respite or vacation and deal with the environmental change in that way. A few think that they are in the wrong place and have a strong desire to go back to a more familiar location. Others believe that they have appointments to keep or job responsibilities to honor and must leave. The residents who are successful in escaping are usually bigger and stronger than the norm. They are more able to climb a fence or force open a window. To manage these residents effectively, exit doors should be disguised, windows should be blocked so that they open only 7–9 inches and the building must maintain a secured perimeter.

Locking the Unit

Depending on the licensing category, the building type, and the attitude of local fire officials, different types of locks and exiting strategies are sanctioned. Because specific building codes often don't take into account this

special circumstance, the final solution is often negotiated with local building and fire officials (Hyde, 1995). The most secure system is one that uses a magnetic lock. In this scenario, the door is permanently locked but can be opened by punching in a key code. During a fire emergency, locks are released automatically. In California and other states that sanction R-type construction, a 13-second delayed egress system is normally used. This is less effective, because residents who engage the door latch can open it after 13 seconds. Some fire officials sanction the use of a fenced garden as a refuge. If this is the case, exit doors can open onto a secured outdoor space.

Disguising the Exit

One very effective strategy is to cover exit doors with the same wall covering and trim used on adjacent surfaces. This makes the doors literally disappear. Another strategy is to use plain flush doors and paint them the same color as the adjoining wall. In one Norwegian facility, a light lace curtain was placed in front of the door, with a plant located to one side (see page 34). The curtain could easily be pulled to one side to allow free access into and out of the building. If an exit door is located at the end of a corridor, one strategy is to place the door on the side rather than at the end of the corridor, which makes it less visible by taking it out of the line of sight. In Denmark, dementia facilities are not allowed to be locked for human rights reasons. This has caused a number of safety issues and produced many creative responses to the issue of disguising entry doors.

Lessons Learned from Woodside Place

One of the most interesting lessons learned from the postoccupancy evaluation of *Woodside Place* in Oakmont, Pennsylvania (Regnier, 1994, page 156) was the exiting conflict created by the entry door. The entry door and vestibule are prominent features of the building exterior and are visible from the inside (see page 138 for plan). Residents were attracted to the entry foyer and often watched family members enter and exit from the parking lot. When the door was open, residents who sought to elope slipped away when someone else entered the building. This problem feature was subsequently adjusted in the Copper Ridge design. It is important to find an unobtrusive place for family members to enter and exit the building. This problem is exacerbated by the often emotional exchanges that occur when a family member leaves. It should be easy for people to enter and exit the building without calling attention to it.

93

The Attraction of Activity and Phototropism in Dementia

◀ *Window walls provide visual access to adjacent spaces:* Because residents with memory loss know only what they can see, it is necessary to link rooms visually. This window wall at the *Vidar Clinic* in Järna, Sweden, has the additional benefit of borrowing light from a skylight in the corridor.

In addition to disguising exits, exit control can be managed by zoning the unit carefully. Residents are naturally attracted to activities that involve other people and to natural light from exterior windows. Activities should be planned far away from exit doors that are used regularly by staff and family members. Also, residents's attraction to natural light can be used to advantage by placing activities near windows that overlook a secured garden. By contrast, a darker area adjacent to the exit door may further camouflage it. Placing staff offices and staff work spaces next to the exit door can also guarantee that the staff will be nearby to monitor the exit. The best example of this is the dementia unit in the *Mission Viejo* (page 181) case study. The unit is located directly below the first floor, so elevator connections are very convenient. The unit is entered from the darker interior side, and most activity spaces are oriented to natural light. With careful planning, a facility can be oriented to its own separate world, thus avoiding the frustration of constantly policing the exit doors. Remember the lesson learned at *Woodside Place* (Regnier, 1994, page 156); if the entrance is visible from the inside, if natural light streams through this entry area, and if it is actively used by staff and family members entering and exiting the building, it will be a problem (Silverman, Ricci, et al., 1996).

94

With Dementia You Know Only What You Can See

◄ *Dementia residents need to see their destination:* Half-walls, columns, ceiling soffits, and floor covering create a looped circulation pathway. Major destinations like this dining room are immediately visible at the *Sunrise of Rockville*, Maryland, dementia unit.

It is important to keep in mind that dementia residents often perceive only what is within their immediate visual field. If a solid door is closed, they may have no idea what lies on the opposite side. What is out of sight is literally out of mind. That is why flush windowless doors work for exit control and why clothing and other items, when located behind a solid closet door, are sometimes impossible for a resident to find. For example, the Shaker-inspired plate shelf and wooden pegs mounted on the two walls of a resident's room at *Woodside Place* (Regnier, 1994, page 156) is very effective because it allows residents to see their wardrobe, which is hung in front them. Wire bins in closets also have been reported to be effective, because residents can see items through the wire mesh.

Designs That Reveal What's Behind

Life-skills kitchens with open shelves or cabinet doors with glass faces facilitate residents' participation in meal preparation because they can see exactly what is located in a pantry or upper cabinet. A graduated dressing cabinet with a glass front is also easier for a resident to identify. Transparent window walls that reveal an adjacent room or a half-wall separation is effective in making adjacent spaces more visible to dementia residents. The furniture and the layout of a room can also provide cues about its use. A living room is easier to identify when it is anchored by a fireplace flanked by book shelves with a couch in front. A dining room makes more sense when it is visually connected to a kitchen on one side with a family-size table for eating. An appropriately proportioned room with the right furniture placements imbues a space with meaning, making it easier to understand.

95

Life Skills Activities

◄ *Dementia residents often engage in ADLs:*   This therapeutic approach to program development works effectively with residents who enjoy tasks like setting the table, bussing dishes, and helping with food preparation.

One of the most innovative approaches to using the environment creatively is making the dementia unit feel like the single-family house most residents came from. This is difficult to achieve with a dozen residents. However, the more residents are comfortable in carrying out activities they associate with a residential setting, the more familiar the environment becomes. Making the building more friendly often centers on the design, specification, and placement of furniture and the layout of work/activity spaces like the kitchen and laundry. The more residents feel they are participants in a life centered on familiar tasks, the more secure and comfortable they feel. This is called *ADL programming* because it seeks to achieve unity between the life of the place and the normal daily activities that occur in any independent household.

Northern European Life Skills Philosophy

The northern Europeans in general are more advanced in their use of the two most important normalizing spaces—the kitchen and the laundry. In the kitchen, one must look beyond the stringent health and safety rules to create a setting where residents can freely participate in meal preparation activities. Some facilities have taken the lead by doing this in a comprehensive way. In the *Hogeway* facility in Weesp, the Netherlands, and in the *Ros Anders Gård* (page 215), food is prepared from scratch in a kitchen adjacent to each unit cluster. Thus, the idea of making the meal a meaningful component of the residents' lives is achieved.

Kitchen Life Skills

Kitchen activities are probably the most crucial of these life skills activities because preparing, consuming, and cleaning up after three meals each day absorb a big part of a normal day. When these activities are carried out in a natural way, they have a major impact on how the unit is perceived by guests as well as residents. Residents find

the kitchen a familiar and comfortable place. It is one of those spaces, especially for women, that is linked to habits created by thousands of hours of use. Everyone is familiar with using a kitchen several times a day for meals and snacks.

Kitchen Activities

Many activities can be carried out in a well-designed ADL kitchen, including but not limited to bussing dishes, setting the table, placing dishes in the dishwasher, putting dishes and flatware away in drawers, cleaning up, and preparing food. Food preparation is a little controversial in the United States because of state health codes. In each state, there are restrictions that limit the amount and type of work a resident is allowed to do. Clean-up activities are also very popular. These can include wiping kitchen counters and cleaning the floor using a hand sweeper or broom. In northern Europe, resident-centered activities are encouraged more often. This is especially true in Denmark and Sweden, where the therapeutic value of these activities is clearly seen. The *Ros Anders Gård* (page 215) and *Virranranta* (page 206) facilities also use the kitchen as an ad hoc nurse's station where medications, charts, notebooks, and residents' records are kept.

Examples of Kitchens in the United States

In *Copper Ridge* (page 201) an open kitchen was designed with appliances that serve two adjacent dining rooms. A combination of residential and commercial equipment was sanctioned here by Maryland state officials to support a plan to normalize activities. Placing the dish, glass, and flatware storage, as well as the dishwasher and the refrigerator, in a separate area in the kitchen makes it easier to encourage residents to participate in ADLs. Placing the more dangerous appliances like the stove, range, servery, coffeemaker, and toaster in a more isolated staff-controlled part of the kitchen increases safety. Appliances including the stove and food disposal should be on kill switches that are kept safe behind a locked door. Some states require NSF (commercially rated) appliances. These are designed for commercial applications and are often difficult to find in a noncommercial finish.

Examples of Kitchens in Northern Europe

The preparation of food from raw materials, common in northern Europe, requires more equipment and space than in the United States, where food is often prepared in a nearby commercial kitchen and then moved precooked to a serving kitchen. The *Ros Anders Gård* (page 215) contains a number of special features. The kitchen has a central island with a grill. Food prepared here can be easily moved in any direction. An interim shelf, located between the countertop and the upper cabinet, is used for convenience items that are left out for easy reference. The dishwasher and stove are both located on platforms approximately 12 inches from the floor in order to make it easier for staff to use them without bending over. Roll-out drawers are located below the counter to ease the transfer of heavy cookware and reduce the need to stoop or bend. Glass-faced cabinet doors make it easier to identify equipment and food. Under-cabinet lighting is used in combination with direct and indirect light fixtures to increase the light level so that it is easier to work.

Laundry Life Skills

Residents also find helping staff with the cleaning of table clothes and napkins to be a satisfying, enjoyable group activity. The most popular activities are placing dirty laundry in the washing machine and folding clean laundry from the dryer. The warm clothing from the dryer feels good to most residents. The sorting and folding of laundry as a group activity can also be a social experience and an opportunity for telling stories and reminiscing. In order for this activity to be most effective, the laundry should be in a central place rather than located at the back of the house. A central location also allows staff to do laundry at night while being on call for residents who might need them. Caution should be exercised in controlling access to laundry detergents and chemicals. A common method is to have automatic dispensing equipment that makes it safer while measuring out the exact amount of laundry detergent needed.

Watching and Doing the Laundry

Doing personal laundry with family members can also be an enjoyable shared activity. Machines for personal and professional use can be intermixed. However, dealing with incontinent laundry may require a machine that operates at a higher water temperature or uses a chemical additive. This type of equipment is often necessary to kill the bacteria from human waste and may need to be located behind a locked door. Sometimes residents enjoy watching the staff and other residents do the laundry. Highly confused or impaired residents might prefer to watch because they cannot easily participate.

Vanity Table for Applying Makeup

Activities such as combing one's hair, putting on makeup, applying lipstick, painting fingernails, testing different perfumes, trying on hats and scarves, and general primping are interesting and fun for many people—especially women. A vanity life skills activity involves a small table with an attached mirror and two or three chairs. If convenient, a clothes tree or pegs suitable for hanging clothing, hats, and scarves should be placed nearby (see page 117). In assisted living, the term *"grooming"* is often used to describe this process in a lifeless, clinical, unimaginative way. Celebrating the act of making residents more attractive elevates a mundane task to an enjoyable activity. This life skill activity can be centered on one person while several others watch and wait for their turn.

Vanity Table Life Skills

Putting on makeup and primping can also lend itself to volunteer or family participation. For most women, putting on makeup is a creative process that doesn't require special training. Because makeup products are thought of as part of a personal hygiene regimen, sharing lipstick and eye shadow may not appeal to everyone. Therefore, having a small, portable container of personal beauty products for each resident may work better. The vanity table can also come in handy for children's face-painting activities during a family event. The ultimate outcome, beautifying the person, is an intrinsically satisfying experience for both the resident and the assistant. This is an activity most staff are enthusiastic about because it is enjoyable and creative.

Vintage and Special-Purpose Clothing

The use of hats, scarves, sweaters, coats, and shawls is popular because these items can be easily worn over street clothing. Dressing up can be a source of spontaneous fun. Hats are particularly effective because they are easy to wear and may relate to specific roles or recall specific places. Wearing hats or trading them with staff and family members can create situations of spontaneous participation that are memorable and enjoyable. Vintage clothing, including military uniforms, and garb for special occasions, like a formal dance or a wedding, can be effective as an aid to reminiscence. For men, participation in military service, and for women, wedding day festivities, are often deeply held salient memories. Very little equipment is needed beyond a range of memory-provoking items, a clothes tree, a shelf with pegs, and a place to sit down. Role playing and whimsical behavior are enhanced by costumes. Different fabrics and furs with soft and coarse textures are also stimulating to the touch. These artifacts are also very interesting to look at and are effective for decorating walls.

Typewriter/Calculator Desk Life Skills

These life skill activities are particularly effective for residents who have worked at a desk all of their lives. Residents who have held jobs as accountants, secretaries, and clerks have spent a lifetime working with numbers and documents and often enjoy the opportunity to practice these past behaviors. Adding a column of numbers or retyping a letter can be very satisfying, especially when they are anxious and are looking for something to do. A desk with an old typewriter, calculator, and/or task lamp can transform a piece of furniture into a workstation. For others, the desk can be a convenient place for writing a letter or signing a card.

Sports Locker Life Skills

A locker that contains sports paraphernalia and active exercise equipment can be a focus for a midmorning exercise activity that gets everyone moving. Located in a wide corridor or a small lounge, the locker can contain many different pieces of equipment. For example, a dart board with "nerf" (Velcro) darts, a collection of plastic bowling pins, and a volleyball net that can be stretched across the room for use with a balloon or an inflatable ball are all possibilities. Exercise equipment can be stored in the locker when not in use and assembled when an activity is carried out. The sports locker itself can be festive, with pennants, stickers, and paraphernalia that represent local university, high school, or professional sports teams. Exercise is appealing to everyone, but the sports theme might be particularly interesting to older men. Baseball cards, videos of special moments in sports, and sports paraphernalia (baseball gloves and autographed baseballs) can be particularly meaningful to men in their eighties. In the future, more women will also find these items interesting and thought-provoking.

Work Bench Life Skill

Men are in the minority in most dementia units, and it is important to have some activities that appeal to them. One effective idea is the creation of a work bench where a resident can carry out various projects. These can be simple tasks like painting a bird house or sanding a piece of wood, or they might be more elaborate craft activities. The work bench can have a stool, a vise, a few tools, and an industrial-looking light source. Tools should be reviewed for safety since residents have been known to use screwdrivers and pliers to dismantle windows and garden gates.

96

Home Within a Home

◄ *Large table in the dementia kitchen is popular:*   This table in the *Sunrise at Westtown*, New Jersey, seats six to eight residents and is used for snacks, for small messy activities, and for people who require frequent reminders to continue to eat.

There are three primary design approaches to the placement and distribution of dwelling units for memory-impaired residents: (1) the dedicated dementia building, (2) the integration of physically and mentally impaired residents, and (3) the continuum or "home" within a home model. Each approach has advantages and disadvantages (Regnier, 1997a). The dedicated dementia building is a stand-alone dementia setting. Residents enter the program after a diagnosis of dementia has been made, and all residents in the building are memory impaired. Examples of this model include *Sunrise of Richmond* (page 196), *Copper Ridge* (page 201), *Harbour House* (page 211), and *Humlehusene* (page 220). The integrated unit, which is less popular today, mainstreams residents with mental and physical impairments in the same building. This model is represented by *Humanitas* (page 158) and *Postiljonen* (page 224). The home within a home model involves the creation of a separate unit cluster for memory-impaired residents in a secured wing or floor of an assisted living building. Examples include *Wilhelmiina* (page 163), *Goddard House* (page 169), *Sunrise of Mission Viejo* (page 181), *Sunrise of Bellevue* (page 191), *Crown Cove* (page 187), *Virranranta* (page 206) and *Ros Anders Gård* (page 215). This is a popular approach that combines the positive attributes of the integrated and dedicated models.

The Integrated Dementia Unit

This housing philosophy is losing favor. During the past decade, a lot has been learned about how to treat residents with memory loss. We are also more aware of the conflicts that occur when the mentally impaired and mentally alert are intermixed. The Danes were strong believers in this approach until recently. Some U.S. providers also believe that mixing the two populations creates benefits for the less mentally capable by placing them in a more stimulating context. This is the approach that most nursing homes take in dealing with memory-impaired residents. Mixing the populations works best with small groups in which no more than a third of the

persons are demented. In general, mixing dementia residents with noncognitively impaired people can often be upsetting to both groups. Staff training efforts and therapeutic interventions associated with the special needs of dementia residents are often harder to accomplish in this context. Security is sometimes a problem, because the security system necessary for dementia residents may exert too much control over assisted living residents.

The Dedicated Dementia Building

These buildings are typically located by themselves in the community. Sometimes they share a campus connection to assisted living or another level of care. The building size can vary from a small remodeled single-family house that supports 6–8 people to facilities that accommodate 60 residents. In northern Europe, it is common to have four to six separate clusters of 6–8 people each (a total of 24–48 residents) sharing one building. In general, a building of this size has enough residents to justify special staff training and more sophisticated program interventions. Residents are normally separated into smaller family-style dwelling unit clusters. In the United States, these clusters are typically larger, with 12–15 residents. This model doesn't work as well with lightly impaired dementia residents who could live in an assisted living environment with a little help. Even though clusters are often separated, it is hard to keep residents from mixing. The limitations of demented residents may make it more difficult for family members to visit if secluded spaces are not available for visitation.

The "Home Within a Home"

This model has some of the positive attributes of the previous two models without many of their problems. The most positive feature is that residents with light mental impairment can be moved into an assisted living environment and later moved to a secured dementia unit when they require more specialized care. A smaller number of dementia residents can be sheltered in a larger building housing assisted living residents. This makes it easier to achieve minimum economies of scale for services, administration, and meals while still maintaining a relatively small dementia unit with no more than 20–25 residents. This setting works best when the percentage of dementia residents is no more than 25–35 percent of the total population. The dementia unit maintains an adjunct status and doesn't dominant the image and character of the building. Entering the dementia unit from the inside of an assisted living building works best for security and for food service delivery.

97

Snoezelen and the Emphasis on Sensuality

◄ *Snoezelen bathing seeks to make the experience a positive one:*   With soft music, candles, dimmable lights, and aromatherapy, the snoezelen bathing room at *Hogeway* in Weesp, the Netherlands, uses sensory techniques to communicate with dementia residents.

Snoezelen is a Dutch word that means "sniff and doze." This communications strategy was adapted from Danish methods that were being used with highly developmentally disabled individuals. It is particularly effective with residents who have lost their ability to communicate verbally and must rely on other emotional and sensory modalities. Some of the most effective and popular snoezelen approaches include the use of (1) music, (2) aromas, (3) bathing and massage, (4) visual displays with lights, images, and bubbles, and (5) dolls and stuffed animals. These are used in conjunction with verbal cues to help residents feel more relaxed and secure.

Snoezelen Process

Snoezelen normally takes place in a small, quiet room. Projection equipment creates abstract, colorful images that are pleasing and visually stimulating. The Dutch utilize a large platform water bed, inviting residents to lay down and relax. The ceiling and the walls are used to display projected images. Soothing music or music that is especially salient or memorable to the resident is often played (see page 241). Aromatherapy can also be carried out in the room while soft music is played. Aromas that have meaning to the resident are selected. The sense of smell and its connection to salient memories may be intact even though the person is unable to communicate verbally. Bathing, with a hydrotherapy massage, might occur in a room that can be darkened for visual displays and music. The added element of a hydro-massage can enhance relaxation. Musical melodies, because they tap one of the last remaining remnants of cognitive function, are also particularly effective in triggering deep-seated memories. Snoezelen rooms are becoming popular in the United States as quiet rooms where agitated residents can relax and individual therapies can be pursued.

98

Access to Outdoor Spaces for People with Dementia

◄ *Woodside garden with a porch can be seen from the living room/dining room:* The integration of indoor and outdoor space at *Woodside* is one of its most successful features

Access to an outdoor garden from the dementia unit is popular in all climates and ecological environments. In northern Europe, where it is cold much of the year, outdoor spaces are highly appreciated and heavily used in late spring, summer, and early fall. Residents who are frustrated and/or feel trapped indoors often find release by walking around outside. Unimpaired access to a garden is very effective for some residents who may go outdoors anytime during the day or night. Some buildings have reported success with the placement of a clothing rack of hats, coats, golashes, scarves, and gloves next to the exit door. This encourages residents to dress up for cold or inclement weather. Being able to see out into a garden can also calm residents. Safety is a paramount concern in the design of an outside garden.

Dementia Garden Fence

A fence should be at least 6 to 8 feet in height, with an exit door located on the perimeter of the fence that is disguised so that residents won't recognize it. The fence can be spaced or solid. A spaced fence can be distracting if residents see activity in the background, such as in a parking lot or walkway around the building. Solid fences are often safer and more popular but, a solid 8-foot fence can be visually restrictive. If an 8-foot fence is selected, then the bottom 6 feet should be stylistically different from the top 2 feet. Six-foot solid fences are perhaps the most popular height. Only about one in ten residents are tempted to think about elopement. Nevertheless, it is necessary to make certain that the fence design does not make it easily scalable. Horizontal supports should be carefully located so that they cannot be used to climb the fence. Some fire districts allow a perimeter fence to be padlocked if there is enough refuge space for residents to assemble 50 feet or more from the edge of the building.

Layout of a Dementia Garden

The garden should have a well-defined looped pathway that allows residents to walk on their own for exercise. A figure eight shape is popular because it provides several different loop options of varying lengths. In optimum circumstances, doors to the garden will be kept unlocked during the day so that residents can exit and enter freely on their own. If the garden is relatively large, then the door from which residents exit the building to enter the garden should be easy to identify from outside. Places for birds, butterflies, squirrels, and other forms of wildlife should be available. A raised planter box can be used to support a gardening activity program. A larger program would benefit from a potting bench, a water source, and a storage place for garden tools, mulch, and soil. Gardening is a very popular pastime with both men and woman. Plants should be selected that are safe to ingest.

Dementia Balcony Above the First Floor

If a dementia unit is located above the first floor, then access to a large balcony of at least 300–400 SF is important. This should be outfitted with seating, activity spaces, and adequate shade control. A covered porch is a well-appreciated feature. The perimeter walls of the balcony surround should be high enough to discourage residents from attempting to climb over them. The generally accepted height for this type of containment wall is 7 to 8 feet. A horizontal trellis can be detailed at the top, making it more difficult for residents who might attempt an escape (see color insert). In addition to a balcony, a securable garden on the first floor should be available where residents can be supervised during the day. The same space can also serve as a larger place for social get-togethers.

99

Environmental Response to Agitation

◄ *High-intensity lighting used to combat sundowner's syndrome:*   At the *Wilhelmiina* (page 163) this 200-SF living room in the dementia unit is outfitted with 28 full-spectrum lights to overcome problems associated with sundowners' syndrome

Some residents are likely to be agitated even in the best circumstances. The best solution is to have a relatively small number of residents in each decentralized cluster. Northern European clusters of six to eight residents are almost always quiet and relaxed. The other environmental strategy is to have plenty of square footage for each resident. In unit clusters of 12 to 15 residents, it is not uncommon to have at least 8000–9000 gross SF of residential and common space. Another strategy is to include a quiet room where residents who are upset can be taken to calm down. The snoezelen room described earlier is particularly effective for this purpose. When not in use for this purpose, the room can be employed for staff training or family conferences.

Sundowner's Syndrome

This is a largely unexplained phenomenon that occurs near the end of the day. Residents typically become agitated as the sun sets late in the afternoon. Some believe that providing additional light to a unit during these hours may help to ease the problem. In *Wilhelmiina* (page 163), several spaces within this service house, as well as the living room in the dementia unit, are outfitted with dozens of additional down-light fixtures. The amount of light is often doubled or tripled in an effort to reduce the

agitated behaviors that result. It is also common throughout Scandinavia to specify full-spectrum lighting, which is used during the long cold, dark winters to counteract depression. It is unclear how effective this strategy is in responding to the problem.

Validation Therapy

The other strategy that is becoming popular in the United States is the use of validation as a therapy. Developed and described in Naomi Feil's book *The Validation Breakthrough* (1993), this philosophy is the opposite of reality orientation. Instead of being confronted with the facts that reflect contemporary circumstances, the validation approach encourages residents to construct their own version of reality. If residents have a belief structure that is intact but not correct (for example, a resident may be living as she did in 1945), the staff is encouraged to support those assumptions. Rather than constantly correcting residents, as is common in reality orientation, they are encouraged to work with residents to understand the world the way the residents perceive it. The staff work with residents to reconcile major inconsistencies. In this approach, life skills stations and outdoor spaces can be wonderful props for implementing validation ideas.

100

Dementia Dwelling Unit Features

◄ *White fixtures stand out against a gray background:* Creating better contrast in the bathroom makes it easier for dementia residents to notice fixtures, especially the commode.

Certain dwelling unit and common space design features that have been tested appear to be useful for residents with dementia. Some are best for providing orientation support, while others can help with ADLs such as dressing and toileting. Dutch doors at the entrance to each dwelling unit have been used in numerous projects with mixed success. In the best circumstances, they allow the unit to be open to the corridor while still providing some sense of privacy and protection. Opening the unit to the corridor makes it easier for residents to find their own room. It also encourages residents to stay in their rooms to be monitored easily by the staff. Windows into the unit also work well for this purpose. At night, staff don't have to enter the unit to check on residents.

Dressing Aids

One of the desires of staff is to encourage dementia residents to dress themselves. In the beginning, a staff member may lay out clothing on the bed in the appropriate order. Later, a graduated dressing cabinet might be useful (see page 129). There are many possible designs for such cabinets. A new armoire manufactured by the Kimball furniture company consists of two 24-inch inch compartments. One compartment holds hanging clothing. The other compartment contains the clothing the resident will be wearing that day. It is laid out laterally in reverse order (underclothing first) to facilitate the process of ordering clothing layers. These arrangements are effective for some residents at a stage during the disease process when this level of cueing is necessary. Wire drawers have been used in closets to reveal the content of each drawer.

Cueing Toileting

Residents with dementia are often incontinent and literally forget to toilet themselves. One method that has been used with some success is the placement of a motion detector switch near the door of the bathroom. As the resident walks by, the motion triggers the switch, which turns on the bathroom light. When the dementia resident sees the bathroom, he or she notices the commode and thinks about toileting. In conjunction with this is the use of a darker paint that contrasts with the white china of the toilet and the lavatory. Sliding barn or pocket doors are also useful in this regard, because they can stay open most of the time. When privacy is desired, they can be easily closed.

Copper Ridge in Sykesville, MD, the central courtyard (Photo: Courtesy Robert Ruschak).

PART III
CASE STUDIES

The ways that a house lets you move, with grace or
confusion, the shelter it puts around you, the things that
it brings to your attention, all establish a substratum of
meaning that accompanies the life that you live there.

—Charles Moore, 1974, p. 143

Case studies are a useful way of learning about the qualities and characteristics of a building type. In contrast to guidelines or directives, case studies utilize a unique integrated, tangible example to communicate a fully realized idea. Even though each example has its limitations based on concept, program, site, and occupant type, it is a fully functioning, holistic entity. The way each building is organized, from the entry sequence to the back of the house, represents a vision of how each architect, along with the client, interpreted ideas about the form of assisted living. In contrast to skilled nursing environments in the United States, which are code and formula driven, assisted living environments demonstrate a range of approaches to the problem of supporting older, mentally and physically frail people. Included are examples that range from nursing homes (*Postijonen*, page 224) that look like assisted living environments to housing and service models (*Gynegemosegard*, page 174, and *Humanitas Bergweg*, (page 158), that are designed to support very frail residents in an apartment-style environment. Each case study embodies ideas about caregiving and architectural form.

PRECEDENTS CAN BE READ LIKE A BOOK

Precedents are useful tools for understanding the application of ideas and techniques. It is almost as if each building, like a book, has a story to tell and a lesson to teach. Knowing how to conduct a Post-Occupancy Evaluation (POE) is like learning a language that allows you to "read" buildings and thus capture what goes beyond the appearance of a building and its functional characteristics. In my experience, visiting each of the 100 buildings I saw in 1991 and the 95 buildings I saw in 1999 was like holding a conversation with a collection of different people. I saw myself as an observer/interviewer gleaning from each example its raison d'être. In that way, each building is like a person with a unique biography influenced by his or her location, financial circumstances, surrounding culture, and personal aspirations. Each building project (environment and staff) seeks to provide older frail people with a better life, and each one has been designed to do that in a purposeful way. Biographies teach us about the similarities and differences between us and other people. In a similar way, a well-described case study can allow us to compare, contrast, and examine the strategies that brought the project to fruition and to understand it better in the context of other settings that strive to achieve similar goals.

FIFTEEN CASE STUDIES

In this examination of 15 buildings, an effort has been made to describe the physical environment through plans, photographs, and statistics, as well as through a description of how the buildings operate for the older person. Knowledge of the characteristics of the residents is also helpful in understanding how and for whom buildings operate. Case studies that focus on just the physical characteristics of the setting miss the important transactional relationship between the environment, the residents, their families, and the staff. Knowing more about the characteristics of residents can help us better appreciate the logic behind design decisions and allow us to contemplate how successful the building has been in enriching the lives of residents.

Each case study has the following format: General characteristics of the building and the residents are described first, flanked by an "establishing shot" of the building. This is followed by a summary description of the building and a list of seven to ten project features. Interspersed are drawings ranging from the site plan to a typical unit plan. Emphasis is placed on the most important floor plan, which is usually that of the entry or ground floor. Usually one or two additional photographs are used to describe special features of the building. Additional cross-referenced photographs of case studies are used to illustrate points made in Chapters 4 to 13.

GENERAL CHARACTERISTICS OF THE CASE STUDIES

These case studies are from five countries. Seven of them are from the United States, representing the Northeast, the South, the Midwest, the Northwest, and the West. All of the domestic projects have distinguished themselves by winning professional recognition in awards programs including those of the National Home Builders Association (NCOSH), the Assisted Living Federation of America (ALFA), Contemporary Long Term Care (CLTC) and Hospitality Design (HD). Several, like *Copper Ridge* (page 201), *Sunrise of Bellevue* (page 191), and the *Sunrise of Richmond* (page 196), have won multiple awards. In northern Europe, three studies are from Finland, two are from Denmark, two are from Sweden, and one is from the Netherlands. These projects were selected on the basis of their status as successful projects with explicit architectural and caregiving lessons to share. They are 8 of the 95 projects I visited in 1999. Selections were based on the desire to represent cultural, contextual (urban vs. small town), scale (14 to 195 units), and stylistic differences. Appendix A lists 100 noteworthy buildings that have been selected from both the 1991 and 1999 investigations. These represent the "best of the best" and were selected from over 200 buildings visited.

The following tables identify 20 characteristics associated with each building. These can be further subdivided into 6 general characteristics, 5 characteristics of the building design or the services provided, and 9 social characteristics of the residents of each building. The case studies are rank ordered by the size of the building, starting with the largest building (Humanitas), which has 195 units, and ending with the Metsatahti, a 14-unit mixed day-care and elderly project in central Finland. The average building size is 72.6 units, with 70 units as the median size. The similarities and differences among the buildings are immediately apparent.

BUILDING CHARACTERISTICS

The sample is drawn from a range of settings, but the majority of the buildings are located in suburban areas of Europe and the United States. The remainder are split between small town and cities. There are seven different types of housing arrangements, with the home within a home combination of assisted living and dementia common to 5 of the 15 cases studies. Building shapes range in complexity, with the simple L shape utilized in three projects. There is great variety in building configurations, with atrium, courtyard, multiple building, X, C, and square parti shapes represented. Building heights range from 1 to 12 stories. A third of the buildings are one story. Two- and three-story buildings are also popular, with three buildings in each category. The majority of the buildings were completed since 1996.

As the table indicates, studio-size units of 250–300 SF are the most prevalent unit. The average size of the 1138 units surveyed is 436 SF. A few buildings, like *Humanitas* (page 158) and *Gyngemosegård* (page 174), have much larger unit sizes. Without these two projects, the average unit size would be 342 SF. All but one of the European projects offer meals or have an adjacent service house or day center that provides meals to people living in the neighborhood. By contrast, only a few of the U.S. projects provide direct services to people in the community. In the United States, most assisted living facilities allow family and friends to take a meal with residents. All the U.S. facilities provide only assisted living services except for *Copper Ridge* (page 201), which also has an adjacent nursing home.

In northern Europe, several buildings are designed to support both the health care and personal care needs of residents. The *Wilhelmiina* (page 183) is not unlike a continuing-care retirement community, with several different types of care located on the same site. *Humanitas* (page 158) represents an "apartment for life" philosophy. It supports residents with a range of frailty levels, from totally independent residents to bedridden residents receiving nursing care services in large, independent apartments. The Postiljonen (page 224) is a nursing home that is designed to the same standards as a U.S. assisted living project.

RESIDENT CHARACTERISTICS

As the following table indicates, most buildings have a uniformly frail population with an average age of between 82 and 86. However, the *Gyngemosegård* (page 174) and *Humanitas* (page 158) buildings appeal to a wider range of older residents and thus have a lower average age (75 and 80, respectively). Residents of *Copper Ridge* (page 201) are also younger, due perhaps to the buildings' emphasis on attracting younger people with dementia. The age ranges in all 15 buildings vary by 50 years, from age 54 to age 104. Due to the average seven-year longevity difference between men and women, the majority of the population in all buildings consists of single women. The large number of couples in the *Humanitas* (page 158) and *Gyngemosegård* (page 174) buildings contributes in part to the younger average age of the residents.

In terms of the level of assistance needed and the general level of service provided, there are some major differences among projects. As might be expected, the two projects with the youngest populations have the lowest percentage of need, as expressed by indicators like bathing and toileting assistance. Also, projects that are designated primarily for people with dementia have very high needs for bathing assistance, toileting help, and help for residents with general incontinence. With a few exceptions, the projects follow the ratios introduced in Chapter 2, where approximately 60 percent of residents were noted to experience problems with bathing assistance, 50 percent to have difficulties with cognitive impairment, 40 percent to require dressing assistance, and 30 percent to need toileting assistance. However, the projects are very diverse, representing quite a range of differences on all measures of resident competence and need. For example, 1–25 percent of the residents in the 15 buildings use a wheelchair, and 31–100 percent of residents require help with bathing.

The 15 buildings surveyed are rank ordered by size, with the largest buildings first. Reading the descriptions and examining the plans should provide a snapshot of each environment and the sample of all 15 should provide a wide range of examples that can stimulate your thinking about the types of models available.

Design Characteristics of Case Study Buildings

Building	Unit Mix	Unit Size	Community Services	Community Meals	HCS/ALS
1. Humanitas	195 1-bdr	750	Yes	Yes	ALS/HCS
2. Wilhelmiina	60 studios	320	Yes	Yes	ALS/HCS
	48 rehab	250			
	26 dementia	250			
	37 service flats	550			
3. Goddard Hse	37 studios	350	No	F+F only	ALS
	34 1-bdr	450			
	4 2-bdr	600			
	40 dementia	300			
4. Gyngemosegård	56 1-bdr	600	Yes	Yes	ALS
	20 2-bdr	725			
	12 3-bdr	850			
	12 co-housing	300			
5. Sunrise of Mission Viejo	38 studios	325	No	F+F only	ALS
	24 1-bdr	550			
	24 companion	450			
6. Crown Cove	75 studios	400	No	F+F only	ALS
7. Sunrise of Bellevue	40 studios	315	No	F+F only	ALS
	15 1-bdr	525			
	15 companion	415			
8. Sunrise of Richmond	32 studios	300	No	F+F only	ALS
	12 1-bdr	500			
	26 companion	425			
9. Copper Ridge	60 studios	200	Day care	F+F only	ALS/HCS
10. Virranranta	40 studios	225	Yes	Yes	ALS/HCS
	10 1-bdr	475			
11. Harbour House	36 studios	268	Lrng. cntr.	F+F only	ALS
	8 companion	412			
12. Ros Anders Gård	40 studios	300	Home care	F+F only	ALS
13. Humlehusene	24 studios	300	Yes	F+F only	ALS
14. Postiljonen	24 studios	325	No	F+F only	ALS/HCS
15. Metsätähti	12 studios	300	Yes	Yes	ALS
	2 1-bdr	450			

ALS = Assisted Living Services are provided.

ALS/HCS = Assisted Living and Health Care (Nursing home) Services are provided.

F+F only = Friends and family only are welcome to take meals.

General Characteristics of Case Study Buildings

Building	Location	No. of units	Context S/U/R	Housing Type	Bldg Shape	Number of Stories	Year Completed
1. Humanitas	Rotterdam, NE	195	U	Apts for life	Atrium	12	1996
2. Wilhelmiina	Helsinki, FI	123	U	Service house	Complex	8	1995
3. Goddard Hse	Brookline, MA	115	U/S	AL + dem	U + L	3	1996
4. Gyngemosegård	Herlev, DK	100	S	Apts + service hse	20 bldgs	2	1993
5. Sunrise of	Mission Viejo, CA	86	S	AL + dem	X	2/3	1998
6. Crown Cove	Corona Del Mar, CA	75	S	AL + dem	C	5	1999
7. Sunrise of	Bellevue, WA	70	S	AL + dem	L	4	1998
8. Sunrise of	Richmond, VA	70	S	AL + dem	H	1	1999
9. Copper Ridge	Sykesville, MD	60	R	Dementia	3 U's	1	1994
10. Virranranta	Kiruvesi, FI	50	R	Service house	Spine	1	1992
11. Harbour House	Greendale, WI	44	S	Dementia	X	2	1999
12. Ros Anders Gård	Vesterhaninge, SW	40	S	AL + dem	L	3	1999
13. Humlehusene	Albertslund, DK	24	S	Dementia	L	1	1997
14. Postiljonen	Holliviken, SW	24	R	Nursing home	Courtyard	2	1994
15. Metsätähti	Hankasalmi, FI	14	R	Service house	Spine	1	1990

U = Urban

S = Suburban

R = Rural/Small town

Social Characteristics of Case Study Buildings

Building	Average Age	Age Range	Number of Residents	% of Couples	% Need Bathing Help	% Cognitively Impaired	% Incontinent	% Need Toileting	% Wheelchair
1. Humanitas,	80	55–96	250	44%	36%	10%	NA	27%	18%
2. Wilhelmiina	85	NA	178	NA	100%	NA	NA	40%	NA
3. Goddard Hse	86	62–96	120	8%	83%	38%	18%	25%	8%
4. Gyngemosegård	75	70–95	64	41%	31%	15%	NA	8%	18%
5. Sunrise of Mission Viejo	86	75–98	85	19%	57%	63%	42%	54%	21%
6. Crown Cove	87	56–96	75	11%	40%	49%	37%	NA	21%
7. Sunrise of Bellevue	84	62–98	81	17%	65%	36%	43%	58%	14%
8. Sunrise of Richmond	84	67–98	81	17%	51%	30%	31%	37%	23%
9. Copper Ridge	77	54–93	60	0%	60%	100%	25%	40%	5%
10. Virranranta	80	68–104	60	3%	100%	27%	38%	80%	10%
11. Harbour House	83	71–96	36	0%	100%	100%	50%	70%	1%
12. Ros Anders Gård	82	60–92	40	10%	75%	45%	62%	62%	13%
13. Humlehusene	82	73–97	24	0%	38%	100%	48%	38%	25%
14. Postiljonen	85	61–94	24	0%	58%	63%	67%	67%	46%
15. Metsätähti	83	65–97	14	0%	100%	22%	43%	57%	14%

14

HUMANITAS BERGWEG

Rotterdam, the Netherlands

Architect   EGM architecten bv | Dordrecht, the Netherlands
Sponsor   Stichting Humanitas

Building Characteristics

Number of units	195
Number of stories	12
Context	Urban
Housing type	Apartments for life
Building parti/shape	Atrium
Unit mixture	195 one bedroom
Size of most common unit (average)	750 SF
Community facilities	Yes
Community-accessible meals	Yes
Date of completion	April 1996

Resident Characteristics

Average age	80
Number of residents	250
Number of couples/men/women	42 men
	98 women
	55 couples
Age range	55–96
Percent requiring bathing help	36 percent
Percent requiring toileting help	27 percent
Percent incontinent	NA
Percent wheelchair bound	18 percent
Percent cognitively impaired	10 percent

Axonometric building plan: Access to the second-floor public atrium is through a pair of escalators located at the north corner of the building. Three stories of single-loaded units overlook both sides of the central atrium. (Courtesy EGM architecten bv)

SUMMARY

Humanitas Bergweg has been classified as a "levensloopbestendige" or apartment for life project. The basic idea is to create a housing and service system that supports older frail people in a normal apartment. The building is located in the central city of Rotterdam. In the surrounding neighborhood, 27 percent of the population is over the age of 65. The 195-unit housing development has a dramatic form that is recognizable from the freeway several miles away. It consists of two housing blocks separated by a conditioned atrium. One housing block is a tower that rises from 4 to 12 stories in its 450-foot length. The other is a four-story, single-loaded corridor housing block. The atrium is three stories in height and is open on both sides to single-loaded corridors. A third of the population receive nursing care, a third receive assisted living, and a third receive no helping services. The rooms are designed to be modified as residents age in place and need more support.

The bathroom is large enough to accommodate not only a wheelchair but a stretcher bather as well. The philosophy of care encourages residents to be highly independent. Residents are asked to take as much responsibility as possible for their self-care needs. Given the emphasis on independence, management believes that the third of the population that receives nursing care services lives far more independently than they would if they were in a nursing home. The three types of residents are scattered throughout the complex rather than segregated on separate floors or in one particular area of the building. The atrium is a public space open to everyone in the neighborhood. A restaurant, lounge, and bar are available for residents and community members, along with an array of professionals such as doctors, physical therapists, and occupational therapists.

Project Features

The "Apartments for Life" Philosophy is Advocated

The apartment for life idea is gaining strength in the Netherlands, which has had a history since World War II of placing older residents in relatively small service flats. This new approach allows residents to move to an apartment and stay there as long as they live. It is particularly appealing to couples who want to stay together, especially if one of them is chronically ill. Residents adhere to a "use it or lose it" philosophy and are admonished when they ask for help in tasks they can carry out themselves. The "apartment for life" philosophy extends the idea of "op maat" or the tailoring of services to the needs of the individual. Care managers are employed to

Central atrium is a public place: The atrium is a reverse bowstring truss structure covered by translucent glass. Landscape features, bridges, a restaurant, a soft-seating lounge, a koi pond, and a bistro bar are a part of this lively, light-filled space. (Photo: Marcel Van Kerckhoven)

Key
1. Escalator
2. Atrium
3. Restaurant
4. Living Room/Lounge
5. Offices

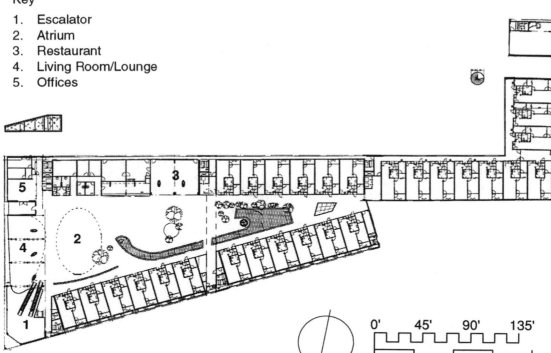

First-floor plan: The triangular theme present in the building's massing is also represented in the floor-plan configuration. Single-loaded units surround three sides of the central atrium. (Courtesy EGM architecten bv)

coordinate care from a variety of sources, including spouses, friends, volunteers, and family members. Home and health care agencies that operate in the building provide formal services.

The Building Was Created as a Neighborhood Center with Housing Attached

The site was formerly a hospital. The neighborhood has many services located within walking distance of the building. The building concept centers on the creation of a large public space where everyone, including people from the neighborhood, is welcome. This atrium is located on the second floor, above a grocery store. The grocery store has a strong retail presence on the street level. Escalators on the northern corner of the site transport participants up to the atrium floor. The restaurant, lounge, and bar located here are open to everyone. Residents can take meals in their own rooms or they can come down to the restaurant. The units are mostly one-bedroom suites with a full kitchen. Although these are rental apartments, Humanitas is currently developing other projects where the units will be sold. Behind the

grocery store on the ground floor and accessible by elevator from the dwelling units are a clinic, therapy office, and day-care center. These services are shared by residents in the building and older people from the surrounding neighborhood.

The Covered Atrium Is Visible from the Units

The atrium is the main meeting space for everyone and resembles a shopping mall. Reverse steel bowstring trusses support glass roof panels. Elevators are centralized, and bridges connect the two sides. The atrium floor is dotted with tables and chairs. The atrium also contains a fountain, a 52-foot koi pond, and mailboxes for residents. It has an open plan, with exotic plant materials designed to be seen from the single-loaded corridors that surround and overlook it. Opening the atrium to the public caused problems at the beginning, when vagrants and drug users frequented it. However, management was committed to keeping the atrium an open public space rather than a private one. Eventually these problems were resolved, and the atrium is highly successful today.

Care and Services Are Geared to Support an Aging in Place Strategy

The approach to this care philosophy relies on separating housing and services. This is done to deinstitutionalize the setting and to open it to a range of residents: rich and poor, healthy and sick, and young and old. Management believes in helping residents do things for themselves—often referred to as "helping with our hands behind our backs." They also believe that too much care is worse than too little. This system works well because it takes advantage of assistance from a spouse, family members, friends, or volunteers. It generally keeps care costs low and keeps residents more motivated to live an independent life. Residents and their families work with a care manager who coordinates needed services. If residents need nursing home care, it is delivered by a home care provider. Some services are planned, while others are ordered on an as-needed basis through the emergency call system. Hospice and day care are available, as well as night care for neighborhood residents. Demented older residents have been a challenge. Approximately five mentally impaired dementia residents were moved because their spouses couldn't manage their care. Twenty-

five younger individuals with developmental disabilities also live here. The apartment for life program is very popular. Humanitas claims to have a waiting list that includes thousands of people. Although the units are much larger than those in a nursing home, the costs are about 35% less. This is due in part to the peripatetic approach to caregiving that characterizes this system. A total of 90 FTEs operate in the building.

Dwelling Unit Features Stress Adaptability

One of the main attractions of the building is the fact that residents need to move only once. Dwelling units are designed to adapt as residents age. If a resident experiences a severe chronic illness, services are provided. Dwelling units are arranged along single-loaded corridors throughout the building. Windows in the kitchen and a glass panel in the entry door allow borrowed light to enter the unit from the corridor side. The entry door is a 36-inch residential door, but adjacent to it is a 10-inch hinged movable panel that, when opened with the door, provides a space wide enough to accommodate a hospital bed. The units are relatively uniform in size. Most of them are 750 SF with a bathroom in the

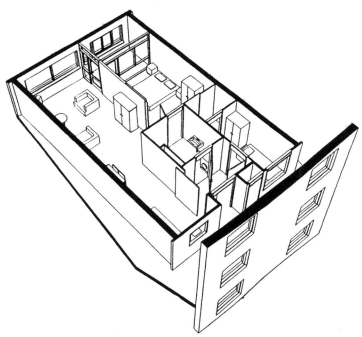

Axonometric unit plan: The unit is designed to adapt to the needs of residents as they age. It features an entrance door wide enough for a bed, a bathroom large enough for a stretcher bather, a kitchen counter that can be raised or lowered, an enclosed serre-style balcony, and an adaptable bathroom. (Courtesy EGM architecten bv)

middle. A few of the corner units are as large as 850 SF. This location allows the bathroom to be accessible from the bedroom and the entry hall. An enclosed balcony or serre is provided adjacent to the bedroom but is also accessible from the living room.

Dwelling Units Are Designed to Encourage Aging in Place

A number of features have been added to the units to make them adapt easily to disability. The kitchen and the bathroom are given the greatest scrutiny. The bathroom is very large and has a roll-in shower. It is big enough to accommodate a stretcher bath, which is typically given to bedridden patients who cannot take a shower. The sliding door to the kitchen and living room is quite large and can be left open. The toilet has grab bars that can be moved, and there are places where additional grab bars can be added. A drop-down shower seat is also provided. Throughout the unit there are wide doors and an absence of thresholds. The kitchen is adaptable and the counter can be moved up or down, depending on the needs of the resident. The kitchen is complete with roll-out shelves. The unit also has lever fixture taps and door handles, smoke detectors, easy-to-use windows and doors, and computerized door keys.

15

WILHELMIINA

Helsinki, Finland

Architect Tuono Siitonen | Helsinki, Finland
Sponsor The Mina Sillanpää Foundation

Building Characteristics

Number of units	123 units + 48 beds (rehab)
Number of stories	3–8
Context	Urban
Housing type	Multilevel service house
Building parti/shape	Complex
Unit mixture	60 long-term care units
	48 rehabilitation beds
	26 dementia units
	37 service flats
Size of most common unit (average)	320 SF (long-term care)
Community facilities	Yes
Community-accessible meals	Yes
Date of completion	September 1995

Resident Characteristics

Average age	85 (long-term care)
Number of residents	60 (long-term care)
Number of couples/men/women	NA
	NA
Age range	NA
Percent requiring bathing help	100 percent
Percent requiring toileting help	40 percent
Percent incontinent	NA
Percent wheelchair-bound	NA
Percent cognitively impaired	NA

Wilhelmiina is an urban project on a tight site: A variety of exterior materials and a lively massing geometry make the building appear smaller from the street.

S U M M A R Y

The Wilhelmiina housing and service center specializes in residential care services: rehabilitation, dementia care, and housing for the elderly. Located near the city center of Helsinki, it is a high-density multiservice building that has three major housing components. It contains a four-story tower with 60 units of cluster housing for the frail, 37 service apartments for older people, 26 dementia units in two small-group clusters, and 48 rehabilitation beds. The service center component is extensive, with a swimming pool, restaurant, physical therapy space, and access to a range of medical specialists. The building varies in height from three to eight stories and utilizes a range of materials including concrete, tile, wood, stucco, and brick (Siitonen, 1996). As a result of the creative application of different materials to different sections, from the street the project appears to be a collection of smaller buildings clustered together. The 60 housing units for the frail are contained in a four-story block, which has 15 dwelling units on each floor. These units are subdivided into three smaller "family clusters" of five units each that define three corners of a typical floor plate. Each family cluster is wrapped around a small living room and dining room where residents take meals. A large patio/balcony space is accessible from the living and dining rooms. A central living room in the middle of each floor provides more shared space for residents to visit. The therapeutic services the building provides are offered to residents, outpatients, and people who live in the surrounding neighborhood.

Project Features

Service House Has a Continuing-Care Format

Wilhelmiina offers many different types of housing to residents. For the most independent segment, there are 37 studio and one-bedroom apartments. Residents liv-

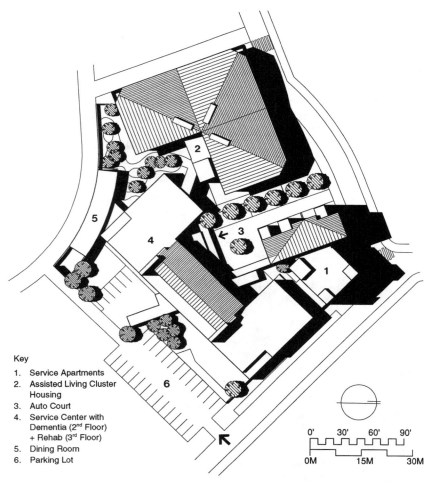

Key
1. Service Apartments
2. Assisted Living Cluster Housing
3. Auto Court
4. Service Center with Dementia (2nd Floor) + Rehab (3rd Floor)
5. Dining Room
6. Parking Lot

0' 30' 60' 90'
0M   15M   30M

Site plan: The building plan takes advantage of the irregular geometry of the site, making the building a contextual response to the neighborhood. A variety of roof treatments and a rich palette of materials give it a natural, pleasing contextual fit. (Courtesy Tuono Siitonen)

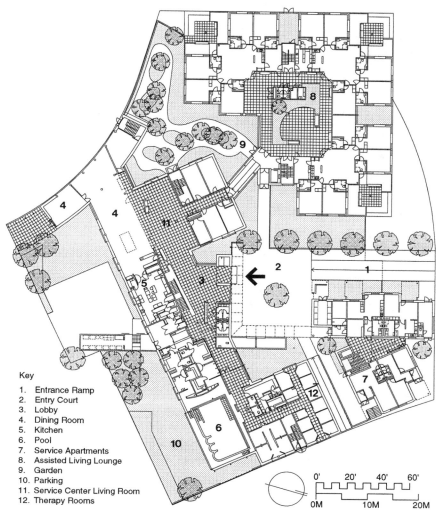

Key

1. Entrance Ramp
2. Entry Court
3. Lobby
4. Dining Room
5. Kitchen
6. Pool
7. Service Apartments
8. Assisted Living Lounge
9. Garden
10. Parking
11. Service Center Living Room
12. Therapy Rooms

First-floor plan: The building complex consists of three major building elements. The service housing on the north, the assisted living building on the west, and the main service center with dementia housing and rehabilitation unit on the upper floors on the south. A central motor court can be used to drop off visitors. (Courtesy Tuono Siitonen)

ing there can prepare meals in their own apartments or take meals in the adjoining restaurant. In another adjacent building, there are 60 units of assisted living housing. These are arranged in 5-unit clusters (15 units per floor) on four floors. Residents here generally take meals in 12 small dining areas shared with 4 other residents in their cluster. Two small-group dementia clusters of 13 residents each occupy 250-SF rooms on the second floor. On the third floor is a 48-bed short stay/rehabilitation unit for brain injury and stroke victims. The main building offers a range of activities and therapeutic services. Treatment is also available from a range of specialists including doctors, dentists, geriatric specialists, and neurologists.

Building Has an Urban Organization with a Central Auto Courtyard

The building parti is a complex shape that involves the layering of three dominant massing elements. A five- and eight-story mass on the north edge of the site flanks the auto court entry. In the center of the compact site is a paved urban courtyard, which can be used by vehicles to pick up and drop off residents. The building's design takes advantage of the polymorphous shape of the site. The first floor of the three-story common building contains the entry, the kitchen, the restaurant, the swimming pool (see page 101), medical offices, and therapy spaces. On the upper floors are dementia and rehabilitation beds.

Corner balconies are shared with five units: The four-story assisted living building has three eroded corners where a shared balcony has been placed. Wood slats have been used to create interesting shadow patterns and to provide shade control. (Photo: Jussi Tianen)

The lower level contains a gym, physical therapy spaces, and occupational therapy rooms. The commons is connected by an enclosed corridor to the assisted living housing. Service apartments are linked to the commons via a short covered walkway. A small landscaped courtyard is sandwiched between the common building and the assisted living housing.

Creative Use of Materials and Color Reduces the Scale of the Building

One of the most striking aspects of the building is how color and materials have been used to make one large mass appear like a collection of smaller buildings. A combination of red brick and white stucco is used in the service apartment tower to reduce its massiveness when seen from the street, However, it presents a uniform look from the courtyard drive and the north elevation. The common building uses white stucco, wood slats, cast concrete, brick of two colors, glass block, and light blue glass to add variety, complexity, and contrast. Continuous wood slats, extended roman brick, and a cast concrete base contain dominant horizontal lines that also cast strong shadow patterns. These horizontal elements mitigate the tall height. Balcony treatments vary from building to building and are used to add emphasis and distinctiveness. For example, the first five floors of the service apartment tower use a cantilevered glass balcony. This transitions to a black rail support for the upper three floors of balconies. The main building, including the dementia and rehabilitation units, utilizes windows that appear to be French balconies with an expanded metal face. In the cluster unit, a large shared balcony with a curved roof supported by diagonal struts adds emphasis to the corners of the building.

Five Dwelling Unit Clusters Exist for Frail Residents

This 60-unit, four-story assisted living building is subdivided into three group clusters of 5 single-occupied units each. Three unit clusters capture the three corners of this L-shaped tower. The eroded fourth corner of the square floor plate contains the entrance, a connection to the common building and access to an adjacent garden. Each five-unit cluster is referred to as a *family group.* Each dwelling unit opens onto a small shared area that consists of a dining room, living room, kitchen, and outdoor balcony. Residents take their meals here or are welcome to use the restaurant in the attached common building. The shared living and dining room opens onto a small communal balcony. The balcony is generous in size and on the first floor has a natural-colored wood slat screen that provides privacy and shade control. Each floor also contains a central shared living room where larger group activities can be planned near the center of the building. This centrally located common space is eroded on the south edge to reveal a multistory atrium with plant materials at the base. This adds spatial interest to the building while allowing natural light to enter all levels at the center of the building. Each floor is color coded (blue, green, and red) for orientation purposes.

Dwelling Unit Design Features Corner Windows

The assisted living dwelling unit is 320 SF. Bathrooms have a built-in vanity with a horizontal window above that borrows light from the bedroom. At night the window glows with light from the bathroom and is used as a night light. The shower is a roll-in type. A large, low sill height corner window in all but a few units supplies natural light and a view in two directions. Another small horizontal window is used for natural ventilation. As in most northern European housing, residents bring their own furniture (except for the bed) as well as their favorite chandelier or pendant light fixture, which is wired into place. A few of the units have armoire cabinets at the entry to create more privacy.

Care Approach Follows the *Op Maat* Philosophy

Services are provided following the Dutch *op maat* philosophy, which means that the care is designed to fit the resident rather than being constrained by staffing requirements. For example, mealtimes are flexible. If someone wants to take a meal in the restaurant, management tries to arrange it. A variety of therapies including massage therapy are available. About half of the individuals using the physical therapy and swimming pool facilities are community residents. One of the unusual treatment

ideas that has been implemented is a full-spectrum "bright light area" in the café and the dementia living room. For example, the cafe has 38 down lights in a 300-SF area. Management believes this helps residents deal more effectively with depression in the middle of the winter.

Service Flats in the Tower Have Excellent Views

There are 37 service flats that vary in size from 430 to 640 SF. They are located in a compact eight-story tower on the northeast corner of the site. There are five units on a typical floor of this building, which has one elevator and one fire stair. Each unit has a spacious balcony and a large kitchen. The bedrooms are small and are separated from the living room by a sliding door. Bathrooms feature roll-in showers and a washing machine and are designed to meet the latest standards for the handicapped.

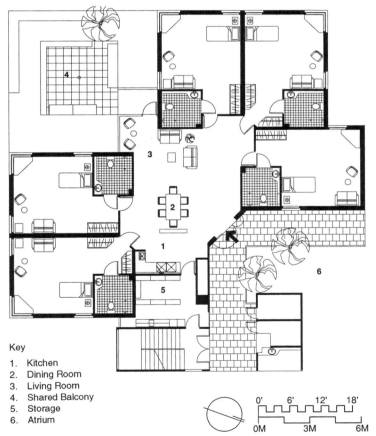

Key

1. Kitchen
2. Dining Room
3. Living Room
4. Shared Balcony
5. Storage
6. Atrium

0' 6' 12' 18'

0M 3M 6M

Assisted living family cluster: Each five-unit cluster shares a small living room, dining room, and balcony outside of their unit where meals are taken. Each unit is single occupied, with its own private bathroom, a large corner window, and a long-low slung ventilation window.

Dementia and Rehabilitation Units Are Provided

The second floor contains two 13-unit dementia clusters. These units, at 250 SF, are small compared to the other units. Short stays and respite care are also accommodated on this floor. Wood floors have been used to make this space very cozy. In the living room, 28 full-spectrum lights have been mounted to create a bright light area (see page 149). Management is evaluating the effect of this feature on depression and sundowner's syndrome. The rehabilitation unit is more like a typical hospital environment. The typical stays here are 2 to 4 weeks, and the clientele consists of people of all ages. Other photos of Wilhelmiina are available on the cover, the color insert and pages 62 and 243.

16

GODDARD HOUSE

Brookline, Massachusetts

Architect Childs Bertman Tseckares Architects | Boston, Massachusetts
Sponsor Goddard House

Building Characteristics

Number of units	115
Number of stories	3
Context	Urban/Suburban
Housing type	Assisted living and dementia
Building parti/shape	U + L
Unit mixture	37 studios
	34 one bedroom
	4 two bedrooms
	40 dementia studios
Size of most common unit (average)	420 SF (one bedroom)
Community facilities	NA
Community-accessible meals	No—family and friends only
Date of completion	December 1996

Resident Characteristics

Average age	86
Number of residents	120
Number of couples/men/women	16 single men
	94 single women
	5 couples
Age range	62–96
Percent requiring bathing help	83 percent
Percent requiring toileting help	25 percent
Percent incontinent	18 percent
Percent wheelchair-bound	8 percent
Percent cognitively impaired	38 percent

Goddard House fits into the surrounding community: The gray shingle siding, white trim, one- and two-story gables, hip roof accents, fireplace chimneys, and attached porch call attention to the entrance and reduce the three-story scale of the building as seen from the street. (Photo: Edward Jacoby Photography)

SUMMARY

The Goddard organization has a long and distinguished history of serving older frail people in the community. The Goddard nursing home, a sister facility located a few miles away, was first incorporated in 1849 and is believed to be the third oldest housing and health care provider in the country. Goddard House, located on the 5.9–acre site of the old Brookline Hospital, is in the middle of a vibrant older Boston community. The building is a gray shingle and white trim three-story traditional building that fits nicely into its surrounding Victorian neighborhood. The building has 75 dwelling units of assisted living and 40 single-occupied units for people with dementia. The unusual configuration of the building footprint and the use of gables, porches, and dormers make the building appear smaller and more intimate in scale. The shape also allows for the creation of several courtyards that are visible from major common spaces.

There are a number of distinctively furnished common spaces including a living room parlor, a café, an activity room, and a country kitchen. The assisted living dwelling units are relatively large and include four two-bedroom units. The dementia program is broken into four small clusters of ten units each. The facility has an active volunteer program that draws from high school students, art therapy interns from Wellesley College, and volunteers from the surrounding community.

Project Features

Complex Building Shape Reduces the Perceived Scale

The building consists of an L-shaped and a U-shaped configuration that are joined together to create a complex shape. This unusual configuration allows the building to fit the site better and minimizes the length of the

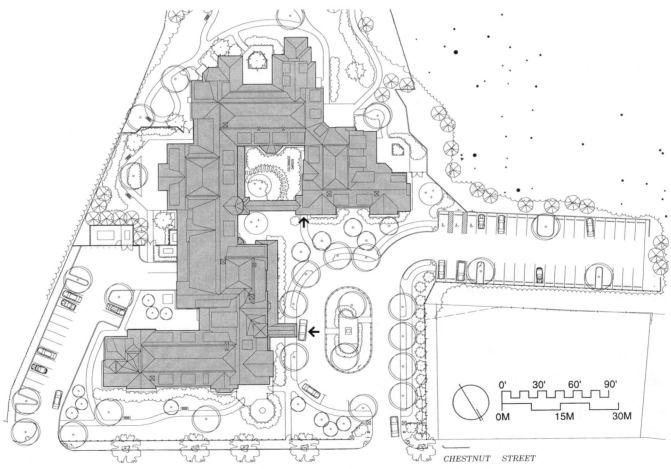

Site plan: The twisted building configuration fits the triangular shape of the site. Short wings result from this complex shape, which make this rather large building appear smaller. The site is surrounded by walking paths and a wetland on the southeast side. (Courtesy CBT Architects)

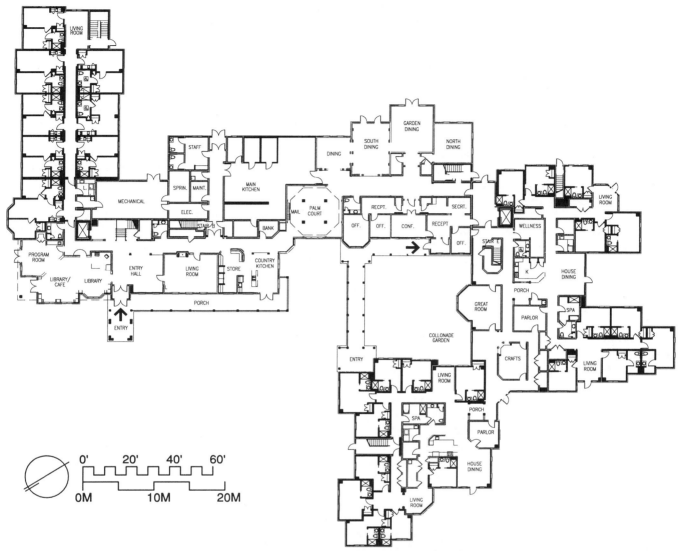

First-floor plan: The plan reduces the perceived corridor length while adding variety to the exterior of the building. First-floor common spaces are linked together by corridors. This creates an event-filled circulation pathway through the building. (Courtesy CBT Architects)

façade that can be seen from one location. This is important because the building, with 115 dwelling units and three stories, is relatively large. The use of a porch on the first floor, several large one- and two-story gables, and a third-floor dormer reduces the scale of the building from the street, making it appear to be less than three full stories. The shingle style of the building blends with the older neighborhood. Gray shingles contrast with white trim around the windows and white columns on the first floor porch (see page 67). The dormers, bay windows, porches, and chimneys add detail and interest to the façade from the street. A drop-off area and ample convenient parking are located in front of the build-

ing. Wood frame construction, allowed in Massachusetts for this building type, adds to its residential character. The program, with both assisted living and dementia represents the home within a home model.

Common Spaces Are Small in Scale and Distinctive

The vast majority of common space, located on the first floor, follows the circulation corridor from one end of the building to the other and links the elevators with a distinctive sequence of common spaces. The spaces along this spine include the entry hall, library, café, activity room, living room, country kitchen, palm court, and dining rooms. Each room is unique in color and character. Strong, bold, rich, warm, and friendly color combinations are used, which are visually stimulating without being overwhelming. The common space rooms, which are small in scale, resemble those one might find in a large mansion house. In fact, the dining room has been divided into three smaller rooms, each of which is furnished and decorated like an attractive restaurant. There is also a private dining room that seats 12.

Each Common Room Supports a Different Behavioral Agenda

The first space one notices when entering the building is the porch, which is heavily used by residents throughout the summer. Once inside, the café/library to the left has the feeling of a bookstore café. This space is used as an activity room, and residents watch TV here. It also serves as an exercise space in the morning. Family and friends use the living room, with its dark blue wall covering and fireplace (see page 106). The country kitchen is perhaps the most popular and successful social space in the building. Its placement near the south edge of the building guarantees that it receives a lot of sunlight during the day. Residents come here to spend time and hangout. It serves as a very successful 100 percent corner. The palm court is a widened corridor area that serves as a small performance space. It can seat 50 people in folding chairs and does so frequently for the music and drama programs that occur once or twice a month.

Care Approach Stresses Independence, Privacy, and Individualism

The Goddard House has a strong reputation for quality care inherited from its sister facility. Each resident is assessed and monitored by the care staff, and a program of individualized service is developed. The facility has a working agreement with a sister nursing facility in Jamaica Plain for residents who need rehabilitation or more intense medical care. The building strongly reflects its local neighborhood, with a mixture of Christian and Jewish residents. About 15 percent of the dwelling units are reserved for low- to moderate-income residents. There are a number of programs with groups from the surrounding community. Seventh and eighth graders from the local high school have formed a discussion group with six residents. Wellesley College has two interns who work with residents during the fall and spring. Goddard also has a strong volunteer program with 25 people who range in age from 14 to 85.

Outdoor Spaces and Walking Pathways Are Provided

The Goddard House neighborhood is friendly, and the site is lovely. In fact, many residents walk daily in good weather to a nearby park and a corner store. The building overlooks a strip of conservation wetland on one side, which is highly unusual for an urban parcel such as this one. Walking paths surround three sides of the building and the fourth side is secured, providing a large outdoor

Common spaces are varied: Each common space takes on a slightly different character, like rooms in a mansion. Strong, rich, bold colors and patterns are used in rooms that are sized to be residential in scale. (Photo: Edward Jacoby Photography)

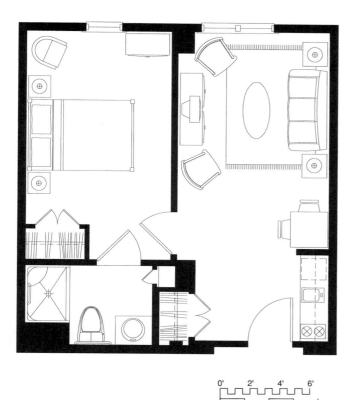

Room plan: Nearly half of the assisted living units are 420-SF, spacious one-bedroom apartments. The tea kitchens in these units have a small two-burner range in addition to a refrigerator. (Courtesy CBT Architects)

garden and walking space for dementia residents. A highly visible gazebo in front of the building is also popular with residents. On a nice summer afternoon, it is not uncommon to see as many as 20 residents sitting on the front covered porch. Outdoor patio extensions connect to the library/café and the dining room. A dementia

garden in a courtyard formed by the building is accessible from the common area of the dementia unit.

Dwelling Units Are Spacious

Units vary in size from 360 SF for studios to 420 SF for one-bedroom units and 680 SF for two-bedroom units. The 40 dementia units, at 250 SF, are much smaller. Assisted living units typically contain a cooktop. The vast majority are one-bedroom units that are large enough for family visits and overnight stays. Many of the units were designed so that the toilet is visible from the bed (see page 265). Larger two-bedroom units have bay windows.

Four Dementia Clusters on Two Floors

The dementia unit is located on the west edge of the site and is split into two stacked floors of 20 residents each. The third floor above it is for assisted living. The dementia program, known as the *homestead* program, accommodates 40 residents in single-occupied units. The 20 units on each floor are subdivided into two 10-unit clusters. Each of these smaller ten-unit arrangements is clustered around a dining room, kitchen, spa, and living room. These clusters are further subdivided into small groups of five units each. Clustering units together stimulates a family-style relationship among residents. Each floor has access to a garden/deck, a crafts room, and a great room. At 250 SF, each dwelling unit is small, but each has a full private bathroom (sink, shower, and toilet). All 40 dwelling units share access to a beauty salon and a wellness office. The program has its own front door, and it is functionally separated from the assisted living program. The outdoor garden is designed for movement and contemplation, with low plantings, birdhouses, birdbaths, and a covered walkway. A ramp from the second-story balcony connects to the area below for residents who want to walk for exercise.

17
GYNGEMOSEGÅRD

Herlev, Denmark

Architect   Thure, Nielsen, and Rubow | Copenhagen, Denmark
Sponsor   Gladsaxe Kommune

Building Characteristics

Number of units	100
Number of stories	2
Context	Suburban
Housing type	Aldrecenter
Building parti/shape	20 buildings
Unit mixture	56 one-bedroom (elderly + family)
	20 two-bedroom (family)
	12 three-bedroom (family)
	12 co-housing (elderly)
Size of most common unit (average)	650 SF (elderly)
Community facilities	Yes
Community-accessible meals	Yes
Date of completion	October 1993

Resident Characteristics

Average age	75 (elderly)
Number of residents	64 (elderly)
Number of couples/men/women	13 couples
	7 single men
	31 single women
Age range	70–95
Percent requiring bathing help	31 percent
Percent requiring toileting help	8 percent
Percent incontinent	NA
Percent wheelchair-bound	18 percent
Percent cognitively impaired	15 percent (mildly impaired)

Pedestrian street links units with the community center: This pathway runs from one end of this thin site to the other. In new urbanism style, units are buffered by a garden space and a fence. Walk-up units are for families and younger people, while grade access units are set aside for older people. (Photo: Martin Rubow)

SUMMARY

The Danish emphasis on integration and normalization is well represented by this housing project. Located in the Copenhagen suburb of Herlev, this 100-unit development has 56 one-bedroom units (44 of which are for the elderly), 12 cohousing units for the elderly, and 32 two- and three-bedroom units for families. Most of the dwelling units for the elderly in this two-story complex are on the ground floor. However, one group of second-story units on the eastern edge of the site has access to an elevator. A community center with a glass-covered two-story atrium contains a café, a large meeting room, a physiotherapy space, an occupational therapy kitchen (see photo 283), and an exercise room. Located near the center of the development for easy access, it has a parking lot drop-off on one side and a parklike outdoor space on the other side. The community center has equipment and personnel to provide a customized physical therapy and exercise program for each resident. Therapists work with residents to develop movement, aerobic, and strength training exercises in several well-equipped rooms. A home care service delivery strategy common throughout Denmark is used to provide help and assistance to the elderly in Gyngemosegård and the surrounding neighborhood. New urbanism techniques have been used to link housing units to pedestrian pathways. Two six unit cohousing clusters provide another lifestyle alternative for older residents who want to lead a more collective life.

Project Features

Social and Service Integration Are Stressed

The general theme here is integration. Connecting older and younger people socially is a priority, as is the integration of housing with supportive services. Nearly half

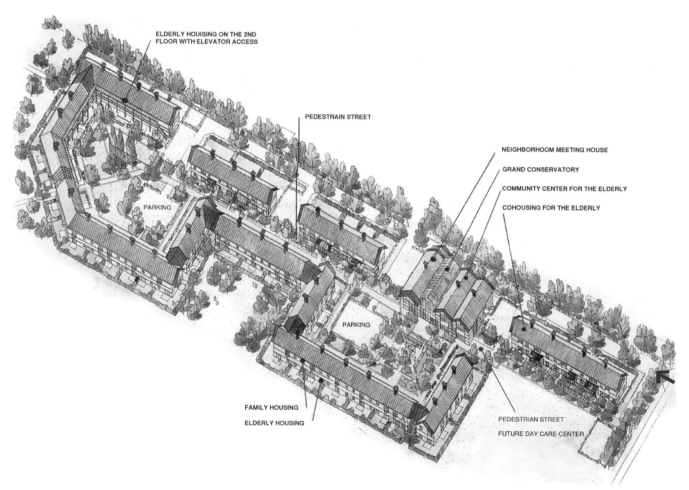

ELDERLY HOUISING ON THE 2ND
FLOOR WITH ELEVATOR ACCESS

PEDESTRAIN STREET

NEIGHBORHOOM MEETING HOUSE

GRAND CONSERVATORY

COMMUNITY CENTER FOR THE ELDERLY

COHOUSING FOR THE ELDERLY

PARKING

PARKING

FAMILY HOUSING

ELDERLY HOUSING

PEDESTRIAN STREET

FUTURE DAY CARE CENTER

Axonometric site plan: The building complex consists of a line of units/common space along the southern edge of the site. The northern edge is formed to create two courtyards, both of which contain parking. Two cohousing clusters are located on the western edge of the site. A community center is located near the center of the site. (Courtesy Thure, Nielsen and Rubow Architects)

Community building is seamed with an atrium: The community building has a two-story glass atrium where residents can take a noon meal. The small garden on the north side of the community building can be seen from both floors. (Photo: Martin Rubow)

of the project consists of families with children (44 units), and adjacent to the development on the western edge is a primary school. There are about 125 residents in the total project. The community center is the main social and service setting. It offers a noon meal, exercise/ physical therapy equipment, and space for meetings. Home help and home health providers are also housed in this building.

Pedestrian Street Is a "New Urbanism" Concept

Special attention has been paid to the relationship of the private dwelling unit to pedestrian pathways. Housing units with friendly outdoor garden spaces flank both sides of a 15- to 20-foot-wide circulation pathway that is used by pedestrians, bicyclists, and emergency vehicles. The units have their more public/social side (kitchen and dining room functions) oriented to the street edge, where social contact is easier to initiate. A short wood fence covered with clematis and wisteria separates the public walkway and each unit's outdoor patio. This patio, large enough for a coffee table and chairs, is accessible to each first-floor dwelling unit kitchen. The public pathway links dwelling units to the community center and a central garden space. Each dwelling unit also has a private side

with access to a small garden patio or balcony and views over the surrounding wetlands.

Community Center Provides Access to Exercise Equipment and Rehabilitation Services

The social center for the complex is a small two-story building that contains a cafe, a meeting space, offices for home care agencies, and an exercise/physical therapy space. Sandwiched between these four uses is a glass-covered, light-filled atrium where residents can take a noon meal surrounded by sunlight and lush plant materials. About 30 people take meals here on a regular basis, and about half of them are older people from the complex. More than 70 percent of the elderly utilize some form of service from the building. Meals on wheels that come from the café are also delivered to residents in their units and to people in the surrounding neighborhood. Food is prepared at a nearby regional kitchen and delivered to the community building for redistribution. Frozen meals, which can be prepared later, are also popular. The café is open during the day. Although the noon meal is the major event, residents also take afternoon coffee here. There is also a large "town meeting" room that accommodates about 50 people. Most group get–togethers occur in the meeting room or the atrium.

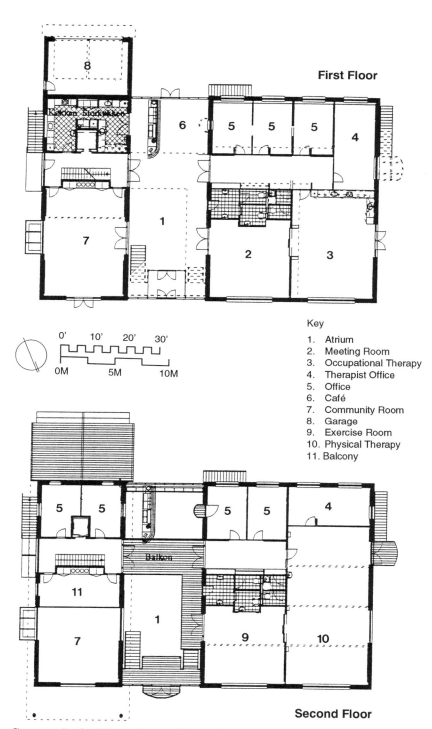

First Floor

Key

1. Atrium
2. Meeting Room
3. Occupational Therapy
4. Therapist Office
5. Office
6. Café
7. Community Room
8. Garage
9. Exercise Room
10. Physical Therapy
11. Balcony

Second Floor

Community building plan: This building contains a small café as well as a meeting room and a community center. On the second floor are a physiotherapy space, a training kitchen, and an exercise room. Offices for home care staff are located here as well. (Courtesy Thure, Nielsen and Rubow Architects)

Supportive Services Are Delivered Using a Home Care Format

Home health nurses stationed at the day center coordinate the delivery of services to older residents in the complex as well as in the surrounding neighborhood. Approximately 20 residents need help with bathing but only 5 need help with toileting. The resident population is relatively young and thus reasonably independent. Although this facility is not designed for a nursing home population, older frail people can be supported here for a long time. People with severe dementia, however, must seek another form of housing, although a dementia day group from the surrounding community meets at the center twice a week. In 1998, only one person left Gyngemosegård for a nursing home.

Physiotherapy and Exercise Are Blended

Management has made a commitment to integrate exercise and traditional physical therapy regimens. They also utilize occupational therapists to rehabilitate and retrain residents. This is important for residents and community members who have experienced weakness and coordination difficulties as a result of a stroke. Five physiotherapists and five occupational therapists work at the community center. The physical therapy room has three mat tables, a chair exercise area, parallel bars, and upper-body weights. The adjacent exercise space has seven pieces of exercise equipment, including two exercise cycles, three upper-body strength machines, and several treadmills. When these two related activities are combined, physical therapy becomes more of a physiological concern than a medical care one.

Dwelling Units Feature Large Windows

Units range from 600–725 SF. These are well designed one-bedroom units with a large kitchen and bathroom. Two large windows (approximately 36 SF) with low sills (14–16 inches high) are located opposite one another in the living room and dining room (see page 125). Their placement in the narrow, 25-foot-deep unit allows light to flood the middle of the unit from two sides. The living room opens onto either a balcony or a first-floor patio. The kitchen, entry, and dining room functions are

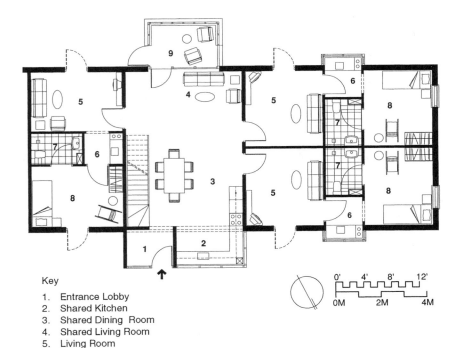

Key

1. Entrance Lobby
2. Shared Kitchen
3. Shared Dining Room
4. Shared Living Room
5. Living Room
6. Kitchenette
7. Bathroom
8. Bedroom
9. Wintergarden

Cohousing dwelling unit on the first floor: The six people who live in these two-story blocks have chosen a more collective lifestyle. They take meals together and have developed close, interdependent friendships. A kitchen, living room, and solarium on the first floor are the main shared spaces.

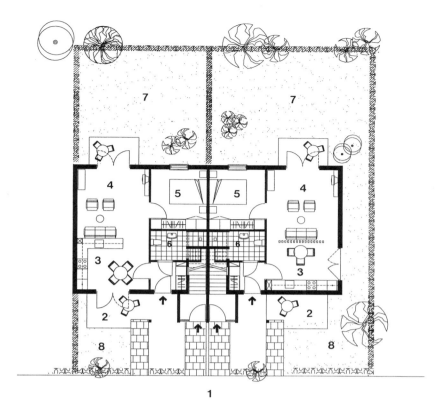

Key

1. Pedestrian Walkway
2. Patio
3. Kitchen
4. Living Room
5. Bedroom
6. Bathroom
7. Backyard
8. Frontyard

Unit plans: These units located along the pedestrian street take full advantage of the surrounding landscape. Patios are located on both sides, with access from the living room and the entry/kitchen. The centrally located stairs lead to the two upper-floor units.

placed on the most public courtyard side of the complex overlooking activity. All units have a small separate entry vestibule. Although this is unusual in the United States, it is a common feature in northern European housing that is considered important for security, privacy, and temperature control. Unfortunately, the placement of the bathroom near the entry requires residents to pass through three doors at night to get to the toilet. Bathrooms feature roll-in showers and a built-in storage area. The dwelling unit floors are wood, giving the space a cozy feeling. The units on the second story at the east end of the project have access to an elevator and a glass overhang that provides protection for residents but doesn't reduce the amount of light entering the unit.

Cohousing Encourages Healthy Interdependence

Danish cohousing for the elderly is a popular program that is offered in a number of different forms. Two cohousing units at the west end of this complex are designed for people who want to live a more social, interconnected life but still value their privacy. The six residents in each of these two-story units are a little older, 78–80 years of age. Each cohousing apartment is 300 SF. Together the six apartments share approximately 1400 SF of common space, which includes a small kitchen, a living room, a greenhouse sunspace (see page 89), and a dining room. Residents in this small six-person arrangement have their own kitchen and bathroom but also share another communal kitchen. Dwelling units are designed so that residents can take meals together or by themselves. These residents live separate lives but come together socially to celebrate birthdays and special occasions. They also share a rich social life with one another.

Cohousing Has Some Limitations for Frail Residents

The two-story configuration is not very effective because there is no elevator, and the stairs are narrow and difficult to navigate. Cohousing works best when residents are in good physical condition and are cognitively intact. In Gyngemosegård the cohousing unit that consists of all single women functions better than the one that contains couples. Social continuity is important to the success of cohousing, and residents normally interview new participants to see if they are compatible with the group before they are invited to join. Because their lives are so interconnected, it is important that residents exhibit tolerance toward one another. In general, six is considered the minimum-size group for social cohesiveness.

18

SUNRISE OF MISSION VIEJO

Mission Viejo, California

Architect   Hill Partnership | Newport Beach, California
Sponsor   Sunrise Assisted Living

Building Characteristics

Number of units	86
Number of stories	2 and 3
Context	Suburban
Housing type	Assisted living and dementia
Building parti/shape	X
Unit mixture	24 one-bedroom
	24 companion
	38 studios
Size of most common unit (average)	425 SF
Community facilities	No
Community-accessible meals	No—family and friends only
Date of completion	November 1998

Resident Characteristics

Average age	86
Number of residents	85
Number of couples/men/ women	20 single men
	49 single women
	8 couples
Age range	75–98
Percent requiring bathing help	57 percent
Percent requiring toileting help	54 percent
Percent incontinent	42 percent
Percent wheelchair-bound	21 percent
Percent cognitively impaired	63 percent

Wraparound porch gives the building a friendly look: The Spanish Colonial revival style fits into the surrounding neighborhood. The attached porch serves to reduce the scale of the building as seen from the street. (Larry A. Falke Photography ©)

S U M M A R Y

The Sunrise of Mission Viejo is an 86-unit, two- and three-story assisted living building with 20 units for dementia care on the lower floor. It is designed in a Spanish Colonial Revival style with stucco walls, dark wood accents, white windows, and a red tile roof. The compact **X** configuration reduces the distance from residents' units to common spaces. Common spaces are concentrated around the front entry on the first floor and along a centralized, skylighted second-floor space known as "Central Park." Seven dwelling units typically surround decentralized common living rooms at the ends of nine residential corridors. The four living rooms on the upper floor have large, centrally located, clear-lens skylights above them. These furnished lounge spaces break up the extruded nature of the corridor. The front of the building has a wraparound porch that reduces the scale of the two-story building, giving it the feeling of a rambling Spanish hacienda. The dementia unit, located on the lower floor, has its own private, secured outdoor garden. This unit operates as a semiautonomous home within a home that is accessible to staff and family members through a centrally located elevator and stair. The dementia area is subdivided into two 10-unit clusters with separate dining and activity spaces. Both clusters share a living room, kitchen, spa, and staff office. There are three types of dwelling units, and nearly half of them are designed to be single or double occupied, depending on the demand. As the building ages and the frailty level of residents increases, the demand for double occupancy may also increase.

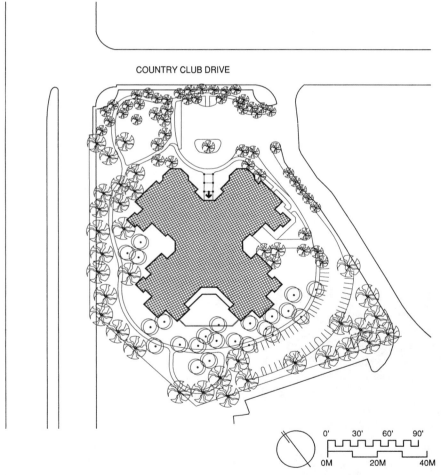

COUNTRY CLUB DRIVE

0'   30'   60'   90'

0M   20M   40M

Site plan: The building is sited so that the entrance is visible from the two adjacent, heavily trafficked streets. An exercise pathway loops around the building, with benches every 100–150 feet. Parking is concentrated at the rear of the site to give the front entry a softer, open, gracious feeling. (Courtesy Hill Partnership)

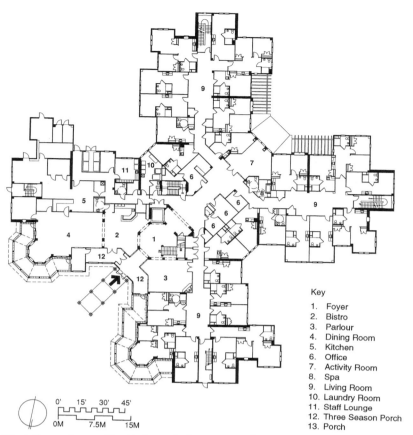

First-floor plan: The X-shaped plan creates three clusters of units that are close to the dining room. Community spaces are clustered around the front entry and along the axis that links the entrance with the activity room. (Courtesy Hill Partnership)

Key
1. Foyer
2. Bistro
3. Parlour
4. Dining Room
5. Kitchen
6. Office
7. Activity Room
8. Spa
9. Living Room
10. Laundry Room
11. Staff Lounge
12. Three Season Porch
13. Porch

Project Features

Building Site Creates an Attractive First Impression from the Street

Planned on a sloping 2.8-acre site, this building is a prototype that Sunrise Assisted Living has used elsewhere. The Spanish Colonial Revival style includes similarly styled interior furnishings giving the building a look that fits into this predominantly Spanish-styled Orange County, California, neighborhood. The colorfully landscaped building entrance, visible from a heavily trafficked nearby street, shares its entry drive with an adjacent country club. Most of the parking spaces are located at the rear of the site to add emphasis to the front door and the trellis-covered entry. The covered porch surrounding the first floor mitigates the overall height of the building and gives it a friendly, inviting feeling. A barbecue area near the front of the building marks the beginning of a walkway surrounding the building that

residents use for exercise. Benches and rest areas including a raised resident garden are located every 100–150 feet to break up the pathway and give residents a convenient and attractive place to rest.

Open Plan Links the Major Common Spaces with the Entry Foyer

The entry sequence begins with a two-story foyer that creates a powerful first impression and gives the first-time visitor views of several adjacent rooms. The fireplace in the parlour, a festive bistro bar, a small-scale dining room with two seatings, an activity room with a view beyond, a friendly concierge, and an open stairway that leads to the skylighted second-floor main street are all visible from a single location a few steps inside the building. The first floor contains the majority of the common shared spaces in an open plan arrangement. Two lengthy, spring-loaded, flexible fire partitions were required to achieve the open feeling on this floor. Special fire-rated windows were necessary to create the desired visual connection between staff offices in the middle of the first floor and the adjacent corridor.

Central Park Is a Skylighted Meeting Space on the Second Floor

On the second floor, located at the top of the foyer stairs in the middle of the building, is a cluster of spaces (wellness offices, activity room, hair salon, laundry, and staff coordinator's office) centered on a wide corridor with two large 5-foot by 5-foot clear skylights. This space, Central Park, is furnished with outdoor-style teak tables and benches. The surrounding offices and the activity room at one end activate the space during the day.

Care and Service Concepts Stress Personalized Care in a Normalized Setting

Sunrise has focused on the frailest sector of the assisted living population, a group that normally has no alternative but a nursing home. Almost all residents pay privately and are generally financially well off. Staff are subject to a rigorous, sequenced, multistepped internal training program. Compensation is tied to mastering the knowledge necessary to serve frail residents appropriately. An individualized service plan is established for each resident, to whom a specific caregiver is assigned. The residents' personal and health care needs, in addition to the dwelling unit they have selected, is the basis for calculating the monthly fee. The eight Sunrise principles of service presented in Chapter 3 are the basis for a philosophy of care that emphasizes personal choice and freedom. For example, two dinner seatings are offered, and fresh coffee, juices, fresh fruit, cookies, and sugar-free candy are available 24 hours a day. Pets are welcome. In fact, every Sunrise building has at least one house dog and cat in residence. Grandchildren have access to a "children's corner" inside the building, as well as to play equipment on the grounds.

Building Stresses Family-Friendly Attitudes and Volunteer Activities

An important priority is making the experience of visiting the building a pleasant one. Family and friends are welcome 24 hours a day, seven days a week, and can purchase a meal whenever they like and eat with a resident. An HVAC system that creates positive pressure in public corridors isolates any odors from public spaces by venting exhaust air through residents' bathrooms. Visitors are encouraged to volunteer time through the "willing hearts volunteer program." Through this program, volunteers can drive residents, walk residents, reminisce, garden, read to residents, assist with arts and crafts, care for the community pet, play an instrument, or bake cookies. Wellness nurses carry out resident assessments each month, working with the family and the resident's personal physician. A full range of services is offered including hospice, respite, and dementia care. Special programs are available to deal with incontinence.

Central Park is a skylighted meeting place: Located in the center of the second floor, this lounge is flanked by an activity room, a residents' laundry space, a beauty shop, and wellness offices. It is a popular meeting space for second-floor residents. (Photo: Larry A. Falke Photography ©)

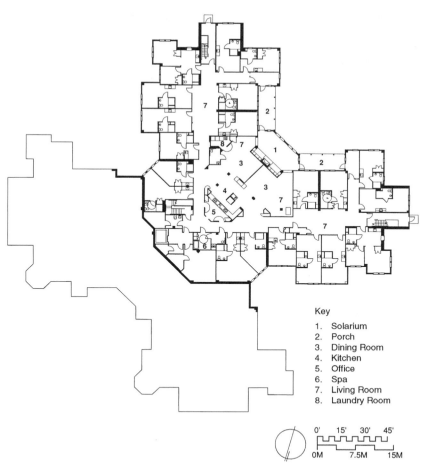

Key

1. Solarium
2. Porch
3. Dining Room
4. Kitchen
5. Office
6. Spa
7. Living Room
8. Laundry Room

Lower-floor dementia unit plan: Located below the entry floor, this dementia unit has its own secured garden. A resident-oriented life skills kitchen, two dining rooms, and a solarium create a looped walking pathway. Family access from the back of the unit helps to maintain excellent exit control. (Courtesy Hill Partnership)

Dementia Neighborhood Is a Self-contained Home Within a Home

Most of the common spaces in the dementia unit are oriented to a secured garden view. Residents literally turn their backs to the elevator and stairs, making elopement from this unit less of a problem. Residents come together for joint activities in the living room but generally take their meals in two separate dining rooms. One of the most interesting interior spaces is the living room/solarium, which is skylighted and surrounded by fixed French doors. This space overlooks the garden and nearby areas, which have bird feeders and plant materials that attract other forms of wildlife. Separating the living room from the dining rooms is a fireplace with open shelving on both sides. The kitchen and laundry are designed for residents to participate in ADLs like setting the table, bussing dishes, and folding laundry. Life skills stations throughout the building stress reminiscence themes and other daily activities like putting on makeup. The unit consists of two 10-unit clusters, each with its own activity space for small-group interactions. Because the caregiving needs of this group are more intense and the amount of common space per resident is greater than in assisted living, the daily cost here is higher. As a result, the frequency of double occupancy is also higher.

Dementia Neighborhood Features an Accessible, Dedicated Outdoor Garden

The outdoor secured garden is an important addition, especially in southern California, because it is usable almost every day of the year. A greenhouse-like living room, a three-season porch, and two trellis-covered ar-

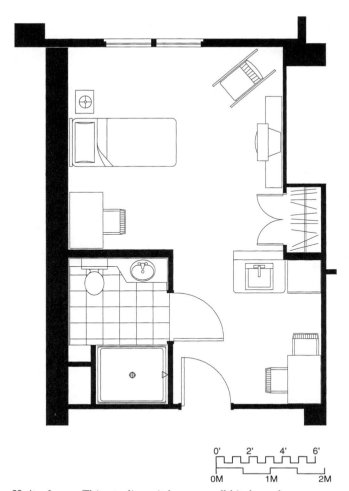

Unit plan: This studio unit has a small kitchen alcove next to the entry and bathroom with a half-wall connection to the adjacent bedroom space. Note the large 6-foot-wide windows.

eas are sandwiched between the building and the garden. The outdoor garden has a looped walking pathway that leads to a small trellis-covered retreat area on the edge of the garden. The space is secured by a 6-foot-high open metal fence that has plant material trained between its vertical bars. Residents walk for exercise and partake in activities like gardening. The building is designed to make it easy for residents to walk inside and outside with caregivers or on their own.

Three Basic Types of Dwelling Units Are Offered

Units are clustered around nine lounges (including two for dementia residents) that are contained in the four wings of the building. The four lounges on the top floor have large 5-foot-square skylights in the center of the space. About 50 percent of the units are studio apartments. Companion suites account for about 25 percent of the total and one-bedroom units the remaining 25 percent. The average size of a unit is 325 SF for a studio, 450 SF for a companion suite, and 550 SF for a one-bedroom unit. Half of the units are designed to be either shared by two people or occupied by one. The typical unit has a bathroom with a shower, toilet, emergency call button, storage space, medicine cabinet, heat lamp, and lavatory with an under-sink cabinet. The bathroom is designed to meet California adaptability standards, so that it can be easily transformed into a space for handicapped residents. The typical unit also has a small tea kitchen with a sink, cabinet, and refrigerator. Units are designed with individually controlled large-dial thermostats. They also have large 6×6-foot windows with low 16-inch-high sills so that residents can easily see outside from their beds. Other photos of Sunrise of Mission Viejo are available on pages 18, 111, 126, and 281.

19

CROWN COVE

Corona Del Mar, California

Architect JBZ Architects | Newport Beach, California
Irwin-Pancake Architects (Alzheimer's consultant) | Huntington Beach, California
Teller-Manok Architects (design consultants) | Laguna Beach, California
Sponsor Birtcher Properties

Building Characteristics

Number of units	75
Number of stories	5
Context	Suburban
Housing type	Assisted living and dementia
Building parti/shape	C
Unit mixture	75 studios
Size of most common unit (average)	400 SF
Community facilities	Day-care program
Community-accessible meals	No—family and friends only
Date of completion	August 1999

Resident Characteristics

Average age	87
Number of residents	75
Number of couples/men/ women	14 single men 53 single women 4 couples
Age range	56–96
Percent requiring bathing help	40 percent
Percent requiring toileting help	NA
Percent incontinent	37 percent
Percent wheelchair-bound	21 percent
Percent cognitively impaired	49 percent

Entry plaza on the street: This five-story building contains a view corridor in the middle of the building. The building steps down a dramatic site overlooking the Pacific Ocean. Shingles, white trim, wide overhangs, and hexagonal corner units give the building a seaside look. (Eric Figge Photography, Inc.)

S U M M A R Y

Crown Cove is an attractive shingle-style building located on a steep hillside site overlooking the Pacific Ocean in Corona Del Mar, California. The building was controversial when it was first introduced, and numerous hearings with the city were required to arrive at a form that was compatible with the neighborhood, functional for seniors, and economically feasible. In order to secure approval, the architects maintained a low two- and three-story scale from the street and created a view corridor through the center of the building. To maintain the required density, they dropped the building down from the street and added an additional story below the entry floor. The scheme looks like a southern California one primarily because of the presence of outdoor decks, courtyards, and patios. The building uses the decentralized nature of the building mass advantageously by creating three separate programs. One program is for ambulatory, independent assisted living residents. The second program, referred to as *enhanced care*, is for those who are more physically impaired and need assistance with transfers and a higher level of personal care. The third program is for residents with dementia. Common spaces are elegantly furnished, and the views of the ocean and the adjacent canyon are strategically developed throughout the building.

Project Features

Multifloor Building Wraps Around a Small, Sloping Site

This 75 unit, five-floor building is located on the bluffs overlooking the Pacific Ocean. Sandwiched between Pacific Coast Highway and a severe grade change, which eventually terminates at the ocean edge below, the building is shoehorned into a very tight site. In addition to massing concerns, the architects had to deal with soils problems and fire code interpretations for licensure. The

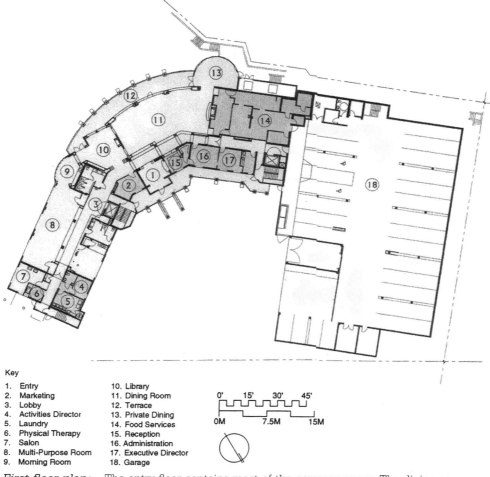

Key

1. Entry
2. Marketing
3. Lobby
4. Activities Director
5. Laundry
6. Physical Therapy
7. Salon
8. Multi-Purpose Room
9. Morning Room
10. Library
11. Dining Room
12. Terrace
13. Private Dining
14. Food Services
15. Reception
16. Administration
17. Executive Director
18. Garage

First-floor plan: The entry floor contains most of the common space. The dining room, library, breakfast area, balcony, and multipurpose room wrap around the edge of the floor and take in a spectacular ocean view. Parking is handled in an adjacent covered garage. (Courtesy JBZ Architects)

Observation deck is created by the view corridor: Adjoining property owners lobbied for a reduction in the building's mass to create a view corridor. This centrally located space is an outdoor deck above the main floor that overlooks the ocean. (Photo: Barbara White Architectural Photography)

building is located in the upscale seaside community of Corona Del Mar. The massing and detailing of its appearance are consistent with the architecture of the surrounding neighborhood, which is a mix of commercial and residential uses. The U-shaped building surrounds a landscaped auto courtyard. A parking garage tucked under the building at the entry level is directly accessible from this courtyard. The roof of the parking lot is used as a sensory garden for the dementia care program.

Building Has a Seaside Look with Natural-colored Wood Shingles

A bridge links the auto court with the main entry door. Clustered around the entry area are the majority of common spaces. A continuous light well on the auto court side of the building brings daylight into seven less desirable units located on a lower floor. Altogether there are 75 units, including 14 on the lowest floor for enhanced care and 17 on an upper level for dementia care. The building is friendly and residential, with distinctive nautical-style turrets with high windows that appear to be lighthouse inspired. The building is covered with cedar shingles that are natural in color. The shingles contrast with the white trim around windows, doors, and columns. Charcoal gray shingles are used on the roof.

Building Massing Creates a View Corridor

The building is carefully massed to ensure a view corridor through the center of the building. This preserves the view of the ocean from adjoining properties and creates an outdoor viewing deck for residents. The massing,

which is one story higher on the north side and stepped back from the street, adds variety to the composition. Shaping the building in this way creates five relatively distinct corridor segments on the upper floors. Elevators from each of these unit clusters lead to the main floor.

Community Spaces Are Clustered on the Entry Floor

One of the most compelling features of the building is the view of the ocean and the surrounding canyon from the dining room. Multiple-level soffited ceilings add variety to the dining room ceiling plane. To the west side of the dining room is a semicircular private dining room for family events. The open dining room is designed so that views are immediately apparent when a person enters the building. Inviting wood grain flooring, subdued light peach colors, and a wood wainscot are featured at the building's entry. Common spaces with different functions, including a library with a fireplace and a shared computer space available to residents, line up along the southern edge of the building. Next to the library is a bistro space for informal snacks and morning coffee. A large lounge space with a parlor and a baby grand piano at one end is used for afternoon socials. The north end of this floor contains office spaces and a family room. A beauty shop and a gift store are also located in this general area.

Care Is Provided for Three Distinct Populations

The three populations served by the building are ambulatory residents, physically challenged nonambulatory residents who need help with transfers, and residents with dementia. Each population is located in a separate wing of the building. The cluster of 14 nonambulatory units is on the lowest floor and has access to an adjacent garden area and a terrace. It is referred to as the *enhanced care* neighborhood. Assisted living is graded into four progressive levels of care that match staff time with the needs of each resident. Individualized care plans are established for each resident, and health assessments are made by a nurse. Service is an important priority for the sponsor, so much so that they provide a guarantee that management will respond to a resident's concern in 30 minutes and correct the problem in 24 hours or they will compensate the resident financially. Room service is available to provide another dining choice for residents. The building also provides a short-stay program for individuals who are convalescing from surgery or illness or who need respite care. A day care program called the "Cove Club" provides care for people from the surrounding neighborhood.

Dwelling Unit Design Provides Many Amenities

The project is broken into six unit clusters that vary in size from 5 to 21 units. The building form was adapted to maximize ocean views, and 40 percent of the dwelling units have one. Balconies were designed into top-floor, single-loaded corridor units to maximize views and the opportunity for outdoor living. All of the units are relatively compact studios, although each unit has a walk-in closet and storage space in the bathroom. Each unit is wired for high-speed computer access, satellite cable television, and emergency response.

Dementia Neighborhood Has a Large Sensory Garden

The dementia unit is L-shaped and surrounds two sides of a secure sensory garden. The garden is accessible from the living room and a family room. The 17-dwelling unit cluster, with a resident capacity of 24, is intimate in scale and is located above the main common area floor. The focus of the program is on reinforcing ADLs. There is a life skills kitchen that is used for baking and other activities. It also functions as the servery for a home-style dining program. Residents take their meals in a small dining room adjacent to the kitchen. The floor also has a living room lounge and a family room with an aviary and patio at one end of the corridor. The facility has developed a program called *memories in the making* to enhance reminiscence activities. The dementia program caters to the needs of each resident, who has a designated caregiver. This makes it less confusing for residents and allows caregivers to learn the likes and dislikes of each resident for whom they have responsibility. There are four graduated levels of care in the dementia program. At each doorway facing the hallway is a large shadow box where residents can display personal items that can be useful for orientation or for expressing identity.

Outdoor Decks and Balconies Have Ocean and Canyon Views

One of the strongest qualities of this design is the decks and balconies created for outdoor use. These are found in one form or another on almost every floor. The main entry floor has a balcony that runs along the outside perimeter of the dining room, permitting views of the ocean. On the next floor above, there are two large decks. One is dedicated to the dementia program, and the view corridor that cuts through the building forms the other. This space, named the Captain Seaward Observation Deck, is large and spacious, with excellent views of the ocean and the neighboring wilderness preserve. However, it is not very convenient from the main entry floor. The upper floors on both sides of the view corridor have large, spacious balconies. Finally, the enhanced-care wing on the lowest floor has access to a courtyard garden. Outdoor spaces at this building are used for special events in the summer.

20

SUNRISE OF BELLEVUE

Bellevue, Washington

Architect   Dietrich-Mithun Architects | Seattle, Washington
Sponsor   Sunrise Assisted Living

Building Characteristics

Number of units	70
Number of stories	4
Context	Suburban
Housing type	Assisted living and dementia
Building parti/shape	L
Unit mixture	40 studios
	15 companion suites
	15 one-bedroom
Size of most common unit (average)	380 SF
Community facilities	No
Community-accessible meals	Family members
Date of completion	September 1998

Resident Characteristics

Average age	84
Number of residents	81
Number of couples/men/ women	12 single men
	55 single women
	7 couples
Age range	62–98
Percent requiring bathing help	65 percent
Percent requiring toileting help	58 percent
Percent incontinent	43 percent
Percent wheelchair-bound	14 percent
Percent cognitively impaired	36 percent

L-shaped plan embraces the entry: This four-story building with wide overhangs and dormer windows has an Arts and Crafts appearance. A porte cochere provides an undercover walkway from the car to the entrance in this rainy northwestern climate. (Photo: Robert Pisano)

S U M M A R Y

The Sunrise at Bellevue is a four-story L-shaped building that contains 70 units. It has been the recipient of several design awards. The building is designed in an Arts and Crafts style, including interior furniture and trim. It is located on a half-acre site bounded by a community center, a park, and a commercial shopping district. The building contains a dementia unit on the fourth floor with an outdoor balcony. There is also a small secured garden with a 5-foot wood fence on the first floor that dementia residents can use for exercise. The floor plate is very compact, and the result is a highly efficient building with relatively short corridors. The short distance between each unit and the elevator makes it easier for residents with physical impairments to reach the elevator from their rooms and to access the dining room. Offices for the caregiving staff are centrally located on the second floor. Three primary unit designs are utilized. About half of the units are studios, a quarter are one bedroom, and the remainder are dumbbell-shaped units with two spaces that can be used for single or double occupancy.

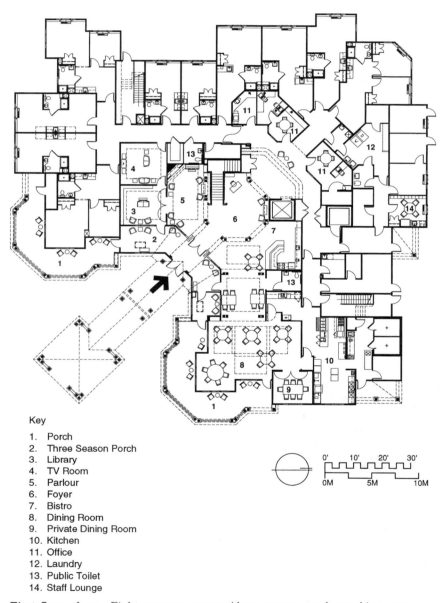

Key

1. Porch
2. Three Season Porch
3. Library
4. TV Room
5. Parlour
6. Foyer
7. Bistro
8. Dining Room
9. Private Dining Room
10. Kitchen
11. Office
12. Laundry
13. Public Toilet
14. Staff Lounge

First-floor plan: Eight common spaces (three season porch, smoking room, porch, library, parlour, bistro, dining room and foyer) clustered around the front entry provide access to a wide range of social spaces. (Courtesy Dietrich-Mithun Architects)

Dining room continues the emphasis on arts and crafts: A dining room sized for two consecutive seatings is relatively small and intimate in scale. Gray-brown trim with dark oak furniture that has green/gold accents in the chair fabric adds to the character of the space. (Photo: Robert Pisano)

Project Features

Compact Building Is Located on a Tight Site

The building is an attractive four-story wood frame structure. Its color is a combination of dark gray and light gray siding, with contrasting white frame windows. Two white horizontal bands occur at the first and third floors to add horizontality to the building mass. In addition to a change in color, the top floor and roof have several features that give it increased interest. Gables are used at the dominant ends and in the middle of the building, with hip roofs over the large, square turrets. Heavy curved brackets at the corners of the turrets, with horizontal purlins between them, give the wide roof overhang greater emphasis. Shed dormers add additional emphasis to the roof. At the ground floor, a wraparound open porch and a three-season porch combine to make the building friendly and approachable from the street. The three-season porch utilizes large windows with low 6-inch-high sills and skylights to create edge spaces that connect visually with the surrounding landscape. The dominant porte cochere signals how to enter the build-

ing from the street and offers protected access into the building—a useful feature in this rainy climate. A sidewalk that loops around the building's perimeter provides a way for residents to exercise.

Open Plan Creates Friendly Visual Connections to Adjacent First-floor Common Rooms

The building uses an open plan to connect visitors visually to a number of different features. A person entering the building can see into the dining room, bistro, living room, and library. Rooms are defined and made distinct through the use of wall coverings, columns, half-walls, floor covering changes, and different ceiling heights. A floating concierge desk is located at the foot of a monumental staircase that connects the first and second floors (see photo 67). Medium-dark wood trim and casework, in combination with Stickley-style furniture and Craftsman style mutton details on windows and doors, give the building its Arts and Crafts look. Interior fabric and carpet colors are primarily gold and green. The major first-floor spaces consist of a two-story foyer, a small-scale dining room with two seatings, a bistro with a wooden floor, a piano and jukebox, a parlor with a corner fireplace, a quiet library alcove, and a TV room. Staff offices and a conference room are located in the center of the building.

Caregiving Offices and Activity Room Are on the Second Floor

The second floor contains the caregiving offices and the activity room. The activity room is split between a carpeted area with a large-screen TV and a vinyl wood-grain hard-surface space where messy activities are staged. The third floor contains the beauty shop and a large lounge space that can be used for meetings and staff training. The fourth floor is a secured dementia unit. A single-sided tub/spa with a drop-down access door is located on the third and fourth floors. This type of tub is preferred over the peninsula-style bather, where residents must be suspended over and lowered into the tub. Newer tub designs are open below to accommodate hydraulic lift devices.

Offices for Care Personnel Are Designed to Make Them Approachable

The amount of care that each resident receives is ascertained through a monthly assessment. This analysis establishes the amount of help needed for bathing, dressing, transferring, eating, basic ambulation, and assistance with incontinence. Activities are oriented to smaller groups and at least six activities per day are available,

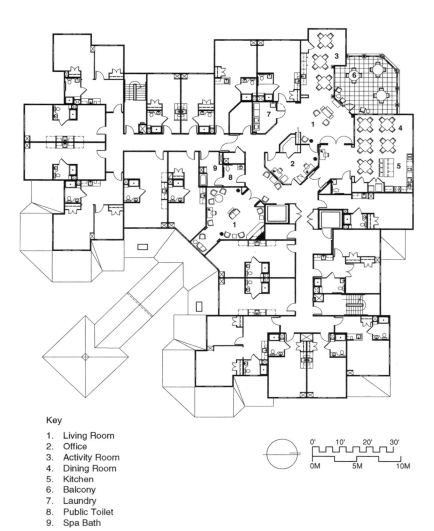

Key

1. Living Room
2. Office
3. Activity Room
4. Dining Room
5. Kitchen
6. Balcony
7. Laundry
8. Public Toilet
9. Spa Bath

Dementia floor plan: Common space is clustered in the center of this compact upper-floor plan. A walking loop around the staff office puts residents in contact with the dining room, an outdoor patio, an activity room, the kitchen, a living room, the laundry, and the bathroom/spa. (Courtesy Dietrich-Mithun Architects)

including a van ride, an afternoon social, and an after-dinner activity. A wellness nurse trained as a registered nurse is on duty 40 hours per week, with the assistance of a licensed practical nurse during the rest of the time. Sunrise's policies and priorities are oriented to residents' desires rather than driven by regulatory considerations. They pride themselves on the personal attention that staff pays to residents and family members. Offices are designed with half-walls, Dutch doors, and windows to make them more approachable from the corridor for family and resident contact. Several programs are in place to encourage family members and friends to volunteer to work with residents who benefit from more personal contact. Finally, in order to guarantee that important policies are implemented in all homes, Sunrise has de-

veloped 22 Sunrise Signatures. These requirements range from a live-in dog and cat to a box of children's toys available for visiting youngsters.

Common Spaces for the Dementia Floor Are Centralized

The fourth-floor dementia neighborhood contains 18 dwelling units split into two nine-unit clusters in each wing. These two clusters connect to the middle of the building, where all of the common space is located. The main common spaces include a living room with a fireplace and a centralized staff office with windows that overlook the common spaces and corridors. The dining room, sized for a single seating, is adjacent to a life skills–style kitchen. Adjacent to the kitchen is a large table for residents who need assistance with eating. The floor also has a shared outdoor balcony, an activity room, a spa and toilet, and a resident laundry with a nearby table where residents can fold laundry. A looped pathway in the center of the floor meanders past all of the common space rooms, including the dining room, living room, kitchen, and activity room. A small alcove is available for snoezelen activities, a Dutch concept that involves the use of multisensory experiences to calm residents and facilitate communication with them. An outdoor balcony with a surrounding trellis for safety purposes is used frequently. A secured garden on the first floor can be reached from a second elevator to facilitate access from the dementia floor. Four large clear skylights are strategically located throughout the floor to provide daylight for rooms and spaces that don't have the benefit of nearby windows.

Philosophy Involves Stimulating Abilities Through Life Skills

The dementia program focuses on creating "pleasant days" for residents. Staff receive specialized training to deal with the complexity and unpredictability associated with dementing illnesses. A family resource library is also available, with books and monographs that describe effective therapies and the latest research findings. Life skills stations and reminiscence kits that focus on themes like sports, handicrafts, gardening, beauty, baby care, weddings, and military service allow family and staff to find something that is of interest to every resident. The stations and kits are used as props to elicit interaction with and responses from residents.

Dwelling Units Have Big Windows

Three unit types are available that vary in size from 315 to 525 SF. A few dwelling units contain firelight glass windows that connect the unit with the corridor. This unusual feature creates a visual connection to the corridor. Residents or their families decorate shadow boxes located outside each room to express their individuality. Dwelling units contain a full bathroom with a raised toilet, a handicap-adaptable lavatory and cabinet, a subdividable medicine cabinet, a 3×4-foot shower with a movable seat, an emergency call cord between the shower and toilet, and nonslip residential-style flooring. In some dwelling units, fully accessible roll-in showers are available. A small tea kitchen contains a refrigerator, a sink, and cabinetry. A large 6×6-foot window with a 24-inch-high sill floods the room with light, making it appear larger. Alzheimer's dwelling units are the same size and type as assisted living units, but they have a few special features. For example, one wall of the bathroom is painted green to make the white toilet and lavatory fixtures more visible. Graduated dressing armoires are available for residents who need help organizing the order of their clothing when getting dressed. Another photo of Sunrise of Bellevue is available in the color insert.

21

SUNRISE OF RICHMOND

Richmond, Virginia

Architect   Berry Rio and Associates | Springfield, Virginia
Sponsor   Sunrise Assisted Living

Building Characteristics

Number of units	70
Number of stories	1
Context	Suburban
Housing type	Assisted living and dementia
Building parti/shape	H
Unit mixture	32 studios
	12 one-bedroom
	26 companion-style
Size of most common unit (average)	380 SF
Community facilities	No
Community-accessible meals	No—family and friends only
Date of completion	July 1999

Resident Characteristics

Average age	84
Number of residents	81
Number of couples/men/ women	14 men
	53 women
	7 couples
Age range	67–98
Percent requiring bathing help	51 percent
Percent requiring toileting help	37 percent
Percent incontinent	31 percent
Percent wheelchair-bound	23 percent
Percent cognitively impaired	30 percent

Building is nestled within a wooded site: One-story buildings with a porch entry that surround two sides of an entry garden combine gable and hip roof patterns. The building is clad with gray shingles and contrasting light trim. (Photo: Stewart Brothers)

SUMMARY

This project consists of three-1-story buildings with a total of 70 units. Two assisted living buildings have 26 units each, while the third building, for dementia residents, has 18 units. The site is heavily wooded and located on the outskirts of the city of Richmond, Virginia. Designed in an Arts and Crafts Style, the building has a simple plan that minimizes corridor lengths and centralizes the main common spaces. Common spaces include a dining room, serving kitchen, living room, bistro, and three-season porch. A large stone double-hearth fireplace separates the living room and dining room. Display niches and lighting brings attention to the fireplace as a major interior feature. Care management is decentralized, but all meals are prepared in the central building and all heavy-duty laundry is handled in the 26-unit west building. A softscape outdoor courtyard is located in front of each building. A covered entry porch overlooks this space. At the rear of the building is a hardscape patio with a trellis that is visible from the dining room.

Units have 10-foot-high ceilings and large windows to increase their perceived size. This wood frame building allows residents who are incapable of self-preservation to live here, allowing the population to age in place.

Project Features

Cottage Concept Stresses an Intimate Social Cluster of Residents

The most interesting feature of this concept is the decentralization of units into three highly approachable, small-scale buildings. The Arts and Crafts style used inside and outside reinforces the philosophy that residents "see nothing they wouldn't see in their own homes." Commercial fixtures, furniture, finishes, and equipment have been carefully avoided. The wooded site and the shingle-style exterior treatment help to reinforce the idea that each building is a small cottage in the woods. The buildings are designed as self-contained environments from a caregiving perspective. A continuous front side-

Key

1. Main Building
2. Twin Building
3. Alzheimer's Building
4. Service Building
5. Detention Pond

Site plan: Three small buildings are planned in a crescent shape with a connecting sidewalk. The parking lot in front was sculpted to save as many trees as possible. It includes two 26-unit buildings and an 18-unit dementia cottage. (Courtesy Berry Rio Architects)

Key

1. Three Season Porch
2. Smoking Porch
3. Living Room
4. Library
5. Resident Laundry
6. Bistro
7. Serving Kitchen
8. Dining
9. Kitchen
10. Community Relations Office
11. Executive Director's Office
12. Work Room
13. Wellness Office
14. Spa
15. Hair Care
16. Staff Room
17. Private Dining
18. Mechanical Room

First-floor assisted living plan: Two wings with 13 units flank a cluster of centrally located common spaces. A softscape garden in the front and a hardscape barbecue plaza in back provide accessible outdoor spaces. Food is prepared in the central kitchen and moved to the other two buildings. (Courtesy Berry Rio Architects)

walk links the three buildings together, while rear service entries and sidewalks allow food and goods to flow in back from one building to another. The sidewalk also wraps around the perimeter of each building and through wooded areas of the site.

Three-Building Configuration Allowed Trees to Be Saved

The three buildings were planned next to one another in an arc configuration. This plan also allowed a tree save area in the middle of the site to be maintained. The result is a double vale of mature trees, which gives the project the feeling of being placed in a forest of existing trees. Additional trees were planted along the outside perimeter to reinforce the wooded character of the site. The wood shingle buildings in gray and natural tones use gable and hip roof forms to add interest and reduce the scale of the buildings. A picket fence in front and an extended entry porch welcome visitors. An accessible front

and rear garden is created as a result of the H-shaped plan. Controlled views of each garden are created from the three-season porch in front and the dining room in back.

Bungalow Arts and Crafts Style Is Reflected in the Wall, Ceiling, and Casework Details

Stylistic continuity was sought between the architecture, casework, trim, lighting fixtures, and furniture. Casework and trim details included (1) a traditional dark-colored banding board treatment above windows and doors; (2) the use of a paired joist *flying header* above portals to corridors and alcoves; (3) the creation of a plate shelf with support knuckles approximately 18 inches from the ceiling in the living and dining rooms; and (4) the application of wood strapwork to the ceiling. Hanging pendant-style incandescent brass chandelier fixtures were utilized in the shared common areas, while pendant-style bowl fixtures that emphasize indirect and soft, direct light were used in offices and residential corridors. Building edge features such as a square bay window in the dining room, a three-season porch with skylights (see color insert), and a covered entry porch were used to emphasize the cozy bungalow character of the building.

Interior Treatments Are Consistent with the Traditional Arts and Crafts Motif

Soft chenille fabrics, which are literally warm and fuzzy, are utilized in rust, peach, and hunter greens. These colors, selected to reflect the glow of the fireplace, are attractive to the eye and to the hand. These fabrics are saturated with polymer bonding solution and moisture-proofed on the back to protect them from problems like incontinence. Tiffany-style iridescent glass lampshades were specified in the living room, along with Stickley-style dark oak furniture. The designs used for chests, chairs, ottomans, armoires, and tables are in the Arts and Crafts style. This style was common in the eastern United States at the turn of the twentieth century.

Circulation Is Compact and Loops Through the Dining Room and Living Room

One aspect of this plan that makes it especially effective is its looped, compact configuration. Two short 6-foot-wide corridors lead from the units to major common spaces in the middle of the building. This arrangement is particularly effective in the dementia building, where residents are able to wander without becoming confused. A central two-sided fireplace visually separates the living room and dining room. The intimate, attractively scaled living room ensemble planned in front of the fireplace is immediately visible when someone enters the building. The fireplace is lighted and terraced to create places where accessories can be displayed. The dining room also takes advantage of the central fireplace, utilizing the dining room side to create an attractive focal feature for this room. Other common spaces that encourage independence or socialization include a laundry, a hair care area, a private dining room, a bistro (see page 73), and an open serving kitchen. The leftover space in the plan between the dining room/living room and the dwelling unit corridor contains the kitchen, laundry, office spaces, break rooms, storage areas, and toilets.

Intimate Scale of the Care Setting Creates a More Personal Caregiving Environment

The more intimate environment created by this three-building, single-story design leads to personal family-style caregiving. This intimate setting is believed to maximize the time spent by caregivers with residents. A designated staffing approach utilizes the *universal worker* philosophy, in which all workers have a direct relationship with residents. Added to this is the fact that everyone knows everyone else. The small scale of the setting also emphasizes the personal characteristics of residents, family members, and the staff in defining the social milieu of each cottage. A small serving kitchen is designed into each building to encourage ADL programming. The kitchen area is designed to support work spaces for the staff as well as activity spaces for the residents. A large eat-in kitchen table is placed here for family-style dining and to provide a convenient place for residents to carry out craft activities, as well as recreational cooking and baking activities.

Centrally located fireplace divides the living room and dining room: Arts and Crafts furnishings, wood strap work on the ceilings, a plate shelf surrounding the room, and a stone fireplace add to the homelike character of the space. (Photo: Jerry Staley Photography)

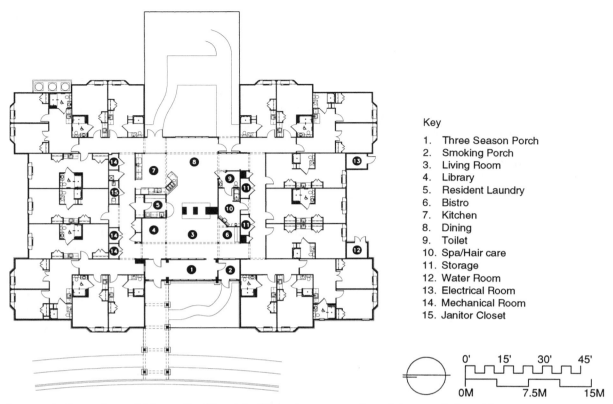

Key

1. Three Season Porch
2. Smoking Porch
3. Living Room
4. Library
5. Resident Laundry
6. Bistro
7. Kitchen
8. Dining
9. Toilet
10. Spa/Hair care
11. Storage
12. Water Room
13. Electrical Room
14. Mechanical Room
15. Janitor Closet

Dementia floor plan: This smaller 18-unit building shares a number of characteristics with the larger building. The garden at the rear of the property is a secured, fenced outdoor space. (Courtesy Berry Rio Architects)

Dwelling Unit Design Features Are Flexible and Adaptable

Residents' rooms have 10-foot-high ceilings and 6 × 6-foot windows, making dwelling units appear larger. Twenty-four-inch-high window sills, which are 80 inches wide and 10 inches deep, were designed above low-profile through-the-wall heating and air conditioning units. The wide sills, used by residents for plants and displays, camouflage the air-handling units. There are three dwelling unit sizes and types. Nearly half of the units are studios, a third are companion-style suites, and the remainder are one-bedroom units. The building has attracted an unusual number of couples, perhaps because of its intimate residential scale. Finally, the bathroom is spacious, with sink base cabinet faces that can be removed for handicapped residents. Roll-in showers are available in 10 percent of the units. Plywood backing adjacent to the toilet wall allows the grab bar to be rearranged at any height or angled to meet the needs and preferences of each resident. Other photos of Sunrise of Richmond are available on page 307 and the color insert.

22

COPPER RIDGE

Sykesville, Maryland

Architect Perkins-Eastman and Partners | Pittsburgh, Pennsylvania
Sponsor Episcopal Health Ministries to the Aging

Building Characteristics

Number of units	126 beds (60 for dementia)
Number of stories	1 story (dementia)
Context	Rural small town
Housing type	Dementia and skilled nursing care
Building parti/shape	complex (three U shapes)
Unit mixture	60 studios (dementia)
Size of most common unit (average)	200 SF
Community facilities	Yes (day-care center)
Community accessible meals	No—family and friends only
Date of completion	July 1994

Resident Characteristics

Average age	77
Number of residents	60 (dementia only)
Number of couples/men/women	16 men / 44 women
Age range	54–93
Percent requiring bathing help	60 percent
Percent requiring toileting help	40 percent
Percent incontinent	25 percent
Percent wheelchair-bound	5 percent
Percent cognitively impaired	100 percent

Axonometric drawing:
Copper Ridge offers both nursing and dementia care. The 60 units of dementia care, located to the left of the entry, consist of three U-shaped houses with 20 residents each. (Courtesy Perkins-Eastman Architects)

SUMMARY

Copper Ridge is a partial continuum of care project that contains skilled nursing and dementia care. It is located adjacent to the campus of Fairhaven, a senior housing development in a small town outside of metropolitan Baltimore. Copper Ridge is best known for its innovative dementia design of 60 dwelling units, which benefited from extensive research that was carried out for an earlier project, Woodside Place (Hoglund and Ledewitz, 1999; Kershner, Roques, et al., 1999; Silverman, Ricci, et al., 1996). One of the most interesting aspects of this project is how the units have been clustered. The 60 dwelling units are subdivided into three U-shaped 20-unit clusters.

Each of these clusters is further subdivided into two ten-unit "houses." These houses, in turn, are split into two 5-unit clusters. The design matches the staffing pattern with the architectural unit layout. The other innovative feature is the use and treatment of outdoor spaces. Each 20-unit cluster defines a small, intimate courtyard and porch that are accessible from the common dining and living rooms. Two larger outdoor spaces with walking pathways are shared by the three clusters. A large courtyard in the center of the building is designed for special events. The caregiving program is fitted to the needs and characteristics of each resident. An ADL philosophy is followed by involving residents in day-to-day tasks like setting the dinner table and making their beds.

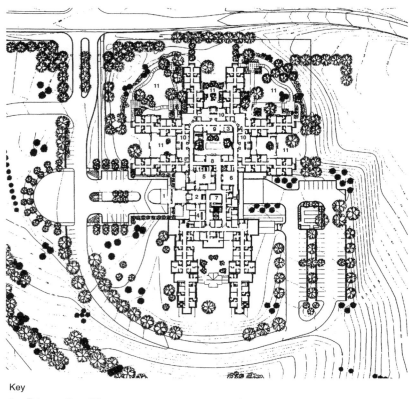

Key

1. Entrance Drop-Off
2. Entrance Lobby / Reception
3. Activity Room
4. Administration
5. Adult Day Care
6. Multi-Purpose Room
7. Coffee and Gift Shop
8. Living Room
9. Garden Room
10. Alzheimer's Resident House
11. Secure Wandering Garden

0' 60' 120' 180'
0M 30M 60M

Site plan: The three U-shaped dementia clusters are connected by a looped pathway that surrounds a central courtyard. Three small gardens are created by each cluster, with two larger gardens with walking pathways in the corners between units. (Courtesy Perkins-Eastman Architects)

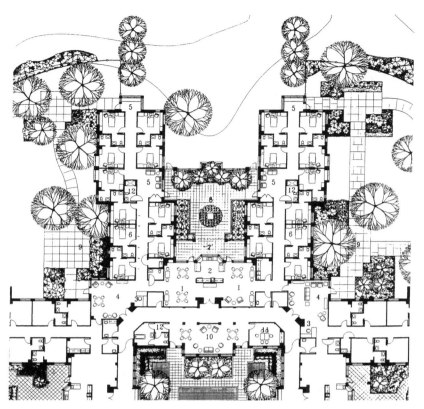

Key

1. Dining Room
2. ADL Kitchen
3. Nurse Alcove
4. Den
5. Sitting Area
6. Private Resident Room
7. Porch
8. Secure Courtyard
9. Secure Wandering Garden
10. Garden Room
11. Activity Room
12. Tub and Shower Room

Twenty-unit cluster: Each wing of this U-shaped cluster contains ten rooms. A fenced outdoor garden with an attached porch allows residents to walk freely inside and outside. Units are single-occupied but contain only a sink and toilet. Bathing facilities are shared. (Courtesy Perkins-Eastman Architects)

These familiar household duties normalize their day. An active day-care program is open to 25 memory-impaired people from the surrounding community.

Project Features

Building Is Broken into Three 20-Unit Clusters

The design of the dementia unit at Copper Ridge centers on (1) the concept of linking designated staff to small clusters of residents and (2) the idea of allowing residents as much freedom as possible to roam the building and the adjacent outdoor gardens. The cluster design is broken into three U-shaped clusters of 20 dwelling units. Each cluster consists of two 10-unit "houses." Each house is divided into two small-group clusters of five units each. The 10-unit houses are better for staffing, and the 20-unit cluster is more efficient for food service. The appearance of the one-story building includes details of the surrounding suburban housing, with yellow siding, white trim, and a brick water table.

Interior Colors and Styles Are Used to Create Differences Between Clusters

The interior design utilizes three distinct styles to differentiate each 20-unit cluster. The designs include (1) an Annapolis-inspired "old town" look that relies on Federal detailing; (2) an "Eastern Shore" style inspired by the informal, relaxed culture of this seaside recreational area; and (3) a "Carroll County" style that reflects the surrounding small-town feel and turn-of-the-century architecture. The central courtyard is used to create an orientation point for all three houses. There are several sitting areas including window seats that overlook the courtyard from the surrounding corridor. This corridor also has an effectively disguised entry door that leads to the building's main entrance. This route is used by family members as a quiet way of entering and exiting the building.

The Cluster Kitchen Is Designed to Be Used by Residents

One of the most unique features of the caregiving plan is its ADL philosophy. This involves the identification of normal, routine daily life activities such as folding napkins, setting the table, bussing dishes, making one's bed, and dusting the common area, which residents are encouraged to perform. Among the most effective architectural props for this program is an open kitchen that residents can use but that also operates as a servery for meals. The kitchen has been designed with familiar-looking fixtures and windows that overlook the courtyard. A cabinet where silverware, napkins, plates, and glasses are kept allows staff to direct residents to help

with meals. The floors are residential-style sheet vinyl to make it appear more like a real kitchen. For safety purposes, the stove, coffee pot, and toaster have been wired to a switch in a locked cabinet.

Courtyard and Circulation Pathway Link the Clusters Together

All three houses share the central courtyard (see page 152) and a series of common spaces around it. The circulation corridor that surrounds the courtyard and links the front doors of the houses also connects residents to several common lounges, a crafts room, a living room, and an activity room. The outside wall surrounding each cluster entry has two large glass windows. These windows bring light from the courtyard into the dining room through the shared corridor. Two corner living room spaces situated between the three 20-unit clusters are popular places for TV watching, game playing, and arts and crafts. Accessible from these living rooms are larger courtyards where residents can walk for exercise. A decentralized nurse's station is also located here.

Three Distinct Outdoor Areas with Different Roles and Purposes Are Available

The weaving of outdoor space with small clusters of units makes Copper Ridge particularly delightful. There are three different types of outdoor space. In the middle of the plan is a central shared courtyard with plants and furniture. This courtyard is used for group events and for orientation purposes. The second outdoor space is a small garden with a porch that each 20-unit cluster is planned around. This garden space is surrounded by the build-

Dining room is adjacent to the kitchen and a covered porch: The kitchen, open to dining rooms on both sides, is designed to encourage residents to participate in the meal preparation and serving process. (Photo: Robert Ruschak)

ing on three sides and by a 5-foot solid wood fence on the fourth side. The third outdoor space consists of two large outdoor areas open off living room lounges between the three 20-unit clusters. This garden is designed for walking and large-group activities. A looped walking path surrounds the perimeter of this garden, and it is secured by a 6-foot-high wrought iron fence. Each of these three types of outdoor spaces is secured separately. Evaluations suggest that they might have better been linked together for a more extensive walking/pathway system.

Care Program Is Negotiated with the Family

The daily life program focuses on fitting services to the needs of residents. This is similar to the *op maat* approach described in the *Humanitas* (page 158) and *Wilhelmiina* (page 163) projects. The personal and social history of each resident is important in developing a plan for working with each resident. Caregivers are particularly sensitive to the relationships of family caregivers who assumed major responsibility for a resident's care before the move to Copper Ridge. Care conferences with family members are scheduled regularly, and the family is invited to volunteer to participate in the program. Universal staff workers are also crucial to increasing efficiency and making care more personal. All staff are involved in working with residents. Staff training is also a high priority. Activities that are carried out with residents include baking, singing, walking, reading the Bible, playing cards, looking through fashion magazines, nail manicur-

ing, working on craft projects, and weeding the garden. One of the most popular activities involves the use of music for singing, dancing, and general entertainment. A day-care center for adults with a capacity of 25 is also available. A respite program called the Carroll Club is administered by the day-care center.

Dwelling Units Feature Dutch Entry Doors, Sliding Barn Doors, and Window Seats

Each single-occupied, 200-SF unit contains a number of interesting features. For orientation purposes, identity boards are located next to each resident's door. A Dutch half-door entry is used for sociability purposes. The bathroom, for accessibility reasons, has a barn-type sliding door, a second medicine cabinet, and a taller toilet. Outside the bathroom is a night light to guide residents from the bed to the toilet. However, the bathroom does not contain a shower—an omission later regretted. Showers located between the unit clusters are shared by ten residents. In each resident's room, a small plate shelf with pegs is mounted to one wall for display purposes. A large window with an attractive window seat and a low sill is adjacent to the bed (see page 24). Residents can easily see the ground plane while lying in bed. This window seat also has a storage space below and is often used for display purposes. There is no built-in closet, but an armoire for clothing with wire shelving is available. Finally, a wainscot of vinyl wall covering is used around the perimeter of the room to make the walls more scuff-resistant.

23

VIRRANRANTA

Kiruvesi, Finland

Architect NVO Architects | Helsinki, Finland
Sponsor Kiruvesi Kommun

Building Characteristics

Number of units	50
Number of stories	1 (partial 2)
Context	Small town
Housing type	Mulitlevel service house
Building parti/shape	Spine
Unit mixture	40 long-term care units
	10 service house units
Size of most common unit (average)	225 SF (long-term care)
Community facilities	Yes
Community-accessible meals	Yes
Date of completion	April 1992

Resident Characteristics

Average age	80
Number of residents	60
Number of couples/men/women	9 men
	49 women
	1 couple
Age range	68–104
Percent requiring bathing help	100 percent
Percent requiring toileting help	80 percent
Percent incontinent	38 percent
Percent wheelchair-bound	10 percent
Percent cognitively impaired	27 percent

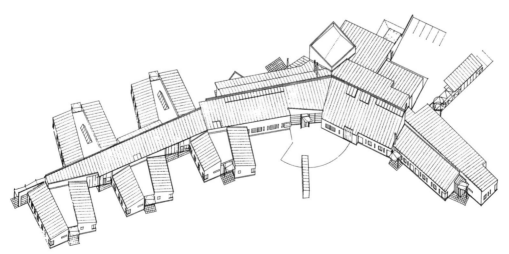

Axonometric drawing: Virranranta is a one-story service house that combines housing for mentally and physically frail people with community services for younger-older people in the neighborhood. The central portion of the building is devoted to community functions. (Courtesy NVO Architects)

SUMMARY

This unusual one-story building combines four elements: (1) a community service center for residents of the service house and for older neighborhood residents, (2) an office for home care and home health delivery, (3) 10 service apartments, and (4) 40 dwelling units for people with physical impairments, dementia, and short-term stays. The site is a beautiful setting adjacent to a picturesque lake and the town center of Kiruvesi. The building is sited to maximize views of the lake and uses a long, thin circulation spine to connect one end of the building with the other. The service center includes a dining room, physical therapy space, and library. These spaces, along with the kitchen and home health offices, are located in the center of the building. Ten service apartments for more independent residents are at one end, and five small-group clusters of eight residents each are at the other end. Of the five clusters, the two most re-

mote ones are for dementia residents. Two other clusters are for the physically frail, and one is increasingly being used for short-stay and respite residents (Verderber and Fine, 2000). The service center is also a resource for older people living in the community as well as others, including youth groups. Centers like this have been developed in small towns throughout Finland because the municipality where the person is born is responsible for taking care of that person in old age.

Project Features

Service House Contains Community Services and Housing for Two Age Groups

The service center is the core of the building, and it offers a range of health and social services to residents of the building and to older people in the neighborhood. The sloped ceilings at this widest section of the building

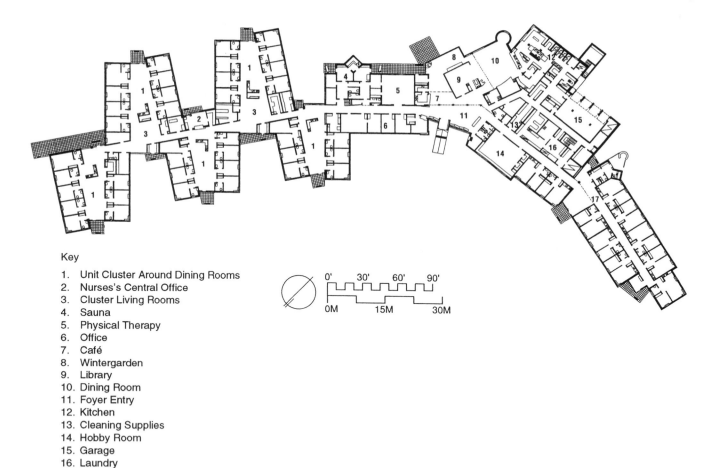

Key

1. Unit Cluster Around Dining Rooms
2. Nurses's Central Office
3. Cluster Living Rooms
4. Sauna
5. Physical Therapy
6. Office
7. Café
8. Wintergarden
9. Library
10. Dining Room
11. Foyer Entry
12. Kitchen
13. Cleaning Supplies
14. Hobby Room
15. Garage
16. Laundry
17. Service Apartments

First-floor plan: Five self-contained small group clusters (total 40 units) are at one end, with ten units of larger service housing on the other. The community spaces in the center include a dining room, winter garden, physical therapy area, library, and multipurpose room. (Courtesy NVO Architects)

create dramatic double-height spaces. A small second floor for administrative offices and storage is in the center of the building. The common spaces here include a kiosk, a winter garden sunroom (overlooking the lake), a library, a hobby/activity area, two saunas, a beauty shop, a physical therapy space, and a dramatic sloped-ceiling dining room with a stage. Two types of housing are located on opposite ends of the building and are easily accessible to the day center. At one end are service apartments. These are larger one-bedroom units for younger, more independent older people. At the other end are smaller long-term care units for frail older people. A day-care program, available twice a week for 50 residents of the community, is targeted to the socially isolated and those with beginning memory loss problems. The service center also monitors 30 to 40 older people in the neighborhood through a telephone-based emergency alarm system.

One-story Building Is Configured to Capture Views of the Lake and the Nearby Town

The building is an elegant one-story structure with one side oriented to the street and the other side open to a view of the lake. The roof is a silver-colored standing-seam metal structure that reflects the color of the sky and adds to the sculptural character of the building. The low-scaled building blends with the site. It was designed to maximize lake views from inside the building. Besides the dining room, one of the more popular places is the winter garden greenhouse (see color insert). It creates a termination of the entry area axis and is distinctly shaped to capture views and provide an intimate place for older people to sit. The building was placed high on a raised plateau to avoid potential problems with spring floods. Its blue color was selected to blend with the sky and create a subtle contrast with the snow in the winter and the green surrounding lawn in the summer. Bolder colors are applied to segments of the building to create interest and call attention to various elements.

Two-story Spine Links the Major Spaces Together

The central spine is a powerful organizing, unifying, and orienting element that links one end of the building with the other. It is broken into three segments to minimize its perceived length and to define three major sections of the building. A two-story height is used to add grand scale to the public spaces. The height of the spine is reduced when the corridor enters the residential portions of the building. Clerestory windows occur at the spine to bath it in natural light during the day. The spine is an indoor space but has the character of an outdoor street.

Multistory circulation spine links the building and daylights the corridor: Community spaces are connected to the housing by a meandering circulation spine that acts like a "shish kabob," connecting spaces together. (Photo: Raino Ahonen)

Brick pavers, light fixtures, and benches are used to reinforce this feeling.

Five Clustered Housing Groups Accommodate Mentally and Physically Frail Residents

The five trapezoidal clusters of eight units are among the most interesting features of this design. Likened to a "shish-kabob" the splaying of each unit cluster on both sides of the spine reduces the corridor's length and creates a series of courtyards. Each cluster is a self-contained small-group residence with a dining room, kitchen, and living room. Nonorthogonal walls were used to add interest to each unit cluster. Skylights located in the center of each dining room introduce natural light. A heavily utilized multipurpose table provides a place for activities and meals. A kitchen located between the dining room and living room in each unit cluster serves as a food preparation space and an ad hoc nurse's station.

Dining room serves the community and the service apartments: This large dining room is used daily by older people in the community and on special occasions by other community groups.

Medications and residents' records are kept in an upper kitchen cabinet. Adjacent to the kitchen is a living room space with a view to an outside courtyard. The two clusters for dementia residents at the end of the spine also have a covered patio and a secured outdoor space for gardening and walking.

Dwelling Units Have Windows with Low Sills

The long-term care dwellings are small, 225-SF, single-occupied units. They contain two small closets for personal clothing and possessions and a relatively large, bathroom with a sliding door and a roll-in shower. Windows are relatively large with low sills so that residents can see the views of the ground plane from their beds. The corner units have large wraparound corner windows (see page 55). A small ventilation door allows fresh air to enter the room in a controlled way in the winter without having to open a window. Each unit door opens directly onto the dining room.

Service House Dwelling Units Have Sloped Ceilings

The ten 1-bedroom units located at the west end of the building, which complement the housing for the frail at the east end of the building, are larger. Varying in size from 425 to 535 SF, they have small kitchens with a two-burner range and a refrigerator. Windows here also have low 14-inch-high sills, and the rooms are made to appear larger by using higher-sloped ceilings. Bathrooms have roll-in shower capability with sliding pocket doors. Residents can bring in their own furniture except for the bed. Hospital-type beds are used to ensure that the staff

Dining occurs in a central location in each small group cluster: Dwelling units surround a skylighted dining table. The kitchen at one end serves as a nurses' station, with residents' records and medications as well as a serving kitchen.

will not strain their backs while transferring residents. In the last few years, it has become clear the frailest population has the greatest needs. Residents who are only slightly more independent than the cluster unit residents have double-occupied the service apartment units. They take their meals in the large dining room because they are too frail to prepare meals in their own units.

Service Center Is Open to the Community

The service center has much the same role as a senior center in the United States. Except in northern Europe, the vast majority of day centers or service centers are attached to housing complexes and are also responsibile for serving neighborhood residents. Having housing for frail elderly people attached to the center allows it to eas-

ily broaden its responsibilities. About 100 older community residents visit this building during a typical week. The building is also shared by the local middle school, which uses the stage to perform plays. A chair exercise program occurs three times per week, and residents walk the length of the spine (approximately 500 feet) for exercise during the winter. There is no swimming pool, but a community pool is available nearby. The building has two elaborate saunas, each containing a dressing room, a shower, and an outdoor space. Residents like the sauna, but its use is a labor-intensive process, so they reserve it for special occasions like Christmas and Easter. The clustering of residents has allowed care management to be decentralized. Each cluster has its own lifestyle. At night two people take responsibility for all 60 residents and for the 30–40 persons in the community who are monitored by emergency alarms. Other photos of Virranranta are available on pages 49 and 302.

24

HARBOUR HOUSE

Greendale, Wisconsin

Architect   KM Development Corporation | Greendale, Wisconsin
Sponsor   Towne Realty Inc.

Building Characteristics

Number of units	44
Number of stories	2
Context	Suburban
Housing type	Dementia
Building parti/shape	X
Unit mixture	36 studios
	8 companion
Size of most common unit (average)	268 SF
Community-accessible facilities	Yes—learning center
Community accessible meals	No—family and friends only
Date of completion	December 1999

Resident Characteristics

Average age	83
Number of residents	36 (capacity 52)
Number of couples/men/women	16 single men
	20 single women
Age range	71–96
Percent requiring bathing help	100 percent
Percent requiring toileting help	70 percent
Percent incontinent	50 percent
Percent wheelchair-bound	1 percent
Percent cognitively impaired	100 percent

Harbour House is an Arts and Crafts–styled building: The building combines brick stone and wood siding in a way that makes it resemble a mansion from the street. Double rough-sawn cedar columns frame the entry. (Photo: Skot Wiedemann Photography)

SUMMARY

The Harbour House is a two-story, X-shaped, 44–unit dementia facility for 52 residents. It is part of a larger continuing-care campus, which includes a retirement residence, an assisted living building, and an adult day-care center. This Arts and Crafts–style building is designed as two L-shaped buildings joined together. Each L has space for 13 residents. A typical two-wing unit has nine single units, which are sized at 268 SF, and two double-occupancy rooms that average 412 SF (206 SF per person). A one-story administration building and learning center serves as the entry pavilion. The learning center is used for training and for community meetings. A concierge to provide information and assistance, a program director's office, and a small fireplace lounge for family members and guests are located here. At night and after business hours, family members and friends have computer access cards that they can use to gain access to the building. On the opposite side of the entry is a service court used for kitchen deliveries and trash removal. The other two courtyards are secured outdoor gardens that are directly accessible from the dining room of each L-shaped cluster. Each L has two shower rooms, two small lounges, a dining room, a living room, a country kitchen, a spa, a staff room, and an outdoor terrace or garden.

Project Features

Arts and Crafts Style Building Appears Residential in Character

The building is an attractive, approachable structure that uses brick, stone, and wood siding in an Arts and Crafts style. The building's footprint has great visual complexity, which makes the building resemble a large house.

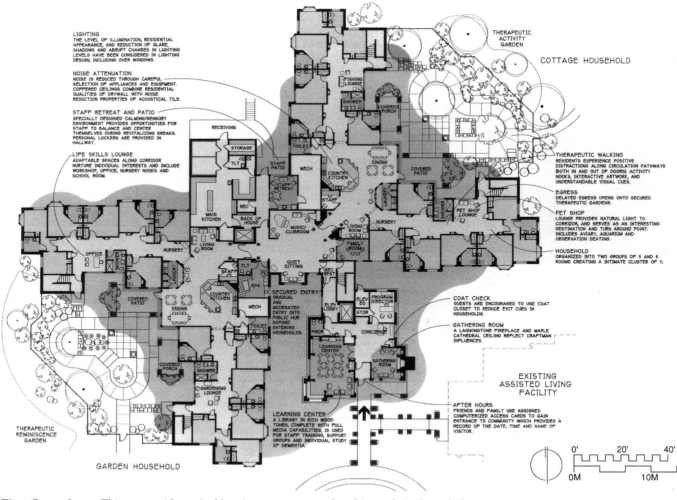

First-floor plan: Thirteen residents in 11 units are accommodated in each L-shaped cluster. Meals are taken in a dining area next to the country kitchen. The clusters share access to a spa and a music room on the first floor. (Courtesy KM Development)

Food service is decentralized in four country kitchens: Each kitchen has the capability of serving food at tables and along a breakfast bar. This kitchen also serves as an ad hoc nurse's station where staff can be outposted. (Photo: Skot Wiedemann Photography)

Bay windows in units near the end of each wing add interest and distinction to the corners of the building. A combination of gable, hip, and shed dormer forms add variety to the roof. A covered walkway that links the assisted living and dementia building to a drop-off area emphasizes the front of the building, further defining the entry. Stone-tapered base supports with double rough-sawn cedar columns frame the entry walk. The combination of stone and cedar, which is stained and not painted, reinforces the rustic character of the building.

Decentralized Clusters Have Distinct Identities

One of four themes is assigned to each of the four wings—Americana, woodland, garden, and cottage. Each wing is clustered around a living room, and each uses different colors, fabric types, and textures to define its separate character. Eight different themed lounge areas use different furniture, fabrics, and accessories to add individuality to each wing. The themes that are used include a workshop, office, nursery, schoolroom, gardening, pet shop, fishing, sports/games, and quilting.

Kitchen Serves as a Focal Point for Each Cluster

The two country kitchens and dining rooms on each floor provide the conceptual center to each L. Food is delivered there from the kitchen three times per day. The kitchen consists of an open servery and a large wraparound bar where residents who need help can sit and be assisted. There is also a small office space for the staff to keep records and organize their work. The kitchen is

a critical work area. The recessed soffit there is illuminated with both indirect and direct light. High, even light levels are used throughout the building to mitigate concerns about sundowning. A window from the adjacent staff room overlooks the kitchen.

Other Common Spaces Provide Opportunities for Enrichment

The staff room is used to store medications and has a Dutch door to make it more friendly and approachable. The adjacent dining room has large windows with low sills that overlook the garden and the terrace. A great room for assembly purposes is located between the two wings of the L on both floors. Upstairs it is designated as an activity space and downstairs it is used as a music room. A wellness space is located upstairs, where it is used for exercise, physician's visits, posting messages, and examinations. The beauty/barber shop is also located on the second floor. Windows allow residents to preview the laundry, beauty salon, and wellness center. Finally, a camouflaged exit door with an attached chair rail and wall covering has been installed to discourage residents from exiting the building.

Spa Bathing Area Is Attractive and Soothing

Another innovative feature is the spa tub. One is located on each floor. The spa has been designed to be a strongly positive experience for residents. It features a whirlpool tub with a side-mounted swing door and a tile ledge surround (see page 109). The use of half-walls, indirect lighting, a generous area allocation, and a separate toi-

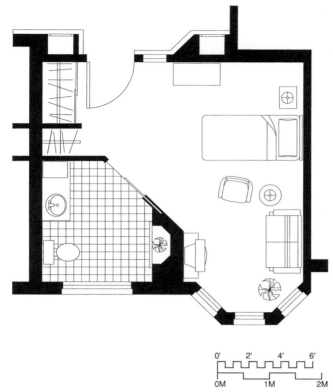

0'   2'   4'   6'
0M   1M   2M

Dwelling unit: Each private room has a closet, graduated dressing bar, bathroom, window to the corridor, and corridor shadow box. A few selected units have bay windows.

let room add to its attractiveness. The space also has adjustable lighting, heat lamps, music, and a place for bubble bath and candles. A shower is also available in each wing for assisted bathing.

Learning Center Is Used for Staff Training and Family Meetings

Programs are designed to stimulate the ability of residents to maintain dignity, identity, and self-worth. A personalized service plan is developed for each resident. The program has six activity components: (1) daily life (cooking, washing clothes, and gardening); (2) cognitive function (reading, games, study groups, story telling); (3) sensory stimulation (music, massage, reminiscing); (4) social/recreational (parties, crafts); (5) physical movement (walking, dancing, wellness); and (6) life skills (reminiscing using special lounge areas). Families are encouraged to take an active role in the community through a volunteer program called "Partners in Care" and monthly care conferences. The learning center seats 20 people at tables and is often used for family support group meetings and educational programming (see page 90). Families are also encouraged to dine with residents,

and they have a magnetic card that allows them to enter the building after business hours. With six residents in each wing, the staff/patient ratio is 1:6.

Dwelling Units Have Large Bathrooms with Windows

There are two sizes of units, and both are relatively small. The private room is 246 SF, and the double-occupancy room, which shares a bathroom, is 412 SF. Bathrooms are large. They contain a window and a niche for storage and display but do not have a shower. They are positioned with sliding pocket doors so that a resident can see the commode from the bed. This is believed to encourage toilet use. Each unit has two windows and a 9-foot 4-inch ceiling to make it seem larger and more spacious. A number of rooms have bay windows with window seats that can also be used for display. Window sills are too high for visual access to the garden from the bed. A built-in closet is available along with a day closet, which is designed to display the clothing the resident plans to wear that day. A plate shelf with a few pegs is located against one wall for display purposes. At the front entry, a large memory box is placed for orientation and display purposes. A fluorescent light located above the door provides direct light for the door and bounces light off the ceiling. In a few units, windows have been installed that link the room with the corridor as an experiment to see how they are used.

Horticultural Therapist Created Lively Outdoor Gardens

The two wings of each L define an outdoor courtyard, which is used as a garden for residents on the first floor. Second-floor residents have access to a balcony, which is surrounded by a vertical and horizontal trellis to safeguard them. Every dining room has a view of either the balcony or the garden. The gardens are lively places, with a good balance of hardscape for special events and activities and softscape for landscape materials and raised planters. In the center of each garden is an area for activities, bird feeders, windmills, and planters. The purpose of the garden is to stimulate sensory experiences. A cutting garden, a wildlife area, and a covered pavilion are connected to a looped pathway that provides an opportunity for exercise. Off to one side is a tool shed for the storage of garden implements, an open lawn with a view of the surrounding landscape, and several places to sit and look out over the garden. A spaced black metal fence creates a secured perimeter. The first floor has a covered porch and a covered space below the balcony, which provides shade in the summer. The column bases of these shelters are stone, reinforcing the Arts and Crafts style of the building.

25

ROS ANDERS GÅRD

Västerhaninge, Sweden

Architect   ANOVA arkitekter ab | Stockholm, Sweden
Sponsor   Haninge Kommun

Building Characteristics

Number of units	40
Number of stories	3 (third floor for offices only)
Context	Suburban
Housing type	Assisted living and dementia
Building parti/shape	L
Unit mixture	40 studios
Size of most common unit (average)	300 SF
Community facilities	Home care coordination
Community-accessible meals	NO—Family and friends only
Date of completion	May 1999

Resident Characteristics

Average age	82
Number of residents	40
Number of couples/men/women	2 couples
	14 single men
	22 single women
Age range	60–92
Percent requiring bathing help	75 percent
Percent requiring toileting help	62 percent
Percent incontinent	62 percent
Percent wheelchair-bound	13 percent
Percent cognitively impaired	45 percent

Ros Ånders Gard is a three-story L-shaped dementia/assisted living community: The staff lounge and administration offices are located in the middle of the third floor. (Photo: Björn Karlsson)

SUMMARY

Ros Ånders Gard is a 40-unit, two-story dementia and personal care home located in the community of Haninge in a suburb south of Stockholm. The building has an L-shape with four clusters of units, two on each floor. This type of building is new in Sweden. It combines the intimacy of a small-group home with the efficiency of a larger cluster of units. Although it is technically not a nursing home, only a few residents with complex medical needs will ever need to move. The building is so new that its capabilities have yet to be determined. The 20 people who live on the second floor are physically impaired. The first floor is reserved for people with dementia. Although the building is a concrete frame structure, it is clad with residential materials and utilizes bay windows on the exterior to give it a softer residential character. One of the most innovative features of this project is the way it decentralizes and humanizes care. A cluster of ten residents in single-occupied rooms surrounds a kitchen and a dining room. The kitchen is the central hub for staff and resident activities and also serves as an ad hoc nurses' station. Residents' records

and medications are kept here for annotation, reference, and distribution purposes. Staff involve residents in the preparation and serving of meals. The kitchen, which provides a fine lesson in universal design, includes a central cooking island and other features that make it easier for residents to participate in meal preparation. Given its location and open design, it would be considered too dangerous by many U.S. regulators. The building is also the hub for community-based home care workers. Home care workers serve about 20 older people in the neighborhood from this building.

Project Features

Four Decentralized Clusters of Ten Units Each Are Provided

Like many of the new Scandinavian and Danish housing models for the frail, this moderate-sized building is designed to feel intimate through the use of small resident clusters. There is great debate about what constitutes the appropriate cluster size. Should a cluster include six, eight, or ten residents? The ten-person clusters in this

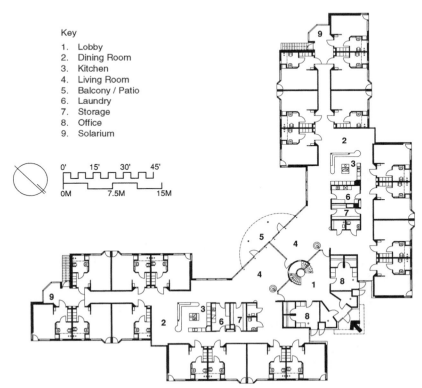

Key

1. Lobby
2. Dining Room
3. Kitchen
4. Living Room
5. Balcony / Patio
6. Laundry
7. Storage
8. Office
9. Solarium

First-floor plan: The building is divided into four clusters of ten units each. Dementia residents are on the first floor, and the physically impaired are on the second. The kitchen is located in the middle of each cluster, with a living room and garden/balcony at one end.

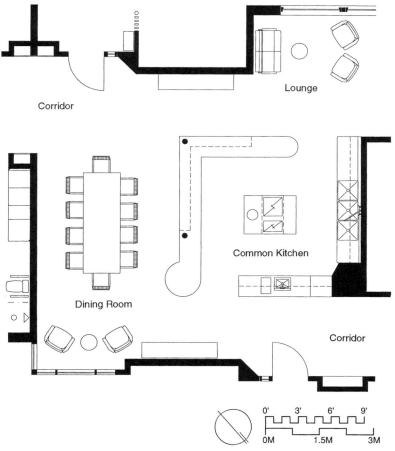

Corridor

Lounge

Dining Room

Common Kitchen

Corridor

| 0' | 3' | 6' | 9' |

| 0M | 1.5M | 3M |

The kitchen and dining room are centrally located: The kitchen was designed to allow older people to participate in food preparation. A central food preparation island with wide aisles allows the staff to work efficiently.

building are considered large by Scandinavian standards. However, with four clusters of ten residents, the building has achieved important economies of scale. The clusters are arrayed in a back-to-back manner that allows easy access from a shared elevator and staircase. A glass window wall separates the two clusters. A curtain covers the glass and can be opened or closed, depending on the need. The kitchen and dining room are located near the center of the cluster (see page 289), with a living room and access to the outdoors at one end. The lower floor is designated for dementia residents and the upper floor for physically impaired residents. Each cluster plan allows for a walking loop, and the centrally placed dining room is positioned to receive light from two sides of the building.

Life Skills Kitchen Is Designed to Involve Residents

One of the most innovative features of this building is its use of the kitchen for both functional and program purposes. The kitchen is the core of each cluster. Food arrives as raw foodstuffs and is prepared in each kitchen. The kitchen attracts residents, and the care approach involves them in as many activities as they would like to experience. Some residents help with cooking, while others set the table or put away dishes. The daily menu is written on an old-fashioned chalkboard and displayed for residents to see. The corridor from each resident's room leads to the dining room, facilitating wayfinding and also guaranteeing that the kitchen will be a popular destination. Because meals occur three times a day, residents often find themselves anticipating a meal, taking a meal, or relaxing after a meal.

Kitchen Also Serves as a Nurse's Station

The kitchen is square (two L-shaped counters), with two corners used for circulation. In the center of the kitchen is a food preparation island where a ventilating hood and a cooktop are located. The kitchen serves as both a meal preparation space and an informal nurse's station. Residents' records bound in notebooks are located in one cabinet, along with medications (see page 284). A stool with an open kick space below allows staff to sit at the kitchen counter and make notes or use the phone. A convenient interim shelf above the counter and below the cabinets surrounds the perimeter of the kitchen. It is used to hold mixing bowls, condiments, spices, and other paraphernalia used in food preparation. The dishwasher and the oven are raised 12 inches above the floor to make them more accessible and to allow staff to transfer heavy containers without bending over. Several under-counter cabinets have roll-out hardware, making access to them more convenient.

Dementia Garden and Balcony Accommodate Physically Impaired Residents

The site is relatively compact but includes a walking pathway that loops around the building. The main outdoor space is a special dementia garden created within the legs of the L-shaped building that is accessible from both first-floor dementia clusters. As in many Danish buildings for demented residents, a 3-foot fence surrounds the garden. A shared balcony that overlooks the garden is available for second-floor residents.

Materials and Features Reinforce the Residential Character

Although this is a concrete frame building, the cladding material is wood. Vertical and horizontal white wood siding is used, with yellow ochre trim around windows and doors. The building also has a steeply sloped roof that reinforces its residential character. The interior floor cov-

ering throughout the building's common spaces and dwelling units is a wood grain material that appears very cozy. A freestanding fireplace located in the living room provides another residential reference. Finally, tall glass, solarium lounges provide a place for sunlight to enter the unit at the corridor end and at the middle of each cluster.

Building Serves the Community with Home-delivered Services

Like most larger Swedish service houses, this project also provides help and assistance to people living in the neighborhood. Offices on the third floor of the building provide a meeting space for home health workers. Home care specialists who travel from the project to visit older neighborhood residents serve about 20 people each week (see page 46).

Unit Design Features a French Door and a Compact Tea Kitchen

The unit plan features a French balcony in half of a bay window (see page 131). When placed back to back with another unit, the bay window is complete. The dwelling unit is approximately 300 SF and is single occupied. If a couple moves in, they usually take two adjacent units using one as a bedroom and the other as a living room. The front entry door is extra wide to accommodate a bed, and a glass window panel is provided on one side to make it easy for caregivers to monitor residents without opening the door. Residents bring their own furniture, and the dwelling unit is large enough to accommodate a bed, a couch, and a small table. There is a

Older memory-impaired resident helps attendant prepare a meal: The kitchen is also used as an ad hoc nursing station where residents' records and medications are stored. Food is prepared from scratch in this kitchen by attendants.

Unit Features a Large Bathroom

The bathroom is designed for ease of manipulation. It has a roll-in shower built into the corner of the room, with a continuous slope to a drain. Staff members can easily help residents bathe, and wheelchair residents can roll into the corner without having to transfer. The bathroom also features a large window, which provides ample light, and a sink that moves up and down to accommodate people in wheelchairs (see page 122). The toilet is wall mounted for easy cleaning and has two dropdown grab bars for ease of transfer. The design of one of the full-height storage cabinets is unique. It has two doors. One opens from the bathroom and the other from the dwelling unit. This adds flexibility by optimizing the utility of this storage space.

Universal Workers Provide Care

The facility has embraced a universal worker approach. All caregivers, with the exception of the nurse, carry out dining, laundry, personal care, and housekeeping tasks. The staff hierarchy is flat. The building has 35 FTEs (41 employees), which is a relatively large number by U.S. standards, but everyone has a direct caregiving relationship with residents. All residents have a contact person who knows their likes and dislikes and is familiar with their family background and history. The lifestyle that the building hopes to provide to residents is 50 percent food and nurturance and 50 percent social interaction and the good life. In this building design the communal tub was eliminated because it required a lot of staff time. They believe that using showers in the room is a better use of staff time and is more private for residents. The second-floor units are designed for people who are physically impaired. They are outfitted with built-in rails in the ceilings for electric lifts. This is becoming an important priority in care homes to avoid potential staff back injuries.

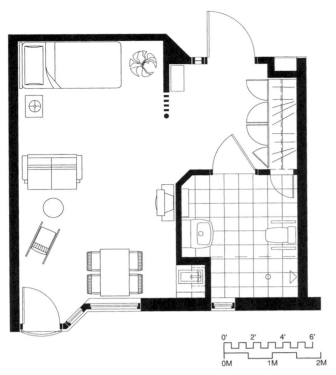

Dwelling unit: Each dwelling unit has a small kitchen and a large bathroom with a window. A screen creates an alcove for the bed near the corridor wall. A small bay window contains a French balcony that, when opened, allows fresh air to enter the unit.

kitchen area, but it is extremely small (30 inches wide), accommodating a small refrigerator and a sink. The dwelling unit is wider than it is deep, with large windows that span about half of the unit's width. Sill heights set at 14 inches are low, and the French balcony and bay window both stretch to the floor. Radiators located adjacent to the exterior wall have built-in shelves above them that can be used to hold plants or to display items.

26

HUMLEHUSENE

Albertslund, Denmark

Architect Domus Arkitekter | Kongens Lyngby, Denmark
Sponsor Albertslund Kommune

Building Characteristics

Number of units	24
Number of stories	1
Context	Suburban
Housing type	Dementia
Building parti/shape	L
Unit mixture	24 studio units
Size of most common unit (average)	300 SF
Community facilities	Yes
Community-accessible meals	Yes—in the adjacent day center
Date of Completion	July 1997

Resident Characteristics

Average age	82
Number of residents	24
Number of couples/men/women	5 men
	19 women
Age range	73–97
Percent requiring bathing help	38 percent
Percent requiring toileting help	38 percent
Percent incontinent	48 percent
Percent wheelchair-bound	25 percent
Percent cognitively impaired	100 percent

Humlehusene is a one-story collection of three L-shaped dementia units: These small units, with eight residents each, are placed together to create a courtyard. The building is a dark gray-blue color with yellow trim. Roof tiles are a bright red-orange.

SUMMARY

Many of the newest projects in Denmark are designed for people with dementia because general long-term care policies assume that most older people with physical impairments can be managed in their own homes and apartments though aggressive home care support. It is generally recognized in this country that people with dementia will likely require the support services of a group living environment. The Danes have gone from advocating larger buildings to preferring smaller decentralized buildings of 18–30 units. These units, are in turn subdivided into six- to eight-person clusters. Humlehusene is a one-story courtyard-style building that consists of three small group homes with eight units each. These three L-shaped build-

ings are joined together to create a three-sided courtyard. However, even though they are interconnected, they are managed as three separate settings. At night, two staff members move among the three eight-person buildings to monitor problems and to care for residents who may need help in the middle of the night. Humelseme is located in the suburban community of Albertslund. It is colocated with a day center (social center) that serves the neighborhood and a housing cluster for developmentally disabled individuals. The project is striking in appearance, utilizing a strong palette of dark gray-blue siding, orange tile, and yellow door and window trim. The care philosophy focuses on a normalized, noninstitutional approach that emphasizes home-prepared meals and small-group interactions between staff and residents.

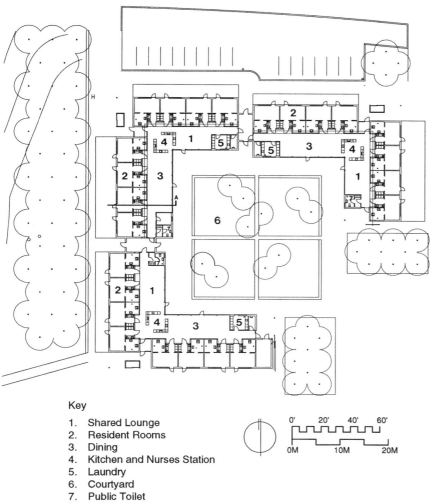

Key

1. Shared Lounge
2. Resident Rooms
3. Dining
4. Kitchen and Nurses Station
5. Laundry
6. Courtyard
7. Public Toilet

0'   20'   40'   60'
0M   10M   20M

First-floor plan: Each L-shaped unit is centered on the kitchen, where medications and records are also kept. Four units on one side open onto an area where living room and dining room furniture is placed. (Courtesy Domus Architects)

Project Features

A Courtyard Is Created from the Three L-shaped Buildings

Humlehusene is a one-story building made up of three smaller eight-unit L-shaped clusters that are joined together to create a courtyard. The dwelling units are on the outside edge, and the common spaces are on the inside (courtyard edge). The most dominant common space is the serving kitchen, which is placed at the intersection of the L. On one side of the kitchen in one wing is a dining room separated by a three-quarter-height partition from an activity space. The other wing has a table game space and a living room. All common spaces have windows that overlook the courtyard. These windows are composed into three large horizontal bands. The window stretches from the ground plane to within 12 inches of the sloped ceiling plane that begins there. This large expanse of glass makes the courtyard feel like an extension of the interior space. Residents frequently use the courtyard.

Building Is Simple in Form but Bold in Color

The complex is located in an outlying suburban neighborhood. The structure is a simple gable building with strong, memorable colors reminiscent of the bold colors often used in rural areas of Denmark. An orange tile roof is used in combination with wood siding that is stained a very dark gray-blue color. The siding almost appears black from a hundred feet away. Window and door trim as well as rafter tails are painted mustard yellow. These three colors together are striking. Plant materials have been trained along a trellis at the gable end of the building. The exterior of the building has permanent horizontal, thickened wood trim bands every 30 inches, giving the elevation scale and interest.

Courtyard Is Used for Both Viewing and Activities

The courtyard has an attractive controlled view and is a functionally important space. The three buildings create the courtyard and share an inward-focused view. Hardscape pavement immediately adjacent to the building's edge and partially covered by an overhang contains seating, umbrella tables, and furniture for residents. Near the center of the courtyard is a landscaped planting area. In the past, residents and staff planted and cultivated vegetables here. The staff is somewhat discouraged because most residents are too frail to participate in this activity. They regularly feed ducks here that fly in from a nearby lake. In the summer, they often have barbecues and eat outside in the courtyard. Difficulties with sun control and errant wind gusts have made the use of the courtyard challenging.

Sloped Ceiling and an Open Plan Furniture Layout Make the Common Space Easy to Comprehend

A sloped ceiling creates an open setting where furniture placements define spaces for meals and shared activities. The tall sloped ceiling gives the shared space prominence, and the open nature of the plan makes it easy for caregivers to monitor where residents spend the day. Large pendent light fixtures located near the center of the building augment skylights at the ridge and provide light

Dining and living room areas arranged in an open plan: The ceiling is sloped, with a skylight in the center. Large window walls toward the central courtyard dominate the view. Finally, the specification of a wood floor creates an attractive residential atmosphere.

Dwelling unit: The unit features a large bathroom with a sliding door, an entry alcove with a large closet, a tea kitchen, and a patio that is accessible from the living room. This wider unit can accommodate a side-by-side sitting area and a bed alcove. (Courtesy Domus Architects)

at night. The building is designed to look and feel like a big house. Centrally located skylights introduce natural light into the darkest part of the common area by reflecting sunlight against the tall wall in the center of the building. Large plants located throughout the building benefit from this source of natural light. Because of the open plan, dwelling units open directly onto adjacent shared spaces.

Residents Are Involved in Food Preparation

One of the most active and engaging spaces in the building is the shared kitchen. It is located in the middle of the building where the two wings meet. The kitchen has access to tables on both sides, which can be used for meals or activities. One of the kitchen counters is designed to be raised and lowered so that residents in wheelchairs can be involved in food preparation activi-

ties. The other counter has a cooking surface, refrigerator, and sink. The focus is on the daily lives of the eight residents who eat family style at a single table. The caregivers join them at dinner, making it a group of ten. They sit in the middle of the table opposite one another, encouraging residents who need help to eat. Prepared food is delivered for the major meal at noon from the day center. However, breakfast and the evening meal, which are both lighter, are often prepared in the kitchen. The kitchen also contains medications, resident's record books, and working space for staff. The normal staffing pattern involves two full-time caregivers during the day. At night, two caregivers monitor all 24 units.

Dwelling Units Make up About Half of the Building's Total Area

The square footage of the building is based on the 67-square-meter standard established for Danish elderly housing. About 45 percent of the space is devoted to private dwelling unit areas and the remainder to shared public space, corridors, and utility rooms. Each dwelling unit has a large window with a door that leads to a small patio space on the outside perimeter of the building. This is counterintuitive given the fact that dementia residents are known to wander away. However, the Danes as a matter of national policy have advocate high levels of freedom for these residents—including a rule against locking doors. An emergency call system has been instituted to make it easier for staff to coordinate with one another. Its red and green lights allow staff members to determine who is responding to a resident's call.

Dwelling Units Are Small but Self-contained

Each single-occupied dwelling unit measures about 300 SF. The floors are wood but can be covered by carpet at the discretion of the resident and his or her family. Residents can bring in their own furniture, but the building furnishes a bed for residents who need help with transferring. The entry area contains a small kitchen with a refrigerator and a two-burner cooktop, as well as wall cabinets for clothing and storage. A bed alcove and a small living room are located in the portion of the dwelling room, with a sloped ceiling. The large bathroom with a barn-style sliding door, is located adjacent to the bed alcove.

27

POSTILJONEN

Hölliviken, Sweden

Architect   White Arkitekter | Malmö, Sweden
Sponsor   Vellinge Kommun

Building Characteristics

Number of units	24
Number of stories	2
Context	Small town
Housing type	Nursing home
Building parti/shape	Courtyard
Unit mixture	24 studios
Size of most common unit (average)	325 SF
Community facilities	No
Community-accessible meals	Family and friends only
Date of completion	July 1994

Resident Characteristics

Average age	85
Number of residents	24
Number of couples/men/women	12 single men
	12 single women
Age range	61–94
Percent requiring bathing help	58 percent
Percent requiring toileting help	67 percent
Percent incontinent	67 percent
Percent wheelchair-bound	46 percent
Percent cognitively impaired	63 percent

Postiljonen is a comfortably scaled two-story courtyard building: A traditional ochre and blue-black combination characterizes the exterior coloration. French doors open to the courtyard, which is designed to support a range of activities.

SUMMARY

Postiljonen is a two-story, 24-bed nursing home organized as four group clusters of six units each. In many ways, it is indicative of future U.S. long term care models. It looks like assisted living, but residents are provided nursing home services. Designed with traditional colors and materials, it has a timeless character that makes it appear as if it was constructed years ago. It is a courtyard building with a corner removed that opens the courtyard to a view of the adjacent library and a heavily landscaped park. The decentralized cluster scheme contains two groups of six units on each floor. Several other common spaces are available for residents, family, and friends. The most dramatic space is a second-floor lounge that overlooks the Baltic Sea. Four decentralized dining rooms are located at the end of each resident corridor. Each dining room overlooks the courtyard on one side and is flanked by a galley kitchen on the other side. With access to the nurse's desk and a three-season porch, the dining room is used for meals and activities throughout the day. Units are arrayed along a wide single-loaded corridor with large windows and doors that overlook the courtyard. In the summer, the courtyard is the hub of many group activities. Each dwelling unit has a small tea kitchen and a large, accessible bathroom. Residents bring their own furniture to outfit each 300-SF unit. However, hospital-type beds are provided to ease the trans-

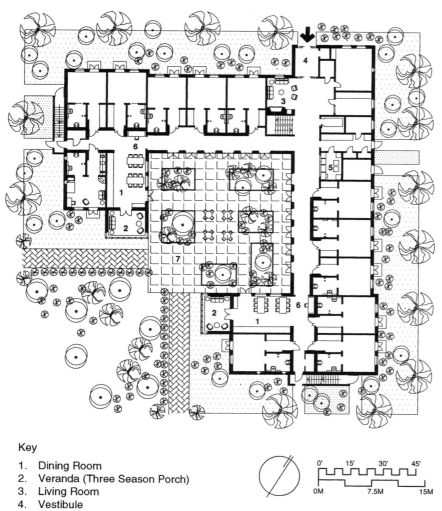

Key

1. Dining Room
2. Veranda (Three Season Porch)
3. Living Room
4. Vestibule
5. Laundry
6. Nursing Station
7. Courtyard

First-floor plan: The L-shaped plan is split into two-six unit wings on each floor. A verandah or three-season porch is located at the end of all four clusters. Each dining room has a view of the courtyard.

fer of physically impaired residents. Wood floors and windows with low sills give the unit a cozy and connected view to the outside. A ceiling-mounted electric lift system facilitates transfers from the bed to the toilet.

Project Features

Building Palette Is Based on Traditional Colors and Forms

The simple courtyard configuration with gable ends is a very pleasing traditional building form. In order to make the building appear to be from another era, ochre-colored stucco was used in combination with black wood siding. Ochre and barn red are traditional colors used in farmsteads throughout rural Sweden. A black stucco wainscot belt stretches from the soil line to the first-floor windowsill and grounds the building to the site. A traditional sloped red tile roof and trimless white windows and doors contrast with the dominant darker colors. Modern ribbon windows are inserted at each three-season porch and on the second-floor living room to create a wider, more panoramic view. Inside the building, antiques are used throughout common spaces to add character and interest. The result is a mixture of old and new that makes the building appear comfortable, familiar, and residential in character.

Decentralized Clusters Have Six Residents Each

A six-unit cluster is located in each wing of this L-shaped building. The wings are stacked to create a 24-unit com-plex. In each cluster, a wide, single-loaded corridor links each unit with adjacent shared spaces. The common spaces in each cluster consist of a dining room, a three-season porch (or veranda) (see page 260), a galley kitchen, and a desk/alcove for the nursing staff. The dining room, with tables and chairs, overlooks the central courtyard. The dining room is the most popular place for residents to sit during the day. The galley kitchen that runs parallel to the dining room facilitates the serving of food.

A six-resident cluster appears to be the smallest practical size for staffing and socializing. In fact, the staff frequently brings all 12 residents together on each floor for the evening meal. This building also contains several other common spaces where residents can go with family members and guests. Thus, it combines all the benefits of a small-group cluster with access to several other spaces that are shared by all residents.

Surrounding Community Is Rich and Varied

One of the best attributes of this building is its central location in the small (population 30,000) town of Höllviken. The site in this resort beach community is adjacent to the town library, the bus station, a service house for the elderly, a city park situated along the coast, and the beach. An adjacent 25-unit service house provides housing for more competent residents who move to Postiljonen when they need more care. The site is located within an active area of the city that contains numerous destinations for summer outings. Most of the services provided here are for residents only; however, four beds are set aside for short-stay respite or palliative (hospice) care.

Single-loaded corridor: A single-loaded corridor wraps the courtyard edge, providing access from residents' rooms to the dining room and verandah. French doors on the first floor and low-sill windows on the second floor create a dramatic view of the courtyard.

Courtyard Is a Heavily Used Outdoor Living Room

The courtyard, which is visible from locations throughout the building, plays an important aesthetic and functional role in the life of this place. Large windows and doors along the exterior corridor wall visually connect residents with the outdoor courtyard as they walk from their unit to the dining room. The courtyard is surrounded on three sides of its perimeter by a two-story building mass that provides excellent shade and wind control. The courtyard floor is about 50 percent hardscape and 50 percent landscape (see page 65). Trellis structures that flank each window/door are designed to create green walls on the inside of the courtyard. The courtyard contains umbrella tables, chairs, and garden plots. Residents who take coffee, host picnics and barbecues, tend a garden plot, and engage in group exercise use it almost every day in the summer. Doors and windows are often opened for ventilation because the building, located next to the sea, doesn't require air conditioning.

Verandah Is a Pleasant, Residentially Scaled, Informal Enclosed Porch

Several features reinforce the residential character of the building. For example, persons enter the building through a two-story space with a stairway that links the first and second floors. To one side is a cozy alcove that contains a brick fireplace and a television. Upstairs is a living room, which is used for group activities including birthday parties and family events. The windows from the activity room look out over a park, the beach, and the Baltic Sea beyond. In each unit cluster, an informal three-season porch (or verandah) has been created where residents can relax. This room uses a brick and wood wall and a green soapstone floor to simulate an enclosed porch space. The indoor/outdoor furniture specified here resembles that on a screened porch in a private house. Windows wrap around the perimeter of this room, connecting residents with a view of the courtyard and an adjacent tree-filled landscape.

Universal Worker Approach Allows These Small Clusters to Work

Swedish housing policy has shifted from big buildings in the 1960s and 1970s (150–200 units) to small buildings in the 1980s (6–12 units), to medium-sized buildings in the 1990s (24–60 units). This building is relatively small compared to the norm but achieves appropriate economies of scale. The FTE of 28 staff includes 5 nurses who are needed to deal with this more frail nursing home population. Residents stay here until they die unless they

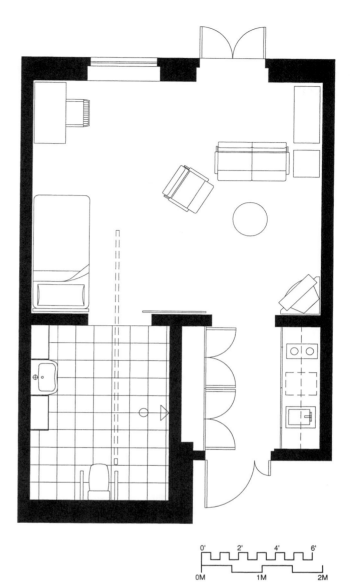

Dwelling unit: Each dwelling unit on the first floor contains a small patio. The entry has a tea kitchen and a storage cabinet. A ceiling-mounted track allows nonambulatory residents to use an electric lift to move residents from their bed to the bathroom.

have a behaviorally difficult mental condition. A universal worker staffing philosophy is used to flatten the staff hierarchy. All staff are assigned hands-on caregiving responsibilities. Physical therapy and activities are available, but there is no single person who takes responsibility for these tasks. Physiotherapists visit periodically and train assistant nurses to carry out various procedures. A doctor visits once a week to see residents. Finally, the building has abandoned tub baths in favor of showers in residents' rooms to save time. Although the staff has received special training in the use of validation therapy for dementia residents, they have chosen to mix mentally and physically frail residents.

Dwelling Units Are Residential in Character but Have Features That Allow Aging in Place

Residents' rooms are designed like small 325-SF single-occupied apartments. Residents furnish their units with their own possessions, which look cozy on the wood grain floor (see page 259). Tall windows with low sills and first-floor units with French-style patio doors connect each unit with views to the outdoors. At the unit entry door a mail slot, name and room number, and doorbell are used to achieve individuality and privacy. The entry door is designed as a two-part hinged opening wide enough to accommodate a standard hospital bed (see page 97). Inside, the dwelling unit includes a small kitchen with a stovetop and refrigerator (see page 120). The large bathroom has a 38-inch-wide sliding door to facilitate access. Grab bars, an adjustable sink, and a no-curb, roll-in shower add to the bathroom's overall accessibility. Rails are attached to the ceiling for lift devices that are used to help transfer residents from their bed to a wheelchair (see page 128).

28
METSÄTÄHTI

Hankasalmi, Finland

Architect   NVO Architects | Helsinki, Finland
Sponsor   Hankasalmi Kommun

Building Characteristics

Number of units	14
Number of stories	1
Context	Small rural town
Housing type	Service house
Building parti/shape	Spine
Unit Mixture	Two 1-bedroom
	12 studios
Size of most common unit (average)	300 SF
Community facilities	Yes—well-baby clinic
Community-accessible meals	Yes
Date of completion	December 1990

Resident Characteristics

Average age	83
Number of residents	14
Number of couples/men/women	4 single men
	10 single women
Age range	65–97
Percent requiring bathing help	100 percent
Percent requiring toileting help	57 percent
Percent incontinent	43 percent
Percent wheelchair-bound	14 percent
Percent cognitively impaired	22 percent

The entrance pays homage to Alvar Aalto: The placement of a high clerestory window in the dining room and an upturned entrance canopy mark the entry to the building.

SUMMARY

The Metsätähti is a unique mixed-use project that combines a day-care center for 21 3- to 7-year-old children with a service house for 14 older people. The concept evolved in response to the need to serve both of these populations in the small rural central Finnish municipality of Hankasalmi. The day-care center and service house are under the same roof and share the kitchen, the laundry, and a dining room/multipurpose space. Most of the activities involving children and residents take place in the dining room or along the corridor spine of the service house. Metsätähti has operated for a decade and has been a success both socially and financially. Residents are screened for compatibility with children but are under no obligation to spend time with them. Shared activities include watching children play, telling stories, baking bread, and celebrating birthdays and special holidays. Residents' dwelling units are clustered into three groups (two groups of five and one group of four) that are arrayed on a north-to-south axis along a two-story circulation spine. The day care center consists of two large rooms for children's activities and a large outdoor play space. The shared dining room is where everyone (older residents and children) takes the noon meal together. Dwelling units range in size from 215 to 465 SF. Although the facility was originally designed as a service house, the population has become frailer over time. To operate these two facilities efficiently, the six personnel working here are shared between the two buildings. Meals prepared here are also delivered to about 50 older people living in the community.

Project Features

Intergenerational Concept and Activities Are Provided

The concept of bringing children and the elderly together is not new, but the idea of mixing these two populations in a single small building is unusual. In this building, these two groups have their own separate territory but share the centrally located dining room/multipurpose space. Large and small tables sized for adults and children are located here. The relatively small sizes of the two groups (21 children and 14 older adults) facilitates interaction. Some of the shared activities consist of the elderly teaching skills to the youngsters like

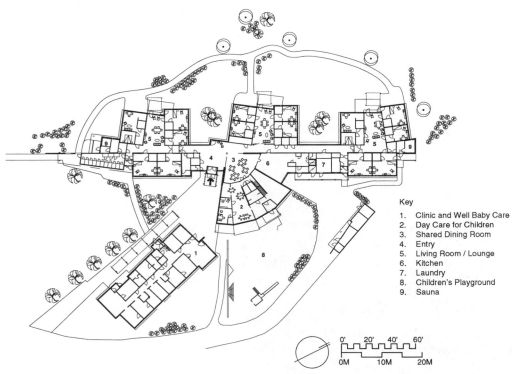

Key

1. Clinic and Well Baby Care
2. Day Care for Children
3. Shared Dining Room
4. Entry
5. Living Room / Lounge
6. Kitchen
7. Laundry
8. Children's Playground
9. Sauna

Site and floor plan: The plan combines a day center for 21 children on one side with 14 units of housing for older people. The dining room is the space where both groups meet to take meals and participate in shared activities. (Courtesy NVO Architects)

Two-story day-care classroom connects with the dining room: A sliding glass door with a movable curtain links the day-care center for children with the shared dining/multipurpose room.

baking bread (see page 113), making birch vastas for the sauna, and creating decorative crafts. (A vasta is a collection of birch twigs used to stimulate circulation in a sauna. The skin is beaten with the birch twigs/leaves.) Other activities include watching the children play, singing together, telling stories, and celebrating birthdays. The elderly are screened for compatibility with children but are under no obligation to spend time with them. The interactions between older residents and children have led to many friendships. In the past, older residents lived here when their grandchildren received day care. They share similar schedules. Both groups start early in the morning, eat lunch together at 11–12, and take a nap in the afternoon. The children leave around 3 to 5 PM, when residents start to end their day.

Dwelling Units Are Clustered in Three Small Groups

Each cluster of four or five dwelling units opens onto a small, decentralized living room. This living room has access to an outdoor patio space on one side and a circulation corridor on the other. The furniture, donated by residents, consists of tables for eating and card playing and chairs and couches for socializing. The relatively small size of the dwelling units encourages residents to spend time with one another in these shared spaces. A two-story, skylighted, north/south corridor connects each of the three clusters with the dining room and the entry.

Dining room has seating for children and adults: The dining room is a dramatic two story space with a clerestory window in one corner that serves as the main meeting space for the children and older residents.

Children's Day-care Center Is Sandwiched Between the Shared Dining Room and the Outdoor Playground

The day-care center consists of a large classroom and a rest area; both have access to a toilet, a computer room, and an office. An outdoor playground is located on one side of the classroom, and the shared dining room is on the other side. A tree house–like mezzanine play space with stairs that overlooks the main classroom is sandwiched between the classroom and the resting space. The lively colors and two-story classroom adds to the light-hearted spirit of the place. A sliding glass window wall with a curtain separates the day-care setting from the dining room. When the curtain is open, residents can look into the classroom and the children can look into the dining room.

Two Buildings and the Playground Define the Site Plan

The site consists of two buildings. One building is the intergenerational day-care center and elderly service house. The other building is a doctor's office and a day hospital, which is used as a well-baby clinic and a pre-natal center. It also hosts older people from the community who visit the center during the day. These one-story structures have wide sloped roofs and are placed on the site at an angle that naturally leads to the front door of the service house. The juxtaposition and separation of the two buildings gives them a small-scale village-like look from the street. A lively sloped overhang announces the entry and the front door of the service center. The exterior material is blue vertical metal siding, and the roof is silver standing seam metal that reflects the color of the sky.

Spine Links All the Main Spaces Together

The building is a low one-story mass. It has a low overhanging roof and lively shade structures that are playful and inviting from the street. A long, thin two-story spine with high clerestory windows links the three unit clusters together. The metaphor of a street is used to enliven the spine with benches, street lamps, birds, and plants. Two saunas located at the north and south ends of the spine are used twice a week by residents and occasionally by the children. The dining room/multipurpose is a two-story heavily utilized space with an angular clerestory window that brings daylight in. The front entry sequence terminates in a nook with a fireplace. Walls joined throughout the building at nonorthogonal angles add a dynamic quality to many spaces. Careful planning and conservation of space were necessary with such a small building. It contains no lounge for the staff or spe-

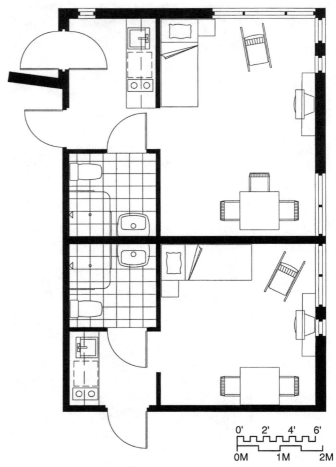

Dwelling unit: Dwelling units have been reduced to a minimum size to accommodate more shared common space. Units vary in size and type. This unit, with a second door that opens from the outside, is made to feel more independent.

cialized hobby rooms for residents. Most spaces are used for several purposes.

Dwelling Units Vary in Size

Dwelling units vary in size from a very small 215 SF to a relatively large 465 SF. Larger units have a separate bedroom and are designed for couples. Two medium-sized units are designed with a separate outside access door to make them function more independently. The majority of the units have several windows located to promote cross-ventilation. Each unit also has a small kitchen with a sink, a two-burner range, and an under-counter refrigerator (see page 124). Unit restrooms are small, but each has a roll-in shower. Residents are encouraged to bring their own furniture.

Staff Is Shared with the Children's Day-care Center

Because the Metsätähti is a small project located in a rural environment, there are a number of care challenges. For example, there is no staff person located here at night. The "night patrol" visits the building periodically and is on call. A physical therapist travels from about 10 miles away. The basic staff of six is shared between the children's day-care center and the elderly service house. Personal care assistance is provided by home care workers who are on call rather than full-time employees. This arrangement is similar to that of many Danish facilities, which share personal care workers with residents of the neighborhood. Most residents have their own phones and security devices. Every home helper has a mobile phone and e-mail. The staff e-mails a shopping list to the grocery store and a home helper picks up the order and delivers it to the building. About seven to ten elderly community residents take a meal at the building and the kitchen prepares 50 meals per day, which are delivered to older people living in the community.

Vickelbygarden, Skarblacka, SW, raised planter bed in the courtyard.

PART IV
CONCLUSIONS AND DIRECTIVES

Repose, cheerfulness, simplicity, breadth, warmth, quietness in a storm, economy of upkeep, evidence of protection, harmony with surroundings, absence of dark passages, evenness of temperature . . . rich and poor alike will appreciate these qualities.

—CFA Voysey, 1909

Conclusions are important statements that summarize the essentials and restate what is most important to remember. Because a range of people with different expectations and interests are likely to be reading this book, I chose to formulate conclusions in four different ways. I start with lessons learned from Europe, which are presented in two separate formats. First, Chapter 29 identifies *20 themes* that are common throughout northern Europe, and that characterize how their systems and practices differ from what we do in the United States. Second, Chapter 30 presents *20 specific program features or ideas* that are unique to the culture, policies, and politics of each country. This discussion restates in one place the most interesting features of various northern European systems.

Following these "lessons learned," Chapter 31 focuses on 20 *design and management considerations* for those who want to know what I consider to be the most important conclusions underlying best practices. Included are 234 specific actions that can be taken to support these broadly stated design considerations. These are clearly the most critical issues and restate important information presented in Chapters 4–13.

Next, in Chapter 32, is a discussion of *30 future trends and predictions* that come primarily from the academic and trade literature, experiences with a range of new building types, and my experiences in northern Europe. These statements examine the material presented from a future perspective, responding to the question "How will all of these new ideas impact the development of buildings and care practices in the future?"

Finally, in Chapter 33, *six broad concluding issues*, which emerge as larger trends and defining characteristics, are identified and discussed. These are *mega-trends*, for lack of a better term, that will likely affect the state of the art during the next decade.

29

LESSONS LEARNED FROM NORTHERN EUROPEAN VISITS

When you examine long-term care systems in different countries, one of the first things you notice are the differences and the similarities. The similarities seem natural and logical because they are an extenuation of your beliefs. The differences, however, are clearly much more profound. When differences contradict your own experience, ambiguity and uncertainty are introduced. These two powerful feelings make it difficult to forget what you have seen and ignore what you have experienced. You feel compelled to reconsider your assumptions as you reconcile what you have seen with your basic beliefs. When I first saw Danish home care nurses providing long-term care services in large one-bedroom, single-loaded corridor buildings, I was forced to rethink why it was necessary for U.S. nursing homes to have double-occupancy rooms along double-loaded corridors in institutional buildings. Discoveries like this are particularly useful because they make you rethink your own assumptions and challenge you to think about how we can provide care to older frail people in a better, more humane way.

The following twenty "lessons learned" represent a compilation of the overlapping experiences gleaned from site visits to facilities in Sweden, Denmark, Norway, Finland, and the Netherlands. These topics represent attitudes, practices, and beliefs that are generally shared by professionals in most of these countries. When I started this assessment, I was interested in two things:

1. Chronicling differences between what I saw in 1991 and in 1998

2. Identifying issues that could stimulate our thinking about the design and organization of long-term care for mentally and physically frail people

What is most interesting are the features that seem sensible but have not been considered in the United States, either because of a regulation that forbids them or a practice that discourages them. When you examine northern European nursing homes, what you see is the U.S. version of assisted living. The rules that govern assisted living in the United States appear to be flexible and free enough to accommodate most of the improvements the northern Europeans offer. I hope that the U.S. system of long-term care will move in the same direction.

Service house provides assistance to residents across the street: The service house in *Monster*, the Netherlands (on the right), provides help to older residents living in the first-floor units of the "lean-on" housing above.

The 20 lessons learned from northern Europe include the following:

1. Housing Is Regularly Linked with Community–Based Facilities
2. Home Health Services Are Organized at Service Houses and Day Centers for Older People Living in the Neighborhood
3. Service Houses Have Day Programs for People with Dementia
4. Most Housing for the Frail Is Made up of Small-Group Clusters
5. There Is Greater Emphasis on Short Stays, Rehabilitation, and Respite
6. Dementia Units Are Increasing in Popularity
7. Op Maat Approach Is Used to Meet Each Resident's Unique Needs
8. A Deep, meaningful Relationship to Outdoors and Nature Is Developed
9. Today's Resident Population Is Sicker, Frailer, Older, and Heavier
10. Most New Buildings Feature Single-Occupancy Units
11. Commonly Found Unit Design Features
12. Recruitment of Nurses and Undernurses Is Difficult
13. Food and Emergency Call Systems Are Becoming Regionalized
14. Excellent Examples of Urban Architecture Exist
15. A Feeling of Coziness Is Important in the Selection of Interior Furnishings
16. More Opportunities to Link with Children Are Provided
17. Lifting Devices Are Becoming More Popular
18. Municipalities Have More Influence on Planning
19. Volunteer Recognition Is Becoming More Important
20. There Are Fewer Extremely Frail Older People

HOUSING IS REGULARLY LINKED WITH COMMUNITY-BASED FACILITIES

Service houses are mixed-use buildings that provide housing and services to residents as well as people who live in the neighborhood. Located throughout the community in separate neighborhoods, they serve as community centers as well as places for older frail people to live (Ministry of Health and Social Affairs, 1997, 1999). They combine the qualities of a senior center with those of assisted living housing. Residents from the neighborhood can take meals there, and home health workers operate out of these places to serve older people living in the surrounding community. Older people living in housing attached to these day centers benefit from convenient access to a range of services available there. It is not at all uncommon for a service house to provide meals for the community, home health services, physical therapy, occupational therapy, recreational rooms, and emergency medical response offices. Many others have convenient retail services, doctors' offices, swimming pools, and extensive rehabilitation facilities.

HOME HEALTH SERVICES ARE ORGANIZED AT SERVICE HOUSES AND DAY CENTERS FOR OLDER PEOPLE LIVING IN THE NEIGHBORHOOD

In general, these countries have made health and home help services available to a broad range of older people in an effort to encourage them to stay at home for as long as possible (Swedish Institute, 1996). Working out of service houses, home care workers meet and organize in the service house and then spend the day in the community delivering services to people living in nearby housing. There is a seamless connection between home care and service houses. Supportive health and personal care services as well as long-term care are paid for by the government. Frailer individuals often move to service apartments when they no longer feel secure in their own homes. Some countries, like Denmark, organize the delivery of services to people in service apartments in the same way they deliver services to people in the surrounding neighborhood.

SERVICE HOUSES HAVE DAY PROGRAMS FOR PEOPLE WITH DEMENTIA

Most service houses/day centers have small day-care programs for people with dementia. These programs usually operate in an area separated from the shared activity spaces available to people living in the neighborhood and in attached housing. These are small programs involving 12 to 15 participants, many of whom are suffering from dementia or are social isolates. Normally, a van picks them up at home in the morning and brings them back in the afternoon. Participants attend sessions one to three days per week, depending on their needs. Programs are designed to stimulate their minds and their social skills. Participants often live independently or with a spouse in the community. These countries believe in encouraging people with dementia to stay as independent as possible for as long as they can in the community (Socialstyrelsen, 1997). To encourage this, they have *night patrols* that make stops in the evening at the homes of individuals who need nighttime help or who must be checked on during the evening.

MOST HOUSING FOR THE FRAIL IS MADE UP OF SMALL-GROUP CLUSTERS

During the 1990s, the Swedish experience with small-group homes encouraged providers to create family-like clusters of 6–8 units. Previous experience with large institutional buildings demonstrated the inhumane outcomes associated with large-scale settings. Today's clusters are more likely to be grouped four to six to a building, with 24 to 40 units total. The *Ros Anders Gård* (page 215), *Humlehusene* (page 220) and *Postiljonen* (page 224) are good examples of this basic philosophy. Typically, there are 5 common spaces including a kitchen, dining room, living room, outdoor patio/balcony, and activity room in each cluster. Residents spend most of their time in these common spaces, using their units mostly for sleeping or napping. In many of the best-designed cluster arrangements, residents take meals family style and participate in meal preparation. Most of these settings have a very flat managerial hierarchy, with one leader and the rest caregivers. A major criticism of this approach is that no other common areas are available for residents to visit. When the only place to go is a small cluster of rooms with the same people, life can be tedious and boring.

THERE IS GREATER EMPHASIS ON SHORT STAYS, REHABILITATION, AND RESPITE

One of the benefits of a community-based system is the interest that housing providers take in helping older people stay in their own homes. There is a strong emphasis on short stays for people who are moving from a hospi-

Entry space has a bar that greets visitors: The *Kopsinrinteen* project in Pyhasalmi, Finland, has a festive-looking bar at the front entry to greet visitors and provides a place for residents to hang out.

tal setting to home. Rehabilitation can sometimes best be accomplished when a resident who has suffered a stroke, for example, moves in for one to two weeks of intensive rehabilitation. Respite is provided to family members who may need some time to themselves or who may be planning a vacation or a trip and need a place where a parent can stay temporarily. A decentralized cluster plan works very well for this type of service. The *Virranranta* (page 206) has five clusters of eight units. One cluster is set aside for short-stay residents. Because average lengths of stay are five to seven days, these rooms are much more likely to be used by a number of people. Hospice arrangements are not as popular as short-stay options in Europe. In the United States, assisted living buildings are often favored as settings to provide end-of-life care.

DEMENTIA UNITS ARE INCREASING IN POPULARITY

One of the major differences between the early and late 1990s is the changing attitude toward dementia care. The Danes have accepted the idea of clustering six to eight residents with dementia together, and the Swedes have discovered the need (for economy of scale purposes) to bunch several group clusters together. In Denmark, some providers believe that older people with dementia will be the only future long-term care population. They believe that with increasing communication technology, most physically impaired residents will be supported through a peripatetic home care program. The Dutch have experimented with many different new therapies including importing the idea of snoezelen from developmentally disabled group homes in Denmark. All coun-

tries recognize the importance of a small family-oriented cluster where meals are taken together, usually at one big table. ADL philosophies that involve residents with meal preparation, laundry, cleanup chores, and other normal daily routines have also become very popular.

THE OP MAAT APPROACH IS USED TO MEET EACH RESIDENT'S UNIQUE NEEDS

In the early 1990s, the Dutch were experimenting with this model of care. It has since become far more popular throughout northern Europe and is considered the care philosophy du jour. Op maat involves creating a care plan to fit the personality, needs, and preferences of each older person. Practices include simple ideas like waking "morning people" and allowing those who want to sleep in to do so. In most long-term care environments, the resident's schedule is forced to fit the institution's schedule. Residents take a meal or a bath when the institution schedules it rather than tieing these events to the resident's past experiences and preferences. The philosophy of self-help often accompanies the op maat approach. Residents are expected to do as much as they can for themselves. Staff members assist residents but are careful to avoid doing tasks for them.

A DEEP, MEANINGFUL RELATIONSHIP TO THE OUTDOORS AND NATURE IS DEVELOPED

Northern Europeans love nature and outdoor spaces (Strange, 1996; Su-Dale, 1995). This relationship can be seen in the way outdoor spaces are designed and related to interior rooms. It is also apparent in the way natural materials like wood are used and in the way the mid-summer holiday is celebrated. During the long, dark winter, people look forward to the short but very pleasant summer months. They take month-long vacations in July and August and many people have small, rustic summer cottages. These cultural patterns have developed over a lifetime and connect the population with nature and natural plant materials. Indoor plants in glass-enclosed winter gardens and exterior landscaping in the summer are lush and varied. Even in dementia units, individual outdoor patios at each unit are a standard element of the Danish nursing home. Unit orientations toward the south and west are prized, and if a balcony is not planned, then an erker (glass bay window) or a French balcony is used. In Sweden, electric heaters are often mounted on shared balcony ceilings to extend the usefulness of the space into the fall and spring.

TODAY'S RESIDENT POPULATION IS SICKER, FRAILER, OLDER, AND HEAVIER

Repeating a pattern that occurred in the United States, the general frailty level of residents increased during the 1990s. Residents who sought group housing arrangements were a more frail, medically dependent population. Emphasis was placed less on larger service apartments and more on the creation of small-group unit clusters for a highly dependent population. An even better and more aggressive home care program allowed residents to stay in their homes for a longer period of time.

The older, frailer population that moved to group housing was more impaired and more passive. Crafts and making things with your hands was replaced with more passive pursuits such as watching, talking, and interacting. An increase in the number of residents who weigh more have required more hydraulic lifts and staff to devote more time to tasks like getting residents into and from the bathroom. In general, today's population is more dependent on medications and less able to do things on their own.

MOST NEW BUILDINGS FEATURE SINGLE-OCCUPANCY UNITS

For more than a decade, the standard for new construction has been 100 percent single-occupied dwelling units. This standard was established in response to the larger multibed wards in hospitals that were deemed unacceptable in the 1950s and 1960s. Private rooms allow residents to personalize their space more effectively. Increased privacy makes it easier for residents to sleep as well as carry out ADLs. Caregivers also appear to have more respect for the personal space boundaries of residents when units are single-occupied. Doors are kept closed, and knocking before entering becomes a common courtesy in all nursing homes. In some countries, like Finland, dwelling units are very small. However, the single-occupancy standard has been rigidly upheld. One side effect of this policy is the lack of larger units for couples or for individuals who would prefer to live together. In some buildings, walls between units can easily be connected by a door so that two studio units can be transformed into a larger one-bedroom unit for two people.

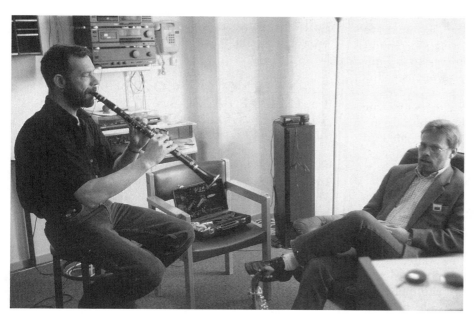

Music snoezelen is also practiced in the Netherlands: In this setup, amplifiers are located in the chairs so that residents can feel as well as hear the music. Tunes that relate to salient past experiences of dementia residents are selected.

COMMONLY FOUND UNIT DESIGN FEATURES

Residents' rooms vary in size and complexity, depending on the age of the person and his or her health or personal care needs. The following are unit features commonly found in many buildings.

▲ Partly as a result of sun-starved northern latitudes, resident units have large windows that are typically 2 meters square.

▲ Low windowsills allow residents to see outdoors from their beds. Sill heights are usually about 12–18 inches above the floor.

▲ Sliding barn or pocket doors are commonly used between bathrooms and bedrooms. These doors are perceived to be more accessible and easier to manipulate.

▲ Showers are designed to be flush with the adjacent bathroom, floor. They are often located in a corner of the room, with a drop-down seat and a surrounding curtain.

▲ Carpeting is rarely used in residents' rooms since it is believed to cause allergic reactions. Sheet vinyl and wood parquet are popular floor surfaces.

▲ Every unit has a small tea kitchen with a refrigerator and a microwave oven or a small two-burner stove.

RECRUITMENT OF NURSES AND UNDERNURSES IS DIFFICULT

The recruitment of caregivers is becoming more of a problem in northern Europe. Countries like Sweden, which have placed controls on compensation, consider this to be a mounting crisis. They often lose nurses to Denmark and Norway, where salaries are higher. Compared to the United States, nurses and undernurses (personal caregiving staff) are paid well and job tenure is much longer. Nursing training continues to be quite good, but there is a concern that replacements will not be readily available. Younger workers in general are harder to recruit. The best care staff employment universe is older women who are returning to the workforce after their child-rearing responsibilities have ended.

FOOD AND EMERGENCY CALL SYSTEMS ARE BECOMING REGIONALIZED

Most countries are organizing more efficient systems for food distribution and emergency response. Service houses typically designate the noon meal as the major meal of the day. Breakfast is often light, and dinner may be cold cuts or sandwiches. In the last decade, many municipalities have established regional kitchens that provide food for schools, nursing homes, and day centers. During the transition, many buildings still utilize their own facility's kitchen for food preparation. Day center kitchens in rural areas are increasingly becoming regional hubs for the distribution of prepared food to the surrounding area. More emphasis is being placed on frozen meals that can be delivered directly to dwelling units and then reheated in microwave ovens when needed. Emergency care providers are also studying how to reduce their overhead. Increasingly, there has been a move to regionalize the communications component of the emergency medical response system. Most buildings that manage their own system take responsibility for monitoring emergency call hardware that is distributed to older people living independently in the neighborhood.

EXCELLENT EXAMPLES OF URBAN ARCHITECTURE EXIST

Sites selected for service-based elderly housing are usually located in mature neighborhoods where older people live. This means that many neighborhoods are urban and many buildings are located in densely populated environments. Mixed-use buildings with commercial uses on the first floor are common. In these buildings, the entrance to the housing is normally located at a corner. A first-floor lobby links the street with the center of the block, which is usually a courtyard. Many buildings have an urban edge and a garden edge, providing resident units with two different orientations. The building's design relies on the surrounding neighborhood for cues to style, materials, and details. In northern Europe, the setting is considered extremely important. Buildings are designed to complement and fit into the neighborhood. Because many sites have a history that can be traced back hundreds of years, there is a tendency to think of every new project as a remodeling of the environment.

A FEELING OF COZINESS IS IMPORTANT IN THE SELECTION OF INTERIOR FURNISHINGS

Gezellig and *huga* are Dutch and Danish terms, respectively, that refer to a sense of coziness (Strange, 1996; White and Boucke, 1989). They are often used to describe the kind of atmosphere the staff hopes to achieve in common spaces. In Denmark, it is a tradition for candles to be used at the dinner table to create a feeling of intimacy. The architectural language of most buildings in northern Europe is modern. The tall ceilings and starkly detailed surfaces often contrast with this feeling. Residents value furniture and finishes that make the

Traditional kitchen bed: This antique piece of furniture was common in households at the turn of the twentieth century, when it was used to sleep in the kitchen during cold nights. It added character to a resident's dwelling unit in the *Wilhelmiina* (page 163) project.

building appear homelike. Specifying antique furniture is a very popular approach for creating interiors with character. Artwork and furnishings that residents bring are often used to decorate public corridors. This gives the building a genuine homey feeling but is often somewhat haphazard from a stylistic perspective.

MORE OPPORTUNITIES TO LINK WITH CHILDREN ARE PROVIDED

Because agencies that work with children and older people are often located at the municipal level, there is often good informal communication between them. Service houses for older people located in a particular community may also need child-care services. Working together to serve the needs of both of these dependent populations, local officials often propose that they be colocated. Day-care centers can also rent a portion of the first floor of a building for the elderly. Rural areas have some of the most successful examples. The *Metsätähti* project (page 229) combines both uses and is managed by one group. Some buildings position the playground so that it can be seen from a heavily utilized space like the dining room.

LIFTING DEVICES ARE BECOMING MORE POPULAR

Incoming residents today weigh more and are more frail than those of the early 1990s. This has prompted the use of electric lifting systems attached to ceiling-mounted tracks. These systems are common in buildings for the physically frail. The track normally runs between the bed and the bathroom. Staff health and safety requirements are one reason they have become popular. Caregivers can easily damage their backs by twisting and turning while lifting a resident. Because caregivers are employed by local municipalities, these public agencies have a vested interest in making the workplace safer. Europeans typically have experienced a higher rate of disability than the United States due to on-the-job injuries.

MUNICIPALITIES HAVE MORE INFLUENCE ON PLANNING

A lot of the excess land available for housing development is owned by local municipalities. Therefore, working with the city is often like working with both a seller and a public agency. Municipalities often seek out developers for a particular parcel of land that may best suit a certain use. For example, they normally plan elderly housing near stores and services. Most developers in northern Europe are nonprofit community providers. They are motivated to create housing as a public good rather than to solely make a profit. Because land purchases often come with a wish list of provisos, developers often coordinate improvements that affect adjacent properties. Although this approach seems positive, it often makes the planning task more complex.

VOLUNTEER RECOGNITION IS BECOMING MORE IMPORTANT

One of the most positive aspects of the U.S. system of elder care is the attitude toward volunteerism. Volunteering time to help others is not prevalent in northern Europe. There have been a number of experiments in these countries to stimulate more volunteerism. In the Netherlands, there has long been an interest in recruiting older people to help one another informally in housing environments. In Denmark, the cohousing movement has explored methods of stimulating informal care and assistance among friends living together.

THERE ARE FEWER EXTREMELY FRAIL OLDER PEOPLE

It was difficult to find the highly impaired segment of the nursing home population that we often find in the United States. Residents with intravenous medications, tube feeds, oxygen dependency, ventilator supports, infusion therapy, and bedridden mobility problems are not very common. A great deal of hands-on care appears to be provided, but making extraordinary efforts to keep an older person alive is discouraged. In Denmark, everyone is dressed and out of bed every day. Someone who has a mobility problem is assigned physical therapy. It is difficult to find a bedridden resident in any nursing home. As medical technology advances and residents live to be older and frailer, there will no doubt be more discussion about this issue. Quality of life rather than number of years is clearly a priority in this system.

30

OTHER LESSONS FROM EACH INDIVIDUAL COUNTRY

I n addition to widely shared practices, each country has its own unique collection of special programs and system attributes. Study trips from one country to another to share information are common, but each country's approach to service provision is colored by its preferences, beliefs, and history. The Swedish experience with small group homes for dementia residents in the 1980s and 1990s greatly encouraged the Danes to explore segregated buildings for residents with identifiable memory loss. The bold Danish approach to combining housing with services has influenced the Dutch in their experiments with the "apartments for life" program. The Finns are experts at copying and refining ideas after they have been well demonstrated by others. It is not uncommon to find Dutch care strategies, Swedish dementia innovations, and Danish attitudes about unit sizes and autonomy embedded in Finnish long-term care settings.

SYSTEM FEATURES THAT COULD BE IMPROVED

The northern European long-term care system is clearly not perfect. Although many of the system attributes described in detail are much better than those in the United States, weaknesses exist.

Interior Design

The understanding of how interior design can be used to create settings with deep and profound connections to past experience has not been recognized. Although residents are strongly encouraged to bring their own furniture into dwelling units, common spaces are often the dumping ground for cast-off furniture or the administrator's personal selections. If the administrator has taste, a sense of design, and some discretionary funds, the interiors can be attractive. However, most settings leave this most important design element to chance.

Family Connections

Many Americans assume that family participation rates in northern Europe are higher than those in the United States. However, from interviews and observation, my sense is that most families have a "hands-off" attitude. This perhaps occurs because the quality of the housing and service is high. Family members come to visit, but they trust the providers to do a good job in caring for the needs of relatives. Northern Europeans pay high taxes for a well-ordered system of care for children and older people, and they expect it to work efficiently. There is less need to provide independent oversight or to provide voluntary assistance in caregiving. We will probably not see great refinements in the integration of family members into the caregiving process until family-based models in Asia and Central and South America are developed and refined.

Volunteerism

The northern European countries have some of the highest female workforce participation rates in the world. One resulting side effect is that caregiving is viewed as a profession and volunteers, although welcome, are not very common. The general attitude is that people should be paid for this type of work. As a result, we don't see the attitude toward volunteerism which is clearly present in the United States. In the United States, volunteerism often starts early, with high school students seeking placements for community service. This type of participation is not common in northern Europe.

Netherlands

▲ "Apartments for Life" Arrangement Combines Services for the Frail with Conventional Housing
▲ Atrium Designs Create Habitable Outdoor Spaces During the Winter
▲ Should There Be Housing with Services or Services with Housing?
▲ Care-Housing Partnerships Combine the Expertise of Housing Developers with Care Providers
▲ Experimental Housing Models Exist

Denmark

▲ Physical Therapy and Exercise Build Residents' Competence
▲ Senior-Only Cohousing Encourages Informal Social Exchange
▲ Vacation Programs Exist for Long-Term Care Residents
▲ Varied Housing Forms Characterize the Housing Stock

Sweden

▲ Anthroposophic Architectural Ideas Are Sensitive to the Human Condition
▲ Unit Clusters Are Consolidated into Larger Buildings
▲ Controlling the Costs of Care and Staffing Difficulties Are Constant Struggles
▲ A Range of Different Therapies Are Used

Norway

▲ The Caring Home Initiative Is Producing Two Types of Housing
▲ Husbanken Maintains Design Standards for Elderly Housing
▲ Cooperative Ownership Is Common in Norway

Finland

▲ Saunas and Swimming Pools Are Essential Parts of the Finnish Lifestyle
▲ Wood Is Used for Floors, Ceilings, and Details
▲ Natural and Artificial Lighting in Northern Latitudes Is Important
▲ Architecture Expression in Finland Is Lively and Expressive

THE NETHERLANDS

"Apartments for Life" Arrangement Combines Services for the Frail with Conventional Housing

One of the most interesting housing types is the apartment for life, or *levensloopbestendige*. The *Humanitas Bergweg* (page 158) is an excellent example of this housing and service philosophy. The basic idea involves the creation of an apartment building where service supports can be increased to a nursing home level to keep residents living independently. Most apartments are one-bedroom units, and residents who are bedridden nursing home candidates are supported here along with completely independent individuals aged 55+. Therapy spaces are located on a lower floor and are linked to residents through two banks of elevators. Common spaces, including a restaurant, are open to building residents as well as to other older people in the community. Dwelling units are designed to be adapted to the needs of residents as they become more impaired. Services are provided on a home-delivered basis. Dementia residents stay in their apartments at night and join a day-care group during the day. This housing concept has caught on in the Netherlands, and Humanitas Bergweg building has a very long waiting list.

Atrium Designs Create Habitable Outdoor Spaces During the Winter

Atrium buildings for the elderly are relatively common in the Netherlands. Forty percent of the Dutch buildings I visited in 1999 and over half of the buildings I visited in 1991 were atriums. This building form has be-

Informal service provision is encouraged: At the *Havenbogen* apartments in Schiedam, the Netherlands, younger residents volunteer to help older residents in programs like the delivery of meals on wheels.

come popular in part because of the desire to shelter outdoor spaces from cold North Sea breezes. Many atriums are glass-covered enclosures that are not conditioned. They have ventilator mechanisms that open sections of the glass roof to allow hot air to escape in the summer and during sunny days to avoid overheating. Atriums are often created between two single-loaded corridor buildings. The resultant interstitial space is finished and furnished for community purposes or is left as a softscape garden with places for residents to sit. Because one side of every unit overlooks the atrium, it is a natural place for social interaction. In 1991, I also visited a number of buildings on *enclosed streets* like the DeBrink in Breda, the Netherlands. These are projects with wide double-loaded corridors that are covered by transparent skylights. In multistory buildings, openings to the floor below bring daylight into these spaces. This strategy is used

to protect residents while walking from their units to common spaces.

Should There Be Housing with Services or Services with Housing?

This debate involves a policy discussion of what future housing model for the elderly should be promoted. Many older people believe that the Danish model of providing home health and personal care services within a normal housing context is the best approach. These services are usually monitored and delivered by a nurse or personal care assistant who comes as frequently as needed to the resident's apartment to provide help and assistance. This peripatetic approach, like the apartment for life model, provides autonomy and privacy. and is very appealing to many older people. Others are concerned that the mentally frail or the highly impaired older person will not be able to maintain a secure, well-supported life without more intensive monitoring. This policy debate is essentially between housing with services and the traditional three-meal-per-day licensed assisted living facility. The answer to the debate is that both types are needed and both provide important choices in servicing a range of resident conditions. The debate is more about which type the system should favor. Should it embrace autonomy and independence, at some risk to the older person, or should it provide a safer, more secure homelike environment?

Care-Housing Partnerships Combine the Expertise of Housing Developers with Care Providers

Partnerships are being encouraged between housing developers and providers of long-term care. The idea is to develop housing approaches and service delivery systems that keep the frail elderly more independent. The hope is to achieve the best of both worlds, including new models and approaches to housing older people with health and personal care needs. In contrast to the United States, most projects are financed over a longer period—50 or 75 years—to make it financially possible to add innovative features to the building. There is also a move to encourage nonprofit housing developers to pursue housing mixed with commercial spaces, as well as more owner-occupied housing.

Experimental Housing Models Exist

The Dutch are perhaps the most adept at conceptualizing, testing, and evaluating a range of different housing types. Government organizations like the Stuurgroep Experimenten Volkshuisvesting (SEV) have provided technical assistance in the development of new housing models by consulting on new projects and evaluating experimental ideas (SEV, 1997). Experiments combining personal-care housing with health-care environments in the late 1980s opened the door for more radical ideas like the apartments for life concept in the 1990s. Most of the experimentation has also been disciplined with regard to cost and implementation issues. Developing new models that are less expensive and more effective has been the goal. The Dutch attitude toward regulation is also enlightened. They have not used regulations and standards to police the industry. Thus, the approach to regulation has a strong "*performance standards*" orientation and is flexible enough to embrace new ways of thinking about old problems.

DENMARK

Physical Therapy and Exercise Build Residents' Competence

The Danes have always been interested in and committed to physical therapy. The big change from the early 1990s has been a stronger focus on formally incorporating exercise regimens into their programs. The increasing sophistication of exercise equipment and the mainstreaming of that equipment into traditional physical therapy treatments has enhanced its effectiveness and changed its focus. The approach today is to intervene before physical therapy is necessary. Using strength and aerobic capacity-building equipment in a specialized regimen for each individual, residents pursue a more proactive approach. The Danes appear committed to both staffing and equipping these spaces, as well as picking up the considerable costs associated with these programs. Physical therapy programs in other cultures appear to be in place but are not integrated into a resident's lifestyle, as they are in Denmark. The Danes often place equipment in public places (lobby spaces, lounge areas, and living rooms) rather than relegate it to a single locked room in a basement. Combining physical therapy and exercise has also increased their emphasis on rehabilitation at *Gyngemosegård* (page 174). Danish service houses have a strong commitment to helping people stay in and return to their own homes. Occupational therapy and physical therapy are key components of a therapy program that eases the transition from the hospital to home for stroke victims and orthopedic patients.

Senior-Only Cohousing Encourages Informal Social Exchange

Denmark is known internationally for its experiments in cohousing. Several books (Boligtrivsel I Centrum, 1993; McCamant and Durett, 1988) have chronicled their success over the last 25 years. Senior-only cohousing is rel-

Shallow riser heights make it easier for residents and staff to use the stairs: The stairs at the *Nybodergaården* nursing home in Copenhagen, Denmark (Regnier, 1994, page 146), utilize 6-inch risers with wider treads.

atively new, and has been mainstreamed into housing projects and promoted by local nonprofit development consortiums. This type of housing is often created by a local group of older people who have a desire to lead a more socially integrated life. These settings vary from ones that rigidly adhere to a system of sharing all responsibilities to ones that are much more informal. The informal examples benefit from friendships and interrelationships that naturally evolve from this lifestyle. They also vary in size, from small groups like those described at *Gyngemosegård* (page 174) to larger buildings with 25–40 residents. In many of these settings, residents take meals together on a weekly or monthly basis and often help one another when they are temporarily sick or need a ride. The Danish home care system provides ongoing help with personal care and health care, thus eliminating the concern residents might have about becoming too involved with the long-term care needs of their neighbors. This type of housing appears to provide the social benefits of group living without sacrificing the independence and autonomy many older people value.

Vacation Programs Exist for Long-Term Care Residents

One of the most interesting programs offered by many Danish nursing homes and service houses are vacations for residents. These trips are offered to residents of housing projects as well as community care service recipients. They can last as long as a week or as short as a weekend. Sometimes they are elaborate, with trips to Germany, Spain, or even Greece. Others involve a seaside resort destination within the same country. The *Dronningens Ferieby* in Greena, Denmark, is an excellent example of a seaside vacation retreat open to developmentally disabled and older frail residents. Caregivers accompany the residents because many are very frail and need assistance with daily activities such as bathing, toileting, and transferring. Residents are selected on the basis of their interest, not their physical ability. Thus, quite impaired individuals make these trips. The Dronningens facility consists of 46 small single and duplex units that can sleep four to six persons each. Rooms, kitchens, and bathrooms are handicapped accessible, and hospital beds are available to ease the transition for highly impaired individuals. The facility is adjacent to the sea and shares a wheelchair-friendly fishing dock. The funding for these trips comes from each facility. Although this vacation is offered to everyone, only a small number of residents generally take advantage of it (see page 95).

Varied Housing Forms Characterize the Housing Stock

Because of their commitment to providing services to people living in the community, the Danes are far less formula-driven in their approach to housing form. Delivering services to a range of different housing settings has resulted in an openness to different arrangements. It is common to find single-loaded corridors and cottage-style groupings of units. Although none of the northern European countries believe in overusing highly compact double-loaded corridors, the Danes are the most liberal in adapting a range of housing forms. One emphasis that characterizes the Danish approach is a focus on small-group clusters. Even in larger buildings, small groups of residents typically take meals together (*Humlehusene*, page 220). The list of Danish projects presented in Appendix A and B includes several buildings that have been adapted for reuse, as well as others that have utilized apartment-style units. The Danes often value independence very highly. There is an emphasis on larger units,

with a more casual relationship to caregiving. Frail residents may see caregivers only a few times per day. In a home care–based system, contact is based on a predetermined schedule rather than on constant periodic observation.

SWEDEN

Anthroposophic Architectural Ideas Are Sensitive to the Human Condition

This approach to architecture, which evolved from the teachings of Rudolph Steiner, was promoted by the architect Eric Asmussen in Jarna, Sweden (Asmussen, 1992; Coates, 1997). The basic approach focuses on ways of humanizing and sensitizing the environment for human interaction. Pastel colors are utilized to stimulate positive behavioral effects. Cold colors (green/blue) are often utilized in corridors to create a contrast with warmer-toned residents' rooms. Common spaces use warmer colors (yellow/rose) to stimulate social interaction. Rectangular right-angle forms are avoided in windows, doors, and rooms. Rooms used for breathing exercises (a Steiner wellness exercise) utilize clerestory windows and rooms with larger volumes at the top than at the bottom. Pendant light fixtures are clad in fabric and when corridors merge they have raised ceilings that open to skylights. Wood and natural materials have an important role to play in making spaces more approachable and warm. Wood is often covered with a light transparent stain that allows the texture of the grain to be visible. This architectural philosophy focuses on satisfying the residents by utilizing forms and materials that are cozy and humane. The buildings that exemplify this philosophy are the *Vidar Clinic* in Jarna, Sweden; *Vigs Angar* in Kopingebro, Sweden; *Pelgromhof* in Zevenaar, the Netherlands; *Gerby-Vastervik* in Vaasa, Finland; and *Romares Housing for the Elderly* in Helsingborg, Sweden.

Unit Clusters Are Consolidated into Larger Buildings

In the mid-1980s, Swedish designers broke with tradition and radically downsized large facilities for the geriatric dementia population. Huge hospitals were replaced by small group homes with 6 to 12 people scattered throughout the country (*Stenungsund*, Sweden; Regnier, 1994, page 171). The theory was that these homes would be residential in character and would calm the residents. By most accounts, these buildings were successful. The small size of the buildings allowed them to be constructed throughout the rural countryside. In the last 10 years, it has become clear that newer buildings would benefit from bringing these small groups together. Cluster sizes also

Nurse's station is a small drop-down desk and cabinet:
The *Guldbröllopshemet*, Stockholm, Sweden, dementia unit
uses a simple, approachable design for the nurse's desk in
this remodeled facility. Each floor in this multistory buiding
is designed to resemble a separate small-group home.

grew from six to eight to ten in some instances. Today these buildings typically have between 24 and 40 residents. Residents still live in small-group clusters, but four to six of these are grouped together to create one building (*Ros Anders Gård*, page 215; *Postiljonen*, page 224). Smaller buildings are generally not large enough to provide services to residents in the surrounding neighborhood unless they are connected to a day center or service house.

Controlling the Costs of Care and Staffing Difficulties Are Constant Struggles

The Swedes seem to be the most conflicted in their desire to continue to provide quality housing for older frail people while countering the pressures of escalating costs.

Facilities have reported that they have more residents with greater needs but less money to support them. The benign social experiment that Sweden has exemplified for decades is being challenged by politicians and consumers who are seeking lower taxes. The belt tightening that has resulted has made it difficult to recruit personnel. Shortages of nurses have been reported in some areas of the country. Few new buildings have been constructed in Stockholm because the cost of construction has outpaced funding. Sweden appears to be at a crossroads. With one of the highest percentages of older populations in the world, its resources are clearly strained.

A Range of Different Therapies Are Used

The Swedish health care system has always been very flexible in providing support for a wide range of therapies for older residents. These include many different types of exercise and massage therapies for older people with chronic impairments. The *Vigs Angar* building in Kopingebro has a warm therapy pool, a sauna, gymnastics classes, and a massage table for residents. The *Mossebergs Kurot* in Falkoping combines a resort-spa hotel and a housing project for the elderly. The therapeutic facilities are shared by hotel guests who come primarily for therapies for back injuries and other chronic problems. The Rudolph Steiner Seminar in Jarna offers a range of therapies for individuals with chronic and acute problems including curative eurythmy, a Steiner breathing exercise. The Swedish approach, which has been copied by others, involves looking beyond the traditional approaches to therapy to embrace new, nontraditional ideas.

NORWAY

The Caring Home Initiative Is Producing Two Types of Housing

Norway's strategy for the coming decade focuses on the creation of two types of housing. One type resembles the Swedish or Danish service house. It is a large, centralized building (100+ units) with housing for the frail and services that are available for older people living in the community. The *Bydel Sondre Nordstrand* in Oslo is a good example. It has 96 units (25 SM each) of housing clustered in 12 groups of eight units each. One-third of the units are for dementia residents, one-third are for the physically impaired, and one-third are for short-stay (rehabilitation) residents. The building has a swimming pool and a comprehensive rehabilitation center and is the central meeting place for home care workers in the district. The second type of housing is targeted to the 55+ population. A good example is the *Smedstuveien* in Trondheim, a 33-unit, three-story atrium project. It is a self-contained cooperative with large 61 SM units. The building is designed to allow residents to age in place. As residents grow older and need more services, 1 of the 33 units can be taken out of service and transformed into a common dining and living room space. These two buildings represent the "bookends" of a strategy that involves building large, centralized service centers for the very frail and smaller, decentralized housing arrangements in neighborhoods where the elderly population is growing.

Husbanken Maintains Design Standards for Elderly Housing

Design standards like the *Seniorlaben* in the Netherlands for elderly housing control the critical judgments that make housing adaptable to the needs of older residents. The Dutch standards are voluntary, but if a building has

Scooters are used to get from one room to another at night: Devices like this are frequently used in single-loaded corridor buildings so that staff can easily move from one unit cluster to another in less time.

followed them, it is generally considered to be of higher quality. In Norway, the state bank or *Husbanken*, controls building quality standards. If a project doesn't follow Husbaken guidelines, it is much harder to finance. Control over financing has turned out to be the most effective way to advocate for higher development standards. Characteristics like the size of balconies, closet sizes, raised receptacles, low sill heights, and kitchen equipment are all covered by Husbaken design standards.

Cooperative Ownership Is Common in Norway

Older residents often live in equity-based housing arrangements called *Borettslag* that are much like cooperatives. A relatively high percentage of owner-occupied housing is owned this way. These units are often 15 to 20 percent larger than standard rental units. The *Smed-stuveien* housing development in Trondheim exemplifies this type of housing.

FINLAND

Saunas and Swimming Pools Are Essential Parts of the Finnish Lifestyle

Saunas and swimming pools are ubiquitous parts of the culture. The tradition of the sauna goes back to the late nineteenth and early twentieth centuries, when many residents of Finland used saunas before they installed indoor plumbing. Many older people enjoy the sauna. In order to make it safer, they reduce the temperature to 60–80 degrees Centigrade. Some service buildings have saunas for community dwellers and a separate sauna for residents. Using a sauna takes time; as a result, it is sometimes used sparingly or on special occasions. The majority of buildings I visited in Finland had a swimming pool or access to a pool nearby. Often pools are open to a broad constituency including the developmentally disabled and babies. They are designed to meet the needs of older residents, with ramps, lifts, and recessed troughs around the perimeter for therapy and exercise instruction. The maintenance cost is often borne by the community, which may also pay for the initial construction. This is another reason why these pools are open to the community and considered a community resource.

Wood Is Used for Floors, Ceilings, and Details

Finland has vast forest preserves that are important to the culture as well as the economy of the country (Ojanen, 1999). The Finns, like other Scandinavians, love the outdoors. In Norway and Finland, strong em-

Saunas are a common feature in Finnish service houses: This one at Oulunsalo, Finland, operates with a reduced temperature for older residents who use it weekly.

phasis is placed on stained wood detailing. Bathrooms and corridors are popular places for wood slat ceilings. This emphasis on wood was popularized by the famous Finnish modern architect Alvar Aalto. His own interpretation of a regionally relevant modern architecture utilized interesting connections with outdoor spaces and wood detailing in the form of exterior screens and interior casework. Genuine wood flooring and Pergo are popular in many units, as is natural wood furniture. Older residents often collect antique wood furniture. This use of wood for floors, ceilings, wall detailing, and furniture humanizes residents' units and common spaces.

Natural and Artificial Lighting in Northern Latitudes Is Important

The Scandinavians are sensitive to the need for natural light, especially during their long, dark winters. Large corner windows, low sills, skylights, and single-loaded corridors all do their part to introduce light into buildings. In the summer, the lack of air conditioning makes it important to design for adequate flow-through ventilation, so window placements must be coordinated in this way as well. Artificial full-spectrum lighting is also popular in the short days of winter. In the *Foibe Service Center* in Vantaa, Finland, residents used light therapy to counteract depression in the winter. In the *Wilhelmiina* project

(page 163), a 450-SF area has more than 30 recessed full-spectrum light fixtures to create a superbright portion of the building for sitting and reading.

Architecture Expression in Finland Is Lively and Expressive

The architecture of Finnish buildings generally appears to be of higher quality than that of other countries. Although the Netherlands had many interesting buildings, Finnish buildings often include a greater variety of ideas about the use of color, texture, pattern, and fenestration. One cannot understate the impact of Aalto's work in these buildings. Entrances are typically understated, marked by a shade structure or a landscape feature. One of the most interesting façade treatments at *Juvakoti* in Juva, Finland, used decorative attached screens constructed from 2 × 2-inch wood slats. These screens were movable and could be used in the summer as shading devices to prevent sun from entering. They also secured building windows and increased the visual interest of the façade. The exterior design of the site was also more related to the building's interior. Exterior outdoor rooms were often developed as extensions of major interior rooms. Major sections of sites were kept in their natural state so that views from units overlooked natural rather than manicured landscapes.

31

20 MOST IMPORTANT DESIGN ISSUES AND CONSIDERATIONS

Translating research into a form that is easy for design decision makers to comprehend and use is necessary if one expects work of this nature to be used in practice. In this book, part 2 is organized around 100 important ideas categorized by scale and subject. In this chapter, 20 high-priority qualities, characteristics, issues, features, places, and policies have been identified. These range from broad issues to specific commentary on particular types of rooms. However, each has been selected and developed in an effort to focus on the critical characteristics that make a setting socially and physically successful. Taken as a whole, they provide a comprehensive checklist for measuring the adequacy of a proposed design. Taken separately, they represent important design review questions that can be used to enhance or sharpen a specific design response.

FORMAT UTILIZED TO CLARIFY AND FACILITATE USE

A format similar to that discussed in *The Pattern Language* (Alexander, Ishikawa, et al., (1977) has been used

to organize each design issue. Each one starts with a brief label that characterizes the topic. This is followed by a more detailed description that captures the main idea of each topic. Next is a rationale describing why the topic is important and what potential impacts it can have on the project. Finally, a variety of specific design and management solutions outline possible actions. These ideas embrace design features, management policies, and care considerations that, when followed, support the general theme of each design consideration. Altogether, 234 design and management directives are presented within the 20 design themes. The 20 design considerations include the following:

1. Residential Appearance
2. Stimulate Social Interaction
3. Develop Outdoor Spaces as Rooms
4. Make Certain that the Bathroom is Safe
5. Respect the Privacy of Residents
6. Create a Friendly, Comfortable Interior
7. Invite Family and Friends
8. Provide Variety and Control of Lighting

9. Provide Ventilation That Eliminates Odors
10. Create an Accommodating Environment
11. Facility Should Be Open and Connected to the Community
12. Provide a Barrier-free Environment for Everyone
13. Provide a Place for People with Dementia
14. Design a Compact Building Plan
15. Provide a Realm Between the Inside and Outside
16. Facilitate Staff Behaviors That Benefit Residents
17. Focus on Sensuous Activity and Beauty
18. Provide Passive and Active Entertainment
19. Ensure Safety and Security
20. Encourage Choice, Control, Autonomy and Independence

ONE

Residential Appearance

The visual character and physical massing of the building should be reminiscent of a house. The building should avoid the institutional look of a health care facility.

Rationale

A residential-looking building appears friendly, familiar, and inviting, often stimulating a positive response from residents, family, friends, and staff. Health care environments that utilize commercial materials and detailing appear institutional and cold. The building should seek to be the opposite of the sterile stereotype we often associate with nursing homes.

Design and Management Solutions

▲ *Residential Building Materials:* Select residential materials and details that conform to the palette of colors and textures present in the surrounding neighborhood.

▲ *Reduce Scale:* Limit the number of units and break down the massing of the building from the street to make it appear smaller and less overwhelming.

▲ *Interior Design Treatments:* These should emphasize residential characteristics rather than health care or hospitality-oriented furnishings, materials, and textures.

▲ *Setback Form:* Consider the use of porches, dormer window treatments, upper-floor setbacks, and bay windows to reduce the perceived height and mass of the building from the street.

▲ *Corridors:* Avoid long, uniform, lifeless, double-loaded corridors that are void of natural light.

▲ *Sloped Roof Form:* A traditional pitched roof is one of the most popular residential features.

Colorful retractable awnings are commonly used in Dutch housing for shade control: In this remodeled Nieuw Doddendaal in *Nijmegan*, the Netherlands, they have been outfitted with automatic controls that raise and lower them from the inside.

▲ *Residential Front Door:* An attractive wooden front door is a memorable feature identified with residential design.

▲ *Fireplace:* The hearth is a feature that has been used symbolically and functionally in housing for centuries.

▲ *Object in the Landscape:* In a rural or suburban location, the building often appears like a country villa or mansion sitting atop a lush green landscape unfettered by cars and pavement.

▲ *Residential Room Scale:* Interior room sizes should reflect a residential scale. Dining rooms should be subdivided, and living rooms and lounges should be scaled for furniture groups.

▲ *Connecting Stairs:* An open staircase that links the second floor with the first floor is common in most elegant multistory houses.

▲ *Public to Private Sequence:* Common spaces should be arranged to move from the most public to the most private spaces—as in a house.

▲ *Friendly Entry:* Staff offices and staff presence should not dominate the entry experience. Entering to find a small desk with a friendly receptionist or volunteer is far more inviting than confronting a nurse's station.

▲ *Noninstitutional Lighting:* Nothing says "institutional" with greater clarity than fluorescent light fixtures in common spaces.

▲ *Acid Test:* Always ask yourself, "Would I consider doing this for my mother's house?" to test for the appropriateness of spaces, fixtures, features, furnishings, and treatments.

TWO

Stimulate Social Interaction

The building's design, including its entry sequence, common space configuration, and unit entry layout, should encourage residents to make friendly contact with one another.

Rationale

The raison d'être for the creation of purpose-built, age-segregated housing is to establish opportunities for residents to meet one another and to nurture ac-quaintanceships and friendships. One of the inevitable side effects of aging is the loss of good friends through death and disability. Many friendships have literally taken a lifetime to cultivate. Creating opportunities for informal social exchange and friendship formation can be a powerful antidote to depression. Social psychologists have found that the number of human contacts we make is often related to our feelings of happiness. The need to maintain

Key

1. Living Room
2. Dining Table
3. Typical Unit
4. Kitchen
5. Fireplace
6. Outdoor Secured Garden
7. Sauna
8. Laundry
9. Entry Space
10. Second Unit Cluster

Small-group cluster increases sociability for dementia residents: Nine residents in the *Villa Viklo Oulu,* Finland share their daily life experiences in this self-contained unit cluster.

privacy and the ability to avoid unwanted social interaction are also important. In fact, supporting options for privacy usually facilitates social interaction.

Design and Management Solutions

▲ *Avoid Uncomfortable Confrontations:* One of the most common problems is a tight entry area design that causes visitors to "run the gauntlet" between residents as they enter the building.

▲ *Cluster Entry Doors:* When several dwelling unit entries are clustered together, there is a greater probability that residents will get to know one another as they enter or exit their dwelling units.

▲ *People-Watching Places:* Create places where residents can watch others informally. This allows them to connect vicariously with the observed activity.

▲ *Triangulation:* Artwork or memorabilia displays in corridors and common spaces can stimulate conversations between individuals. These are especially effective when the content can be shared between generations.

▲ *Observing Busy Pathways:* The pathway between the front door and the elevator and between the dining room and the elevator in a multistory building are likely to be good places for observation and informal social exchange.

▲ *Dining Room Socializing:* The three mealtimes provide excellent opportunities to converse with friends and tablemates. Dining rooms with relatively low ceilings, carefully controlled acoustics, and good light levels make it easier for residents to talk with one another.

▲ *Friendly Common Spaces:* Most assisted living buildings have 40 to 50 percent of their total square footage devoted to common spaces and corridors. These places should be designed to encourage residents to bump into one another.

▲ *Spaces for Family Conversations:* Shared common spaces should be available where families can engage residents in a conversation outside of their dwelling units.

▲ *Meals with Family Members:* The building's policy should make it easy for a resident to take a meal with family members without a reservation.

▲ *Open Plan:* A well-designed, open first-floor plan makes it easier for residents to see one another and thus prepare to interact with or avoid one another.

▲ *Planned Socializing:* The first priority of planned activity programs is to create enjoyable opportunities for social interaction between residents.

▲ *Introduce Newcomers:* Programs and announcements that serve to introduce new residents to old-timers can break down communication barriers.

▲ *Retreat Spaces:* These are good places for residents to go when they want to be alone. Having places that provide for solitude makes it easier for residents to feel that privacy and communal interaction are both accommodated.

▲ *Encourage Small-Group Activities:* Activities and clubs should be created for small and large groups that share particular interests.

▲ *Intergenerational Exchange:* Allowing grandchildren to be an important part of the life of the place adds variety and interest. Places for play should be located inside and outside the building.

▲ *Mailboxes Are a Popular Destination:* Distributing the mail is a lively event in most assisted living buildings. If the mail is placed in a locked box or is distributed from a central location, residents will come down promptly to retrieve it.

THREE

Develop Outdoor Spaces as Rooms

Outdoor spaces are important sources of views from rooms inside the building. Treat outdoor site areas as destinations for residents to visit or places to walk to and through for exercise.

Rationale

Sites can be sources of beauty, inspiration, and stimulation. Outside elements include landscape materials for color and texture, hardscape surfaces for activities, and pathways for exercise. Landscape materials shouldn't be used just to decorate the perimeter of a building. They should be used to create three-dimensional destinations for residents to visit and spend time. Using plant materials, exterior furniture, and objects, rooms can be given definition, character, focus, directionality, and purpose. The design of outside rooms should always be contemplated from inside the building, from an exercise pathway around the building, and from the edge of the site.

Design and Management Solutions

▲ *Walking Around the Building:* One of the most important and productive ways of using the site is as an exercise pathway. A pathway should surround the building, leading from the front door around the building and back to the front door.

▲ *Views to the Site:* Each common space with an exterior window wall has the ability to support an adjacent outdoor patio or balcony. The views from these spaces are often more memorable, and they give residents a sense of connection with the outdoors.

▲ *Entry Landscape:* Landscape treatments at the front door can make a lively, colorful first impression on both visitors and residents. Because this space is heavily utilized, landscape treatments here often benefit the greatest number of people.

▲ *Benches to Rest:* In order to encourage residents to walk around the site for exercise, benches should be provided every 100–150 feet. If these places are transformed into shaded, landscaped places to rest, they can encourage residents to walk as well as providing them with a place to spend time outdoors.

▲ *Barbecue Plaza:* A large outdoor space should be

Service house and dementia garden overlook children's play space: The rural *Sternberga* service house in Vetlanda, Sweden, combines these three uses in a way that allows everyone to benefit from the views of children playing.

available for group events during good weather that can comfortably seat half of the residents for a meal.

▲ *Exterior Retreat Places:* These are attractive places for residents who would like to meditate by themselves or be with family members who want to get away from the crowd.

▲ *Dwelling Unit Windows:* These should be large (at least 9 to 10 SF) and oriented to a favorable long or short view. The sill should be low enough (12–17 inches) for residents to see the ground plane from their beds.

▲ *Resident Gardens:* Cultivating flowers and vegetables is a popular activity with a small number of people. Garden beds that are raised 26–30 inches keep residents from having to bend over and make them accessible to people in wheelchairs. A nearby water source should also be available.

▲ *Shade Control:* Older residents often want to use outdoor spaces when the weather is pleasant and sunny. However, shade control is necessary if residents are to inhabit a space for any length of time. Porches, shade structures, and umbrella tables are effective in providing shade.

▲ *Outside Storage Places:* Storage areas near large assembly spaces can be used for chairs, tables, games, audio equipment, and recreation paraphernalia.

▲ *Attracting Wildlife:* Areas designed to attract birds, butterflies, squirrels, and other sources of wildlife can animate places on the site and views from the inside.

▲ *Watching Activities and Children:* Visual connections to activities that occur on site or on adjacent

properties can provide hours of enjoyable observation. Visually accessible playgrounds for children hold a special fascination for residents.

FOUR

Make Certain That the Bathroom Is Safe

One of the most dangerous places in the dwelling unit is the bathroom. Residents transfer to the commode, they take baths, and they often come here when they feel ill.

Rationale

The bathroom has a great deal of symbolic meaning to older frail people who are struggling to maintain their independence. It must not only be designed to facilitate its continuing use by residents, but it must also accommodate caregivers who help them. Staff may provide partial assistance or be heavily involved in the toileting and bathing process. Safety devices like grab bars, nonslip floor surfaces, and emergency call hardware must be specified and placed in the right location to be effective. Adequate heat and light are also very important components of a successful design.

Design and Management Solutions

▲ *Adequate Light:* The bathroom should have plenty of light over the vanity, near the shower, and in general throughout the room.

▲ *Bathroom Storage:* A place for medication and towel storage should be provided. Decentralized storage and display space in the bathroom is considered very useful and is popular when provided.

▲ *Emergency Call:* Emergency call hardware should be placed so as to be equally accessible from the shower and the toilet. A string that reaches to within a few inches of the floor can be used by residents who have slipped and fallen on the floor.

▲ *Adequate Heat:* Heat lamps or wall heaters should be specified to warm the bathroom quickly. Older residents often refuse or resist taking a shower when the bathroom is too cold.

▲ *Water Temperature Regulation:* Antiscald regulators on showers or a 110 degree Fahrenheit hot water

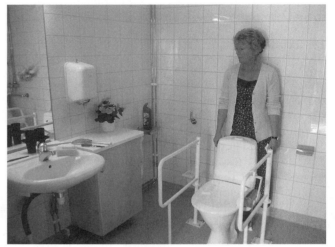

Toilet designs for accessibility vary: In the *Kv Stryrkan* project in Malmö, Sweden, space has been created behind the toilet to give caregivers more room to help residents who require two-person assistance.

supply limit should be specified to reduce the possibility that a resident will be scalded.

▲ *Bathroom Flooring:* Falls in the bathroom can be reduced through the use of slip-resistant floor surfaces in the shower and on the bathroom floor, as well as grab bars located inside and outside the shower and adjacent to the toilet.

▲ *Toilets and Grab Bars:* Toilets should be higher than normal to assist residents in getting on and off the commode, and toilet tissue holders should be conveniently mounted. However, the handicapped height (17 inches) is often too high for shorter female residents. Grab bars can be mounted on a heavy plywood-backed wall so that the height and angle placement of the bar are fitted to each resident's reach and strength capacity.

▲ *Sliding Doors:* Pocket or barn-style sliding doors that are 36 to 40 inches wide make it easier for a resident in a wheelchair or someone who is being assisted by a caregiver to enter the bathroom easily.

▲ *Showers:* These are much safer than bathtubs. Most showers have a hand-held shower wand in addition to a wall-mounted showerhead. Roll-in showers are very useful but much less popular in the United States than in northern Europe. A portable shower seat is often preferred to a built-in one because it can be placed anywhere and can be raised or lowered in height.

▲ *Spacious Bathrooms:* The bathroom should be large enough for wheelchair access and for caregiver assistance. The fair housing standards outline two types of acceptable bathrooms: accessible and adaptable.

▲ *Faucet Controls:* Water supply controls should be levers to facilitate manipulation.

▲ *Lavatory:* In northern Europe, the lavatory sink is often cantilevered and adjustable in height. In the United States, cabinets are often designed with removable fronts so that they can be made handicapped accessible if needed. A larger mirror is also a useful addition; it has the side effect of making the room seem larger.

FIVE

Respect the Privacy of Residents

When residents are living in a group environment and receive personal care assistance from staff, privacy can be an issue. The design of the unit, the configuration of social spaces and policies regarding staff interaction can do much to ensure privacy.

Rationale

Residents should be able to achieve privacy from the staff and from other residents. Staff policies and the physical environment should be configured to facilitate privacy as well as social interaction. The dwelling unit is the most important private retreat for residents. It should be large enough to serve as a setting for entertaining friends and accommodating children and grandchildren. Common spaces in the building and outdoor places on the site should be available where residents can be by themselves or with another person for a private conversation.

Design and Management Solutions

▲ *Dwelling Unit Size:* Residents' units should be large enough and self-contained enough to be perceived as a dwelling unit and not just as a bedroom. In general, the larger the unit, the more time residents will spend there.

▲ *Separate Bedroom:* A separate bedroom provides a private place for the display of personal objects and photographs. The bathroom is sometimes the only place where privacy can be assured.

▲ *Unit Designed for Privacy:* Single-occupancy units go a long way toward ensuring privacy. When a

Unit personalization is encouraged in northern Europe: This small studio unit in the *Postiljonen* nursing home (page 224) looks very cozy with the ten or so pieces of furniture this resident has brought to turn her unit into a home.

double-occupied unit is designed to save money or to allow two people the option of living together, it should also be designed to ensure as much privacy as possible. Using side-by-side beds with a privacy curtain is not a good enough solution.

▲ *Management Should Respect Residents' Privacy:* We often forget that residents in assisted living who need personal care assistance with ADLs like toileting, bathing, and dressing have already had to compromise their standards of privacy. Staff should always knock before they enter a resident's room. Sometimes the presence of a doorbell or door knocker can routinize this protocol, making it easier to signal the desire to make contact.

▲ *Noise Should be Minimized:* Having enough insulation in the walls between units, between units and common spaces, and between units and outdoor street noise can make it easier to sleep at night.

▲ *Private Places for Family Conversation:* There should be places where family conversations can be freewheeling. Residents should be able to express their true feelings about the place, the staff, and fellow residents without feeling that they will experience retribution.

▲ *Windows to the Corridor:* When units have features like windows to the corridor or bathroom doors that are visible from the corridor, they should be configured with doors that shield views and window curtains that close.

▲ *Dining Room Options:* Dining rooms with two-, four-, and six-person tables provide options for controlling the size of a social group.

▲ *Privacy for Couples:* Couples often have a special relationship with one another and therefore have less reason to interact with others. There should be adequate opportunity for them to spend time with one another—including sleeping together in a large bed. Intimacy can be a form of privacy for two people.

▲ *Eating in the Room:* In northern Europe, it is not uncommon for residents to take breakfast in their rooms rather than as a group.

▲ *Staying in the Community:* Encouraging and helping residents to stay in their own homes or apartments is another way to ensure privacy. This is especially true for people who are not ready to move to assisted living.

▲ *Watching Without Obligation:* Residents should be able to watch activities without feeling obligated to be direct participants.

SIX

Create a Friendly, Comfortable Interior

The interior design of the building should exude a friendly, familiar, dignified, residential character. It should be the antithesis of the institutional nursing home.

Rationale

While the model for interior design in nursing homes is often the hospital, the model for assisted living design should be a comfortable and attractive manor house. Residents greatly prefer rich fabrics, wood furniture, and carpets to plastic-covered sofas, sturdy metal furniture, and shiny vinyl flooring. The obsession inherited from hospitals is to create a maintenance-free, easy-to-clean, commercial-style building rather than a residence. Variety with continuity allows the building to be distinct without being too garish. Comfort is also important for individuals with lower back problems and strength deficits. Furniture should be relatively easy to get into and out of, and should be placed to accommodate both the need for rest and the desire for social interaction.

Design and Management Solutions

▲ *Artwork:* Artwork is an important component of an interior design treatment. It should be used to stim-

The verandah provides an informal living room for residents: This fully conditioned, enclosed porch has a view of the courtyard. It is located immediately adjacent to the dining room at the *Postiljonen* nursing home (page 224).

ulate emotion and to add variety and interest to spaces and corridors.

▲ *Affect-laden Images and Accessories:* Emotionally tuned artwork and accessories often feature children, animals, and intergenerational scenes that are upbeat and positive.

▲ *Residential Features:* Candles, stuffed baby animals, and collectibles are often associated with cozy settings that have great appeal to those who are seeking a noninstitutional environment.

▲ *Variety of Rooms:* Rooms with variations in style, color and texture of furniture, wall coverings, and floor coverings add interest and distinctiveness to a building's interior.

▲ *Plant Materials:* Plant materials of various sizes, when placed, mounted, and hung in highly visible locations, add to the humane character of the space.

▲ *Unit Interiors:* Dwelling units should be large enough and configured in a way that allows residents to bring in important furniture items and objects like books, photos, or collectibles.

▲ *Symbolic Residential Features:* A fireplace, like a library, is a symbolic feature that reflects past associations, values, and expectations. Both elements create potentially positive behavioral settings.

▲ *Carpets:* Carpets should be resilient, moisture-backed, and dense enough for wheelchairs and walkers. Colors and patterns should look residential and should be dark enough for ease of maintenance but light enough to reflect an adequate amount of light.

▲ *Dining Room Chairs:* These should have lumbar support, heavy seat padding, arms to ease exiting, and castors on the front legs to move easily. Approximately 60 percent of the body's weight is supported on the ischial tuberosities (Koncelik, 1976), two bony protuberances on the hip where the older person has less fat and muscle tissue.

▲ *Incontinence Concerns:* Chemical moisture-proofing and special fabrics like textured Krypton allow a range of colors and textures to be specified in situations where incontinence is a problem.

▲ *Salient Furnishing Items:* Furniture and accessories, especially antiques, from the surrounding region can stimulate positive associations with places and people.

▲ *Personalizing Corridors:* Allowing residents to personalize the hallway immediately outside their room is a common practice in northern Europe. It makes the setting more personal and more connected to the resident population.

▲ *Pendant-Style Light Fixtures:* In northern Europe, residents often bring a favorite hanging light fixture of their own when they move. Some fixtures are antiques that have been handed down from generation to generation.

▲ *Historic Photographs:* Interiors should utilize historic photographs of the community, as well as other references to its life and history.

▲ *Residential Materials and Associations:* Some materials and treatments, like wood flooring, a stone fireplace hearth, stained wood casework, and divided light windows, have strong residential associations.

SEVEN

Invite Family and Friends

The building's design should make family members feel welcome by creating continuity between their previous residential situation and their new one.

Rationale

There should be places in the building and on the grounds where residents and family members can spend time together. Family members should feel that they are welcome, just as they would if the resident was living at home. The dwelling unit should be large enough to accommodate an overnight stay. Respite, hospice, and adult day-care programs are additional ways an assisted living facility can support family members who want to care for their parents at home.

Design and Management Solutions

▲ *Places for Children to Play:* A children's corner somewhere in the building and outdoor play equip-

Café reproduced in an old-style historic dining room: Creating unusual character and interest in a room can be done by replicating an existing historic place, as was the case in this service house meeting space.

ment on the grounds encourage small children and their parents to visit.

▲ *Places for Family Members to Converse:* Areas in the building like a decentralized lounge or a porch are good common spaces for residents and family members to talk freely and somewhat privately.

▲ *Retreat Spaces:* Places on the site like a gazebo or a garden that are relatively close to the building can be good places to get away from everyone else for conversations.

▲ *Taking a Meal:* There should be enough space in the dining room and policies that encourage family members to take an occasional meal with residents.

▲ *Covered Drop-off Area:* A porte cochere that shelters the path at the front entry from the car to the building can encourage family members to take residents out more frequently.

▲ *Private Dining Room:* A space should be available for birthday parties, celebrations, and special family events. A private dining room works well for this purpose.

▲ *Parking:* Adequate parking should be provided to encourage family members and friends to visit.

▲ *Informal Participation in Caregiving:* Some facilities are organized so that family members can take on limited caregiving duties like doing personal laundry or helping with caregiving tasks.

▲ *Volunteering:* Family members and friends often make great volunteers. They should be invited to participate in special programs and may seek association with other family members for peer discussions and friendship.

▲ *Respite Care:* This is an important service for family members who are taking responsibility for caregiving at home and need more than a week of time off for a vacation or to accomplish something else.

▲ *Adult Day Care:* This service helps to provide relief for families who may need time during the day or week to rest or to do other chores.

▲ *Protection:* Some residents have serious family problems, which may require more active participation by management to protect them from danger.

EIGHT

Provide Variety and Control of Lighting

Natural and artificial light is necessary for basic illumination, mood lighting, and aesthetic purposes.

Rationale

Older frail residents are often in need of more light to see at the same level of visual acuity as younger-older people. They also are more likely to experience problems from glare, which can be caused by too much light. Lighting needs to be used strategically for clinical, functional, and aesthetic purposes. Lighting can also have an impact on mood and behavior, especially with dementia residents.

Design and Management Solutions

▲ *Pools of Light:* Uniform light levels are not always a good idea. Wiping out the natural pooling of light as it enters a room or a corridor makes the environment appear flat and undifferentiated.

▲ *Balance Natural and Artificial Light:* The right combination of natural and artificial light is impor-

Anthroposophic architectural ideas humanize the environment: The fabric light fixtures, wraparound greenhouse window, fireplace hearth, and wood floor were specified to make the *Vigs Ängar* dementia unit in Köpingbro, Sweden, more cozy.

tant in balancing the need for light of the right color and consistency.

▲ *Skylights and Clerestory Windows:* These can introduce natural light into the darkest areas. Transparent glass, tinted for protection, still allows direct sunlight and shadows to enter. If controlled properly, a transparent surface is often more aesthetically attractive.

▲ *Bathroom Light:* The dwelling unit's bathroom requires a higher level of light for safety, personal hygiene, and skin inspection.

▲ *Avoid Conventional Fluorescent Strip Lighting:* The right combination of fluorescent and incandescent lighting can affect mood and facial coloration. Fluorescent lighting, unless it is balanced or skewed toward the warmer end of the color range, can appear flat and sickly.

▲ *Window Shape and Placement:* On an exterior wall, punched openings, corner windows, large windows, and low sills can vary the amount and direction of light.

▲ *Light Level Control:* Sometimes it is important to vary the amount of light for functional purposes. In an activity room, the light level may need to be high for crafts and card games but low for watching TV, videos, or projected images.

▲ *Mood Lighting:* In other rooms, such as a private dining room, the amount of light may vary, depending on the mood or the occasion. Candlelight can be an attractive source of light in the dining room or in the spa, where it has positive associations.

▲ *Control of Natural Lighting:* The control of natural light through shades, curtains, and awnings is important in the late afternoon, when the sunlight is least welcome.

▲ *Porches and Overhangs:* These are popular because they are excellent devices for sun control, and they create pleasant places for residents to sit in good weather.

▲ *Site Lighting:* At night this can be important for walkways, parking lots, and the aesthetic lighting of trees and bushes. The direct lighting of a building is often the least effective form of site lighting. Lights should lead from the front door to the end of the parking lot.

▲ *Variety of Light Sources:* Utilizing a range of artificial light sources often makes a building more residential in character. Table lamps, floor lamps, pendant lighting, sconce lighting, down lights, and indirect cove lighting can all be used interchangeably.

▲ *Avoid Direct Exposure to Light Sources:* Any form of lighting that avoids visual contact with the light source usually reduces glare. Indirect lighting, pendant lighting, and floor and table lamps with shades are some of the best choices.

▲ *Light for Therapy:* In northern Europe, high light levels are used to counteract mood disorders in the winter and sundowning in dementia units. We don't know much about how this form of therapy works, but it appears promising.

NINE

Provide Ventilation That Eliminates Odors

The heating, ventilating, and air conditioning system in the building should exhaust air through common spaces, by exiting it through residents' unit bathrooms.

Rationale

One of the most disconcerting experiences is entering a building and smelling the odors of feces and urine. This unpleasant experience keeps family members from visiting more frequently and generally makes the visit less than pleasant. Ventilation systems, new fabrics and carpet materials, and new cleaning equipment are available today that all but eliminate this problem. Management of incontinence should start with a staff program and a commitment to respond immediately to problems when they occur.

Design and Management Solutions

▲ *Odors Should Not be a Problem:* Given the fabrics currently available for furniture and carpets and the technology for climate control, odors should never be a problem.

▲ *Ventilation Systems:* The best ventilation systems supply fresh air to common spaces and corridors under positive pressure. This oversupply of air naturally migrates around unit doors to bathrooms, where low-pressure ventilation fans continuously exhaust air. In this system, odors from residents' rooms are kept from migrating to common spaces.

▲ *Carpet:* New carpet technologies utilize new materials and moistureproof backing systems that keep liquids from being absorbed into the carpet fabric or the underlying backing material. These materials are often easy to clean and sanitize.

▲ *Natural Fresh Air Systems:* In some countries, like England and those of northern Europe, ventilation in dwelling units is natural. Radiators are used for heat, and windows are structured with *trickle vents* to allow fresh air to enter without having to open a window.

▲ *Air Fresheners:* For difficult situations in which residents exhibit problem behaviors, air fresheners and other chemical treatments are available that absorb

French balcony design is simple but elegant: This window grill design for the Bydel *Søndre Nordstrand* service house in Oslo, Norway, allows residents to place plants outside. The wooden dowel provides security and creates a two-window composition.

and recondition the air rather than just mask the odor.

▲ *Control Is Important:* Odor control starts with staff diligence and a well-managed incontinence program.

▲ *Cleaning Equipment:* Today's professional cleaning equipment is excellent. Assuming that high-quality carpeting has been installed, the devices should be very effective in removing stains and odors.

▲ *Moistureproof Fabrics:* Today's new fabrics, solvents, and cleaning methods allow much greater protection than in the past.

▲ *Running Water:* Sometimes environmental causes of incontinence can be identified. Running and splashing water from interior fountains has been identified by some as promoting resident incontinence.

▲ *Replace Furniture and Carpeting:* If all else fails, the removal of soiled carpeting and furniture should be part of a regular capital budget process. Problem areas should be identified and the furniture and carpeting replaced on a regular basis.

TEN

Create An Accommodating Environment

Toilet is visible from the resident's bed: In the *Goddard House* (page 169), a wide pocket door has been situated so that a view into the bathroom is possible. (Photo: Edward Jacoby Photography)

The building should be adaptable and modifiable so that as residents become more frail, the physical environment and the amount of service needed can be changed to suit their needs.

Rationale

In most assisted living environments, there is a strong desire to maintain residents for as long as possible, allowing them to age in place. One way to achieve this goal is to consider the environment as a fluid one that can to be adjusted and made safer and more supportive. Rooms like the bathroom and kitchen are the most likely candidates for these types of adjustments. One of the major changes occurs when residents need a wheelchair to get around. They can move from an environment where walking was aided by furniture to one where extra furniture gets in the way.

Design and Management Solutions

▲ *Bathroom Changes:* Adding grab bars, increasing the light level, and making the shower and toilet easier to transfer to and from are some of the most important changes to be made in the bathroom.

▲ *Service Adjustments:* In addition to environmental changes, the frequency and intensity of personal care service can be ramped up.

▲ *Wheelchair Adaptations:* Dwelling unit designs should be adaptable for the use of handicapped residents. For example, the shower should have a removable dam, and the toilet should be high enough to accommodate an easy transfer. Transitions between different floor materials should also be smooth, and the lavatory sink should have a removable face.

▲ *Lift Rail Technology:* In northern Europe, ceilings are structurally reinforced so that steel rails for a rolling electric lift can be attached. This makes it easier to transfer a resident from the bed to a wheelchair or to the toilet.

▲ *Bathroom Size:* Bathrooms should be large enough to accommodate a wheelchair and another person providing assistance. Oversized (42-inch) sliding pocket or barn doors can open up the bathroom wall to the surrounding corridor, providing more space for residents and caregivers to maneuver.

▲ *Demountable Bathroom:* Some strategies for bathroom designs start with a more intimate environment containing storage cabinets. These are designed to be removed when wheelchair tolerances are necessary.

▲ *Building Population Ages in Place:* In general, the age of the population in congregate housing increases an average of between 0.3 and 0.5 year for each calendar year the building is open (Lawton, Moss, et al., 1985). Strategies should be in place that allow the building to accommodate a frailer population as it ages.

▲ *Apartments for Life:* In the Netherlands, "apartments for life" dwelling units are designed to adapt from independent housing to heavy nursing use. Bathrooms are large enough to accommodate a stretcher bather, and the front entry door has two leaves (36 + 10 inches) that can be opened wide enough to accommodate a person in a hospital bed. Kitchen counters and the bathroom sink can also be adjusted in height through a motorized lift.

▲ *Increasing Care or Moving?* The continuing-care retirement community is based on the concept of physically moving residents to a higher level of care when they need more assistance. In northern Europe, the service level is increased but residents stay in the same dwelling unit.

▲ *European Roll-in Showers:* The typical northern European bathroom has a continuous tile bathroom floor with a drain in one corner. With this design, residents can easily roll in with a wheelchair or transfer to a drop-down seat. The rest of the bathroom can become a staging area for the shower.

▲ *Toilet Adaptations:* The continued independent use of a toilet is basic to one's sense of competence. Backing the bathroom wall with plywood allows an occupational therapist to select the best location for a grab bar. The height and angle of the bar should be based on the resident's muscle strength and the resident's desire to either pull or push when entering or exiting the commode.

▲ *Hospital Beds:* These make it much safer for a caregiver to assist in a transfer or to turn a resident. In northern Europe, the specification of a hospital bed is a standard modification made when a resident needs more help with ambulation.

ELEVEN

Facility Should Be Open and Connected to the Community

The building and its services should embrace the needs of older residents living in the neighborhood. An assisted living building should be a place to solve a range of problems rather than just a place where people can go to live out the last few years of their lives.

Rationale

The idea of making each assisted living building responsive to the needs of the neighborhood has been fully implemented in northern Europe. Each building is a service center first and a housing environment second. The typical northern European service house spends as much time keeping people in their own homes as it does supporting the needs of frail residents in attached housing. Currently, U.S. assisted living environments tend to be single-focused entities with the potential but not the motivation to serve the surrounding community.

Design and Management Solutions

▲ *Day Care for Children:* This is a popular mixed-use feature that can provide great benefits for residents. It also changes the image of the assisted living facility in the community. It is no longer viewed as only a place for older frail people.

▲ *Short Stays and Rehabilitation:* Rehabilitation services that involve short stays of seven to ten days are particularly helpful for stroke victims and for others who need to leave the hospital but are not well enough to go home. These services reach a

Atrium is used to accommodate a weekly "farmer's market": The *Humanitas* project in Hengelo, the Netherlands, hosts this event for residents who have a difficult time getting out to shop for fresh fruits and vegetables.

broader population that needs personal care on a temporary basis. Physical therapy and exercise services can also be shared with this group.

▲ *Hospice Care:* End-of-life care is another community-based service that assisted living facilities are particularly well situated to provide. This service works well in an assisted living environment because staff can be made available and more extensive personal and health care services can be added when they are needed.

▲ *Zoning Difficulties:* One of the major barriers to implementing mixed-use programs is zoning and entitlement difficulties. Often parking counts and traffic flows are unknown when a public use like a community center is added to a program. This often discourages providers from considering mixed uses like child care.

▲ *Emergency Call:* In northern Europe, it is not uncommon for service houses to have a contract to monitor the emergency call system for people living in the nearby community. Because they know the residents from previous service calls, they can often assess the seriousness of a situation more accurately.

▲ *Community Restaurant:* Also common in Europe is the creation of a restaurant/dining room that is open to people in the community. This makes the assisted living environment far more approachable to a range of people in the community.

▲ *Swimming Pools:* In Finland and Sweden, service houses often contain a swimming pool. Because the service house is open to people in the community, the capital and ongoing operational expenses of the pool are shared by the municipality. It is common for the swimming pool in an elderly service house to be open to preschoolers, to the developmentally disabled, and for baby care.

▲ *Visit the Neighborhood:* Occasionally, buildings are too self-contained. It is important that residents get out and experience the surrounding neighborhood—by going to the local bank to carry out personal business or to a favorite local restaurant.

▲ *Mixed Use:* Mixing retail and housing uses is becoming more popular in the United States. It has been the mainstay of urban housing in Europe for decades. Mixing housing with a doctor's office, pharmacy, or small, supportive retail setting is particularly useful.

▲ *Link to Adjacent Compatible Uses:* Connecting the building to the street through a sidewalk or through a gate to an adjacent shopping area makes the building seem connected to the surrounded neighborhood rather than isolated from it.

▲ *Hosting Events:* When the community uses the building for public purposes like voting and for social events to which neighbors and family members are invited, the building is seen as a community resource.

TWELVE

Provide a Barrier-Free Environment for Everyone

Universal design principles should be the basis for making decisions about the accessibility of the environment

Rationale

As many as 25–40 percent of residents in a mature assisted living facility use a walker or a wheelchair to ambulate. Both of these devices require careful attention to the height of adjacent floor surfaces, surface friction differences between materials, and the amount of floor area and corridor width. The seven principles of universal design are equitable use, flexibility in use, simple and intuitive use, perceptible information, tolerance for error, low physical effort, and size and space for approach and use (Mace, 1991).

Design and Management Solutions

▲ *Floor Level Changes:* Differences in surface friction and level changes make it difficult for residents in walkers and wheelchairs to navigate.

▲ *Sills and Thresholds:* Transitions from inside to outside often cause barriers or a tripping hazard.

Two sliding pocket doors provide access: These two door in the *Ensjøtunet* project in Oslo, Norway, link the bedroom with the living room but also allow caregivers to reach the bed from both sides, facilitating transfers.

The threshold height should be no more than ¾ inch and should be beveled, with a slope of no more than 1:2.

▲ *Interior Thresholds:* Changes in material should be as flush as possible. In no case should they be more than ¼ inch without being beveled or tapered. If a tapered threshold is used, the maximum level change should be ½ inch.

▲ *Public Toilets:* These should be large enough for wheelchair manipulation, with a 5-foot-diameter turning circle between fixtures. Keep in mind that an attendant may accompany a resident to provide help.

▲ *Achieve Spatial Variety:* One of the best ways to achieve this is by making adjustments to the ceiling plane rather than the floor plane.

▲ *Adaptable Dwelling Units:* These usually have wide doors, low-mounted switch controls, and grab bar reinforcement. If needed, grab bars can be added and knee space can be provided by removing the bottom of a base cabinet.

▲ *Select Resilient Materials:* Older people have balance control problems that often put them at risk

for falls. Many have osteoporosis. Carpets and non-slip, resilient sheet vinyl are good floor surface materials.

▲ *Ramps:* Whenever a ramp is being considered, it is a good idea for stairs to be present. Ramps are needed for wheelchairs, but some older people prefer stairs to an inclined surface. A 5 percent maximum slope is preferable.

▲ *Adequate Light:* Light in bathrooms and corridors is very important for safe ambulation. A night light that lights the path from the bed to the bathroom is particularly helpful.

▲ *Controls That Are Easy to Manipulate:* Lighting, HVAC, and water supply controls should be configured to make them easy to manipulate. Single-lever handles, large, easy-to-twist dials, and loop pulls are easier for a resident with arthritis to manipulate.

THIRTEEN

Provide a Place for People with Dementia

Caring for residents with memory loss often requires a smaller, self-contained setting with fewer residents and a carefully trained staff.

Rationale

Good dementia environments are small-scale settings that subdivide the population into small clusters of 8 to 15 residents. Dwelling units are often smaller, with more space devoted to shared common areas. A security system that prevents residents from leaving is important. Access to outdoor garden spaces should be easy to achieve. Being able to walk inside and outside the building can reduce the anxiety level of residents who have an incessant need to wander.

Design and Management Solutions

▲ *Access to Outdoors:* Access to an outdoor garden or balcony is necessary. It is always better to have ground-floor access, but this is not always possible in urban environments.

▲ *Separate Secured Unit Cluster:* Dementia residents seem to do better when they are clustered with residents who have similar memory loss problems. Some of the best assisted living buildings have a separate secured section for people with dementia.

Dementia resident shops for food with a caregiver: The *Hogeway* dementia facility in Weesp, the Netherlands, has a basement grocery store where caregivers and residents can shop for food that will be prepared later in a small kitchen that serves 11 residents.

▲ *Walking or Wandering Route:* Having a looped circulation pathway in the building provides residents with a place to walk if they are frustrated and feel the need to constantly be on the move.

▲ *Dwelling Units Are Used for Sleeping:* Dementia residents spend most of their time in common spaces. The dwelling unit is used primarily as a place for personal hygiene tasks and sleep.

▲ *Window Guards and Balcony Enclosures:* Openings like windows and balconies should be protected so that residents will not be tempted to elope and in the process hurt themselves.

▲ *Fence Height:* Fences should be 6 feet in height, and outdoor garden areas should be visible from major interior common spaces so that caregivers can monitor them.

▲ *ADL Programming:* Using ADL programming (setting the table, folding laundry, limited food preparation, bussing dishes, making beds, etc.) as the basis for interaction is a common strategy in the United States and in Europe.

▲ *Secured Perimeter:* The unit cluster should have delayed egress or magnetic lock protection for securing residents. Some frustrated residents, especially after they have first moved in, may feel the need to search for their former homes.

▲ *European Clusters:* Northern European dementia facilities utilize small-group clusters of six to eight residents. These settings usually have a minimum of five shared spaces including a living room, dining room, kitchen, outdoor area, and activity room.

▲ *Space for Music:* Music activities and sing-alongs are often very popular, in part because residents often retain the ability to understand music late into the disease. Equipment and places where music can be played should be available.

▲ *Staff Training:* Dealing with dementia residents can be difficult and complicated. Special staff training is often needed to reduce frustration and redirect their focus.

▲ *Dementia Onset is Unique:* Each dementia resident is unique. A strategy that works with one person may not work with another or may not work with the same person a week later. Constant reassessment and testing new ideas is necessary for success.

▲ *Sensory Communication Strategies:* The Dutch idea of snoezelen, or communication through the physical senses, was imported from Danish therapies for severely developmentally disabled children. It is an effective approach for residents who are frustrated with or have lost the ability to communicate verbally.

FOURTEEN

Design Compact Building Plan

Minimizing corridor lengths or planning for decentralized small clusters allows residents with mobility difficulties to be more independent.

Rationale

One of the major problems that limit the independence of older people is their inability to ambulate. The distance from the dwelling unit portal to the dining room is a critical measurement. This route often establishes the limit of independence for residents with ambulation difficulties. When this happens, they are more likely to be moved in a wheelchair and will become even less ambulatory. Residents often prefer units on the first floor or close to the elevator. They value access to shared common spaces.

Design and Management Solutions

▲ *Decentralized Clusters:* Many long-term care facilities that have experienced a problem with access to

Long corridors need variety to break them up:
Variety is created here through the use of furniture, artwork, skylights, and plant materials located throughout these relatively narrow corridors. (Photo: Jerry Staley Photography)

the dining room have adopted a decentralized approach. This involves delivering food to several different dining rooms throughout the building. In northern Europe, a typical design often relies on two back-to-back unit clusters on each floor.

▲ *Food Quality May Suffer with Decentralized Unit Clusters:* Units clustered around a small kitchen/dining room can suffer from a lack of control. Food quality is reduced when reheating, and the ability to improvise is limited.

▲ *Relocate or Move Residents:* Buildings with long corridors often have to move residents with ambulatory problems by wheelchair or relocate them to a dwelling unit that is closer to the dining room.

▲ *Avoid a Passive Lifestyle:* When a decentralized cluster approach is taken, it is important to look for ways that residents can continue to walk for exercise. Avoiding a passive lifestyle by keeping residents walking is one of the most important ways to maintain a high degree of physical competence.

▲ *Personal Conveyance Vehicles:* These large, bulky vehicles are increasingly being used in large buildings to get from one place to another. This is often not a good idea. They take up a lot of space, they can be dangerous to others, and they discourage residents from walking for exercise.

▲ *Place to Rest:* A bench or chair should always be available every 50 feet so that residents who need to rest and recharge can do so. Corridor lengths between the elevator door and the farthest dwelling unit door should be no more than 150 feet.

▲ *Extra Staff Time Required to Move People:* When residents need help to get from their dwelling units to the dining room, extra staff time is needed to move them. At the beginning of a meal is usually the time when the staff is busiest. Adding more staff may be necessary as residents become less ambulatory.

▲ *Centralize Elevators:* Centralizing the elevator and the dining room simplifies access and minimizes travel distances.

▲ *Reduced Travel Distance Is Valued by Residents:* In a multistory building, the units on the first floor and the units closest to the elevators are normally the most popular and the first to be rented. A good plan should optimize the number and placement of units on the first floor.

▲ *Double-Loaded Corridors:* Reducing the corridor length usually means more dependence on double-loaded corridors. Mixing the use of single- and double-loaded corridors can be accomplished in most buildings. This allows sections of the corridor to be daylighted.

FIFTEEN

Provide a Realm Between the Inside and Outside

Social spaces sandwiched between the inside and outside of a building hold special fascination and are often heavily used.

Rationale

In-between spaces include arcades, open porches, enclosed porches, screened porches, bay windows, solariums, winter gardens, window seats, and trellis structures. These "sandwich" spaces typically occur on both sides of the building's edge. They can occur in either a conditioned space, an outdoor space, or a partially conditioned space. When these spaces are adjacent to active entry and exit doors, they are more heavily used. They can be great spaces for social in-

Balcony window wall opens for fresh air: This French balcony at the *Vidar Clinic* in Jarna, Sweden, when opened, connects this space to the surrounding landscape. Note the anthroposophic mullion design and the low sill.

teraction or "away spaces" where individuals can be by themselves.

Design and Management Solutions

▲ *Continuum of Indoor/Outdoor Experiences:* Edge spaces can be linked together, providing a continuum of indoor/outdoor settings.

▲ *Continuity of the Ground Plane:* Indoor winter garden spaces that connect with adjacent landscaped areas are more effective when they have low sills. This provides greater continuity between the inside floor and the outside ground plane.

▲ *Large Viewing Windows:* Unimpeded views of the outside are very effective in a dining room. Residents regularly use this room three times a day. They appreciate views of the landscape, as well as views to porches and patios with comfortable furniture and shade control.

▲ *Landscape Views Are Compelling:* The view of nature is something most human beings have an intrinsic interest in experiencing. Inspect the views from each unit to see if it captures a near or far landscape view.

▲ *Erker or Bay Window:* In northern Europe and especially in the Netherlands, the erker (a three-sided bay window) is frequently used to connect the inside with the outside. It also is an attractive feature that adds to the architectural interest of the building.

▲ *Front Porches:* These are very popular in the United States but are less heavily used in northern Europe. They are friendly-looking appendages that have been made even more popular by the new urbanism movement.

▲ *Enclosed and French Balconies:* Enclosed dwelling unit balconies (the French serre) or French balconies are effective ways of introducing views from protected spaces that can be opened during good weather.

▲ *Single-loaded Corridors That Serve as Balconies:* In northern Europe, there is much less concern about exiting conflicts that occur when furniture is placed in a widened single-loaded corridor. These are good places to take in a view or to interact with people walking along the corridor.

▲ *Arcades and Porches:* There is something compelling about sitting next to the outside edge of a building. If the space has good shade control, an interesting view, a wind break, and convenient access to the building, it is almost always used.

▲ *Edge Spaces Seem Very Secure:* These spaces often appear secure and protected. When they are located close to the street or the main building entry, social contact often arises between residents and visitors.

▲ *Single-Loaded Corridor Dwelling Unit Access:* A single-loaded corridor (open or closed) provides the possibility of views, light, and access to the outdoors. When windows into the corridor are used, borrowed light can make the entry experience more friendly and enjoyable.

SIXTEEN

Facilitate Staff Behaviors That Benefit Residents

The building's design and configuration should facilitate the provision of care.

Rationale

Staff labor costs account for most of the daily expense of long-term care. If the building's design is not co-ordinated with the deployment of staff, inefficiencies can result. Office spaces, break rooms, unit cluster sizes, and the philosophy of care management need to be reflected in the architectural design. A staff office design can encourage employees to stay in their offices or thrust them into public spaces and corridors, where they are more likely to make contact with residents and family members. In addition, dwelling unit cluster sizes should be related to the staff/resident ratio.

Design and Management Solutions

▲ *Private but Approachable Offices:* Office spaces with half-walls, windows, and Dutch doors can be seen from public corridors but have the potential to be zoned so that staff can have a private space to get their work done.

▲ *Dutch Doors and Half-Walls Encourage Previewing:* These features facilitate conversations with family and residents. They also encourage previewing, the process of seeing into a space before making a commitment to enter. It is important to make the offices of staff members easily approachable to family members.

▲ *Small Offices Discourage Cocooning:* One useful management philosophy that mirrors the approach of former General Electric President Jack Welch is the idea of "management by walking around" (Slater, 1999). Administrators and managers should be walking around, seeing staff and residents, rather than spending most of their time in the office. Small offices located adjacent to major circulation pathways foster this approach.

▲ *Designated Caregivers:* Caregiving staff should be assigned to a specific cluster of units and specific residents. When the cluster size matches the staffing ratio, a more efficient plan results. When caregivers are assigned, they get to know the preferences and problems of residents on a more personal basis.

Dutch door is used to make nurse's office more approachable: This dementia office uses a fixed-pane glass window and a Dutch door to facilitate interaction between staff, residents, and family members at the *Sunrise at Severna Park*, Maryland.

▲ *Single Seating Facilitates Universal Worker Approach:* A single seating for dining promotes the universal worker approach to management. This makes it easier for all caregiving staff to move to the dining room during mealtimes.

▲ *Activity Director in the Activity Room:* Some work-stations, like that of the activity director, are best located in the activity space rather than in a separate office.

▲ *Comfortable Staff Room:* Providing a comfortable staff room with a refrigerator, table, microwave oven, vending machine, toilet, and lockers is important for staff, who work very hard and need a place to relax and recharge.

▲ *Staff Training Should Encourage Improvisation:* Staff training should encourage brainstorming about how best to use the building and its common spaces for activities and events. Improvisation is required in most buildings because a building is never perfectly designed for every activity. However, having adequate decentralized storage areas and convenient common spaces with hard and soft surface flooring can increase program flexibility.

▲ *College and High School Interns/Volunteers:* Involving young people in the program is a great way to bring the optimism and enthusiasm of youth into the building. Interns in the areas of gerontology, social work, art therapy, physical therapy, and exercise are all possible candidates.

▲ *Create a Culture That Values Volunteers:* Individuals who help others and do so without the benefit of compensation are special people who should be cultivated, encouraged, and rewarded. Some of the best volunteers come from the families of residents. A formal program can provide a vehicle to channel and encourage volunteerism.

SEVENTEEN

Focus on Sensuous Activity and Beauty

Focusing on the aspects that give pleasure to life is gaining support from residents and their families.

Rationale

One of the most dehumanizing aspects of institutionalization is the lack of focus on pleasure. Health care environments often focus on health, excluding the simple pleasures of daily life. Pleasures like good food, a sensuous bathing experience, human sexual contact, access to a beautiful garden, and a focus on personal appearance and beauty are often overlooked or discounted in importance. These are issues that in the past were considered somewhat hedonistic and outside of the realm of good medical care. However, they have always been important to people and are becoming increasingly important.

Design and Management Solutions

▲ *A Pleasant Bath:* A bather with a whirlpool feature can relax a resident. This should be completely different from the bathing process that often occurs in a cold, impersonal shower/bathing room in a nursing home.

▲ *Auxiliary Heat Needed in the Bathing Room:* One of the biggest problems with nursing home bathing spaces is that they are large and covered with cold materials like ceramic tile. They often lack equipment such as radiant heaters or heat lamps to quickly warm the room.

▲ *Food Quality:* The quality, texture, and taste of food are very important to older people. Many have so few other sensuous outlets that food takes on even more meaning. Food also triggers memories and associations.

▲ *Looking Good and Feeling Good:* The focus on beauty and attractiveness will become even more important as baby boomers move into older age co-

Warm-water spa is part of the therapeutic approach: At the *Vigs Ängar* in Köpingbro, Sweden, residents can receive a message after exercising in this spa.

horts. This includes hair dressing, makeup, clothing, perfume, manicures, and pedicures.

▲ *Massage Therapy:* This service is becoming more popular. It is quite common in northern Europe—the home of the Swedish massage. Stretching muscles and connective tissue can be a form of therapeutic massage.

▲ *Snoezelen Therapy:* The use of snoezelen techniques with dementia residents in the Netherlands focuses on various forms of nonverbal sensory communication.

▲ *Aromatherapy:* This form of therapy is effective with some residents because it evokes past associations and because smell is one of the last senses diminished by old age.

▲ *Soft Materials:* Soft fabrics, fur sheepskin, chenille, and stuffed animals feel good to the touch and are often not used because of the fear of incontinence. However, many of these fabrics, if used properly, can be "loose" items that are easily cleaned or replaced.

▲ *A Comfortable Bed:* Because residents spend a lot of time in bed and often suffer from sleep disorders, it is important that the mattress, the linens, the pillows and the light near the bed be designed to provide comfort.

▲ *Music Therapy:* Music is very soothing for some residents because of its association with the past. Because it can be understood by even late-stage dementia residents, it is very enjoyable for many older people.

▲ *Humor and Affect:* Nursing homes are notoriously stiff and sober environments. Making a place or a situation funny or using animals, children, plants, and pets to stimulate positive emotions adds variety and life to the setting.

EIGHTEEN

Provide Passive and Active Entertainment

Social interaction often needs a catalyst. Activities provide a medium for social interaction.

Rationale

Older people with time on their hands can easily become bored and depressed. A variety of activities should be available. Activities should also be targeted to small groups of residents. Watching movies and listening to music are simple, passive pursuits that appeal to most people. Active pursuits like gardening and tai chi exercises often appeal to smaller numbers of people. Other activities like card playing, word games, and memory games stimulate mental activity.

Design and Management Solutions

▲ *Entertainment Room:* With more than 100 cable television channels, residents can watch a variety of programs. Large-screen televisions outfitted with surround-sound speakers can have electronic links to video, DVD, and CD players.

▲ *Encourage Small-Group Activities:* Focusing on the interests of smaller groups through a system of informal clubs is an excellent way to broaden the appeal of an activities program. Bingo may be popular with large groups, but it has limitations. Sometimes accommodating the interests of just one person is important.

▲ *Listening to Music:* Music appeals to many residents. Both prerecorded and live performances are popular. A room dedicated to entertainment can include space for a piano, a juke box, and a large-screen television. The same room can be used for

The "South Seas Corner" is a wacky bit of improvisation: A corridor alcove at the *Hogeway* dementia facility in Weesp, the Netherlands, has a painted beach scene and rattan furniture. A motion detector triggers bird and surf sounds when anyone approaches it.

lectures, church services, staff training, and small-group discussions.

▲ *Computer Applications:* Each year the use of computers for basic entertainment and communication grows. Depending on the resident's average age and past experience level, computers can be employed for games, e-mail, music retrieval, and a range of other applications. Many facilities support e-mail exchanges between residents and family members. In northern Europe, computers are used for sharing traditional folk music.

▲ *People Watching:* Watching the daily activities of other people is an attractive and curiosity-provoking pastime for many residents. This includes watching deliveries, staff members, other residents, and family and friends.

▲ *Summer Holidays and Vacations:* In northern Europe, residents often take vacations away from their service house or nursing home. These can last for a few days or for several weeks. In Denmark, resort communities have been established to care for frail residents. Because of their need for help, residents travel with caregivers from their building.

▲ *Family Events:* These are most popular during the summer holidays of Memorial Day, July 4th, and Labor Day. when they can be staged outside. However, they are also popular at important family holidays like Thanksgiving, Christmas/Hanukah, and Easter/Passover.

▲ *Daily Activities:* Many facilities plan three to five activities each day for residents. These are used to structure the day while giving residents adequate opportunity for social interaction.

▲ *Trips:* Getting away from the building is often a welcome change. Shopping, sightseeing, and day trips are stimulating and interesting for most residents.

NINETEEN

Ensure Safety and Security

The building should be safe from hazards like fire, smoke, and natural disasters, with an up-to-date emergency call system.

Rationale

Safety is an important concern that many older people and family members voice when considering a move to a group living situation. They are often concerned about safety from fire and smoke, the type and quality of emergency care available, the presence of crime (internally or externally motivated), and the protection provided for residents with dementia. Building and licensing regulations have done a good job of ensuring safety. Residents of licensed buildings can rest assured that appropriate safety standards have been met or exceeded.

Design and Management Solutions

▲ *Emergency Call System:* An emergency call system with a voice response is reassuring to the staff and the older resident. The call can be activated by an emergency call button or a pendant the resident wears. In a system that is hard-wired, call devices should be in the bathroom and next to the bed. This is one of the most basic forms of security a resident can have. A two-way communications system allows the staff to quickly discover the nature of the problem.

▲ *Fire Sprinklers and Smoke Detectors:* The entire building should be sprinkled and alarmed for staff and the local fire department to respond. Fire sprinkling and smoke detection are the most effective ways of protecting residents from a fire hazard.

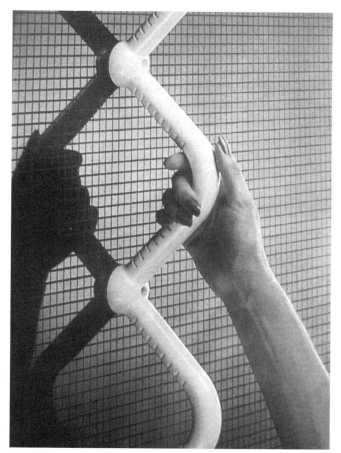

Grab bars can look attractive: Designer grab bars like this one do not have the stigma of disability, which a more conventional stainless steel design is likely to convey.

▲ *Fire-Rated Corridors:* Most buildings require corridors that are fire and/or smoke protected. Openness in the plan between corridors and rooms can be created by fire doors on hold-openers, shutters, flexible fire partitions (won doors), fire sprinkler mitigations, and rated windows and doors.

▲ *Emergency Generators:* These can be important additions in places where power is not predictable and where there is a relatively high probability of a natural disaster that would disrupt power delivery. Emergency generators are particularly important in multistory buildings and should also power the elevator and basic kitchen equipment, as well as provide heat and basic safety lighting.

▲ *Avoid Evacuating the Building:* The best safety systems allow the fire department to fight a fire in place by moving residents to a safe haven on each floor. This is important for older frail people, who should not be required to leave the building during a fire emergency or a fire drill.

▲ *System Reliability and Quality:* Today's fire systems are safer, more reliable, and less expensive than those of the past. There is no excuse for not having a first-rate fire and smoke prevention system.

▲ *Dementia Security Systems:* Exit control can be achieved through the use of magnetic locks or delayed egress doors. New systems are being de-

vised that have the capability of tracking individual residents.

▲ *Safety That Stifles:* It is important to give residents independence. When too many rules are employed to control every situation, residents are treated paternalistically. This can lead to learned helplessness and a passive resident population.

▲ *Security from Crime:* In some environments, safety from intrusion is an issue. However, most projects that experience theft experience it from the inside. The building should be designed so that residents and staff can easily monitor who is entering and exiting.

▲ *CPR Training:* The staff should be trained to deal with emergency situations by stabilizing the resident and immediately calling 911.

▲ *Bathroom Injury:* The bathroom is the most dangerous room in the house. Residents are often in there alone, making transfers, taking a shower, or getting on and off the commode. It is important that residents be able to call for emergency help if they need it from this location.

TWENTY

Encourage Choice, Control, Autonomy, and Independence

The design of the building and the policies associated with resident care should always be oriented toward supporting residents' autonomy.

Rationale

Residents should feel that they have choice and control over their environment. The building should allow residents to maintain continuity with choices that facilitate their pursuit of habits and interests they may have developed over a lifetime. The amount of care assistance and the way it is provided should fit the needs and lifestyle of each resident. A good facility is one that celebrates the diversity of its population rather than adopting a one-size-fits-all attitude.

Transition space links the dining room with the corridor: This works quite nicely as a previewing space for dementia residents who want to see into the room before they enter it.

Design and Management Solutions

▲ *Northern European Op Maat Philosophy:* The care regimen and the way it is delivered should fit the habits and experiences of residents. If they want to sleep late, stay up late, take a bubble bath on Saturday night, take their meal in front of the TV, or have wine with dinner, it should be possible to do this. In some settings, the concern with staff efficiency overshadow the needs of the residents.

▲ *Smoking Room:* A smoking room allows the handful of residents who have smoked all their lives to continue doing so safely.

▲ *Flexibility in Occupancy:* The option of having a single-occupancy or a double-occupancy unit should be available, especially for couples and relatives (sisters). Double-occupancy units should be designed to allow each person as much control as possible over HVAC, bathroom access, natural light, and ambient lighting.

▲ *Dignity and Respect:* Older residents should be treated with dignity and respect rather than infantilized with demeaning pet names. Affection is wonderful, but it should be delivered with dignity rather than treating an older person like a child.

▲ *Encourage Independence:* The care philosophy should encourage residents to do as much as they can for themselves. Like the northern Europeans do, U.S. staff should provide care with "their hands in their pockets."

▲ *Preview Shared Spaces:* Allowing residents to preview common spaces before making a commitment to enter gives them more control over their interactions with other residents and staff. French doors with glass panels or side windows can facilitate this.

▲ *Unit Furniture:* Residents should be encouraged to bring in their own furniture, and to decorate and personalize their dwelling units with objects and possessions that have meaning to them.

▲ *Adaptable Environments:* Residents should retain the ability to make modifications to their unit, especially the bathroom and bedroom, as they age to make it more accessible, safe, and supportive.

▲ *Roles for Residents:* There should be volunteer jobs and leadership roles for residents who want to serve others.

▲ *Few Restrictions:* Basic freedoms like a pet policy, no restrictions on visiting hours, and the ability to host an overnight guest should be possible.

32

30 FUTURE TRENDS

M‍aking predictions about the future is always risky. Directions that appear to make sense often dead-end, while new discoveries provide previously uncharted directions for innovation. However, students and professionals always want to know what the future has in store. These trends and predictions are offered in the spirit of good intentions that, I hope, will spark discussion and debate about their probability of execution. Monitoring their evolution over time will provide a sense of how history has developed. Ten years ago, it seemed premature to identify trends in the assisted living industry. Those presented in this chapter may turn out to be of questionable utility ten years from now, but they currently appear to be plausible. If I have the opportunity to write an update of this work in 2010, these suggestions may help us to better understand what has worked and what has not.

These thirty topics are divided into three groups. The first group consists of 10 general trends, which focus on the development of assisted living. They are based on articles in trade magazines, general issues discussed at conferences, and my discussions with clients, researchers, and policy makers. These trends are generally associated with the growth of assisted living and the factors affecting its future conceptual development. The second group of ten trends concerns building form, development, and design. They are gleaned from years of experience, observations of the field, and knowledge of research that reflects the current strengths and weaknesses of the existing building stock. The third group of ten trends are insights from my experiences in northern Europe. Some of these are ideas that seem ripe for U.S. implementation, while others are system features that would improve our caregiving approach to the elderly population.

FORMAT: A "BECAUSE OF" RATIONALE

Three to four rationale statements follow each prediction/trend. These statements provide additional evidence about why these trends appear to be solid. Some of these trends are clearly present today; others may seem a bit farfetched. Keep in mind that they have been assembled in an effort to articulate hypotheses based on today's experience. Furthermore, they provide another way for the conclusions of this work to be articulated. No one has a crystal ball, and only time will reveal how influential these trends will be in the future. They do, however, at this moment, reflect the general assumptions of many other industry watchers.

1. A more chronically ill and health dependent population will be attracted to assisted living.
2. There will be more regulatory concern about caring for highly impaired residents
3. More states will consider Medicaid waivers and other forms of subsidy
4. Greater attention will be paid to the training and recruitment of workers
5. There will be consolidation in private sector ownership
6. More diversification will occur into independent and congregate housing
7. More effective medications for Alzheimer's disease and other medical problems will change the type of resident who chooses assisted living.
8. Consumer demand for a good, well-managed environment at a fair price will continue to characterize the marketplace.
9. Customer service will evolve and continue to be informed by feedback from older people and family members.
10. The assisted living model will be exported from the United States to other countries.
11. Purpose-built buildings will continue to be the preferred choice of providers.
12. Buildings will be increasingly related to a philosophy of caregiving.
13. Building features and spaces also will continue to cater to volunteers and family members
14. The location and visibility of the building will continue to be important attributes of success.
15. Future projects will be more diverse and will appeal to the specific interests of residents.
16. There will be more dependence on robotic devices for aid and support.
17. Increasing computer-based technology will make it easier to monitor and communicate with residents and diagnose their problems.
18. Buildings will continue to be safer.
19. The emphasis on a residential, friendly context will continue to be important.
20. The cultivation of and focus on beauty and sensuality will grow in importance.
21. There will be more emphasis on rehabilitation, physical therapy, and exercise.
22. There will be more emphasis on short-stay populations, like those requiring respite, hospice, and rehabilitation services.
23. More preassisted living services will be provided by assisted living buildings to older people in the neighborhood.
24. Future dwelling units will be bigger, with larger, more elaborate bathrooms.
25. Individuals with higher service needs will be accommodated in a residential-style building.
26. More single-occupancy housing in nursing homes will resemble assisted living units.
27. Day care for the elderly will become more common.
28. Wellness programs will develop that focus on medications, vitamins, healthy foods, exercise, and healthy behaviors.
29. Lift devices will make it easier to move residents from the bed to the bathroom.
30. Decentralization of units into small-group clusters will continue.

GENERAL FUTURE TRENDS IN ASSISTED LIVING IN THE UNITED STATES

These 10 trends are based on the author's observations of changes we are beginning to see today and forecasts that others in the industry have made.

A More Chronically Ill and Health Dependent Population Will Be Attracted to Assisted Living. This is likely because:

▲ Facilities will continue to encourage residents to age in place providing more services to support their needs.
▲ Advances in home care technology will allow residents to stay at home longer and thus will delay their move to assisted living until they are more frail.
▲ New medications for memory loss will allow residents to stay home longer and delay entrance into assisted living.
▲ Relocation from assisted living to a nursing home will continue to be seen as disruptive and potentially harmful.
▲ Selected states will develop policies that allow residents to stay in assisted living longer.

Stuffed animals for dementia residents: The *Silviahemet* dementia day-care center in Drottningholm, Sweden, has experimented with stuffed animals that contain a water bottle. The extra weight and heat make them feel more realistic.

There Will Be More Regulatory Concern About Caring for Highly Impaired Residents. This is likely because:

▲ To date, the vast majority of assisted living residents have paid privately. If assisted living becomes more broadly supported by public expenditures, then oversight protection will be considered necessary.

▲ As assisted living residents continue to resemble nursing home residents, concerns will center on the adequacy of regulatory oversight for this frail population.

▲ It will take only a few well-publicized examples of bad practice to motivate the political process to respond. One of the few ways politicians know how to respond is through stiffer regulations.

▲ New regulations will likely take the family's perspective into consideration, given the failure of nursing homes to provide a family-friendly environment.

More States Will Consider Medicaid Waivers and Other Forms of Subsidy. This is likely because:

▲ As much as 35–60 percent of the elderly population is unable to afford private-pay assisted living.

▲ As assisted living becomes the long-term care alternative of choice, states will seek to fund it in order to discourage the development of a two-tier system.

▲ As long-term care insurance becomes more popular, assisted living will be added to all policies.

▲ The popularity of a less expensive but more acceptable alternative to skilled nursing care will motivate states to support assisted living.

Greater Attention Will Be Paid to the Training and Recruitment of Workers. This is likely because:

▲ More specialized and sophisticated training will be necessary, and staff turnover will become increasingly costly.

▲ Work in these settings is difficult, the pay rate is modest and workers are increasingly more difficult to find.

▲ Therapeutic strategies, new drug regimens and higher consumer expectations will require a more sophisticated knowledge base and better trained personnel.

▲ Turnover is a problem which higher salary levels and a more professional orientation may help to thwart.

There Will Be Consolidation in Private Sector Ownership. This is likely because:

▲ As in most industries, there will be consolidation resulting from stronger companies achieving greater market share.

▲ Start-up companies that constructed buildings in poor locations and expanded too quickly in the mid-1990s will continue to experience problems with occupancy and financing.

▲ However, the vast majority of properties are not owned by proprietary chain operations.

More Diversification Will Occur in Independent and Congregate Housing. This is likely because:

▲ Many companies that manage assisted living buildings can also manage housing with fewer services.

▲ A well-earned reputation in a community can be extended to other building types and other service products.

▲ Independent buildings can be located and positioned to refer residents to assisted living.

▲ Demand for other types of housing that combine independent housing with services will increase.

Skylights with hanging plant materials: This treatment used at the *Sunrise of Mission Viejo* (page 181) creates a miniature greenhouse-like space out of this cluster living room on the upper floor.

More Effective Medications for Alzheimer's Disease and Other Medical Problems Will Change the Type of Resident Who Chooses Assisted Living. This is likely because:

▲ New medications will be designed to keep older people at home for a longer period of time.

▲ Dementia care will continue to be in high demand because home care service programs will probably not be as effective in supporting individuals with this condition.

▲ Medications will likely extend life and thus extend the period of chronic dependence as well.

Consumer Demand for a Good, Well-managed Environment at a Fair Price Will Continue to Characterize the Marketplace. This is likely because:

▲ Assisted living has brought a stronger consumer-oriented marketplace perspective to the long-term care field.

▲ The public is more educated and aware of the differences in long-term care choices, and it will continue to be sophisticated.

▲ Consumers will become more aware of the differences in assisted living alternatives and will seek settings that best meet their needs.

▲ More choices will be available to residents, including those who want to stay in the community.

Customer Service Will Evolve and Continue to Be Informed by Feedback from Older People and Family Members. This is likely *because*:

▲ The success of assisted living has evolved out of a customer-driven paradigm that requires customer feedback to function properly.

▲ Consumers' preferences will continue to stimulate the development of new services and environmental innovations.

▲ The success of new ideas is totally dependent on how well they are received.

The Assisted Living Model Will Be Exported from the United States to Other Countries. This is likely because:

▲ Very few countries (with the exception of those in northern Europe) have the unique reputation and the experience of the United States with this building and service type.

▲ U.S. industries are aggressive players in the global marketplace, with strong financing and sound training.

▲ Increasing affluence, an increasing population of the older old, and a decreasing number of families who care for older parents and/or grandparents will make assisted living compelling throughout the world.

BUILDING TRENDS FROM THE UNITED STATES

These 10 trends are based on the author's observations of building trends and innovations that have occurred in the last decade.

Purpose-built Buildings Will Continue to Be the Preferred Choice of Providers. This is likely because:

▲ Purpose-built buildings are generally worth more than buildings that have been remodeled.

▲ Purpose-built buildings are often placed in better locations and are designed to work more efficiently and effectively.

▲ The future will likely require that building performance and efficiency be increased. These buildings are clearly better designed for caregiving and service provision.

Staff photos make designated caregivers easier to identify: This attractive board near the entry to the *Petäjävesi* service house in Petäjävesi, Finland, connects faces with names for family members, residents, and staff.

▲ Innovative approaches will continue to be tested in new buildings, which will be more sophisticated than older buildings.

Buildings Will Be Increasingly Related to a Philosophy of Caregiving. This is likely because:

▲ Staff efficiency is contingent on factors like the use of designated caregivers, the acuity level of residents, and the size of unit clusters.

▲ The more we understand about problems like sundowning and wandering, the more effectively we will be able to respond by providng environments designed to support the older person.

▲ Universal worker staffing, for example, generally require decentralization, while a two-seating dining room normally implies a different approach to staff organization.

Building Features and Spaces Also Will Continue to Cater to Volunteers and Family Members. This is likely because:

▲ Much of the success of assisted living is based on its appeal to family members.

▲ The best buildings are those that attract volunteer help from the community. Allowing greater participation of family members often leads to more program enhancements.

▲ Older residents are happier and more satisfied when they see family members and friends on a regular basis. A building designed to support them will motivate them to visit more frequently.

The Location and Visibility of the Building Will Continue to Be Important Attributes of Success. This is likely because:

▲ Successful projects are well located in strong markets they can readily serve.

▲ The visibility of a project is an important attribute that often accounts for its success.

▲ Successful buildings in visible, high-status locations have a higher financial value.

Future Projects Will Be More Diverse and Will Appeal to the Specific Interests of Residents. This is likely because:

▲ Assisted living buildings are much more diverse than skilled nursing homes. As with other forms of housing, their appeal is based on their appearance, location, and size.

▲ Projects with different-sized units, which contain different service mixtures and operate with different policies regarding residents' abilities, will be available from which to choose.

▲ Future buildings will evolve that are targeted toward narrower resident and family preferences.

▲ The perfect assisted living building will never be designed, because there is no one single answer. The future will bring a range of different possibilities.

There Will Be More Dependence on Robotic Devices for Aid and Support. This is likely because:

▲ Expensive and less available human staff will be replaced by electromechanical devices that provide help and assistance.

▲ Health and safety concerns are likely to increase in the future. Thus, lifting devices of various sorts will be used more frequently to reduce staff back injuries.

▲ Lift and wheelchair technology is likely to be combined with computer-aided mobility devices. It is hoped that these devices will also be designed to help the person exercise as well as transfer.

▲ Tomorrow's older residents will likely be heavier and more dependent; thus, devices will be necessary to keep them ambulatory.

Increasing Computer-based Technology Will Make It Easier to Monitor and Communicate with Residents and Diagnose Their Problems. This is likely because:

▲ Systems for monitoring security and vital signs and for diagnosing problems will save the expense of additional labor. Fewer people who are more technically trained will result from this shift.

▲ Monitoring systems will allow dementia residents more freedom and the possibility for residents to stay at home longer.

▲ With the merging of computer, telephone, and television technology, older people will be able to manipulate more sophisticated computer devices.

▲ Older residents and/or their families will be able to order care when needed and thus be more independent.

Buildings Will Continue to Be Safer. This is likely because:

▲ Fire and smoke detection and response systems will do more, will be easier to manipulate, and will be more affordable.

▲ Smoke detectors, fire sprinklers, emergency power generators, building security, and emergency call systems increase in sophistication every year.

▲ Safety will continue to be a national priority, as reflected in regulations and standards.

The Emphasis on a Residential, Friendly Context Will Continue to Be Important. This is likely because:

▲ Assisted living will continue to offer a residential environment that is attractive to residents and families, while nursing homes and subacute facilities will continue to be driven by institutional standards.

▲ Housing is related to feelings of comfort and familiarity. Residents in the future will continue to be attracted by these characteristics.

▲ A design that stimulates social interaction between staff, other residents, and friends makes the building more socially satisfying.

The Cultivation of and Focus on Beauty and Sensuality Will Grow in Importance. This is likely because:

▲ The next cohort of residents will be very concerned about their appearance. Residents feel better about themselves when they know they look good.

▲ It is not uncommon to see facility beauty shops outfitted with equipment for hair dressing, hair coloring, and manicures. In the future, pedicures, facial treatments, massage therapy, spa baths, and other forms of beauty treatment are likely to be popular.

▲ This trend is also likely to be reflected in the increased amount of space needed for clothing storage in the unit.

TRENDS FROM NORTHERN EUROPE

Following are 10 current qualities or best practices in northern Europe that I believe will eventually become typical of assisted living projects in the United States.

There Will Be More Emphasis on Rehabilitation, Physical Therapy, and Exercise. This is likely because:

▲ Exercises, including movement exercises, weight-bearing exercises, and walking clubs, have been shown to be beneficial to older people.

Training kitchen and table: This kitchen alcove is used by occupational therapists at *Gyngemosegård* (page 174) to work with stroke victims and other rehabilitation patients. The kitchen is outfitted with devices that help residents to gain back lost abilities.

▲ Rehabilitation and physical therapy allow residents to come for short stays based on an acute need. Examples include individuals who are recovering from a difficult surgery or who are undergoing treatment for a stroke.

▲ Connecting exercise, physical therapy, and rehabilitation creates a very beneficial synergy that counters the detrimental effects of a passive lifestyle.

▲ It is relatively easy to open a building to the neighborhood for these types of services.

There Will Be More Emphasis on Short-stay Populations, Like Those Requiring Respite, Hospice, and Rehabilitation Services. This is likely because:

▲ These services allow an assisted living building to help older people in the community to remain independent. Thus, the setting has a broader role to play and is often chosen when (or if) an assisted living placement is required.

▲ This attitude creates a better partnership between the facility, family members, and the older person.

▲ In northern Europe, one-quarter to one-third of the typical resident population is made up of short-stay residents.

More Preassisted Living Services Will Be Provided by Assisted Living Buildings to Older People in the Neighborhood. This is likely because:

▲ This reduces the institutional stigma of the building in the community by allowing it to play a role in helping everyone in the community.

▲ Opening the building for physical therapy, day care, and a noon meal for people in the community is a relatively easy adjustment and is common in northern Europe.

▲ Home care and home modification services organized by a community-based assisted living setting for people living in the community creates a bridge to the community.

Future Dwelling Units Will Be Bigger, With Larger, More Elaborate Bathrooms. This is likely because:

▲ Northern European dwelling units for the younger elderly have grown approximately 100 SF over the last ten years, anticipating what boomers will require.

▲ One of the most successful innovative programs has been "apartments for life." This program is characterized by large dwelling units (average, 650–750 SF) with high-level service capabilities.

▲ An emphasis on design for accessibility occurs in these settings. Sliding doors, roll-in shower enclosures, and toilets positioned for ease of transfer (assisted and independent) are carefully considered.

Individuals with Higher Service Needs Will Be Accommodated in a Residential-style Building. This is likely because:

▲ The northern European nursing home unit is almost identical to today's U.S. assisted living dwelling. Nursing home units are single occupied, average about 275 SF, and often have a small kitchen with a range.

▲ It appears to be relatively easy to ramp up services from assisted living to skilled nursing by changing the numbers and training levels of the staff.

▲ In the future, residents and family members will insist that a more pleasant residential environment be the basis for skilled care. Ventilator-dependent, tube-fed, and extremely sick patients will likely reside in a subacute hospital environment.

Kitchen alcove is used as a nurse's station: In *Ros Anders Gård* (page 215), this work space in the corner of the kitchen functions as a nurse's station, with residents' care books, medications, a phone, and a place to sit down and write notes.

More Single-occupancy Housing in Nursing Homes Will Resemble Assisted Living Units.   This is likely because:

▲ Currently, single-occupancy skilled nursing home rooms are rare in the United States, while 80–90 percent of assisted living rooms are designed as single-occupancy units.

▲ Nearly all of the skilled nursing homes built in the last ten years in northern Europe have single-occupied units.

▲ The success of single occupancy in assisted living is good evidence that single-occupied nursing units are feasible.

▲ Single-occupied units foster more privacy, so that family interaction is easier to sustain.

▲ Nursing homes will either be transformed into single-occupancy units or assisted living buildings will begin to take sicker, more medically dependent residents.

Day Care for the Elderly Will Become More Common. This is likely because:

▲ Most buildings with dementia residents have the expertise and the programs in place to serve day-care recipients.

▲ This allows the move to assisted living to be delayed because residents can stay at home longer with family members or a spouse.

▲ However, to be highly successful in the United States, day-care programs will need to have more external financial support through some form of subsidy.

Wellness Programs Will Develop That Focus on Medications, Vitamins, Healthy Foods, Exercise, and Healthy Behaviors.   This is likely because:

▲ As our understanding of what promotes longevity, wellness, and healthy aging evolves, more providers will adapt these programs and lifestyles.

▲ Northern European settings are oriented more to an active lifestyle, with emphasis on physical movement, rehabilitation, and physical therapy.

▲ The anthroposophic architecture movement in northern Europe focuses on creating an environment that supports a more humanistic approach to life.

Lift Devices Will Make It Easier to Move Residents from the Bed to the Bathroom.   This is likely because:

▲ Northern European regulations for occupational health and safety require that aides use lifts for residents who are heavy and need assistance in transferring.

▲ These regulations are likely to be implemented in the United States in the next three to five years.

▲ In northern Europe, most of these applications involve ceiling-mounted rails that connect the bed with the bathroom. The lift can be used to move the resident across the room or transfer them from the bed to a wheelchair.

▲ Life devices in the United States are likely to evolve from robotics and current hydraulic lift technologies rather than ceiling-mounted systems.

Decentralization of Units into Small-group Clusters Will Continue.   This is likely because:

▲ Universal worker and designated caregiver strategies work best at a smaller scale when the environment and the care assignments are coordinated.

▲ Small groups are intimate and familylike. They are also calmer, and create less noise and distraction.

▲ Small groups can be made more flexible by allowing residents to attend clubs with residents from other clusters who share the same interests.

▲ Small groups, however, by themselves are boring. Residents need other common spaces in the building to visit and be with others.

33

CONCLUDING ISSUES

These last six concluding issues summarize some of the major themes presented in this book. It is always difficult to reduce the focus of a broad-based work to a few items, but these appear to reflect both important trends and themes that have emerged from this work. None of these issues should come as a surprise to anyone who has read this book in its entirety. In fact, they emerge in the chapters that describe demographic trends, in the analysis of northern European models, and in the characteristics of the innovative buildings described in Part III.

▲ Family participation is central to the success of assisted living.
▲ Residents move to assisted living based on the environment.
▲ Skilled nursing facilities will be replaced by assisted living.
▲ People with dementia will be viewed as a de-medicalized population
▲ Assisted living facilities will have a community-based orientation.

▲ Residents will be encouraged to pursue an active lifestyle through exercise and physical therapy.

FAMILY PARTICIPATION IS CENTRAL TO THE SUCCESS OF ASSISTED LIVING

In contrast to traditional skilled nursing care, assisted living has sought to be much more family friendly. The needs and preferences of families are met, and as a result, families often feel more welcome. For this reason, they often visit and participate more fully in the life of the place. The building's design is attractive and inviting to families, and the staff values the participation of family members. When handled well, the move to assisted living improves family relationships because concerns about safety are relieved. Programs that encourage volunteerism and family participation should be promoted, just as partnerships like parent-teacher associations in grammar schools have helped to create greater family participation. A similar care partnership between staff and family members could also open new avenues for family participation. One helpful side effect is the opportunity it would provide family members to meet others who are going through the stress of dealing with a chronically ill parent. Creating a formal staff-family partnership would move one step closer to a more integrated family model of participation.

RESIDENTS MOVE TO ASSISTED LIVING BASED ON THE ENVIRONMENT

Beyond location, the building's design is one of the most important attributes consumers cite when describing why they moved to a particular assisted living building. The environment is a far more important influence than caregiving and service provision in this initial assessment. Once a move has taken place, then aspects of a facility's care giving approach and philosophy increase in importance. In fact, if people move to assisted living because of the environment, they often move out because they experience problems with the provision of services and caregiving. Therefore, last-minute value engineering adjustments that downsize landscape materials and reduce the quality and quantity of interior furniture are bad practices that can have disastrous consequences. A $300,000 reduction in the cost of the building translates into only a $3 per day reduction in the overall cost, which, based on the average daily cost of assisted living ($72), repre-

sents a savings of less than 5 percent. This is hardly enough to justify the damage done to the appearance of the building.

SKILLED NURSING FACILITIES WILL BE REPLACED BY ASSISTED LIVING

One of the most eye-opening observations in northern Europe is that skilled nursing environments there look exactly like assisted living environments in the United States. The northern Europeans now provide single-occupied dwelling units with private full bathrooms and small tea kitchens for skilled nursing care. The residents in these nursing homes are more dependent on medication and the staff ratios are higher, but the environments are just like those of U.S. assisted living buildings. Following this lead, we should expect that in the future assisted living buildings will become the long-term care alternative of choice. The only reason this won't happen immediately is the myriad rules and regulations that control the design of nursing homes in the United States. Most if not all of the buildings constructed today for licensed assisted living are safe enough to support residents who require heavier care. In most cases, the only changes needed would be an increase in the services available and in the expertise and training of a few key staff. Hospitals and subacute settings will increasingly be the domain of sicker residents. In northern Europe, assisted

Amsterdam House is for the "urban group": The *Hogeway* dementia facility in Weesp, the Netherlands, is separated into 15 different 11-person clusters based on the backgrounds and lifestyles of residents.

living (as we know it in the United States), is increasingly being defined as a larger setting (600- to 800-SF unit sizes) where home-delivered health and personal care services are delivered. In the United States, skilled nursing care will become subacute care, assisted living will become skilled nursing care, and congregate housing will become assisted living.

PEOPLE WITH DEMENTIA WILL BE VIEWED AS A DEMEDICALIZED POPULATION

Dementia residents will increasingly be treated as a population with a memory disorder rather than a group that needs to be institutionalized. Medications and new technologies will allow us to maintain more control but pro-

Special museum-like room for reminiscence therapy: The *Lohjan Vanhainkoti* in Lohja, Finland, has outfitted a room with household items and antiques that can be used to stimulate discussions with dementia residents.

vide residents with greater freedom. Sooner or later, we will view dementia as we do arthritis, considering it as an annoying disturbance that can be treated with medications. In the past older people were routinely sent to nursing homes when they started to experience incontinence. Innovations including a range of inexpensive and effective incontinence products have forever changed the way we view the nature of this problem. With new medications that are on the way, we will soon view dementia in the same way. More people with dementia will stay at home or in assisted living, and only the most physically frail persons with end-stage disease progression will require skilled nursing services.

ASSISTED LIVING FACILITIES WILL HAVE A COMMUNITY-BASED ORIENTATION

Assisted living facilities and continuing care retirement communities are increasingly recognizing the opportunity to serve the neighborhood populations with knowledge, home-delivered services, and personal care assistance. Provided through assisted living buildings, mobile services and electronic communication links, as well as logistical and monitoring assistance, will keep residents functioning independently in the community for a longer period of time. As their counterparts in northern Europe already do, the best organizations will shed the narrow role of providing only assisted living care to frail people in licensed facilities. They will be viewed as organizations that help families deal with the many choices associated with keeping an older person happy, independent, and safe. They will provide a range of services including home care assistance, emergency care monitoring, home modification analysis, and, in the future, electronic monitoring and electromechanical devices.

RESIDENTS WILL BE ENCOURAGED TO PURSUE AN ACTIVE LIFESTYLE THROUGH EXERCISE AND PHYSICAL THERAPY

One of the best qualities of northern European skilled and personal care housing is the emphasis on movement therapies. Use of exercise equipment is often combined with physical therapy, occupational therapy, and other rehabilitation regimens. In contrast, assisted living buildings in the United States are often passive environments, with an emphasis on social interaction and activities like card playing, television viewing, and birthday parties. Residents who have struggled to maintain their inde-

Dining table is an extension of the kitchen: In the *Ros Anders Gård* (page 215), residents take meals family style in four decentralized dining spaces. The style is meant to be informal and relaxed.

pendence often move into a setting where most things are done for them. This is a problem because it appears quite benign when, in reality, residents are often "being killed with kindness" because they are not staying fit. Muscle deterioration, bone density loss, and decreased aerobic capacity result from this passive lifestyle. Ultimately, loss of ambulation occurs. This requires a change in the way assisted living housing is conceptualized. For decades, "rest homes" have been seen as places for relaxation rather than rehabilitation. Emphasis must be placed on modest activities such as chair exercises, gardening, and walking. However, to be most effective, the clinical perspective of physical therapy must be linked with more informal access to exercise equipment. This practice is what has made northern European assisted care so effective.

CONCLUDING REMARKS

A middle-aged woman with an engaging smile came up to the dais after a recent presentation at a conference on aging. She shook my hand and told me she was very happy that someone was thinking about these issues. She said, "I hope that you can make some of these changes in time for me when I need it." I laughed nervously, but she didn't. She is not unlike many middle-aged to older persons who think realistically about the probability of moving to a nursing home. No one wants to think about that possibility, but the majority of people will spend some time in a nursing home before they die. In fact, this woman has a much higher probability than I do of

spending time in a nursing home simply because of her gender.

I wrote this book to encourage architects, administrators, facility sponsors, financiers, students, and policy makers to think about how to create better environments for older, frail people to live out their final years. As an architect, I believe that the work, home, and neighborhood environments in which we operate make a huge contribution to our quality of life. In long-term care, the "environment" is often reduced to one place. Moving from one's own home in the community to a nursing home is one of the most difficult moves anyone will ever make. Older people often move from a setting where they have lived for many years. Often the structure, the furniture, the surrounding outdoor space, and the neighborhood contain deeply embedded memories. Imagine moving from a place of security, predictability, and comfort to one that robs you of some of your most precious possessions—privacy, autonomy, and independence.

The contrast between a home and an institution is one of enormous difference. The social geographer Graham Rowles talks about the difference between place and space (Rowles, 2001). A place is embued with meaning. A space is defined simply as a three-dimensional geographic entity. Others use the word *home* in contrast to *house* as a way of differentiating shelter from a more personal and affect-laden surrounding.

The question at the heart of this book is, how do we design health and personal care settings so that they are more like the homes people must leave when they can no longer maintain their independence in the community? We have made some progress in this direction in the last ten years, and I hope that ten years from now we will be a little closer to that goal.

I hope this book has challenged some of your assumptions. I hope that the examples of successful projects in the United States and northern Europe have sharpened your thinking about the possibilities that exist. I hope it has left you with better ideas and practices that will be reflected in your own professional work. Finally, I hope you are convinced that our current practices desperately require improvement.

We need bold thinking that questions the status quo and calls for more humane interventions. Between now and the end of this decade, millions of people will enter environments for the frail. Let us hope that these places will be more like the homes they have left and less like the institutional environments they fear.

Appendix A

NOTEWORTHY BUILDINGS

I am frequently asked by people considering a trip to northern Europe, "What buildings would you recommend that I visit?" Following are the names, addresses, and contact persons for the 100 best northern European projects I visited, including facilities from the Netherlands, Denmark, Sweden, Finland, and Norway. After reviewing the list from my 1991 trip and the 95 buildings I visited in 1999, I arrived at this list of 100 *priority* projects. Also listed are 20 projects from the United States. Some of these have been referenced in the text, and others are examples from larger building programs by major providers. The short descriptions are meant to resemble a travel guide. They highlight the defining features and some of the unique qualities of these buildings.

THE NETHERLANDS

1. Anton Piekehofje
Anjstraat 1
2034 ML. Haarlem
Niek de Boer, Medical Director

Two-story building with family housing on the upper floor and six small group homes for dementia residents (36 residents) on the first floor. The group homes are linked by a enclosed common walkway (social wandering pathway) that creates an open, landscaped courtyard in the center of the site. Each resident cluster operates as a separate distinct "home."

2. Bergzicht (Regnier, 1994, page 136)
Alexberg 2
4800 DG Breda
Jacques Smit, Housing Director

A four-story enclosed street consisting of 42 units linked to 16 units of lean-to housing. It provides services to people living in the building and the surrounding neigh-

borhood. Bridges and corridors that connect the floors together are popular settings for social interaction. A home health agency recently moved in to coordinate the growing health care needs of residents.

3. De Drie Hoven
Louis Bouwmeesterstraat 377
1065 NS Amsterdam
Herman Hertzberger, Architect

A large geriatric hospital, this was Hertzberger's first internationally recognized elder care facility. The two-story atrium acts as a "town center" for residents and staff. The "brown café" here is picturesque and popular. The units have a small alcove in front that act as a "front porch." This design was the inspiration for the Captain Eldridge Congregate House in Hyannis, Massachusetts.

4. Flesseman Center
Nieumarket 77
1011 MA Amsterdam
Anita Kinebanian, Manager

Located adjacent to historic Nieumarket Square in Amsterdam, this adaptive remodeling of a historic "New Amsterdam"-style building creates a friendly and heavily used courtyard. Erkers along the street are cantilevered into the right-of-way above the street traffic. They are transparent square bay windows that provide excellent visual access to activities along the street below (see color insert and page 55).

5. Havenbogen
Kerklaan 33
3121 KC Schiedam
Cees Reyers, Architect

This is an elegant, curved, 100-unit, five-story apartment building. It is designed as a new addition to the Frankeland elderly service center, which has been in operation for 150 years. The new building contains a swimming pool, an exercise room and a putting green. Residents were selected from three age cohorts (55–65, 65–75, and 75+). Volunteer helping is encouraged, with younger residents helping older ones. The hope is that this will create a tradition of informal care that will reduce the need for formal help in the future while making the residents a more socially cohesive group (see page 247).

6. Hof Van Orden
Laan Van Orden and Teutonenstraat
7300 AL Apeldoorn
Hans van Beek, Architect

Two separate four-story atrium apartment blocks are placed next to one another on the site. Each building has an atrium that is a nonconditioned but ventilated light-frame glass enclosure. Collectively they accommodate 120 units of social housing. The atrium, framed by two single-loaded corridor blocks, is given a dynamic shape as a result of one curved side and one flat side. The exterior material on the curved side is natural wood siding, while the other side is brick.

7. Hofje van Staats
Jansweg 39-1
Haarlem
S.C. Goetemelk, Contact Person

A beautifully restored 20-unit *hofje* originally constructed in 1731 around a large, peaceful courtyard with a single large tree in the center. (Hofjes were sixteenth- and seventeenth-century examples of Dutch social housing often planned for widows of the merchant marine.) It is located in the middle of the central city, and each remodeled unit is two stories high. Some units are outfitted with chair lifts to accommodate stroke victims. Unit interiors are adaptively remodeled to fit modern life to this historic context (see page xvi and color insert).

8. Hogeway
Heemraadweg 1
1382 GV Weesp
Pauline Baart, Directiesecretaris

The 160 memory-impaired residents who live here are grouped into 15 "lifestyle" clusters of 10–11 residents each. Each lifestyle group is related to a salient aspect of the residents' previous lives (religion, social class, urban/small town, homemakers, etc). More than 30 clubs are available for residents with special interests to attend outside of their group cluster. A basement grocery store is used to retrieve food (with residents) that is brought back and prepared from scratch in each cluster. Lively designs have been added to the interior of the building (see pages 39, 147, 268, 274, and 287).

*9. Humanitas (page 158)
Bergweg Plantsoen 10
3037 SK Rotterdam
Dick Pettinga, Marketing

An intriguing 4- to 12-story, 195-unit "apartment for life" tower in downtown Rotterdam. The project has a range of residents who are divided into 55+, assisted living, and skilled nursing care units throughout the building. A large central atrium provides a public meeting place for residents and older people from the community. The housing is built on air rights above a grocery store. Therapy rooms and staff spaces are located on the first floor at the rear of the building, connected by elevators to the units above (see pages 158–162).

10. Jan van der Ploeg (Regnier, 1994, page 126)
Hooglandstraat 67
3036 PD Rotterdam
Elly Ham, Project leader

This four-story garden atrium, which is ventilated but not conditioned, is located on a tight urban site in the middle of Rotterdam. A bar and a meal service program run by volunteers are also open to people in the neighborhood. A curved balcony decorated with hanging red geraniums gives residents a place to sit adjacent to their unit entry doors (see page 40).

11. De Kiekendief
Kolkplein 1
1315 GW Almere-stad
Lammert Meyer, Head Nurse

A large, light-filled, four-story central atrium with units on two sides is located adjacent to a shopping mall. A cafeteria and grocery store activate the atrium floor. Roof perches are created over both of these spaces that overlook the activity below. The roof is designed so that it can be retracted in good weather. Units are designed so that residents can age in place, with wide doors that accommodate bedridden residents.

12. De Kortenaer
Kortenaerstraat 78
5703 EN Helmond
E. V. Moorsel, Director

A *stenpunt* (or "point of support") project with a long, straight, enclosed two-story mews-style street and a beautiful light-filled atrium. A semicircular acrylic dome over the second-floor central corridor gives the street a tall, spacious scale. It introduces plenty of light, which passes on both sides of the central walkway to the first floor, where plants have been placed against the walls.

* Case study featured in more depth and detail in Part III of this book.

13. Moerwijk

Twickelstraat 120
2539 RB Den Haag
Hans van Beek, Architect

A skillful remodeling of an older facility. A sloping greenhouse garden atrium at one end of a Y-shaped corridor is a popular retreat space for residents to visit. Canals of water are intertwined with building forms, creating excellent long and short, controlled views. Units are flexibly designed, with a movable armoire closet that can open up to the bedroom or the living room (see color insert).

14. De Muzen

Louis Davidsstraat 166
1311 LW Almere
Hans van Beek, Architect

Dramatic four-story, 165-unit condominium development for people aged 55+. A nonconditioned but ventilated atrium is created between two single-loaded corridor buildings. The atrium is about 50 percent hardscape and 50 percent landscape. Deep terra-cotta is the dominant color, which is attractive in both shade and full sun. The immediate environment includes a small commercial center on one side and a large urban park on the other (see page 293).

15. NZH Terrein Voorburg

Van Wassenaer Hoffmanplein
Parkweg, Voorburg
Hans van Beek, Architect

Situated on the former depot of the bus company, this facility contains 98 units for persons aged 55+ in three- and four-story blocks. The plan defines a central elliptical courtyard where rail lines from the original roundhouse are used in a landscape design. Units contain two large sliding glass French balcony doors in place of a balcony. The units are designed to be adaptable as the population ages.

16. Oklahoma

Ookmeerweg and Reimerswaalstraat
Amsterdam-Osdorp
Peter Stolwijk, Het Oosten

A housing complex for persons aged 55+ with 100 apartments features an unusual design by MVRDV Architects. Because only 87 apartments could fit in the single-loaded, nine-story building envelope, 13 apartments were cantilevered above the parking lot. This project, with an average resident age of 75, is linked to a nearby service house. Balconies at the ends with transparent, colored acrylic sides give new meaning to the concept of hanging out.

17. De Overloop

Boogstraat 1
1353 BE Almere-Haven
Herman Hertzberger, Architect

Designed by the Dutch architect Herman Hertzberger, this project has attracted international attention. Of note are the clustered entries. Four units with Dutch doors, windows, and a plate shelf create an alcove in the corridor. A large central atrium links the two floors. A controversial morgue/chapel on the top floor creates an expressive curved mass from the street. Lean-to housing on the perimeter of the site is also noteworthy (see pages 9, 33, and color insert).

18. De Pelgromhof

Molenstraat 7
6900 AB Zevenaar
Mr Lucassen, Director

An interesting 215-unit, anthroposophic-style building with bright exterior colors and muted interior pastel colors. It contains 169 apartments and 46 assisted living units. The four- to six-story building is curved around a courtyard with a central water feature. "Green" architecture ideas including a sedum sod roof were incorpo-

De Muzen

rated. Residents of the apartments were able to design their own units—each of which is unique. Residents who move in can choose independent housing with services or a more conventional assisted living program.

19. De Toonladder
Carousostraat 36
1301 Almere
Fenna Zuurman, Director

A two-story, 200-unit central courtyard project in the "music district" of this suburban enclave. Half of the building is a single-loaded block and the other half consists of small two-story individual four-plexes. The building complex contains a range of housing types including two small-group homes for people with dementia. A central green contains a small petting zoo with a goat, chickens, rabbits, and pigs.

20. Verzorgingshuis de Gooyer
Von Zesenstraat and Dapperstraat
1093 BJ Amsterdam
Martin Spyker, Director

Service house on an urban site adjacent to a busy market street. Mixed retail use on the first floor completes the streetscape. A group home for dementia residents and voluntary technical assistance from a local nursing home allow management to keep most residents here until they die.

21. Dr. W. Drees
Morsestraat 19
2517 PM Den Haag
Wim van Schalk, Managing Director

A 119-unit, five-story project serves a frail nursing home population in residential units. A large four-story atrium is operable during good weather. It provides daylight for an activity center below that is open to the neighborhood. Dutch doors are used throughout the building along single-loaded corridors.

22. Wieldrecht
74-108 H. Chabotstraat
Sprange Capelle
Wil Bongers, Architect

A combination of 20 townhouse units and 18 units in a four-story, curved-block midrise tower. This housing for individuals aged 55+ is designed for two different living circumstances. The townhouses have unusual multistory angular erkers that add to the interest of the housing while providing daylight for the upstairs areas. Anticipating the needs of the new 55+ boomers, the housing is 10–20 SM larger than the 67 SM that is the common standard.

23. Woonheuval De Brink
41-89 Talmastraat
Breda
Jacques Smit, Housing Director

A three-story atrium apartment block for people in the 75–80 age range. It consists of 57 units of lean-to housing and is connected to a recreation center. Residents are encouraged to decorate the corridors by placing their own artwork there. The units are 74-SM one-bedroom dwellings that have attracted 20–25 percent couples.

24. WZV Anholtskamp
Hovestraat 1
7475 CZ Markelo
A. Otten, Manager

Located in a small town, this building shares its common space with community organizations. Committed to maintaining older local residents, the building combines nursing home residents and assisted living residents in a hybrid scheme that has been successful in allowing residents to age in place.

DENMARK

1. Bofælleskabet Sandvejen
Sandevejen 50
8600 Silkeborg
Anne Frederiksen, Manager

This one-story, ten-unit, T-shaped building has a mews-style arrangement with an atrium "street." It is designed for developmentally disabled adults, but its scale and the atrium make it a compelling form for older people as well. The ability to have both a private life and a communal life with friends is what makes this design interesting. Terra-cotta coloring is used for the atrium walls, which are handsome in direct sunlight.

2. Degneparken
Degneparken 15
4293 Dianalund
Kjeld Sørunsen, Technician

A small-town 37-unit service house that provides extensive health, therapy, and respite care to community members and older people living there. A two-story atrium provides an open-plan community area with good natural light. A range of recreational and therapeutic activities for service house and neighborhood residents are offered here.

3. Dronning Anne-Marie Centret
Solbjerg Have 7
2000 Frederiksberg
Niels Gjarstrup, Managing Director

A nursing home (96 units) site planned with a large social housing program (412 units). The nursing home has developed some intriguing policies for decentralized management. Older residents serve on the personnel committee and meet with staff on a biweekly basis to discuss ward policies and programs (see page 133).

4. Dronningens Ferieby
8500 Grenaa
Claus Espeholt, Manager

This is a unique one-story, 46-unit "holiday village" for older frail and developmentally disabled adults and children. Located adjacent to the sea, it is composed of detached units measuring 75 SM that sleep four to six people. There is a communal house with a kitchen, dining room, activity room, and fireplace. The site also has a wheelchair-accessible dock from which residents can fish or enjoy the views. There are several other special settings like this throughout Denmark that are reserved for special populations (see page 95).

5. Egely
Egebjerg Bygade 34-72
2750 Ballerup
Birgit Lintrup, Nurse

This two-story, 32-unit atrium courtyard contains three different housing types. Fourteen nursing home units are combined with ten units of social housing and eight units of private housing. The atrium is a combination of hard materials, landscape, and a pool. It is not conditioned, but it is ventilated. Movable shades are used in the summer to reduce the amount of direct sunlight. A café located at one end of the complex is for residents of the apartments. Nursing home residents take meals together in a separate dining room (see page 295 and color insert).

Egely

6. Gulkrögcentret
Gulkrög 9
7100 Vieje
Anne Marie Henriksen, Physical Therapist

This project has been master-planned to encourage pedestrian through-traffic. Generous community facilities are shared with neighborhood residents. Social areas and lounges overlook the sidewalks and plazas used by employees from a nearby hospital, who cut through the site to catch a train on the other side (see pages 44 and 59).

*7. Gyngemosegård (page 174)
Mørkhøjvej 154
2730 Herlev
Annette Nicolaisen, Physical Therapist

This two-story, 100-unit project focuses on integrating housing with services and younger people with older people. Designed with concepts of new urbanism in mind, a pedestrian spine links the dwelling units with the community center, where physical therapy, occupational therapy, and home help/health care are centered. A light-filled atrium serves as the dining space for a restaurant also located here. Eight units of cohousing are offered for older residents who want to share a more interdependent life (see pages 89, 125, 174–180, and 283).

*8. Humlehusene (page 220)
1-3 Humlehusene
2630 Albertslund
Karin Rostgård, Nurse

This complex for memory-impaired older people consists of three L-shaped buildings arranged around three sides of a spacious landscaped courtyard. Each unit stands alone, but at night two staff circulate between the buildings. The dwelling units, at 310 SF, are relatively large, and residents are encouraged to bring their furnishings with them. The building shares the site with a day center and a small-group home for developmentally disabled children (see pages 220–223).

9. Laerkegaard
Persillehaven 28
Herlev
Tove Kjær Jensen, Director

This modern one-story building contains 24 housing units for physically and mentally frail people. Residents are divided into three groups of eight in L-shaped clusters. The 67 SM, dwelling units, are spacious and contain tall bay windows. The day center has a range of services for residents as well as for short-stay and respite residents. It also has a day program for residents with

* Case study featured in more depth and detail in Part III of this book.

dementia. A wide corridor is used extensively for physical therapy and exercise purposes.

10. Margrethelund

Kong Georsvej 9-13
2970 Horsholm
Sis Hansen, Administrator

This is a 35-unit adaptive-reuse courtyard building. The building uses a portion of the two-story façade of an old factory building. The rear of the site is a one-story addition. Units are clustered into three groups with separate decentralized dining spaces. The op maat principle of giving residents choices about the scheduling of their care is advocated. The facility also has a good physiotherapy program.

11. Mariendalsvej

Mariendalsvej 14-18
2000 Frederiksburg
Ole Hersfeldt, Resident

This five-story, 21-unit, H-shaped building is designed for the 55+ "third age" population. About two-thirds of the units have one bedroom and one-third have two bedrooms. The building has a lively, modern massing configuration that is low in front and builds up to five stories in back. It has several "green architecture" features including a gray water system that recycles rainwater for toilets and washing machines and solar energy panels. A swimming pool is located on the roof.

12. Mølleparken

25 Årslev Møllevej
8220 Brabend
Bent Sjöstedt, Resident

This 28-unit, two-story, seniors-only, L-shaped cohousing building has an atrium plan. A hard-surface atrium created between two rows of single-loaded corridor units is a nonconditioned but ventable social space. Each unit has its own kitchen, but residents also have a large dining room/multipurpose space where they regularly take meals together once or twice a month. The purpose of cohousing is to create a setting that encourages greater interdependence (see page 91).

13. Nybodergaården (Regnier, 1994, page 146)

Kronprinsenssgade 61
1306 Kobenhavn K
Lisbeth Andersen, Manager

A 48-unit, three-story atrium nursing home designed to conform to the shape of sixteenth-century housing in the Nyboder district of Copenhagen. Wide balconies allow residents to place furniture here that overlooks activities below. A neighborhood program cares for six off-site residents (see pages 79, 84, 248, and color insert).

14. Olivehaven

Munkevænget 10
6000 Kolding
Jyette Elkjær, Director

A 60-unit project that has been subdivided into ten separate houses with six residents each. Each building is L-shaped, with three units in each wing. Four of the houses are for people with dementia and they share a secured outdoor garden. These houses surround a large day center that primarily serves older people in the neighborhood. The day center also contains a training facility that caregivers use to learn how to operate the ceiling-mounted electric lifts installed in every unit.

15. Omsorgscentret Egegården

Klausdalsbrovej 213
2860 Søborg
Lone Streibig, Administrator

A 112-bed nursing home with an open linear community building. Services and activities are arrayed along a main corridor. Clear glass transitions between the common building and residential wings provide places for residents to socialize, exercise, and read (see color insert).

16. Rosenborg Centret

Rosengade 1
1309 Kobenhavn K
Sif Galagain, Assistant Manager

A nursing home in Copenhagen with a courtyard and enclosed atriums. The atrium is covered by a pyramid-shaped skylight and is used for morning and afternoon coffee. It fits well into the surrounding environment (see color insert).

17. Rygårdscentret

Niels Andersens vej 22
2900 Hellerup
Jannie Urban Hansen, Physical Therapist

An 87-unit service house with a substantial community services program. The outdoor courtyard is used for a range of physical therapy programs. Extensive use of turf block gives automobile access to most units (see color insert).

18. Sophielund

Sophielund 25-27
2970 Hørsholm
Dan Poulsen, Administrator

Sophielund includes 24 units for people with dementia, 127 units of service housing, and a large day center that serves people from the neighborhood. The day center is very lively, with a range of programs. It runs very effectively with volunteer support from members. A special demonstration house called "Sophie's Place" has been developed to demonstrate equipment and design approaches for severely handicapped older people.

19. Solbakken

Ole Hansenvej 10
4100 Ringsted
Inge Petersen, Nurse

This is a one-story, 36-unit clustered housing arrangement linked to a two-story day center. Five small group clusters housing six to eight persons are arranged in an L shape. Each home is sized to a comfortable family scale and operates in a semiautonomous way. Residents have physical impairments. Two additional group clusters are soon to be added for people with dementia.

20. Strandlund

Strandvejen 146
2920 Charlottenlund
Borge Koll, Director

An equity-based project in a park adjacent to the Baltic Sea, which separates Denmark from Sweden. Housing is clustered in rows that overlook a beautiful park on one side and a combined pedestrian and vehicular turf block path on the other side.

21. Sundheds-og Kulturcenter (aika, Frederiksberg Aldrecenter)

Ankersgade 21
8000 Åarhus C
Grethe Krist, Activity Director

This 87-unit complex consists of four L-shaped four-story towers that are arranged from east to west along a linear park. At one end is a day center with a large restaurant that attracts 300–400 people per week. The day center contains a full range of activity programs including a physiotherapy room and a training kitchen. The center is open to residents as well as to people in the neighborhood. Adjacent to the elderly day center is a children's day-care center and playground (see pages 63, 98, and 119).

SWEDEN

1. BRF Kaptenen

Gråbovägen 37a
441 51 Alingsås
Karin Kastberg, Nurse

This building combines 41 apartments with 24-units of housing for the frail in a courtyard-style building. The oval-shaped center courtyard, with a fountain and a terraced patio, is heavily landscaped. The housing for frail older people is on one side of the courtyard and is split into three separate clusters of eight units each. One cluster is set aside for people with dementia. Small outdoor

gardens linked to each living room are located on the opposite side of the courtyard.

2. Gruppboënde Orustgatan

Orustgatan 16
414 74 Göteborg
Elisabeth Andersson, Manager

This group home for six dementia residents is located on the top floor of a five-story building. This new building is a recent addition to an older suburban neighborhood that contains a number of multistory housing blocks from the 1970s. Many of the residents of this post–World War II suburb are older.

3. Gruppboëndet Strand

Skeppargatan 15
671 30 Arvika
Barbro Wilson, Director

L-shaped group homes, grouped in a cluster plan, are two stories in height. Families live on the second floor, and six physically or mentally frail older residents live below. Sloped ceilings and the extensive use of wood paneling give the units a residential appearance.

4. Grupphemen Solbacken

Bergsmansveg 10-12
430 90 Öckerö
Rut Ludvigsson, Director

Two 8-unit group homes for dementia residents are located on a small fishing island. A spacious kitchen provides an effective setting to involve older residents in meal preparation. Locating two homes together allows for economies at night because only one person is needed to monitor both settings.

5. Guldbröllopshemet

Tideliusgatan 16
Sodermalm, Stockholm
Ulla Nybons, Administrator

This building was recently remodeled but still retains the charm of its early-twentieth-century architecture. A 44-unit, five-story nursing home, each floor is designed as a separate group home with its own living room and dining room. Most residents have dementia, but a first-floor unit is dedicated to older residents with psychiatric problems. A generous outdoor balcony linked to the dining room is large enough for a full-sized dining room table (see page 250).

6. Hasselknuten (Regnier, 1994, page 171)

Hasselknuten 5 A-F
444 44 Stenungsund
Inga Britt Johansson, Director

This dementia home for six residents is located on the first floor of a two-story, L-shaped housing block, which also accommodates 15 families. The project has a fenced outdoor garden and uses clear glass partitions between the kitchen, living room, and dining room to help orient confused older residents.

7. Kvarteret Karl XI

Källegatan 3
302 43 Halmstad
Stellen Eriksson, Architect

This large service house has a glass corridor that runs through the center of the first floor linking a number of activity spaces. The U-shaped courtyard contains a portion of the medieval wall that originally enveloped the city. In one housing block, a single-loaded enclosed glass corridor has encouraged residents to creatively capture this space as an extension of their dwelling unit (see pages 58 and 88).

8. Näverbyn Sternberga

574 98 Vetlanda
Rolf Andersson, Administrator

This rural village, located in central Sweden, contains a rich mixture of housing and services for the community. A service house with a restaurant and other activities is open to the community. Attached to the rear is a small group home for people with dementia. Off to one side are 12 detached dwellings that are clustered together. A day-care center for 20 children and a small grocery store round out the community uses. An outdoor patio accessible from the group home and the day center overlooks the children's playground (see page 257).

9. Nicktistein

Ernst Jacobsgäten 7
Malmö
Inger Moller, Administrator

This two-story square courtyard building has 40 small (350 SF) apartments for a frail population that averages 85 years of age. The courtyard is a very visible outdoor area due in part to a single-loaded corridor that overlooks it. An outdoor balcony on the second floor and the shady space below the balcony on the first floor are very popular in good weather. The facility has a very active social program, with one major event planned each month.

*10. Postiljonen (page 224)

Videholms 3
236 31 Höllviken
Lotten Modeer, Administrator

This two-story, 24-unit nursing home is wrapped around a small courtyard. The courtyard, referred to as an "out-

Riksdalern

door living room," is heavily used in the summer, when the weather is good. Single-loaded corridors link the units, which are clustered into four groups of six residents each. Each cluster has a dining room and an informal verandah. All four clusters share an entry lounge with a fireplace and a second-floor multipurpose room that overlooks the Baltic Sea. Rooms are designed to allow residents to age in place, with extra-wide entry doors and a ceiling-mounted track system for an electric hoist that links the bed to the bathroom (see pages 65, 97, 120, 128, 224–228, 259, and 260).

11. Riksdalern

Ekebergsgätan 3
417 03 Göteborg
Lisbeth Jensen, Administrator

The 20 units in this building are distributed within two point towers that contain four rooms per floor each (Goteborgs Stad, 1992). The first floor is dedicated to common space and contains a service center and meeting rooms for a neighborhood-based adult day-care program. An elevated garden patio has been created between the two towers. The point tower design allows every unit to have cross-ventilation. The design of the commode was the result of an innovative design from an industrial engineering program (see page 298).

*12. Ros Anders Gård (page 215)

Rosgården 5
137 S6 Västerhaninge
Rose-Marie Geijer, Nurse

This 40-unit, two-story building is located in a Stockholm suburb. It is split into four wings with ten units each. Dementia residents are located on the first floor and physically impaired residents on the second floor. The kitchen is the center of activity and contains the nurse's station. Features like raised appliances, roll-out drawers, and a center food preparation island are designed to make it easier to engage residents in food

---

* Case study featured in more depth and detail in Part III of this book.

preparation. The L-shaped building defines a small, secured garden in the back. The third floor has offices where home care personnel meet (see pages 46, 122, 131, 215–219, 284, and 289).

13. Runby Servicehus

Runby Torg 9
194 40 Upplands Väsby
Birgitta Pettersson, Director

An interesting mixed-use building located over a neighborhood shopping center in a Stockholm suburb. The first floor contains doctors' offices and a library for the community. A large sloped atrium brings daylight into the common spaces on the main floor including a dining room.

14. Snöstorps Servicehus

Ljungbyvägen 28
302 Halmstad
Stina Åsen, Leader

This small eight-unit service house overlooks the rolling countryside, with a beautiful garden defined by the U-shaped configuration of the one story building. A south-facing service house porch with a trellis shade covering invites sun in the morning (see page 57).

15. Solgård Nursing Home

Storgattan 40
51400 Tranemo
Anette Åkesson, Director

A good example of a local nursing home design that clusters four resident units around a sitting room and 16 units around a dining room. Courtyard designs are used to maximize views and access to outdoor spaces. An old Swedish ceramic fireplace is used to give the dining room character and warmth.

16. Tornhuset

Åvägen 20
412 51 Goteborg
Barbro Thor, Manager

A six-story, 121-unit urban project located on a 1923 site used originally as a soap factory. The administration building, with the original clock tower, was saved and redesigned for use as a community services building. The project surrounds and protects a garden on the inside of the courtyard (see page 64).

17. Vastersol

Fabriksgatan 17
Jönköping
Anna Brita Nilsson, Director

This older hospital was recently remodeled for nursing care purposes. Each floor is treated like a separate group home cluster, and residents eat with staff around small dining room tables. The wide double-loaded corridors have been decorated with antiques to make the environment more friendly.

18. Vickelbygården

Sågvägen 10
617 00 Skärblacka
Lars Selevik, Administrator

This Swedish nursing home is modeled on Danish ideas. Small, decentralized unit clusters are wrapped around landscaped courtyards with raised gardens beds. Each resident unit has access to its own private patio space with a small raised garden bed. Courtyards are open on one side so that they can be linked together through a walking path that loops the building (see page 234 and color insert).

19. Vidar Clinic (Vidarkliniken)

153 91 Järna
Sten Kristiansen, Administrator

The Vidar Clinic, although not designed for older people, is one of the best examples of anthroposophic architecture. The healing architecture designs of Erik Asmussen (Coates, 1997) are represented in a variety of building types. The clinic uses a combination of colors, materials, fenestration details, daylighting techniques, and fabric-covered light fixtures to give it a warm and attractive feeling. The central courtyard created for views and activities is an important element of the program and the organizational scheme (see pages 141 and 270).

20. Vigs Ängar

Vigavägen 18
270 33 Köpingebro
Lillemor Husberg, Administrator

This one-story double-courtyard building has 32 dwelling units, 8 of which are dedicated to a small-group dementia cluster. Many of its design features (pastel colors, lush landscaping, daylighting, and fabric light fixtures) are based on anthroposophic architecture. One courtyard is primarily landscaped, while the other has more paving for staging events. Both courtyards are very visible because corridors that run east and west are single-loaded and overlook them. The building also features a massage area and a hot therapy pool (see pages 52, 70, 262, and 273).

FINLAND

1. Apian Palvelukeskus

Kangaskan 21
37600 Valkeakoski
Sinikka Paty, Leader

This project is centered around a large U-shaped courtyard opening onto an urban plaza that links the project to the surrounding urban context. A glass observation space on top of the building is lighted at night, forming a highly visible beacon (see page 59).

2. Brahenpuiston Asuintalo

Porvoonkatulo
00510 Helsinki
Kaarina Sainio, Director

This 55-unit, four-story urban project is a mixed-use facility that combines first-floor retail stores with a health center, a child care center, and housing for the elderly. Approximately half of the apartments overlook the internal courtyard, where a children's playground is located.

3. Foibe Service Center and Apartments

Sairaalakatu 7
01400 Vantaa
Tarya Maenpaa, Director

In addition to a large service house, Foibe (Heikkinen, 1995) contains 2-five-story housing blocks and nine one-story triplex terrace units. Altogether it has 51 units, 35 of which are owner occupied, and 16 of which are rental units. One tower contains apartments, and the other contains four- to five-person small-group homes and a dementia facility for ten residents. The large service center has a restaurant, a gymnasium, a swimming pool with a sauna, and a beauty shop. It serves residents of the attached housing and older people living in the community.

4. Folkhälsen

Mannerheimintie 97
Helsinki
Viveca Hagman, Administrator

Designed for Swedish-speaking people in Finland, this large service house and group home complex is in a central location. The four- and five-story buildings contain 77 service apartments that range from 375 to 770 SF. About two-thirds are sold and one-third are rented. There are three groups homes for frail residents that accommodate 38 people. The outreach program in the community is vast, and many Swedes come to the building for its therapeutic programs. An ongoing research program has explored a range of issues related to dementia. A rehabilitation room, lecture hall, swimming pool, library, and restaurant are among the largest spaces available (see page 23).

5. Gerby Västervik Vanhustentalo

Kirjurintie 11
65280 Vaasa
Kati Saksman, Director

Inspired by the anthroposophic architecture of Asmussen, this small collection of 21 service flats is planned around a small courtyard. Roughly in the form of a spiraling P, the courtyard is defined by one-story dwellings and a two-story leg that contains a few apartments on the upper floor and a commons below. The average age of residents is only 75, but the building is designed to allow them to age in place. The building's color is a red-ochre, which fits the rural character of this part of Finland. The site is unimproved, which allows views from the units into the surrounding rugged landscape of fallen trees and overgrown grasses.

6. Juva

Sairaalatie 6
51900 Juva
Heli Muttilainen, Head Nurse

This projects combines seven service apartments (450 SF) with two small group homes that support seven residents each (Siven, 1995). The building has a long, thin circulation spine that links residents at both ends of the building with service center functions in the middle. In addition to a restaurant, the building provides a day-care program for social isolates and memory-impaired people in the community. At one end of the building are two small-group homes with units that are considerably smaller, at 225 SF. The connecting corridor, which daylights the building, varies from a low resident scale at one end to a more monumental scale in the central public areas. Service apartments have outside exit doors (as well as interior doors to the corridor) to make them feel more independent.

7. Kamppi Service Center

Salomonkatu 21B
00100 Helsinki
Helena Järvi, Administrator

This dramatic service building is located in the middle of a densely populated neighborhood in downtown Helsinki. The service center directly controls 30 service flats. However, hundreds of older people who live in the neighborhood come to Kamppi for a range of activities. There are a dozen social and activity rooms including a large festival hall that seats 350. Adjacent to the building is a swimming pool and gymnasium. A children's day-care center is located in the center of the block, which various program spaces overlook. The center of Kamppi is a dramatic multistory atrium that links the entry floor with spaces on the upper floor.

8. Kuuselan Palvelukoti (Regnier, 1994, page 141)

Nuolialantie 46
33900 Tampere
Anni Lvokkala, Director

This garden atrium project has a swimming pool on the lower level that overlooks the central atrium. Two dementia group homes for four residents each are located on the fourth floor. Community services, like meals-on-wheels and emergency response, are coordinated in this building (see page 92).

9. Lohjan Vanhainkoti

Ojamonkatu 34
08100 Lohja
Heli Virtanen, Administrator

This setting contains 57 units for older frail people, with a focus on dementia care that has been well received. One room has been remodeled into a place where various items of historic and cultural significance are placed. These are used to elicit stories and responses from residents. A recent remodeling has involved the use of antique furniture and colors/patterns from the early twentieth century. There is also a small group dementia home for seven residents. It was constructed in the 1940s, and many residents identify with the style and the scale of the setting. The group home program is normalized to encourage ADLs (see page 288).

*10. Metsätähti (page 229)
Suokatu 5
41500 Hankasalmi
Leena Kurra, Leader

This unique project, located in a small town in southern Finland, combines a day-care center for children with a 14-unit service house for older people. In this one-story structure, the service house component is split into three-unit clusters. A large central spine links the buildings together. Children and older people come together in the dining/multipurpose room for meals and for joint programs. Both groups (older people and children) have their own space to which they can retreat. The building also provides meals for older people living in the neighborhood (see pages 113, 124, and 229–233).

11. Old Peoples Home and Health Center
Kuusitie 10-18
12100 Oitti
Päivi Terävä, Social Services Director

This dramatic 42-unit project resulted from an architectural competition. The program combines housing and an outpatient health center. Housing is centered in four "village" clusters grouped around a two-story pyramidal skylight. A continuous corridor, broken in several places, links the separate villages.

12. Palvelukeskus Merikaari
Pohjoiskaari 9
00200 Helsinki (Island of Lauttasaari)
Paula Pohto-Kapiainen, Director

This is a day center that is linked through an enclosed walkway to a 54-unit, single-loaded corridor service apartment building and two small-group homes that accommodate 20 people on an upper floor. The day center contains a dining room, swimming pool, an exercise room, a billiards room, a bank, and a sauna. The small-group homes accommodate 13 memory-impaired residents and 7 short-stay respite care residents. An outdoor space is available for the group home residents that overlooks the city of Helsinki.

13. Palvelutalo Esikko
Uitta Montie 7
20810 Turku
Markku Jyväs, Director

This equity cooperative project has a cost-sharing agreement with the local municipality that allows its swimming pool and restaurant to be shared with neighborhood residents. The central four-story atrium has a wall of viny plant materials adjacent to balcony corridors.

14. Petäjävesi
Teollisuustie 1
41900 Petäjävesi
Helky Koskela, Director

This building combines a service center with three small-group homes that accommodate 30 residents (28 units). The small-group homes are at one end of the building, which branches in three directions. They are self-contained, and each has its own outdoor garden. At the other end of the service house, which is connected by a dramatic two-story circulation spine, is a small hospital infirmary and doctor's office. Residents like the idea of being close to the hospital. The service house has a dining room, living room, sauna, gym/physical therapy room, chapel, meeting room, and beauty shop (see page 282).

15. Saga Seniorikeskus
Vähäheikkiläntie 2
20700 Turku
Anne Simola, Marketing Director

This large, three-story, 128-unit, Y-shaped atrium building is designed with three large, dramatic landscaped atriums that intersect around a two-story entry space. The building is designed as a private housing option, with units that range in size from 350 to 675 SF. Each unit has a balcony or a patio in addition to access to the central atrium. The project features a large indoor/outdoor pool, library, gymnastics area, beauty shop, hobby space, and dining room. A small-group home is provided for residents with dementia, and four levels of service are available for residents as they age (see page 15).

16. Vanhainkoti-Parvakeskus Himmeli
Palokunnantie 39
28130 Pori
Irma Roininen, Director

This home for the aged contains an interesting corridor configuration that terminates in a two-story fireplace. A child-care center attached to the home has introduced joint programs for children and older people. The large, well-landscaped site provides opportunities for exercise.

---

* Case study featured in more depth and detail in Part III of this book.

Virranranta

17. Viherkoti
> Kuusiniemi 13-15
> 02710 Espoo
> Maire Koski, Head Nurse

This 50-unit nursing home contains a three-story atrium. Half of the atrium space is devoted to physical therapy and exercise. A garden adjacent to the atrium allows large areas to be combined and devoted to events that involve residents with families.

18. Villa Viklo
> Hanhitie 15
> 90140 Oulu
> Maaija Skaffari, Administrator

This one-story building is split into two 8-unit small-group homes. About half of the residents have memory impairment. The clusters are beautifully laid out, with a small kitchen, living room, and dining room space. A large outdoor patio is accessible to both unit clusters. Large windows with low sills and bathrooms with wood ceilings make the units attractive and upbeat. The project relies on an adjacent service center for food and other logistical supports.

*19. Virranranta (page 206)
> Kuorevirrankatu 13
> 74700 Kiruvesi
> Erkki Strommer, Director

This 50-unit service house and day center in a small southern Finnish town is beautifully sited overlooking a nearby lake. Units are split into five group clusters of eight units each at one end of the project and ten units of larger service housing at the other end. In the midddle are the common spaces and services that are available to older people in the community. A dining room, winter garden, library, and physical therapy and activity space are available. The group home clusters are designated for physically impaired, memory-impaired, and rehabilitation/respite residents (see pages 55, 206–210, 302, and color insert).

*20. Wilhelmiina (page 163)
> Taavetti Laitsenkatu 4
> 00300 Helsinki
> Leena Välimäki, Director

This large project contains a range of programs including a rehabilitation center, dementia housing, service flats, and assisted living units. The tightly configured plan responds beautifully to the surrounding environment. The materials chosen for the buildings vary with the height and massing of each component. The exterior treatments, especially at the first and second floors, give the building greater detail and make it appear smaller than it is. Each assisted living floor is split into three small clusters of five residents each. The common spaces include a range of therapeutic spaces, as well as a large swimming pool and an exercise/physical therapy room. The dementia floor has experimented with high-intensity, full-spectrum lighting for residents with sundowner's syndrome (see pages 62, 101, 149, 163–168, 243, and color insert).

* Case study featured in more depth and detail in Part III of this book.

NORWAY

1. Boliger Pa Banken
Nedre Bankegatan
1750 Halden
Thinh Huu Nguyen, Resident

This is a beautifully restored eighteenth-century courtyard housing arrangement with 23 units located in the middle of a small town. The central courtyard contains a mixture of private and communal spaces and is a successful social space. It is an age-integrated setting with a majority of older residents (see page 303).

2. Bydel Søndre Nordstrand
Mortensrudveien 185
1283 Oslo
Arilo Fossli, Architect

This is a new five-story hillside project constructed under a recent building initiative. It contains 16 units of service housing and 96 units for the frail that are subdivided into 12 small-group clusters of 8 units each. Four of the clusters are for dementia residents, four are for short-stay (rehabilitation and respite) residents, and four are for the physically impaired. The building also contains a café, swimming pool, rehabilitation center, library, and offices for home care personnel. Each cluster has a large balcony, and most of the units have French balconies. Located on a hillside site, it has a dramatic view of the city of Oslo below. The larger service housing units are designed so that they can be remodeled into four small-group clusters for the frail if needed in the future (see page 264).

3. Ensjøtunet Bo-og Servicesenter
Malerhaugveien 10/12
0661 Oslo
Gurilngvaldsen, Director

Boliger Pa Banken

This complex has recently been remodeled. The common service building is a charming mansion house from 1860. The building has 21 units of service housing and 48 nursing units including 16 units for memory-impaired residents. An activity center added in the last remodeling is located partially underground. The roof serves as a large plaza and green space for the old house, which is a more informal social setting for neighborhood residents. The building provides housing and services, as well as nursing and dementia care (see pages 34 and 267).

4. Forsmannsenteret
Dronningsgatan 24
3200 Sandefjord
Solveig Walloe, Resident

This active service center contains a number of special-use recreation spaces for older people who live in the neighborhood. The building's façade creates a strong urban edge, with retail uses on the first floor. A courtyard greenhouse and a restaurant overlooking the south edge of the site provide attractive places for residents to sit.

5. Hasselbakken Seniorboliger
Hasselbakkveien 5a-5c
7053 Ranheim
Solveig Dignne, Realtor

This housing for persons aged 55+ is split into three groups of 20, 28, and 16 units, respectively. This atrium housing scheme has two parallel lines of units bridged by an atrium that steps down the hill to the sea. The atrium is not conditioned but can be ventilated. The units average 850 SF. The residents are in their 70s and have no need for services yet. Balconies and patios serve as extensions of the units (see pages 127, 130, and color insert).

6. Havstein Bo-og Servicesenter
Stabells Vei 4B
7021 Trondheim
Hans Frederik Selvaag, Leader

A relatively large complex with 60 dwelling units, Havstein also contains a swimming pool, ergo therapy room, physical therapy/exercise room, restaurant, large multipurpose assembly space, and kindergarten. The housing includes 32 service apartments, a 9-unit dementia cluster, 10-units for assisted living/nursing, 5 units for the mentally handicapped, and 8 units for young handicapped individuals. The building is a wood two- and three-story structure that looks residential in character. The day center serves older people in the neighborhood.

7. Hôyas Bo-og Rehabiliteringsenter

Valhallaveien 74
1413 Tårnåsen
Inger Nyhus, Leader

Located on a hill overlooking the city, Hoyas is a two-story building consisting of eight clusters of eight units that are color-coded to aid orientation and staff assignments. The bold colors give each cluster its own identity. Half of the clusters are for people with dementia; one cluster is for short-stay residents, and the remaining three are for physically impaired residents. The facility has a day-care program and a number of common facilities including a swimming pool, physiotherapy and ergo therapy center, restaurant, beauty shop, and home care offices. A large two-story corridor spine links the clusters together (see page 82).

8. Ilevollen Bo-og Servicesenter

Ilevollen 28
7018 Trondheim
Arve Wold, Leader

This 20-unit, two-story courtyard building is constructed in the old tradition of open courtyard housing. The housing is toward the rear, with the service center facing the main street. The courtyard is heavily landscaped, but there are also places for residents to sit. An open single-loaded corridor rings the perimeter. On the top floor, small alcoves have been created that overlook the courtyard below. A new remodeling will expand and cover the courtyard with an atrium so that it will be more comfortable for residents in the winter.

9. Lesjatun (Regnier, 1994, page 166)

2665 Lesja
Hans Hesthagen, Social Services Director

This small service house of 15 units on the edge of a dramatic valley represents the best in the Norwegian tradition of building in wood. Units have rustic wood walls and ceilings. The south-facing balcony provides views of the surrounding mountains. The service house is colocated with a nursing home for residents who need more care as they age.

10. Melhus Omsorgsenter

Nedre Melhus
7224 Melhus
Gravas Per, Leader

This new 34-unit service center contains 16 units for dementia residents, 9 units for the physically impaired (nursing/assisted living), and 9 short-stay units. It also contains a swimming pool, doctors' offices, a café, an adult day-care program, home care offices, and a physical therapy space. The housing for the frail is organized around two U-shaped courtyards that provide visual and physical access to the outdoors. The housing and service center are linked together by a semicircular corridor.

11. Midtløkken Bo-og Servicesenter

Kong Oscargätan 15
3100 Tønsberg
Ellen Otterstad, Director

This 57-unit service house contains a pool, extensive community space, and a restaurant below an air rights equity condominium. The U-shaped courtyard opens onto a park, which encourages residents to walk to the city center a few blocks away.

12. Raufosstun Eldresentret

Severin Olsens Vei 15
2830 Raufoss
Line Kjosbakken, Director

This 32-unit home for the aged is planned around small courtyard *tuns* that connect rear patio areas. It is painted a traditional bright red, which contrasts with the green landscape of the summer and the white snow of the winter (see color insert).

13. Skytta Bo-og Servicesenter

Brennaveien 24
1481 Nittedal
Turid Henriksen, Leader

This 30-unit building has a mix of residents including younger disabled residents and short-stay, memory-impaired and physically disabled residents. The building has wood detailing throughout the interior that gives it a warm, residential feeling. The service center offers a woodworking shop, cafeteria, physiotherapy, ergotherapy, arts and crafts, beauty shop, and a living room with a fireplace. There are 30 additional units of lean-to housing connected by a covered walkway.

14. Smedstruveien

Smedstuveien 7
7040 Trondheim
Solveig Dignne, Realtor

This three-story, 33-unit cooperative is an atrium-style building. It is located in a neighborhood with a growing older population. The local municipality bought ten units, which it plans to rent to residents. It also reserves the right to remodel those units in the future to create more common space for services. A typical 650-SF unit features a large bathroom, a walk-in closet, a large balcony, two doors to the bathroom (from the living room and bedroom), a large eat-in kitchen, and low 12-inch windowsill heights. It follows the Husbakken (financing agency) standards for adaptable housing.

15. Ulvoya Eldreboliger

Pans Vei 1-5

0139 Ulvoya Oslo 1

Wilhelimae Warness, Resident

This small 16-unit village is located on a small island near Oslo. A main arcade links porches and entry spaces together. A common room has been loaned to the district doctor, who sees patients here every week, including children and families from throughout the island. The landscaped linear garden/courtyard between the units is attractive and friendly.

UNITED STATES

1. Annie Maxim House

700 North Avenue

Rochester, MA 02770

Karen Greene, Director

This horseshoe-shaped congregate house is linked together by an enclosed porch that allows residents to observe activities on the site and take a sheltered walk to the main common spaces. A central commons has spaces for reading, socializing, dining, and game playing. The scale of the 12-unit setting and its rural location amid cranberry bogs add to its charm.

2. Arden Court

2505 Musgrove Road

Silver Springs, MD

Marty Kinkead, Executive Director

This prototype of housing for persons with dementia developed by the Manor Care Corporation owes much to Woodside Place. The building is spider-shaped, with a central rectangular mass and four L-shaped legs that emanate from each corner. Four clusters of 12 units are decentralized, with their own serving kitchen, dining room, and living room. A central area contains an activity room, staff lounge, outside entry, and main kitchen. A looped walkway connects the four clusters. A small porchlike space is located at each cluster entry door to give it identity. One unit in each cluster is designed to be double occupied, for a total occupancy of 52 residents (48 units).

3. Sunrise of Bellevue (page 191)

15928 Northeast 8th Street

Bellevue, WA 98008

Barbara Nopen, Executive Director

This four-story L-shaped building is on a tight site surrounded by a community center, a park, and retail stores. It has 70 units, 18 of which are for people with dementia on the secured fourth floor. The building has a friendly Arts and Crafts style that is reflected in the selection of furniture. There are three unit types: studios, companion suites (for single or double occupancy), and one bedroom dwellings. The dining room, parlor, bistro, foyer, and library are residential in scale, giving first-time visitors the sense that they are entering a mansion (see pages 67, 191–195, and color insert).

4. Brighton Gardens by Marriott

2500 S. Roslyn Street

Denver, CO 80231

Judi Del Ponte, Counselor

This facility is typical of the H-shaped, three-story *generation three* prototype that the Marriott Corporation has constructed throughout the country. This building combines ninety units of assisted living and 25 units for residents with dementia. Forty-five units for skilled nursing care are located in an adjacent one-story building. The first floor contains all of the common spaces including a living room, library, dining room, activity space, and beauty shop. Decentralized lounges are also located on upper floors.

5. Captain Clarence Eldridge Congregate House (Regnier, 1994, page 161)

30 Pine Street

Hyannis, MA 02601

Bonnie Goodwin, Administrator

This congregate house designed to accommodate 20 people is an expansion of a nineteenth-century sea captain's dwelling on Cape Cod. A central atrium and dwelling units with double-hung windows and Dutch doors open the unit interiors to natural light. Residents here know one another and have created important informal helping networks (see pages 75 and 81).

6. ClareBridge of Williamsville

6076 Main Street

Amhearst, NY 11412

Adrian Guszkowski, Architect

This 36-unit, one-story building is a stand-alone facility for dementia residents only. Two courtyard buildings are joined together to create a two-story entry space resembling a small town center. Each courtyard building stands alone, with its own dining room, courtyard, outdoor secure garden, activity room, and TV lounge. Units are clustered into three groups of six residents each where care is provided in a more intimate environment. Each resident cluster shares a bathing room and laundry. Dining rooms located adjacent to one another share access to a centralized kitchen.

*7. Copper Ridge (page 201)

719 Obrecht Road

Sykesville, MD 21784

Carol Kershner, Executive Director

The 60 units for dementia care located here are divided into three "houses" of 20 units each. Each house is a

* Case study featured in more depth and detail in Part III of this book.

U-shaped building with 2 ten-unit residential wings and a kitchen/living room/dining room space that connects them together. The three houses are linked together around a courtyard. Various shared spaces are placed here adjacent to a looped circulation pathway. Each house has an outdoor space with a garden, paved plaza, and covered porch. Two larger outdoor spaces contain walkways for exercise. Copper Ridge involved a number of explorations using an ADL lifestyle. Residents are involved in helping with meal preparation (see pages 24, 152, and 201–205).

*8. Crown Cove (page 187)

3901 E. Coast Highway
Corona Del Mar, CA 92625
Sandy Fleschman, President

This shingle-style 75-unit building is located on a dramatic site overlooking the Pacific Ocean. The building has five stories and steps down the side of the hill. A view corridor created in the center of the building provides a sheltered open space for residents to overlook the view. The building is split into six segments/clusters and contains a special care unit for people with dementia as well as a unit cluster for people with ambulatory difficulties. The units were sited so that 40 percent have ocean views and top-floor units have balconies (see pages 187–190).

9. ElderHomestead

11400 4th Street North
Minnetonka, MN 55343
Jan Stenzel, Manager

This small-scale 29-unit project was designed to resemble a rambling rural Minnesota farmhouse. Four individual units share a cluster parlor. Common spaces are in scale with the residential nature of the building. A three-season enclosed porch allows residents to view the surrounding street (see page 102 and color insert).

10. Sunrise of Fairfax (Regnier, 1994, page 151)

9207 Arlington Road
Fairfax, VA 22031
Cody Tower, Executive Director

This three-story Victorian house accommodates 47 units in an L-shaped building. The exterior and interior design is consistent with ideas about residential imagery. Spaces are small in scale. An intergenerational program with the Merritt Academy on the same site brings residents in contact with children (see page 50).

*11. Goddard House (page 169)

165 Chesnut Street
Brookline, MA 02445
Janet Cody, Marketing Director

Goddard house is a three-story, 115-unit building with 75 units of assisted living and 40 units of dementia housing in an older Boston neighborhood. The building has a complex shape that breaks up what could have been a massive building. Gables, porches, shed roofs, and dormers also create a building that looks friendly in scale from the street. The dementia housing is subdivided into 4 ten-unit clusters. Each common space is unique and distinctive. The spaces connect together to create a variety of social opportunities for residents as they move from the entry to the dining room (see pages 67, 106, 169–173, and 265).

*12. Harbour House (page 211)

5900 Mockingbird Lane
Greendale, WI 53129
Kevin Mantz, Architect

This is a 44-unit, two-story housing arrangement for memory-impaired people. The X shape allows the building to be easily subdivided into four neighborhoods and eight wings. The neighborhood size is related to staffing requirements. Each wing is developed around a particular theme that gives it a unique identity. Two secure outdoor gardens are created, and a range of gardening activities are available. Upper-floor units have access to large shared balconies. Residents take their meals in four dining rooms that are designed to accommodate a small staff desk and a counter for residents who need assistance (see pages 90, 109, and 211–214).

13. Maple Ridge by Marriott

1177 Palm Avenue
Hemet, CA 92543
Larry Meyer, Community Relations Director

This one-story, cottage-style development consists of six separate cottages of 14 units each (84 units). An extra unit in each building is devoted to a live-in house manager. Two of the six cottages are for memory-impaired residents. The only major difference in these cottages is the lack of a shower in each resident's bathroom. A separate community building has space for larger events and a kitchen. The cottages are dumbbell-shaped, with a dining room and serving kitchen at one end and a living room at the other.

*14. Sunrise of Mission Viejo (page 181)

26151 Country Club Drive
Mission Viejo, CA 92691
Barbara Morgan, Executive Director

This 86-unit, three-story building combines dementia housing with assisted living in a "home within a home" scheme. The lower floor for dementia residents has 2 ten-unit clusters that open onto a secure garden. The Spanish-style building, with porches and trellis attach-

* Case study featured in more depth and detail in Part III of this book.

ments, has a number of skylights on the top floor that daylight cluster neighborhoods and a large social gathering space. The entry sequence creates a powerful connection between the six or so spaces/features that are visible upon entering the building (see pages 126, 181–186, and 281).

15. Rackleff House (Regnier et al., page 168)

655 SW 13th Avenue
Canby, OR 97013
Keren Brown Wilson, Contact Person

This 25-unit, single-story courtyard buidling in a small rural Oregon town is the original prototype for Assisted Living Concepts. The square courtyard has four sides. Two corridors are single-loaded and open onto a view of the central courtyard. The other two corridors are double-loaded for maximum efficiency.

*16. Sunrise of Richmond (page 196)

1807 North Parham Road
Richmond, VA 23229
Cameron Oglesby, Executive Director

This plan consists of three separate one-story buildings located next to one another in a crescent pattern. Two 26-unit buildings are for assisted living, and one 18-unit building is for dementia residents. The buildings use a combination of hip and gable dormers to create a friendly residential appearance. The Arts and Crafts interior style is complemented by a large central fireplace that separates the living room and the dining room. The H-shaped building has two gardens. The one in front is heavily landscaped, with an adjacent covered porch. The one at the rear has a paved area for outdoor activities. The corridor plan is a loop that connects the units to the main central space (see pages 73, 196–200, 307, and color insert).

17. Rosewood Estate (Regnier, 1994, page 131; Regnier et al., 1995, page 194)

2750 N. Victoria Steet
Roseville, MN 55113
Arvid Elness, Architect

This 68-unit alternative nursing home is designed around a housing and services home-care model that maximizes residents' independence. A physical massing configuration divides the building into three pieces, giving it the look of a mansion from the street.

18. EPOCH Assisted Living (formerly Sunbridge Assisted Living)

4901 South Monoco Road
Denver, CO 80237
Kate Miller, Counselor

* Case study featured in more depth and detail in Part III of this book.

Sunrise of Richmond

This prototype building is a three-story X-shaped building with 96 units. It does not have a dementia unit, but subsequent buildings added a small 12-unit cluster on the first floor. Major common spaces include a central living room, ice cream parlor, and dining room located on the first floor. Upper floors have a library, exercise room, barber/beauty shop, arts and crafts shop, and country kitchen. The building is designed to be site adapted, with wings of various lengths.

19. Woodside Place (Regnier, 1994, page 156; Regnier et al., 1995, page 188)

1215 Hulton Road
Oakmont, PA 15139
Arlene McGannon, Administrator

This one-story, 30-unit residential facility for dementia residents allows residents free reign to wander. The massing involves three small cottages linked through a wandering pathway to a large multipurpose room that resembles a barn. The Shaker details used for interior treatments give it a homey feeling (see pages 9, 121, 137, 138, and 148).

20. Wynwood of Meridian

660 Woelfel Rd.
Brookfield, WI 53045
Kristin Hernandez, Resident Director

This 60-unit, two-story building is an Alterra Assisted Living prototype. Units are distributed to three orthogonal wings that are subdivided into six neighborhoods of ten units each. Each neighborhood cluster stands alone and contains a living room, card alcove, bathing room, laundry, and dining room. Universal workers are assigned to the residents in each cluster. A large entry parlor and an upstairs living room constitute the shared common spaces. Dining rooms are located close to the center core of the building to facilitate the distribution of food.

Appendix B

ADDITIONAL IMPORTANT BUILDINGS

The following 100 projects are either cited in the text or were visited during the first and second site visits. They are not described in the previous collection of 100 noteworthy buildings. They are mentioned here in an effort to be as comprehensive as possible. Although these buildings did not make the first list, most of them have very interesting qualities and are well worth visiting.

THE NETHERLANDS

De Aanleg
Albert Verweyplein 30
3842 HH Harderwijk

De Boogerd
I-87 Prieelstraat
1628 Lt Hoorn n.h.

De Dennen
Huizerweg 140a
1402 AK Bussum

Dr. W. Drees
Morsestraat 19
2517 PM Den Haag

De Gooyer
von Zesenstraat and Dapperstraat
1093 BJ Amsterdam

Heksenwiel
Heksenwiellaan 2
4823 HA Breda

Het Wamlink
Kottenburg 66
7102 AL Winterswijk

Humanitas
Hennepstraat 4
7552 DN Hengelo

De Klinker
Borgenstraat 45
1053 PB Amsterdam

Kruistraat
14-128 Kruistraat St.
3581 G.K. Utrecht

De Landrijt
Drosserstraat 1
5623 ME Eindhoven

De Mering
Kerkplein 29
1777 CD Hippolytushoef

Nieuw Doddendaal
Parkdwarsstraat 34
6511 DL Nijmegan

De Opmaat
van Goghlan 2
2681 UA Monster

Saint Bartolomeus Gasthuis
Lange Smeestraat 40
3511 PZ Utrecht

Soenda Zorgcentrum
Soendalaan 2
3131 LV Vlaaringen

Stichtingete Bouwacher
Leidseweg 140
3533 HN Urecht

De Vaste Burcht
De Vaste Burcht 45
5328 ES Rossum

Verpleeghuis de Schildershoek
J. Catsstraat 325
2515 GK Den Haag

Vereniging Anders Wonen
Madame Curieplein 86
4834 XS Breda

WZV Anholtskamp
A Ten Hovestraat 1
7475 CZ Markelo

De Westerweeren
Burger Huybrechtstraat 66
DB Bergambacht

Zonnetrap
Molen vliet 572
Rotterdam

DENMARK

Aktivitetscentret Baunbo
Skolegade 27 Lunde
6830 Nr. Nebel

Eskegården
Byagervej 115
8330 Beder

Frederiksbroën Aldrecenter
Georgsgade 61
5000 Odense C

Fyensgadecentret
Fyensgade 25
9000 Ålborg

Lille Gläsny
Kanslergade 12
5000 Odense C

Lokalcenter Skelager
Skelagervej 33
8200 Åarhus N

Lyngtoften
Ternevej 4
6920 Videbaek

Nymosegård
Sognevej 39
2820 Gentofte

Pindstrup Centret
Perlevej 3
8550 Ryomgård

Plejecentret Munke Mose
Allegade 94
5000 Odense C

Rygårdscentret
Niels Andersens vej 22
2900 Hellerup

Bofælleskabet Sandvejen
Sandvejen 50
8600 Silkeborg

Sibeliusparken
Tæbyvej 39
2610 Rødovre

Skansebakken
Vestergade 1
7080 Børkop

Taarbæk Aldreboliger
Taarbæk Strandvej 82B
2860 Klampenborg

Tulipan vej Pensionatet
Tulipanvej 100
8600 Silkeborg

Wiedergårdens
Wiedergården 2
2791 Dragør

SWEDEN

Altplaten
Box 123
421 22 V. Frolunda—Goteborg

Aspens Servicehus
Bartotegatan 1
582 22 Linkoping

Atrium House for Pensioners
Carlslund Park
194 22 Upplands Väsby

Baltzargården
Eenatriska Eliv Lasavettet
591 85 Motala

Båtsmangärdet
Bagaregatan 2-4
442 32 Kungälv

BNF Kranen
Oskarsrogatan 9
Solna

Fabriken
Östra Storgatan 109
551 11 Jönköping

Fargärdet
Breviksgatan 15
575 39 Eksjo

Framnäsgården
Glasmästaregatan 6
412 62 Göteborg

Gruppboëndet Lönngården
Granviksgätan 8
571 41 Nassjo

Hornskrokens
Hornskroken 1
117 26 Stockholm

Humlans Gruppbostader
Humlevagen 98
461 65 Trollhattan

Katarinagården
Tideliusgatan 7-9
118 69 Stockholm

Kullëngens Sjukhem
Kullëngsvagan 1
694 00 Hallsberg

Lilldalshemmet
Lilldalsvagen 16
471 94 Kållekärr-Tjorn

Lundagården
Lundagårdsvagen
533 72 Lundsbrunn

Mårtensund Servicehus
Brunnsgatan 11B
223 60 Lund

Mösseberg Spa
Box 733
521 22 Falköping

Rio Servicehus
Sandhammsgatan 6 and 8
115 40 Stockholm

Romares Housing for the Elderly
Romares vag 20
254 51Helsingborg

Servicehuset Hornstall
Lignagatan 6
117 34 Stockholm

Skinnarvikens Servicehus
Heleneborgsgatan 2 A-F
117 32 Stockholm

Silviahemmet Dementia
Gustaf 111 s
Vag 7 Box 142
178 02 Drottningholm

Sörgården
Lopanasvagen 5
360 40 Rottne

Sternberga Servicehus
Näverbyn township
574 97 Vetlanda

Kv Stryrkan
Spånehusvägen 83
Malmö

T-1
Överstegatan 22
581 03 Linköping

Uddängen
Katrinebergsgatan 5
431 61 Mölndal

FINLAND

Anjalankoski Inkeroisten
  Palvelukeskus
Valtatie 10
46900 Anjalankoski

Helmiranta
Helmikuja 3
62200 Kauhava

Köpsinrinteen Palvelukeskus
Köpsintie 19
86800 Pyhasalmi

Kotikallio Service Center
Kyläkirkontie 6-10E
00037 Helsinki

Kurjenmäki Home
Kurjenmäenkatu 4
20700 Turku

Oulusalon Paivakeskus
Kouluti 7
90460 Oulunsalo

Munkkiniemi
Laajalahdentie 30
00330 Helsinki

Riihimäen Vanhainkoti
Kontiontie 73
11100 Riihmäki

Turun Ukkokoti/Gubbhemmet
  I Abo
Multavierunkatu 5
20100 Turku

NORWAY

Aldersbustadane Service
Sentret
3841 Flatdal

Furubakken Service Boliger
Ovre Torggatan 2
2800 Gjøvik

Lårdal Alderspensjonat
3860 Høydalsmo

Holmestrand Eldersenter
Rådhusgaten 11
3080 Holmestrand

Søreidtunet Eldrescentret
Søriedtunet 2
5060 Søreidgrend

Sportsvenien Borettslag
Lyseagan 50
0383 Oslo 3

Zion Housing
Ole Hogstads vei 16
7046 Trondheim

UNITED STATES

The Argyle
4115 W. 38th Avenue
Denver, CO 80212

John Bertram House
29 Washington Square
Salem, MA 01970

Eaton Terrace II
323 South Eaton
Lakewood, CO 80226

Hearthstone at New Horizons
402 Hemingway Street
Marlborough, MA 01752

Heritage at Cleveland Circle
50 Sutherland Road
Brighton, MA 02135

Heritage at Framingham
747 Water Street
Framingham, MA 01701

Heritage at Vernon Court
430 Center Street
Newton, MA 02458

Motion Picture and Television
  Country Home and Hospital
2338 Mulholland Drive
Woodland Hills, CA 91364

Palmcrest Nursing Center
3355 Pacific Place
Long Beach, CA 90806

Sedgewood Commons
22 Northbrook Drive
Falmouth, ME 04105

Stride-Rite Intergenerational
  Center
Five Cambridge Center
Cambridge, MA 02142

Sunrise at Fair Oaks
3950 Joseph Siewick Drive
Fairfax, VA 22033

Sunrise at Findlay
401 Lake Cascade Parkway
Findlay, OH 45840

Sunrise at Gahanna
775 Johnstown Road
Gahanna, OH 43230

Sunrise at Norwood
86 Saunders Road
Norwood MA 02062

Sunrise at Severna Park
43 W. McKinsey
Severna Park, MD 21146

OTHER FACILITIES

Minna Murra Lodge
Toowoomba Garden
Queensland Austrialia

Sunrise at Frognal House
Sidcup Township
London, England

Appendix C

GLOSSARY OF HOUSING TERMS

Each culture has its own label and name for housing for the frail. The following 18 types are not an exhaustive list but represent most of the examples selected for this book. They represent different approaches to bringing physical environments and social service programs together. Additionally, several different housing types are targeted to a range of different resident competence levels.

Aanluen Woning or "Lean-to" Housing: This is a Dutch housing invention that involves the construction of independent housing next to service houses/day centers. This housing is usually not linked by a covered walkway. In fact, it often looks like conventional neighborhood housing. The major difference is that it is electronically linked (emergency response system) to a nearby service house, and home care workers visit everyone in the building on a regular basis. This housing type is particularly appealing to couples and to persons who have experienced a major problem in the past and need monitoring.

Andelsleilighet Borettslag Housing: Traditionally in Norway, a relatively high proportion of the housing stock is owner occupied. Dwellings are normally purchased in a form that is similar to cooperative housing in the United States. Although this arrangement is less popular in other countries, ownership has been promoted and is becoming more popular in the Netherlands.

Apartment for Life: This concept involves accepting residents over the age of 55, but with a commitment to keep them in their apartments regardless of their level of need. Residents stay in the same apartment even though they may need skilled nursing care. This is a new housing type that started in the Netherlands. Care is provided by home care workers who visit on a scheduled or as-needed basis. Residents with different levels of need are randomly distributed throughout the building.

Assisted Living Housing: This is the term used to describe housing for mentally and physically frail older people in the United States. It includes residents with a wide range of capability levels. In most cases, residents have personal care needs but do not require 24-hour medical supervision. Assisted living targeted to the most frail population is often referred to as *high-acuity* assisted living. These are residents who have multiple problems (e.g., memory loss, wheelchair bound, insulin-dependent diabeties), major disabilities and ambulation difficulties, or a psychiatric condition. These are complicated cases that require extra staff attention.

Atrium Housing: This is common in all countries but particularly in the Netherlands, where glass enclosures often create an enclosed protected area between units. These buildings are normally surrounded by single-loaded corridor housing with a transparent roof. The spaces are usually nonconditioned but have large roof ventilators that allow the space to be cooled naturally when temperatures rise above a certain level. The floor of the atrium usually contains a combination of soil and plants, sidewalks and pavement, and pools of water.

Caring Home Initiative: Norway's new policy approach to housing the frail elderly has two tracks. One involves the creation of large rehabilitation centers and service houses in the community. These are much like the traditional service center, but housing involves primarily frail dementia residents, short-stay rehabilitation/respite participants, and physically impaired residents. The second track involves independent housing for the community that can be adapted as the population ages in place. This normally means that over the life of the program, the dwelling unit and the housing common space allocations adjust to the changes in residents and the shifts in the composition of the neighborhood.

Home for the Aged or Personal Care Housing: This housing is designed for older frail people who need assistance. Before the term *assisted living* came into vogue, these two terms were commonly used to describe residents who had primarily a need for help rather than health needs. *Intermediate nursing care* is another older term that generally refers to the same population.

Home Within a Home: The placement of a small-group home for people with dementia within an assisted living building. Generally, the dementia units account for less than 25–30 percent of the total number of units. Residents are usually confined to a secure area of the building where they take their meals and spend the day together. These homes generally have access to an outdoor garden or a large patio space.

Intramural versus Extramural Housing: Currently being debated in the Netherlands, this involves the choice between housing with services integrated with a more collective lifestyle versus a more traditional housing and service package (similar to the Danish home care model). Residents who seek autonomy and privacy prefer the extramural model, while those who are more interested in security and predictability opt for the intramural type of dwelling.

Life-Span or 55+ Housing: These terms are used to describe housing for more independent, younger persons. Normally, this housing follows the requirements established in Norway (*Husbanken*) and the Netherlands (*Seniorlaben*), which allow the dwelling units to adapt to the needs of the residents as they age in place. The boomers for whom this housing is intended are also referred to as the *68 generation* and *new agers* in Europe.

Local Nursing Home: This is a Swedish prototype of the early 1980s that experimented with basic concepts of decentralization. Very few of these nursing homes were constructed. Today the term has little meaning, but many of the ideas embodies in the best contemporary facilities (small clusters, orientation to landscape/outdoor spaces, courtyard organizational form, single-room occupancy, etc.) grew out of these early local nursing home experimental models.

Mews Atrium Housing: These projects bring two single-loaded rows of apartments close enough together to share a single central corridor. In multistory applications daylight filters down to the lowest levels through spaces between the walkway and the units. Skylights or a glass roof cover the top floor roof. These facilities are almost always nonconditioned but ventible spaces that are pleasant and can be used year round.

Plegehem: This is a Danish term for a nursing home. In the last ten years, as traditional nursing homes have been replaced by housing with services, this term has become less commonly used. Some of my interviewees thought it had a somewhat negative (old-fashioned) connotation.

Point of Support (Stenpunt) Housing: This Dutch housing model is designed to provide limited services to residents of the project and older people living in the neighborhood. It usually involves a protected (sometimes enclosed) "dry feet" walkway between the housing and an adjacent service center. Services vary from a single meeting from to a full scale dining program.

Seniors-Only Cohousing: This Danish housing model is oriented to a collective lifestyle. Two types exist—one for seniors only (55+) and one for persons of all ages. The individuals who move into these facilities usually agree to share some meals together and to look after one another, although most of the heavy personal care responsibility is borne by the Danish home care system. This form of housing encourages interdependence.

Service House: This type of housing is common in all five northern European countries, although it is used most frequently in Sweden and Denmark. It combines housing for the frail with a range of other community services including but not limited to a restaurant, multipurpose social (senior) center, adult day-care program, home-care services, occupational therapy, activity/crafts rooms, physical therapy, and swimming pool. Home care workers are stationed here and provide care and assistance to people in the neighborhood. In Finland and Denmark, the portion of the building that contains services is called the *day center*. When an attached housing unit has a full kitchen and supports an independent lifestyle, it is often referred to as a *service apartment*.

Small-Group Housing or Clustered Units: This Swedish invention for residents with dementia has been eliminated and replaced by four to six clusters of units (six to ten residents in each cluster), usually in a single two- to three-story building. The small-group cluster defines a functioning household that is normally operated by a team of universal workers. In most dementia facilities, residents participate in the life of the place by helping with laundry and meal service.

Social Housing: This is subsidized housing that is available to lower-income residents. In northern Europe, a relatively high percentage of the housing stock for the elderly is fully or partially subsidized by the government. Although the amount of this stock decreases every year, it is still a significant component of the total housing inventory for people over the age of 75.

REFERENCES

Alexander, C., S. Ishikawa, and M. Silverstein (1977) *A Pattern Language*. New York: Oxford University Press.

American Association of Retired Persons (AARP) (1993) *Life-Span Design of Residential Environments for an Aging Population*. Washington, DC: AARP.

American Association of Retired Persons (AARP) (1996) *Understanding Senior Housing into the Next Century: Survey of Consumer Preferences, Concerns and Needs*. Washington, DC: AARP.

American Seniors Housing Association (ASHA) (2000) *Seniors Housing Statistical Digest 2000–2001*. Washington, DC: ASHA.

Asmussen, E. (1992) *Husbehov*. Haderslev, Denmark: Forlaget Privattryk.

Assisted Living Federation of America (ALFA) (1996) *An Overview of the Assisted Living Industry, 1996*. Fairfax, VA: Coopers and Lybrand.

Assisted Living Federation of America (ALFA) (1999) *The Assisted Living Industry, 1999: An Overview*. Fairfax, VA: PriceWaterhouseCoopers and the National Investment Center.

Assisted Living Federation of America (ALFA) (2000) *ALFA's Overview of the Assisted Living Industry*. Fairfax, VA: PriceWaterhouseCoopers and the National Investment Center.

Boligtrivsel I Centrum (1993) *Co-Housing for Senior Citizens in Europe*. Copenhagen: BiC Conference Report #94.

Brawley, E. C. (1997) *Designing for Alzheimer's Disease: Strategies for Creating Better Care Environments*. New York: Wiley.

Brummett, W. (1997) *The Essence of Home: Design Solutions for Assisted Living Housing*. New York: Van Nostrand Reinhold.

Calkins, M. (1988) *Design for Dementia: Planning Environments for the Elderly and Confused*. Owings Mills, MD: National Health Publishing.

Calkins, M. (1995) "The Corrine Dolan Alzheimer Center," in S. Marberry (ed.) *Innovations in Healthcare Design*. New York: Van Nostrand Reinhold.

Carstens, D. (1985) *Site Planning and Design for the Elderly: Issues, Guidelines and Alternatives*. New York: Van Nostrand Reinhold.

Center for Business and Policy Studies (EVA), (1999) *Spectrum of Finnish Opinion*. Helsinki: EVA.

Centers for Disease Control and Prevention (CDC) (1999) *Targeting Arthritis: The Nation's Leading Cause of Disability*. Atlanta: CDC.

Centre for Accessible Environments (1998) *The Design of Residential Care and Nursing Homes for Older People HFN 19*. London: The Centre.

Chappell, N. (1990) "Aging and Social Care," in R. Binstock, and L. George (eds.), *The Handbook of Aging and the Social Sciences*. San Diego: Academic Press.

Coates, G. (1997) *Erik Asmussen, Architect*. Stockholm: Byggforlaget.

Cohen, U. and K. Day (1993) *Contemporary Environments for People with Dementia*. Baltimore: Johns Hopkins University Press.

Cohen, U. and J. Weisman (1991) *Holding on to Home*. Baltimore: Johns Hopkins University Press.

Cooper-Marcus, C. and M. Barnes (1999) *Healing Gardens: Therapeutic Benefits and Design Recommendations*. New York: Wiley.

Cooper-Marcus, C. and C. Francis (1998) *People Places: Design Guidelines for Urban Open Space*, 2nd edition. New York: Wiley.

Dannenmaier, M. (1995) "Healing gardens," *Landscape Architecture*, 85(1), pp. 76–79.

Day, K., D. Carreon, and C. Stump (2000) "The therapeutic design of environments for people with dementia: A review of the empirical research," *The Gerontologist*, 40(4), pp. 397–421.

Evans, D. (1990) "Estimated prevalence of Alzheimer's disease in the United States," *The Milbank Quarterly*, 68(2), pp. 267–289.

Feil, N. (1993) *The Validation Breakthrough: Simple Techniques for Communicating with People with Alzheimer's-Type Dementia*. Baltimore: Health Professional Press.

Fiatarone, M. A. (1994) "Exercise training and nutritional supplementation for physical frality in very elderly people," *New England Journal of Medicine*, 330, page 1769.

Fich, M., P. Mortensen, and K. Zahle (1995) *Old People's Houses*. Copenhagen: Kunstakademiets Forlag.

Friedlob, A. (1993) *The Use of Physical Restraints in Nursing Homes and the Allocation of Nursing Resources*. Unpublished doctioral dissertation, University of Minnesota, Minneapolis.

Golant, S. (2000) *Assisted Living: A Potential Solution to Canada's Long-Term Care Crisis*. Vancouver: Simon Fraser University.

Gordon, P. (1998) *Seniors' Housing and Care Facilities: Development, Business and Operations*. Washington, DC: Urban Land Institute.

Gotesborg Stad (1992) *Bostader for Aldre (Homes for the Elderly)*. Gothenborg: City Publishing.

Gottschalk, G. and P. Potter (1993) *Better Housing and Living Conditions for Older People*. Horsholm: SBI-Danish Building Research Institute.

Guralnik, J., M. Yanagishita, and E. Schneider (1988) "Projecting the older population of the United States: Lessons from the past and prospects for the future," *The Milbank Quarterly*, 66(2), pp. 283–308.

Hansen, E., A. Dahl, G. Gottschalk, and S. Jensen (2000) *Ældre I Bofællesskab*. Copenhagen: AFK.

Harrigan, J., J. Raiser, and P. Raiser (1998) *Senior Residences: Designing Retirement Communities for the Future*. New York: Wiley.

Hiatt, L. (1987) "Designing for the vision and hearing impairments of the elderly," in V. Regnier and J. Pynoos (eds.), *Housing the Aged: Design Directives and Policy Considerations*. New York: Elsevier.

Hildebrand, Grant (1991) *The Wright Space: Pattern and Meaning in Frank Lloyd Wright's Houses*. Seattle: University of Washington Press.

Hines, Thomas (1982) *Richard Neutra and the Search for Modern Architecture*. Berkeley: University of California Press.

Hoglund, D. (1985) *Housing for the Elderly: Privacy and Independence in Environments for the Aging*. New York: Van Nostrand Reinhold.

Hoglund, D. and S. Ledewitz (1999) "Designing to meet the needs of people with Alzheimer's disease," in B. Schwarz and R. Brent (eds.), *Aging Autonomy and Architecture: Advances in Assisted Living*. Baltimore: Johns Hopkins University Press.

Houben, P. and A. Mulder (1999) *The Future of Housing for the Elderly: What We Can Learn from Europe*. Delft: Department of Housing and Urban Renewal, Delft University of Technology.

Howell, S. (1980) *Designing for Aging: Patterns for Use*. Cambridge, MA: MIT Press.

Hyde, J. (1995) *Serving People with Dementia: Regulating Assisted Living and Residential Care Settings*. Boston: Hearthstone Press.

Jensen, S. (1997) *Byg om byg godt*. Copenhagen: Boligselskabernes Landsforening.

Kane, R., and K. B. Wilson (1993) *Assisted Living in the United States: A New Paradigm for Residential Care for Frail Older Persons*. Washington, DC: AARP.

Kaplan, Stephen (1987) "Aesthetics, Affect, and Cognition: Environmental Preference from an Evolutionary Perspective," *Environment and Behavior* 19(1) pp. 3–32.

Kershner, C., C. Roques, and C. Steele (1999) "Dementia care in assisted living," in B. Schwarz and R. Brent (eds.), *Aging Autonomy and Architecture: Advances in Assisted Living*. Baltimore: Johns Hopkins University Press.

Koncelik, J. (1976) *Designing the Open Nursing Home*. Pennsylvania: Dowden, Hutchinson, and Ross.

Krauss, N. and B. Altman. (1998) "Characteristics of nursing home residents—1996." *MEPS Research Findings No 5*. Rockville, MD: Agency for Health Care Policy and Research.

Kristiansen, E. (1997) *Forms of Accommodation for the Physically and Mentally Handicapped*. Åarhus: Ministry of Housing.

Lawton, M. P., M. Fulcomer, and M. Kleban (1984) "Architecture for the mentally impaired elderly," *Environment and Behavior*, 16, pp. 730–757.

Lawton, M. P., M. Moss, and M. Grimes (1985) "The changing service needs of older tenants in planned housing," *The Gerontologist*, 25(3), pp. 258–265.

Leibrock, C. (1999) *Design Details for Health: A Visual Guide*. New York: Wiley.

Leibrock, C. and J. Terry (1997) *Beautiful Universal Design: A Guide to Making the Most of Interior Design's Healing Potential*. New York: Wiley.

Lindstrom, B. (1989) *Gode boliger til aeldre.* Copenhagen: Byggeriets Udviklingsrad.

Lindstrom, B. (1995) *Ka' du rock'e I din bolig.* Åarhus: Arkitektskolen I Åarhus.

Lynch, K. (1960) *Image of the City.* Cambridge, MA: MIT Press.

Mace, R. (1991) *The Accessible Housing Design File.* New York: Van Nostrand Reinhold.

McCamant, K. and C. Durrett (1988) *Cohousing: A Contemporary Approach to Housing Ourselves.* Berkeley, CA: Ten Speed Press.

Ministry of Health and Social Affairs (1997) *Responding to the Elderly.* Stockholm: Fritzes.

Ministry of Health and Social Affairs (1999) *National Action Plan on Policy for the Elderly.* Stockholm: The Ministry.

Mollica, R. (1995) *Guide to State Assisted-Living Policy.* Portland, ME: National Academy for State Health Policy.

Mollica, R. (2000) *State Assisted Living Policy.* Portland, ME: National Academy for State Health Policy.

Moore, J. (1996) *Assisted Living: Pure and Simple Development and Operating Strategies.* Fort Worth, TX: Westridge.

Moore, J. (2000) *Assisted Living 2000.* Fort Worth, TX: Westridge.

Moore, J. (2001) *Assisted Living Strategies for Changing Markets.* Fort Worth, TX: Westridge.

Moore, K. (1998) *Towards a Language of Assisted Living.* Milwaukee: University of Wisconsin-Milwaukee.

Moore, C., G. Allen, and Donlyn Lyndon (1974) *The Place of Houses.* New York: Holt, Rinehart and Winston.

Moos, R., S. Lemke, and T. David (1987) "Priorities for design and management in residential settings for the elderly," in V. Regnier and J. Pynoos (eds.), *Housing the Aged: Design Directives and Policy Considerations.* New York: Elsevier.

Mueller, J. L. (1997) *Case Studies on Universal Design.* Raleigh: Center for Universal Design, North Carolina State University.

Myers, G. (1990) "Demography of aging," in R. Binstock and L. George (eds.), *The Handbook of Aging and the Social Sciences.* San Diego, CA: Academic Press.

National Academy on an Aging Society (2000) *Caregiving: Helping the Elderly with Activity Limitations,* #7. Washington DC: The Academy.

National Association of Home Builders (NAHB) Research Center (2000) *Directory of Accessible Building Products.* Upper Marlboro, MD: NAHB Research Center.

National Institute of Aging (NIA) (1999) *Progress Report on Alzheimer's Disease, 1999.* Bethesda, MD: National Institutes of Health.

National Investment Conference (NIC) (1998) *National Survey of Assisted Living Residents: Who Is the Customer?* Annapolis, MD: NIC.

Ojanen, H. (1999) "Finland in Europe," in (anon) *Facts About Finland,* Helsinki: Otava Publishing Co.

Paulsson, J. (1997) *Det nya Äldreboendet.* Goteborg: Chalmers tekniska högskola.

Pearce, B. (1998) *Senior Living Communities.* Baltimore: Johns Hopkins University Press.

Peterson, M. J. (1995) *Universal Kitchen Planning.* Hackettstown, NJ: National Kitchen and Bath Association.

Peterson, M. J. (1996) *Universal Bathroom Planning.* Hackettstown, NJ: National Kitchen and Bath Association.

Pirkl, J. J. (1994) *Transgenerational Design: Products for an Aging Population.* New York: Van Nostrand Reinhold.

Porter, D. (1995) *Housing for Seniors: Developing Successful Projects.* Washington, DC: Urban Land Institute.

Pynoos, J. (1998) "Improving the delivery of home modifications," *Technology and Disability,* 8, pp. 3–14.

Pynoos, J. (2000) *Home Modifications.* Los Angeles: Andrus Gerontology Center.

Pynoos, J. (in press) "Elders and the right to housing," in R. Bratt, C. Hartman, and M. Stone (eds.), *The Right to Housing.* Philadelphia: Temple University Press.

Pynoos, J. and P. Liebig (1995) *Housing Frail Elders: International Policies, Perspectives and Prospects.* Baltimore: Johns Hopkins University Press.

Raschko, B. B. (1982) *Housing Interiors for the Disabled and Elderly.* New York: Van Nostrand Reinhold.

Regnier, V. (1985) *Behavioral and Environmental Aspects of Outdoor Space Use in Housing for the Elderly.* Los Angeles: School of Architecture, University of Southern California.

Regnier, V. (1991) *Best Practices in Assisted Living: Innovations in Design Management and Financing.* Los Angeles: National Eldercare Institute on Housing and Supportive Services, University of Southern California.

Regnier, V. (1994) *Assisted Living Housing for the Elderly: Design Innovations from the United States and Europe.* New York: Wiley.

Regnier, V. (1997a) "Design for assisted living," *Contemporary Long Term Care,* 20(2), pp. 50–56.

Regnier, V. (1997b) "The physical environment and the maintenance of competence," in S. Willis, K. W. Schaie, and M. Hayward (eds.), *Societal Mechanisms for Maintaining Competence in Old Age*. New York: Springer.

Regnier, V., J. Hamilton, and S. Yatabe (1995) *Assisted Living for the Aged and Frail: Inovations in Design, Management and Financing*. New York: Columbia University Press.

Regnier, V. and J. Pynoos (1992) "Environmental interventions for cognitively impaired older persons," in J. Birren, B. Sloane, and G. Cohen (eds.), *Handbook of Mental Health and Aging*, 2nd edition. New York: Academic Press.

Rivlin, A. and J. Weiner (1988) *Caring for the Disabled Elderly*. Washington, DC: Brookings Institution.

Rodin, J. and E. Langer (1977) "Long-term effects of a control-relevant intervention with the institutionalized aged," *Journal of Personality and Social Psychology*, 35, pp. 897–902.

Rowe, J. W. and R. L. Kahn (1998) *Successful Aging*. New York: Pantheon Books.

Rowles, G. (2001) "History, habit, heart and hearth: On making spaces into places in old age," paper presented at the conference "Aging in the Community: Living Arrangements and Mobility," Heidelberg, Germany.

Rybczynski, W. (1986) *Home: A Short History of an Idea*. New York: Penguin Books.

Salmon, G. (1993) *Caring Environments for Frail Elderly People*. New York: Wiley.

Schaefer, R. (2000) *Housing America's Seniors*. Cambridge, MA: Joint Center for Housing Studies of Harvard University.

Schwartz, B. and R. Brent (1999) *Aging Autonomy and Architecture: Advances in Assisted Living*. Baltimore: Johns Hopkins University Press.

Seligman, M. (1975) *Helplessness: On Depression, Development and Death*. San Francisco: Freeman.

Siitonen, T. (1996) "Asumispalvelukeskus Wilhelmiina," *ARK Finnish Architectural Review*, 2(3), p. 96.

Silverman, M., E. Ricci, J. Saxton, S. Ledewitz, C. McAllister, and C. Keane. (1996) *Woodside Place: The First Three Years of A Residential Alzheimer's Facility*, 2 vols. Oakmont, PA: Presbyterian SeniorCare.

Siven, K. (1995) "Palvelukeskus Juvakoti," *Arkkitehti*, 92(2/3), pp. 62–67.

Slater, R. (1999) *Jack Welch and the GE Way*. New York: McGraw-Hill.

Sloan, P., G. Weisman, M. Calkins, J. Teresi, and M. Ramirez (1993) *Therapeutic Environment Screening Scale, 2+*. Unpublished assessment protocol.

Socialstyrelsen (1997) *Social and Caring Services in Sweden, 1996*. Stockholm: National Board of Health and Welfare.

Spirduso, W. and P. Gilliam-MacRae (1991) "Physical activity and quality of life in the frail elderly," in J. Birren, J. Lubben, J. Rowe, and D. Deutchman (eds.), *The Concept and Measurement of Quality of Life in the Frail Elderly*. New York: Academic Press.

Steinfeld, E. and S. Danford (1999) *Measuring Enabling Environments*. New York: Kluwer Academic/Plenum.

Stone, R. (2000) *Long-Term Care for the Elderly with Disabilities: Current Policy, Emerging Trends, and Implications for the Twenty-First Century*. New York: Milbank Memorial Fund.

Story, M., J. Mueller, and R. Mace (1997) *The Universal Design File*. Raleigh: Center for Universal Design, North Carolina State University.

Strange, M. (1996) *Culture Shock: Denmark*. London: Kuperard.

Stuurgroep Experimenten Volkhuisvesting (1997) "Ik woon hier eigenlijk niet." Rotterdam: SEV.

Su-Dale, E. (1995) *Culture Shock: Norway*. London: Kuperard.

Swedish Institute (1996) *Housing and Housing Policy in Sweden: Fact Sheet FS 84.1 Ohc*. Stockholm: The Institute.

Thomas, W. (1996) *Life Worth Living: How Someone You Love Can Still Enjoy Life in a Nursing Home*. Acton, MA: VanderWyk and Burnham.

Treas, J. (1995) "Older Americans in the 1990's and beyond," *Population Bulletin*, Population Reference Bureau: Washington DC 50(2).

Tyson, M. (1998) *The Healing Landscape*. New York: Wiley.

Ulrich, R. S. (1984) "View through a window may influence recovery from surgery," *Science*, 224, pp. 420–421.

Ulrich, R. S. (1995) "Effects of healthcare interior design on wellness: Theory and recent scientific research," in S. Marberry (ed.), *Innovations in Healthcare Design*. New York: Van Nostrand Reinhold.

U.S. Bureau of the Census. *World Population, 2001*. Accessed online at: www.census.gov/ipc/www/idbsum.html on July 3, 2001.

U.S. Senate Select Committee on Aging (1991) *Aging America: Trends and Projections*. Washington, DC: U.S. Department of Health and Human Services.

Valins, M. (1988) *Housing for Elderly People: A Guide for Architects and Clients*. London: Architectural Press.

Verderber, S. and D. J. Fine (2000) *Healthcare Architecture in an Era of Radical Transformation*. New Haven, CT: Yale University Press.

Voysey, CFA. (1909) *Ideas in Things*. London: Batsford.

Wallman, K. (2000) *Older Americans 2000: Key Indicators of Well-Being*. Washington, DC: Federal Interagency Forum on Aging Related Statistics.

Weal, F., and F. Weal (1988) *Housing for the Elderly: Options and Design*. New York: Nichols.

Weisman, J. (1987) "Improving way-finding and architectural legibility in housing for the elderly," in V. Regnier and J. Pynoos (eds.), *Housing the Aged: Design Directives and Policy Considerations*. New York: Elsevier.

Weisman, J. and M. Calkins (1999) "Models for environmental assessment," in B. Schwarz and R. Brent (eds.), *Aging, Autonomy, and Architecture: Advances in Assisted Living*. Baltimore: Johns Hopkins University Press.

Welch, P. (1995) *Strategies for Teaching Universal Design*. Boston: Adaptive Environments Center.

Welch, P., V. Parker, and J. Zeisel (1984) *Independence Through Interdependence: Congregate Living for Older People*. Boston: Department of Elder Affairs.

White, C. and L. Boucke (1989) *The UnDutchables*. Lafayette, CO: White Boucke.

Whyte, William H. (1980) *The Social Life of Small Urban Spaces*. Washington, DC: Conservation Foundation.

Wilson, K. B. (1990) "Assisted living: The merger of housing and long term care services," *Long Term Care Advances*, 1, p. 208.

Wolfe, D. B. (1990) *Serving the Ageless Market: Strategies for Selling to the Fifty-Plus Market.*, New York: McGraw-Hill.

Wylde, M. and S. Zimmerman (1999) *A Guide to Research Information for the Long-Term Care Industries: Assisted Living Communities and Nursing Homes*. Fairfax, VA: International Assisted Living Foundation.

Young, L., R. Mace, and G. Sifrin (1996) *Fair Housing Act Design Manual*. Raleigh, NC: Barrier Free Environments.

Zahle, K. (1998) *Boliger til Gamle*. Copenhagen: Arkitekten and Boliglaboratoriet/Kunstakademiets Arkitektskole.

Zeisel, J. (1981) *Inquiry by Design*. Monterey, CA: Brooks-Cole.

Zeisel, J. (1999) "Life quality Alzheimer's care in assisted living," in B. Schwartz and R. Brent (eds.), *Aging, Autonomy, and Architecture: Advances in Assisted Living*. Baltimore: Johns Hopkins University Press.

Zeisel, J., J. Hyde, and S. Levkoff (1994) "Best practices: An environment-behavior (E-B) model of physical design for special care units," *Journal of Alzheimer's Disease*, 9, pp. 4–21.

Zimmerman, S., P. Sloane, and J. Ekert (2001) *Assisted Living: Needs, Practices and Policies in Residential Care for the Elderly*. Baltimore: Johns Hopkins University Press.

INDEX